P9-CKX-121

DATE DUE

DEMCO 38-296

ASIAN/OCEANIAN HISTORICAL DICTIONARIES
Edited by Jon Woronoff

Asia

1. *Vietnam,* by William J. Duiker. 1989
2. *Bangladesh,* by Craig Baxter and Syedur Rahman, second edition. 1996
3. *Pakistan,* by Shahid Javed Burki. 1991
4. *Jordan,* by Peter Gubser. 1991
5. *Afghanistan,* by Ludwig W. Adamec. 1991
6. *Laos,* by Martin Stuart-Fox and Mary Kooyman. 1992
7. *Singapore,* by K. Mulliner and Lian The-Mulliner. 1991
8. *Israel,* by Bernard Reich. 1992
9. *Indonesia,* by Robert Cribb. 1992
10. *Hong Kong and Macau,* by Elfed Vaughan Roberts, Sum Ngai Ling, and Peter Bradshaw. 1992
11. *Korea,* by Andrew C. Nahm. 1993
12. *Taiwan,* by John F. Copper. 1993
13. *Malaysia,* by Amarjit Kaur. 1993
14. *Saudi Arabia,* by J. E. Peterson. 1993
15. *Myanmar,* by Jan Becka. 1995
16. *Iran,* by John H. Lorentz. 1995
17. *Yemen,* by Robert D. Burrowes. 1995
18. *Thailand,* by May Kyi Win and Harold Smith. 1995
19. *Mongolia,* by Alan J. K. Sanders. 1996
20. *India,* by Surjit Mansingh. 1996
21. *Gulf Arab States,* by Malcolm C. Peck. 1996
22. *Syria,* by David Commins. 1996
23. *Palestine,* by Nafez Y. Nazzal and Laila A. Nazzal. 1997
24. *Philippines,* by Artemio R. Guillermo and May Kyi Win. 1997
28. *People's Republic of China: 1949–1997,* by Lawrence R. Sullivan. 1997

Oceania

1. *Australia,* by James C. Docherty. 1992
2. *Polynesia,* by Robert D. Craig. 1993
3. *Guam and Micronesia,* by William Wuerch and Dirk Ballendorf. 1994

4. *Papua New Guinea,* by Ann Turner. 1994
5. *New Zealand,* by Keith Jackson and Alan McRobie. 1996

New Combined Series (July 1996)
25. *Brunei Darussalam,* by D. S. Ranjit Singh and Jatswan S. Sidhu. 1997
26. *Sri Lanka,* by S. W. R. de A. Samarsinghe and Vidyamali Samarsinghe. 1997
27. *Vietnam,* 2nd ed., by William J. Duiker. 1997
28. *People's Republic of China: 1949–1997,* by Lawrence R. Sullivan, with the assistance of Nancy Hearst. 1997
29. *Afghanistan,* 2nd ed., by Ludwig W. Adamec. 1997.
30. *Lebanon,* by As'ad AbuKhalil. 1997.

Historical Dictionary of the People's Republic of China: 1949–1997

Lawrence R. Sullivan
with the assistance of Nancy R. Hearst

*Asian/Oceanian Historical
Dictionaries, No. 28*

The Scarecrow Press, Inc.
Lanham, Md., & London
1997

SCARECROW PRESS, INC.

Published in the United States of America
by Scarecrow Press, Inc.
4720 Boston Way
Lanham, Maryland 20706

Copyright © 1997 by Lawrence R. Sullivan

British Library Cataloguing in Publication Information Available

Library of Congress Cataloging-in-Publication Data

Sullivan, Lawrence R.
    Historical dictionary of the People's Republic of China : 1949–1997 /
Lawrence R. Sullivan, with the assistance of Nancy R. Hearst
        p.   cm.—(Asian/Oceanian historical dictionaries ; no. 28)
    Includes bibliographical references.
    ISBN 0-8108-3349-2 (alk. paper)
        1. China—History—1949—Dictionaries.   I. Hearst, Nancy R.   II.
    Title.   III. Series: Asian/Oceanian historical dictionaries ; no. 28.
    DS777.55.S85   1997
    951.05'03—dc21   97-15875
                                                                        CIP

ISBN 0-8108-3349-2 (cloth : alk. paper)

∞ ™ The paper used in this publication meets the minimum requirements of
American National Standard for Information Sciences—Permanence of Paper
for Printed Library Materials, ANSI Z39.48–1984. Manufactured in the United
States of America.

For My Family:
Lawrence Sr., Virginia, and Carole Sullivan

Contents

Editor's Foreword   *Jon Woronoff*   ix

Spelling and Alphabetization Note   xi

Acronyms and Abbreviations   xiii

Chronology   xv

Map and Charts   xxxi

Introduction   1

THE DICTIONARY   9

Selected Bibliography   251

About the Authors   279

Editor's Foreword

China, one of the world's biggest countries, with by far the world's largest population, today has a booming economy and is gradually becoming a major player in regional and, soon, global politics. This book on the People's Republic is thus a welcome addition to the series of Asian Historical Dictionaries published by Scarecrow Press.

It offers an array of entries on significant persons, places, and events, as well as political, economic, social, and cultural aspects. The introduction sums up the present situation quite clearly and the chronology makes it easier to follow the tortuous path leading to the Communist takeover in 1949 and the even more confusing period since then. The selective bibliography provides greater detail on a wide range of topics. Reference works on China can be cumbersome; yet this one-volume *Historical Dictionary of the People's Republic of China* has been written in a straightforward, thorough style that gives the reader a strong background on the country.

The author of this volume is Lawrence R. Sullivan. He teaches political science at Adelphi University where he specializes in comparative politics with an emphasis on the People's Republic of China. In addition to the many articles he has written and the papers he has presented, he is the coauthor or coeditor of several books. Recently he edited *China since Tiananmen: Political, Economic, and Social Conflicts.* He was assisted by Nancy R. Hearst who, as librarian at the John K. Fairbank Center for East Asian Research at Harvard University, was in an excellent position to survey the literature.

Jon Woronoff
Series Editor

Spelling and Alphabetization Note

The Romanization employed in this dictionary for Chinese terms is the pinyin system developed and currently used in the People's Republic of China. Names and places of some well-known figures (e.g., Sun Yat-sen) and of terms associated with the Republic of China on Taiwan are, however, written according to the Wade-Giles system of romanization. In Chinese and East Asian culture generally the family name precedes the given name.

Acronyms and Abbreviations

APC	Agricultural Producers' Cooperatives
CAC	Central Advisory Commission
CASS	Chinese Academy of Social Sciences
CCP	Chinese Communist Party
CDIC	Central Discipline Inspection Commission
CITIC	China International Trust and Investment Corporation
CPPCC	Chinese People's Political Consultative Conference
CYL	Communist Youth League
KMT	Kuomintang (Nationalist Party)
MAC	Military Affairs Commission
MAT	Mutual Aid Team
MOFERT	Ministry of Foreign Economic Relations and Trade
NPC	National People's Congress
PLA	People's Liberation Army
PRC	People's Republic of China
ROC	Republic of China (Taiwan)
TVE	Township Village Enterprises
SAR	Special Administrative Regions
SEPC	State Environmental Protection Commission
SEZ	Special Economic Zone

Chronology

1644–1911   Qing Dynasty, China's last.

1912   The Republic of China is proclaimed with Sun Yat-sen as president. He is soon replaced by the warlord, Yuan Shih-kai.

1919   May 4. The May Fourth Movement breaks out among students and workers in protest against the Chinese government's acceptance of the Versailles Treaty ending World War I, which turned over Chinese territory in Shandong province formerly under German control to Japan. The movement inaugurates modern Chinese nationalism and gives birth to the CCP in 1921.

1920   Comintern envoys from the new Bolshevik regime in Russia arrive in China.

1921   July. The CCP is formally organized at a girls' school in the French sector of Shanghai.

1923–1931   Period of the First United Front between the CCP and the KMT

1925   Death of Sun Yat-sen.

1927   April. Anti-Communist coup in Shanghai led by Chiang Kai-shek, KMT leader and successor to Sun Yat-sen.
November. Mao Zedong sets up Soviet government in Hunan province.

1928   Sixth CCP Congress is held in Moscow.

1931   Chinese Soviet Republic established in Jiangxi province. Japanese occupy Manchuria.

1935–1946   The Yan'an Period

1934–1935   Communist armies retreat from KMT forces in historic Long March.

1937   Japan invades China. Second United Front is established between KMT and CCP.

1942–1944   First CCP Rectification.

1945   April. Seventh Party Congress. Mao outlines his plan for a "New Democracy" based on an alliance of workers, peasants, and bourgeois elements.

August. War with Japan ends.

1946–1949   **The Chinese Civil War**

1946   Mission headed by General George C. Marshall is sent to China to mediate KMT-CCP armistice.

May. Communists issue first Land Reform directive.

August. United States assists KMT forces to occupy key sites in central, south, and east China.

1947   July. Communists launch major counteroffensive against KMT forces, thus turning the tide of the civil war.

1949–1957   **Period of Economic Reconstruction and Political Consolidation**

1949   January. Communists occupy Beiping.

April. PLA captures Shanghai.

October 1. Mao Zedong formally proclaims the founding of the PRC.

December. KMT forces with Chiang Kai-shek flee to Taiwan.

1950   February. Sino-Soviet Pact of Friendship and Alliance is signed in Moscow between Mao Zedong and Josef Stalin.

April. China's Marriage Law is promulgated.

October. China enters the Korean War.

1952   October. Land Reform completed.

1953   February. MATs are organized in the countryside.

March. Josef Stalin dies.

July. Korean War armistice.

December. CCP Central Committee authorizes formation of APCs.

1954   September. First NPC promulgates the Chinese state constitution. State Council is established.

1955   March. Gao Gang and Rao Shushi are purged from CCP in first post-1949 leadership struggle.

July. Mao Zedong intervenes to speed up formation of rural APCs.

September. Anticounterrevolutionary campaign carried out in CCP.

October. CCP departments are established for Party central, provincial, and local-level committees that function the same as the administrative organs in the government, thereby insuring Party control of state economic decision making.

1956   "High tide" of rural cooperativization produces vast increase in number of APCs and with it severe disruption in agricultural production.

February. Nikita Khrushchev denounces Stalin in "secret speech" at Twentieth Soviet Communist Party Congress held in Moscow. China issues editorial tepidly endorsing Khrushchev's criticisms.

April. Mao calls for stability in his speech "On Ten Major Relationships."

May. Hundred Flowers policy announced by Lu Dingyi.

September. CCP Eighth Party Congress indicates liberal direction in economics and politics.

October. Anticommunist revolt breaks out in Hungary.

December. China issues editorial defending Josef Stalin against attacks by Khrushchev.

1957   February. Mao's speech on internal "contradictions" among the people signals greater tolerance of intellectuals and free speech.

May. Three weeks of free expression by Chinese intellectuals.

June. Anti-Rightist campaign launched against outspoken intellectuals.

August. CCP cadres sent to countryside for "study."

October. Soviets launch first space satellite. China and USSR sign nuclear sharing agreement.

November. Mao Zedong visits Moscow.

1958–1965   **Period of the Great Leap Forward and Its Aftermath**

1958   Spring. Decision to amalgamate APCs.

May. Second plenum of the Eighth Party Congress reverses policies and endorses Maoist radicalism.

August. Politburo meeting of top leadership at Beidaihe announces formation of people's communes in the countryside.

September. People's militia is established.

December. Sixth plenum of the Eighth Party Congress held in Wuchang announces retreat on formation of the people's communes. Mao Zedong announces his forthcoming resignation as head of state at the 1959 NPC.

1959   Spring. Economic stabilization policy is enacted.

March. Revolt in Tibet.

August. Eighth plenum of the Eighth Party Congress in Lushan announces shift in the focus of agricultural

	decision-making power from the people's communes to the brigades.
	September. Khrushchev stops off in Beijing after visiting United States.
1960	The second Great Leap Forward resumes campaign to send cadres down to the countryside. Food crisis that began in 1959 intensifies.
	August. Soviet advisers withdraw from China.
	September. Decentralization of rural decision making to the level of the production team.
1961	January. Ninth plenum of the Eighth Party Congress announces full retreat on the Great Leap Forward. Rectification of basic-level cadres is announced.
1962	Beginning of Socialist Education Movement.
	March. Liu Shaoqi emerges as primary leader in period of recovery as liberalization is announced for economic and cultural sectors.
	September. Attack on "modern revisionism" at CCP Tenth plenum of the Eighth Party Congress signals return to more radical Maoist policies. Mao insists "never forget class struggle."
1963	April. Directive on political work in the PLA.
	July. Sino-Soviet conflict worsens.
1964	Spring. Political departments organized in various government ministries and bureaus signaling tighter political control.
	June. Campaign to train "revolutionary successor generation."
	October. China tests its first atomic bomb. Khrushchev is overthrown in the USSR.
1965	Escalation of war in Vietnam.
	June. China eliminates all ranks in the PLA.
	September. Lin Biao gives speech calling for worldwide "people's war."
	November. System of part work and part study is proposed for Chinese schools. The play by Beijing vice mayor Wu Han, *Hai Rui Dismissed from Office*, is attacked by Yao Wenyuan.

1966–1976	**Period of the Cultural Revolution**
1966	March. Attack on "bourgeois authorities" in academic and cultural circles.
	May. May 16 Circular dissolves Five-Man Group for being insufficiently radical and establishes a new Cultural

Revolution Small Group headed by Chen Boda. First big-character poster appears at Peking University.

June. Work teams sent into China's universities.

July. Mao swims the Yangtze River.

August. The Eleventh plenum of the Eighth Party Congress replaces Liu Shaoqi with Lin Biao as second in command and heir apparent. Liu is demoted from second to eighth position in the Party hierarchy. Mao Zedong greets Red Guards at a number of rallies in Beijing.

October. Deng Xiaoping is attacked at CCP Central Work Conference.

1967   January. Mao Zedong orders PLA to intervene in Cultural Revolution on the side of the leftists. "January storm" by Red Guards in Shanghai signals collapse of authority.

February. "February Adverse Current" calls for end to Cultural Revolution radicalism.

April. Deng Xiaoping and Liu Shaoqi are accused of committing "crimes" against the CCP.

July. Wuhan incident brings China to brink of civil war.

Fall. Height of factional fighting and violence among Red Guards.

1968   July. Mao Zedong attacks Red Guard leaders for excessive factionalism and orders students sent to the countryside.

October. At the Twelfth plenum of the Eighth Party Congress Mao Zedong calls for "getting rid of the stale and taking in the fresh" in the CCP.

Army veteran Zhu De is attacked for purportedly opposing Mao Zedong.

1969   March. Sino-Soviet border clashes break out along the Ussuri River.

April. Ninth Party Congress selects Lin Biao as Mao's official successor and proclaims "victory" of the Cultural Revolution.

1970   August. Conflict between Mao Zedong and Lin Biao over the reestablishment of the position of head of state, which Mao opposes. Lin Biao offers his theory of genius.

December. Radical leftists criticized as Beijing Military Region is reorganized.

1971   April. Lin Biao supporters subject to open criticism.

September. Lin Biao purportedly attempts to assassinate Mao Zedong and dies in plane crash in Outer Mongolia while fleeing China.

December. Top CCP leadership learns of proposed trip to China by U.S. President Richard Nixon.

1972	February. Richard Nixon makes historic trip to China and signs Shanghai Communiqué.
	May. Purported coup attempt by Lin Biao is revealed to CCP rank and file.
	June. Attacks against Zhou Enlai begin.
1973	May. Veteran CCP leaders purged during early years of the Cultural Revolution are rehabilitated. National economic plan is reviewed.
	August. Tenth Party Congress is held and elects radical worker Wang Hongwen into top leadership post. PLA representation on Central Committee is reduced.
	November. Jiang Qing criticizes Zhou Enlai's handling of foreign affairs.
	December. Mao Zedong warns of civil war in China and proposes appointment of Deng Xiaoping as PLA chief of staff. CCP Central Military Commission rotates regional PLA commanders.
1974	July. In letter to Jiang Qing, Mao criticizes her and warns against engaging in factional activity.
	October. Radical leaders resist appointment of Deng Xiaoping as China's first vice premier.
	November. Mao orders return to task of economic modernization.
1975	January. Deng Xiaoping is reappointed as CCP vice chairman and as member of Politburo Standing Committee.
	February. Deng Xiaoping criticizes neglect of production in China's rural and urban economy.
	May. Mao Zedong warns Jiang Qing and three supporters against forming a "Gang of Four."
	July. Deng Xiaoping calls for modernization of PLA.
	October. Conference calls for learning from Dazhai brigade in agricultural policy.
	November. Criticism of Deng Xiaoping by radical faction. Emergence of Hua Guofeng as national Party leader.

1976–1977   Period of Late Maoism

1976	January. Death of Zhou Enlai.
	February. Hua Guofeng appointed acting premier.
	April 5. Mass demonstrations break out in memory of Zhou Enlai on Tiananmen Square in Beijing and are suppressed by state militia controlled by radical faction led by Jiang Qing.
	April 7. Deng Xiaoping is suspended from all work.
	September 9. Death of Mao Zedong.

October. Arrest of the Gang of Four (Jiang Qing, Zhang Chunqiao, Yao Wenyuan, and Wang Hongwen).

1977 February 7. *People's Daily* editorial lauds the pro-Maoist "two whatevers."

March. Central Work Conference reaffirms the "two whatevers" supported by Hua Guofeng and Wang Dongxing. Wang Zhen and Chen Yun demand Deng Xiaoping's rehabilitation.

July. Third plenum of the Tenth Party Congress restores Deng Xiaoping to the Politburo Standing Committee. Hua Guofeng is confirmed as Mao's successor.

August. At Science and Education Work Forum, Deng Xiaoping pushes for major reforms and praises the work of intellectuals.

1978–1997 **Period of reform and political crises**
1978 April-June. All-Military Conference on Political Work is held, at which Deng Xiaoping criticizes leftists in Party leadership.

May 12. *People's Daily* editorial "Practice is the Sole Criterion of Truth" attacks leftist ideological orthodoxy.

October. Democracy Wall movement begins in Beijing.

November. Central Party Work Conference focuses on debate over the "criterion of truth." Deng Xiaoping gives speech supporting shift of Party work from promoting "class struggle" to socialist modernization.

December. Third plenum of the Eleventh Party Congress inaugurates major reforms in agricultural and economic policies focusing on the "four modernizations."

1979 January. Democracy Wall movement peaks in Beijing. Deng Xiaoping travels to the United States.

February. China invades northern territory of Vietnam.

March. Chinese forces retreat from Vietnamese territory. At Conference on Guidelines in Theory Work, Deng Xiaoping gives hard-line speech on "Upholding the Four Cardinal Principles." Democracy Wall activist Wei Jingsheng is arrested.

April. At Central Work Conference Party conservatives criticize reforms inaugurated by the December 1978 Third plenum. Three-year period of "readjustment" is proposed.

September. Fourth plenum of the Eleventh Party Congress promotes Zhao Ziyang to the Politburo and adds senior cadres to the CCP Central Committee. Agricultural policies are revised.

1980 February. Fifth plenum of the Eleventh Party Congress elevates Zhao Ziyang and Hu Yaobang to the Politburo and reestablishes the Party Secretariat as the de facto decision making body of the Party. Radicals Wang Dongxing, Ji Dengkui, Wu De, and Chen Xilian are removed from Party posts.

April. Hu Qiaomu attacks Party Propaganda Department. At All-Military Conference on Political Work Wei Guoqing pushes leftist slogan to "promote proletarian ideology and eliminate bourgeois ideas." Deng Xiaoping refuses to attend the meeting.

May. Deng attacks "feudalism" in the Party but critical elements of the speech are later excised from his *Selected Works*.

June. Politburo Standing Committee holds special meeting to discuss eliminating "feudalism" from the Party.

July. Political crisis in Poland.

August. Enlarged meeting of the Politburo decides to replace Hua Guofeng as premier with the reformist Zhao Ziyang. Proposals are made for a bicameral NPC and tricameral CCP, complete with checks and balances. Third session of the Fifth NPC allows open debate among delegates over the issue of reforming the political system. Deng Xiaoping endorses fundamental institutional political reform.

September. Central Secretariat meeting decides to apply flexible and open policies in Guangdong and Fujian provinces. Agricultural responsibility system is strengthened.

November. Hu Yaobang is charged with routine work of the Politburo and Deng Xiaoping is put in control of the CCP Central Military Commission. Gang of Four are put on trial. Hu Qiaomu at Central Work Conference launches "struggle against bourgeois liberalization" while Deng Xiaoping, Zhao Ziyang, and Chen Yun endorse economic retrenchment.

1981 March. Deng Xiaoping mentions the "struggle against bourgeois liberalization" for the first time. State Council call for diversified agricultural economy.

June. Sixth plenum of the Eleventh Party Congress issues document "Resolution on Certain Questions in the History of our Party" criticizing Mao Zedong's excesses during the Cultural Revolution (1966–1976). Hu Yaobang is promoted to Party chairman.

July. Party conservatives attack Special Economic Zones (SEZs).

August. Forum on Problems on the Ideological Battlefront is held to launch attacks on "bourgeois liberalization."

December. At Central Committee discussion meeting Chen Yun criticizes Hu Yaobang's alleged mistakes in economic policy. Chen also asserts a primary role for the state in the economy and opposes any further expansion of the SEZs.

1982　January. CCP chairman Hu Yaobang calls for utilizing foreign investment in China's economic modernization. Chen Yun asserts that economic planning must remain supreme in the countryside, despite the creation of the agricultural responsibility system.

February. Open forum on Guangdong and Fujian provinces. Hu Yaobang focuses on the problem of corruption.

April. Politburo meeting discusses "economic crimes" and calls for harsh punishments to be meted out by the Central Discipline Inspection Commission of the CCP.

July. Enlarged Politburo meeting discusses ways to end life tenure for leaders.

August. At Seventh plenum of the Eleventh Party Congress Hua Guofeng attacks the slogan "practice is the sole criterion of truth."

September. Twelfth Party Congress. Party chairmanship is abolished and replaced by weaker post of general secretary. Chairmanship of the Central Military Commission is strengthened.

December. Enlarged Politburo meeting emphasizes the importance of raising divergent views at inner-Party meetings.

1983　January. At National Conference on Ideological and Political Work Hu Yaobang and leftist leader, Deng Liqun, clash over the role of ideology in China's modernization.

March. At an academic forum at the Central Party School to commemorate the centennial of Marx's death, China's former cultural "czar," Zhou Yang, raises the issues of humanism and alienation in a socialist society.

October. Chen Yun calls for purging from the CCP former Red Guards known as the "three categories of people."

November. Enlarged meeting of the Politburo decides to limit the "anti-spiritual pollution campaign" to the fields of art and literature.

1984   January. Deng Xiaoping tours several southern SEZs and voices support for continued economic reform.

February. Central forum on the role of SEZs produces "heated" discussion on the policy of opening up to the outside world.

March/April. Forum convened by the Central Secretariat and the State Council on the SEZs opens fourteen more coastal cities to foreign investment.

April. *People's Daily* calls for a fundamental negation of the Cultural Revolution.

June. Central Committee Document Number One on agriculture calls for strengthening and improving the rural responsibility system. Rural surplus laborers are allowed to travel into the cities for "temporary" work.

October. Third plenum of the Twelfth Party Congress adopts liberal "Resolution on the Structural Reform of the Economy," marking the beginning of the urban reforms.

December. Fourth Conference of the All-China Writers' Association in Beijing calls for greater autonomy for writers. China and Great Britain sign an agreement to restore China's sovereignty over Hong Kong on July 1, 1997.

1985   January. CCP and the State Council jointly issue "Ten Policies on Further Enlivening the Rural Economy," calling for expansion of the free rural economy.

March. National Forum on Science and Technology in Beijing calls for radical changes. Third session of the Sixth NPC takes initial step toward price reform.

May. Central MAC decides to reduce the size of the army by one quarter by demobilizing up to one million PLA troops and to retire older officers.

June. Restructuring of the administrative organs of the people's communes is completed. State Council decides to enlarge the Xiamen (Amoy) SEZ.

September. At National Conference of the CCP Chen Yun attacks "Resolution on the Structural Reform of the Economy" and criticizes Party members for a loss of communist ideals.

1986   January. Central Cadres Conference focuses on "instability" in the national economy and criticizes "lax" work among Party organs.

June. At Politburo Standing Committee meeting Deng Xiaoping gives speech on reform of the political structure and on strengthening legal consciousness.

September. Sixth plenum of the Twelfth Party Congress

adopts "Resolution on the Guiding Principles for Construction of Socialist Spiritual Civilization." Zhao Ziyang sets up Political Reform Research Group charged with enacting systemic institutional reforms in China's political system.

December. Student demonstrations break out in Hefei, Anhui province, and quickly spread to other cities, including Beijing. Deng Xiaoping criticizes Hu Yaobang's handling of liberal intellectuals in the CCP.

1987   January. Enlarged Politburo meeting relieves liberal reformer Hu Yaobang of his duties as general secretary of the CCP. Dissidents Fang Lizhi, Wang Ruowang, and Liu Binyan are expelled from the CCP for allegedly advocating "bourgeois liberalization."

April. Series of conferences on ideological and political work are convened by leftists to continue criticism of "bourgeois liberalization" as direct CCP control is established over previously semi-independent newspapers and periodicals.

July. Zhao Ziyang initiates Central Work Conference to discuss comprehensive plan for political reform.

October. Seventh plenum of the Twelfth Party Congress appoints Zhao Ziyang as general secretary of the CCP and approves "General Program for Political Reform" calling for separation of Party and government, creation of an independent judiciary, and a shift in authority within state economic enterprises from CCP committees to professional managers.

October/November. At Thirteenth Party Congress Zhao Ziyang characterizes the current state of China's development as the "primary stage of socialism," thereby allowing for further market reforms. Politburo replaces Party Secretariat as the center of CCP decision making. Party departments established in the mid-1950s are abolished.

1988   March. At Second plenum of the Thirteenth CCP Central Committee, Zhao Ziyang proposes the establishment of a professional civil service and calls for greater internal Party democracy.

March/April. First session of the Seventh NPC formally approves Li Peng as state premier, Yang Shangkun as president, and Wang Zhen as vice president. State Statistical Bureau warns of inflation.

July. *Red Flag* ceases publication and is replaced by *Seeking Truth* (*Qiushi*).

August. After fierce debates among top leadership at Beidaihe summer retreat, commitment is made to pursue price reform, but the decision is quickly withdrawn after panic buying occurs in the cities.

September. Third plenum of the Thirteenth Party Congress calls for emphasis on stabilizing and rectifying the economy, with some leaders calling for greater "centralism."

1989   December 1988–February. Petition drive by Chinese dissidents seeking amnesty for China's political prisoners.

April 15. Death of Hu Yaobang.

April 22. On official day of mourning for Hu Yaobang, massive crowds of students fill Tiananmen Square.

April 26. A *People's Daily* editorial, based on a speech by Deng Xiaoping, condemns student demonstrations as "anti-Party, anti-socialist turmoil."

May. At Asian Development Bank meeting in Beijing, Zhao Ziyang speaks positively about the student movement. More than three hundred journalists demand freedom of the press. Students initiate a hunger strike that leads to a failed dialogue on nationwide TV between Premier Li Peng and student leaders. Mikhail Gorbachev makes historic visit to Beijing. Martial law is declared.

June 3–4. PLA troops force their way into Tiananmen Square and outlying parts of the city, killing several hundred or perhaps thousands of students and city residents in Beijing. Killings also occur in Chengdu, Sichuan.

June 24. Fourth plenum of the Thirteenth Party Congress votes to strip Zhao Ziyang of all his posts and appoints Jiang Zemin as general secretary of the Party.

November. Deng Xiaoping resigns as chairman of the CCP MAC, his last official position.

December. Ceausescu government in Romania is overthrown.

1990   January. Two-year economic austerity program is announced as Chinese police are put on alert following the collapse of the Communist government in Romania.

March. At Third session of the Seventh NPC Li Peng calls for tighter control of "hostile elements."

April. Jiang Zemin is named chairman of the state MAC. Basic Law for Hong Kong is passed by the Seventh NPC.

June. In the *People's Daily* Wang Zhen attacks moderates in the government as "hostile anti-Party forces."

October. *People's Daily* announces a new campaign

against crime and such "liberal" influences as pornography.

December. Economic blueprint for the Eighth Five-Year Plan stresses stability and self-reliance.

1991   January/February. Trials are held of leading 1989 democratic movement participants.

March. At a national meeting on economic reform, Li Peng supports further reforms to decentralize the economy.

April. Shanghai mayor Zhu Rongji and head of the State Planning Commission Zou Jiahua are appointed vice premiers.

May. New press code encourages journalists to spread Marxism-Leninism. Secret emergency directive issued to all Party and government offices to guard against hostile forces that seek to overthrow the government.

July. Jiang Zemin views the country's "central political task" to be opposition to Western plots against China that are dubbed "peaceful evolution."

August. Attempted coup d'état against Soviet leader Mikhail Gorbachev collapses.

September. Chen Yun's son, Chen Yuan, draws up document on "Realistic Responses and Strategic Options for China Following the Soviet Union Upheaval."

October. Internal CCP document accuses the Bush administration of attempting to bring about the collapse of communism through "peaceful evolution."

1992   January. Deng Xiaoping tours Shenzhen SEZ in southern China and calls for further economic reforms.

February. The *People's Daily* attacks hard-line views and calls for bolder economic reforms.

March. Supporters of economic reforms attack conservative attempts to reverse economic reform policies. Finance Minister Wang Bingqian reveals a projected budget deficit of $3.8 billion for 1992 and announces a 13 percent increase in military spending.

April. The NPC approves construction of the controversial Three Gorges Dam project.

June. Liberal scholars hold unofficial forum to condemn continuing power of the hardliners in the CCP. More than one million workers are laid off from money-losing state enterprises.

August. Outbreak of strikes by industrial workers.

October. Fourteenth Party Congress enshrines the principle of a "socialist market economic system" for China's future development. CAC chaired by Chen Yun is abolished and Yang Shangkun is dropped from the CCP MAC. November. Deng Xiaoping gives speech admonishing people to follow the "three don'ts," that is, don't revise the political interpretation of the 1989 Beijing massacre, don't tolerate "bourgeois liberalization," and don't replace any more leading leftists.

1993   March. Death of Wang Zhen. CCP General Secretary Jiang Zemin is appointed president of the PRC.

April. The World Bank announces that China is the world's fastest-growing economy, estimated at 12 percent a year.

June. Peasant riots break out in Sichuan province over taxes and other exorbitant fees.

August. The United States imposes trade sanctions on China and Pakistan, charging Chinese companies with selling missile technology to Pakistan.

October. Governor Chris Patten of Hong Kong announces that his efforts to get China's approval for democratic political reforms in the colony have failed.

December. China marks 100th anniversary of birthday of Mao Zedong.

1994   March. President of China's Supreme Court reports significant increases in serious crimes—murder, robbery, and rape—and economic crime. Taiwanese tourists in Zhejiang province are robbed and murdered precipitating a crisis in PRC-Taiwan relations.

May. Chinese intellectuals call on the government to reappraise the 1989 democracy movement. Clinton administration extends Most Favored Nation status to China, delinking human rights and trade issues.

June. In midst of a crisis over North Korea's nuclear program, China's Foreign Ministry urges the North Korean government to desist from "fruitless military conflicts."

October. Confrontation between a U.S. Navy aircraft carrier battle group and a Chinese submarine occurs in Yellow Sea.

1995   February. Beginning of a petition movement by Chinese intellectuals, which continues throughout the spring, seeking political reform, an end to corruption, a reevaluation of the 4 June 1989 crackdown, and more openness in government.

April. Death of Chen Yun.

1996	March. Taiwan (ROC) conducts first direct election for president in Chinese history as the PRC conducts war games in the Taiwan Straits.
1997	February 20. Deng Xiaoping dies.
	July 1. Hong Kong reverts to Chinese rule.

Sources used in preparing this chronology include: Kenneth G. Lieberthal and Bruce J. Dickson, *A Research Guide to Central Party and Government Meetings in China, 1949–1986* (Armonk, N.Y.: M. E. Sharpe, Inc., 1989); the annual editions of *China Briefing* (Boulder: Westview Press, 1984–1992 and Armonk, N.Y.: 1997), Richard Bush, Steven M. Goldstein, William A. Joseph, Anthony J. Kane, John S. Major, and Robert Oxnam, eds.; "Quarterly Chronicle and Documentation," *The China Quarterly*, School of Oriental and African Studies, London; and Franz Schurmann, *Ideology and Organization in Communist China* (Berkeley and Los Angeles: University of California Press, 1966).

Map and Charts

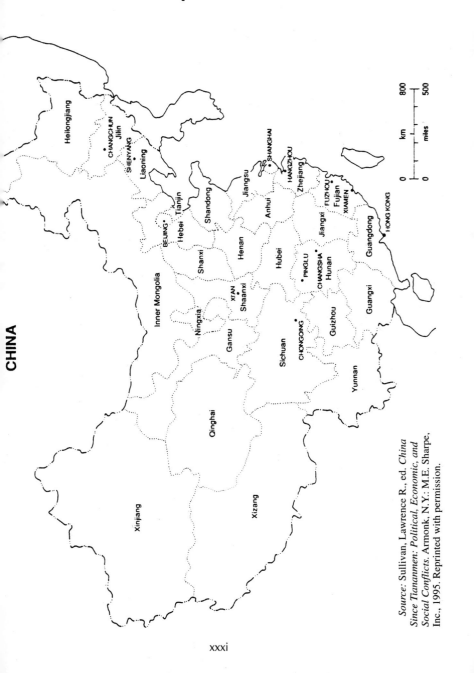

Source: Sullivan, Lawrence R., ed. *China Since Tiananmen: Political, Economic, and Social Conflicts.* Armonk, N.Y.: M.E. Sharpe, Inc., 1995. Reprinted with permission.

Government of the People's Republic of China*

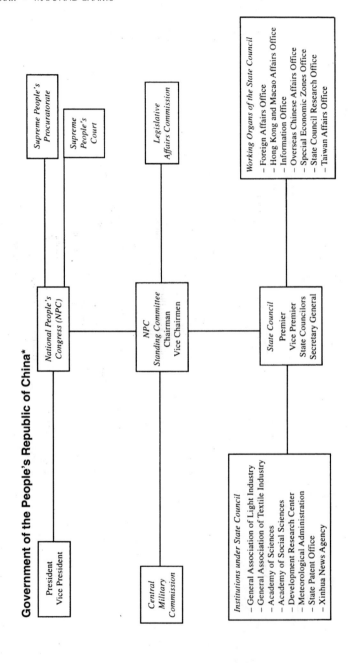

Supreme People's Procuratorate

Supreme People's Court

National People's Congress (NPC)

President
Vice President

Legislative Affairs Commission

NPC Standing Committee
Chairman
Vice Chairmen

Central Military Commission

State Council
Premier
Vice Premier
State Councilors
Secretary General

Working Organs of the State Council
- Foreign Affairs Office
- Hong Kong and Macao Affairs Office
- Information Office
- Overseas Chinese Affairs Office
- Special Economic Zones Office
- State Council Research Office
- Taiwan Affairs Office

Institutions under State Council
- General Association of Light Industry
- General Association of Textile Industry
- Academy of Sciences
- Academy of Social Sciences
- Development Research Center
- Meteorological Administration
- State Patent Office
- Xinhua News Agency

Commissions
- Science, Technology and Industry for National Defense
- State Economic and Trade
- State Education
- State Family Planning
- State Nationalities Affairs
- State Physical Culture and Sports
- State Planning
- State Restructuring of the Economic System
- State Science and Technology
- People's Bank of China

Ministries
- Agriculture
- Chemical Industry
- Civil Affairs
- Coal Industry
- Communications
- Construction
- Culture
- Electronics Industry
- Finance
- Foreign Affairs
- Foreign Trade and Economic Cooperation
- Forestry
- Geology and Mineral Resources
- Internal Trade
- Justice
- Labor
- Machine-Building Industry
- Metallurgical Industry
- National Defense
- Personnel
- Posts and Telecommunications
- Power Industry
- Public Health
- Public Security
- Radio, Film, and Television
- Railways
- State Auditing Administration
- State Security
- Supervision
- Water Resources

Organizations under the State Council
- Civil Aviation Administration
- Counsellors' Office
- General Administration of Customs
- Government Offices Administration Bureau
- National Tourism Administration
- Administration for Industry and Commerce
- General Administration of Taxation
- Environmental Protection Bureau
- Land Administration Bureau
- Legislative Affairs Bureau
- Press and Publications Administration
- Religious Affairs Bureau
- Statistical Bureau

Source: Sullivan, Lawrence R., ed. *China Since Tiananmen: Political, Economic, and Social Conflicts.* Armonk, N.Y.: M.E. Sharpe, Inc., 1995. Reprinted with permission. Prepared by Nancy Hearst.

Chinese Communist Party Organizations*

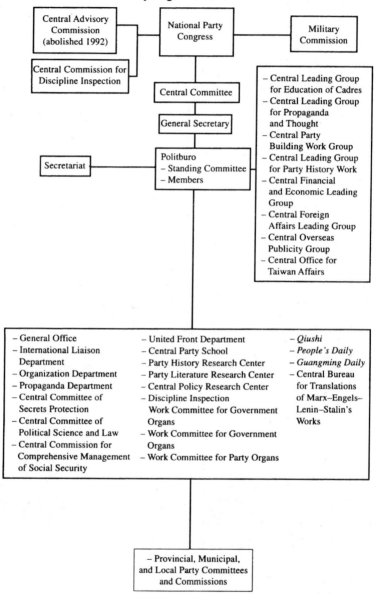

Source: Sullivan, Lawrence R., ed. *China Since Tiananmen: Political, Economic, and Social Conflicts.* Armonk, N.Y.: M.E. Sharpe, Inc., 1995. Reprinted with permission. Prepared by Nancy Hearst.

Introduction

Geography and Topography

The People's Republic of China (PRC) is located in eastern Asia, bounded by the Pacific Ocean in the East. The third largest country in the world behind the Russian Republic and Canada, it has an area of 9.6 million square kilometers, or fully one-fifteenth of the world's land mass. From east to west, China's territory extends about 5,200 kilometers, and from north to south it measures some 5,500 kilometers. Approximately 98 percent of China's total land area is situated between latitude 20 and 50 degrees North, the greater part belonging to the temperate and subtropical zones. The PRC is bordered by the Democratic People's Republic of Korea (North Korea) in the northeast; Russia and Mongolia in the north; Kazakhstan, Tajikistan, and Kyrgyzstan in the west; Nepal, Sikkim, Bhutan, and India in the southwest; and Burma, Laos, and Vietnam in the south.

Topographically, China is similar to a gradient staircase, high in the west and low in the east. Mountains, plateaus, and hills account for about 65 percent of the country's land area, 20 percent of which is more than 5,000 meters above sea level. This region is located primarily in the western Qinghai-Tibet plateau, the highest and largest plateau on earth. Seven of the world's highest mountains are in China, including Mt. Everest (known in Chinese as *Zhumulangmafeng* and also as Qomolangmo), the world's highest. The terrain in the central part of the country drops to between 2,000 and 1,000 meters above sea level, and in the east the terrain is low, generally less than 1,000 meters above sea level, where the country's vast farmlands and major cities are located.

China has a vast river system that totals 220,000 kilometers in length and consists of three major systems, the Yellow River in the north, the Yangtze in the central part of the country, and the Pearl River in the south. River flow is unevenly distributed, with the higher part lying in the south. The Yangtze (*Changjiang*, or "Long River") is the third largest river in the world (after the Amazon and the Nile) and accounts for almost 40 percent of China's entire water runoff. With a catchment area of 1.8 million square kilometers, the Yangtze is also the major water transport artery in China. The Yellow River, generally considered the cradle of Chinese civilization, is the second longest in China. The total volume of water per capita in China is only 3,000 cubic meters, one-fourth of the world's average.

China can be divided into three major physical districts based on the primary elements that affect regional differentiation—geographical position, climatic characteristics, and geological features. About 45 percent of the country, primarily in the eastern region, consists of a monsoon district that is characterized by a humid and semi-humid environment with abundant rainfall. Here lives 95 percent of the total population (over 1.1 billion people) and is 90 percent of the country's farming area. The northwest arid district consists of 30 percent of the land area, 10 percent of the total cultivated land, and about 4 percent of the population. It is composed of deserts, desert steppe, and steppe and includes the country's major pastoral areas in Inner Mongolia. The third area consists of the Alpine-cold region of Qinghai-Tibet, which constitutes about 30 percent of the country's land mass and less than 1 percent of its cultivated land and population.

In terms of cultivated land, China has approximately 250 million acres (or about 100 million hectares). There is only about one-quarter acre per capita of cultivated land in the entire country (in the United States the comparable figure is two acres per capita). Ninety percent of the cultivated land is concentrated in the eastern region, with 30 percent of the total in the middle-lower Yellow River region, 21 percent in the middle-lower Yangtze River region, and 7 percent in the Pearl River region in the south. In terms of mineral resources, China has one of the world's largest coal reserves (approximately 770 billion tons), which is the major source of energy for the country and the number one factor in China's growing environmental pollution. Onshore and offshore oil reserves are also substantial, as is natural gas.

Population and Administrative Divisions

At 1.162 billion people in 1994, China has the largest population in the world. By the year 2000 it is estimated that China will have a population of 1.255 billion people and by 2025, 1.471 billion people. These figures are based on a population growth rate from 1980 to 1992 of 1.4 percent and a projected growth rate of 1.0 percent from 1992 to 2000. Currently, China has an average life expectancy of 69 years, which is quite high for a country with a low per capita income. The geographical distribution of the population is very skewed, with 95 percent living in the eastern region of the country. Approximately 80 percent of the population lives in rural areas, primarily in villages and towns that can be as large as several thousand people. Chongqing, located in the interior province of Sichuan, is the country's largest city (14 million people) followed closely by Shanghai (meaning literally "on the sea") on the eastern seaboard with a population of more than 13 million people. The capital of the country is Beijing (literally "northern capital") and has a population of over 11 million people. China's most populated province is Sichuan (literally "four rivers"), with a population of over 112 million people. Ninety-two percent of the population is composed of the dominant Han ethnic group, who live in the densely populated eastern region. Ninety-one million people in China (or about 8 percent of the population) are members of more than 50 officially recognized minority groups. They are concentrated in the thinly populated, outlying provinces and regions in the strategically important southwestern and western parts of the country.

Administratively, China is divided into 22 provinces, five autonomous regions, and four centrally administered municipalities (Chongqing, Beijing, Shanghai, and Tianjin). There are over 2,900 cities and towns in China, fifteen of which have more than two million people each, 102 between one and two million each. There are also more than two thousand counties and 91,000 townships (*xiang*), which is the basic level of administrative organization in the country. Between the formation of the PRC in 1949 and 1978, the population distribution was centrally controlled, resulting in very little of the rural to urban migration that characterizes most Third World countries. The inauguration of economic reforms in 1978, however, substantially weakened central controls on population mobility and residence, resulting in large migrations of the "floating population" (estimated to be as high as 100 million people in 1995) moving from countryside to city and city to city in search of employment and higher income. This has created a growing problem of housing and social services support in China's increasingly hard-pressed urban areas, especially as government support for a broad range of social services—health care, housing, education, and transportation—has declined. Large cities, such as Beijing, now have upwards of one million unregistered people living in the environs who do not have adequate housing, nutrition, or health care. In addition, rural areas are increasingly losing young males such that agricultural production is increasingly carried out by women and the very old and very young.

Economy

China's economy in 1996 consisted of a combination of state, collective, and privately owned industry and agriculture. From 1949 to 1978 the entire economy was under the control of the state planning system in a socialist system similar to that of the Soviet Union. Emphasis on heavy industrialization and collectivization of agriculture produced major structural changes in the Chinese economy as it moved from an over-whelmingly agricultural economy in 1949 to an economy in which industry was the largest component in 1975. Under the state planning system, prices were set by the state for virtually all products, and production quotas for industry and agriculture were assigned by planning agencies, with economic distribution highly egalitarian. Internationally, China pursued an autarkic economic policy with trade restricted primarily to Soviet bloc countries.

Since 1978 economic reforms in China have created a mixed economy with the socialist (state) sector concentrated in heavy industry and the collective and private sectors restricted to agriculture and services. In 1994, total gross domestic product (GDP) was about $550 billion, 27 percent coming from agriculture, 34 percent from industry, and 38 percent from services. Average annual economic growth from 1980 to 1992 was over 9 percent (in 1994 over 11 percent), one of the highest growth rates in the world. Per capita annual income in 1994 stood at $470; from 1980 to 1992, it had grown on an annual basis of 7.6 percent. Major industries include textiles, cement, pig iron, steel, and silk. In terms of foreign trade, China's exports in 1994 totaled $115 billion and imports amounted to $120 billion, producing a small but troublesome trade imbalance. China is a major exporter of textile yarn and fabrics, clothing, oil, machinery and transport equipment, and agricultural products. It imports grains, chemicals, mineral fuels, fertilizers, machinery and transport equipment, and iron and steel. China's largest trading partner is Hong Kong (which reverted to Chinese sovereignty on July 1, 1997), followed by Japan. In 1995 internal government debt was approximately $15 billion while total external (or foreign) debt in 1994 was $100 billion. China's currency is the *yuan*—also referred to as *renminbi* (literally, "people's money")—which in 1994 was officially valued at 8.52 to $1. Since 1978, stock markets have been established in Shanghai and the Special Economic Zone of Shenzhen in the south.

History

The history of the PRC from 1949 to 1996 has been marked by political turbulence and transformation but with substantial progress in economic growth, public health, and social-economic infrastructure. Five distinct periods mark this history: 1) economic reconstruction and political consolidation, 1949–1957; 2) the Great Leap Forward and its aftermath, 1958–1965; 3) the Great Proletarian Cultural Revolution, 1966–1976; 4) Late Maoism, 1976–1977; and 5) the era of reform and political crisis, 1978–1997.

The first period witnessed the takeover of China by the Chinese Communist Party (CCP) after its defeat of the Nationalist (Kuomintang) Party in the Chinese civil war (1946–1949). Domestically, the CCP consolidated its rule by employing military and political resources to bring large swaths of territory (including Tibet, but not Taiwan) under CCP direct control. The Communist Party's political support among the peasantry was reinforced by the promotion of Land Reform from 1946 to 1953 and among workers by the socialist transformation of the Chinese economy. Political opponents of the regime, including many Western-educated intellectuals, were subject to severe persecution in a series of political campaigns, such as the "Three Antis and Five Antis" in the early 1950s, that often resulted in long periods of imprisonment or execution of the victims. State party control over the media and all institutions of learning was initiated and a grassroots structure of "units" (*danwei*) and personal dossiers (*dang'an*) was put into place. Regional layers of state organization and collective ownership of land gradually gave way to a more highly centralized structure that allowed for CCP control over the economy. Among the Party elite, political differences during this era were largely muted, except for one instance when a top regional leader in the northeast, Gao Gang, was purged from the CCP. Internationally, China aligned itself to the Soviet Union and became embroiled in the three-year war on the Korean peninsula (1950–1953) that was provoked by North Korean leader Kim Il-sung and involved direct military confrontation with the United States.

The second period (1958–1965) involved a dramatic change in domestic economic policy and rural organization that produced an economic and demographic catastrophe. At the urging of Party chairman Mao Zedong, the CCP attempted to increase dramatically the production of agricultural goods and steel through the reorganization of the countryside into massive people's communes and the introduction of so-called backyard steel furnaces. Designed to catch up with major industrial powers, particularly Britain, within fifteen years, and to achieve "communism" in the near term, the Great Leap Forward led to drastic reductions in food supply and the production of millions of tons of virtually worthless steel. By the early 1960s, China was in the grips of a severe economic crisis that ultimately led to the deaths of an estimated 30 million people and the political eclipse of Mao Zedong.

During the third period (1966–1976), after regaining his political standing in the top leadership of the CCP, Mao Zedong took revenge against those Party leaders and rank-and-file personnel who had failed to support his vision of Chinese socialism. In three years of political turmoil and conflict (1966–1968), rampaging groups of young Red Guards were licensed by Mao Zedong and his wife, Jiang Qing, to persecute Party leaders (including Mao's first successor, Liu Shaoqi) and to transform the CCP into a radical leftist organization bent on revolutionizing Chinese society along the lines of Mao Zedong Thought. Spurred on by a Mao Zedong personality cult that equaled in intensity and irrationality the Stalin cult in the Soviet Union during the 1930s, radical Red Guard factions tore the CCP apart from top to bottom and essentially brought China to the brink of civil war. By 1968, after the Red Guards had become increasingly and destructively factionalized, these youth groups were banished to factories and the countryside to "learn from the workers and peasants," while Mao gradually allowed the CCP to be rebuilt along conventional Leninist lines. In 1971, Mao's second successor, Marshal Lin Biao, allegedly attempted to assassinate the Chairman and was subsequently killed in a plane crash, while attempting to flee to the Soviet Union.

This so-called Lin Biao affair brought a new political crisis during which the authority of civilian leaders was increasingly challenged by the military. In 1972, however, China broke its long-standing political isolation from the United States by inaugurating official contacts that began with the historic trip to China by President Richard Nixon and the signing of the "Shanghai Communiqué."

In the period of Late Maoism from 1976 to 1977, the aging Mao grew increasingly frail and struggled against the attempts by his wife, Jiang Qing, and her supporters (later dubbed the "Gang of Four") to take over after his death. Deng Xiaoping, an early victim of the Cultural Revolution, was restored to power by Mao only to be purged once more in 1976 following the first outbreak of democratic sentiment in China.

Mao's death in 1976 led to the appointment of his third designated successor (a provincial CCP leader named Hua Guofeng from Mao's home province of Hunan). Joined by the security forces, Hua executed the arrest of Mao's wife and her supporters while at the same time allowing Deng Xiaoping to return to a position of leadership. Although loyal to Maoist thought and policies, Hua Guofeng began the process of shifting the focus of state policy from radical politics and internal turmoil to economic growth and development. By 1977, however, Hua had been completely outflanked by Deng, who by mid-1978 took effective control of the CCP.

The period of reform in China began in late 1978 at a historic CCP meeting at which the Party leadership endorsed fundamental economic reforms. Agriculture was freed from oppressive state control and China followed up its political opening to the West with an international economic policy designed to encourage exports and foreign investment in the Chinese economy. Deng supported the creation of so-called Special Economic Zones and allowed for the growth of a service economy that had previously been dominated (and suppressed) by bureaucratic control. Politically, Deng even toyed with the idea of radical democratic and constitutional reforms, but quickly pulled back from such dramatic changes under pressure from more conservative-minded political leaders, such as Chen Yun, and the political fallout over China's failed invasion of Vietnam in 1979 that Deng had promoted. At the same time, throughout the 1980s China witnessed greater economic and social freedom, but with few changes in the totalitarian political structure headed by the CCP. In 1986 and 1989, such fundamental "contradictions" led to massive outbursts of popular discontent, especially among students, that challenged CCP authority and called on more liberal CCP leaders, such as Party General Secretary Hu Yaobang and his successor Zhao Ziyang, to inaugurate liberal reforms. Under pressure from conservative leaders, however, Deng blunted popular demands and instead purged Hu Yaobang in early 1987 and then Zhao Ziyang in 1989.

When student and popular protests reached a crescendo in spring 1989 (prompted in good part by the sudden death of Hu Yaobang), Deng Xiaoping refused to yield to student demands and instead called in the army to crush the pro-democracy movement with lethal force. The "Tiananmen massacre" in the capital city of Beijing resulted in an estimated three thousand casualties and all but destroyed the democracy movement in China as dissident leaders either fled the country or were imprisoned. This wanton violation of human rights created tensions with the United States that continued into 1996, though the United States, under the Bush and Clinton administrations, refused to cancel China's Most Favored Nation status. After purging his two previously designated successors, Deng Xiaoping decided on former Shanghai mayor, Jiang Zemin, to become the "core" of the third generation of leaders. Yet whether Jiang, and the entire CCP, can survive Deng Xiaoping's death in 1997 still remains to be seen.

The Dictionary

A

"A Q SPIRIT" (*A Q JINGSHEN*). From the 1921 short story by Lu Xun (q.v.) entitled "The True Story of A Q," this "spirit" refers to the self-deception and fear of the truth that Lu Xun believed was part of China's national character and a major reason for its weakness. The story concerns a peasant named A Q, a despicable bastard who repeatedly cheats and is constantly being cheated and yet refuses to admit that he has lost face. He is a perennial optimist, believing that things will turn in his favor but is generally disappointed. The 1911 Republican revolution raises great hopes for A Q (and, by implication, for the Chinese people), but the lowly peasant quickly realizes that the new rulers are no different from the previous dynastic overlords. A Q is finally charged with stealing and is sentenced to death, even though in this particular case he is not guilty. The "A Q Spirit" refers to anyone who fears the reality of his own suppression but engages in self-deception by declaring himself a "victor." But it also may refer to those outcasts who see through political and cultural hyperbole and reveal the hidden truths, even when a "new era" under a "new leadership" has been declared. In this sense, the "A Q Spirit" is very subversive of any political authority in China. Lu Xun was venerated by the CCP (q.v.), but some of his works, including "The True Story of A Q," have been censored or, at times, banned. *See also* DAI QING.

"ACT ACCORDING TO PRINCIPLES LAID DOWN" (*AN JIDING FANGZHEN BAN*). This political phrase was propagated in China during the internecine struggle among top CCP (q.v.) leaders that followed the death of Party Chairman Mao Zedong (q.v.) on September 9, 1976. Its intent was to bolster the political forces of Mao's designated successor Hua Guofeng (q.v.) in his struggle with Mao's widow, Jiang Qing (q.v.), and her radical faction, who were subsequently referred to as the "Gang of Four" (q.v.) following their arrest on October 6, 1976. According to the editorials of the CCP official newspaper, the *People's Daily* (q.v.): "To 'act according to principles laid down' means to act according to Chairman Mao's proletarian revolutionary line and policies." In practical political terms, this meant that the CCP and the PLA (q.v.) should support Hua Guofeng as Mao's successor in line with the chairman's purported statement shortly before his death that with "You [Hua Guofeng] in command, I am at ease." In a vain attempt to oust Hua Guofeng, the radical faction, led by Jiang Qing, offered the alternative political line that the Party should "act according to past principles." In the arcane language of Chinese political discourse, this was interpreted to mean that because Mao had originally promoted the Cultural Revolution (1966–1976) (q.v.), the mantle of leadership should pass to the radical faction led by Jiang Qing and not the more pragmatic Hua Guofeng, and, more important, that the radical policies of the Cultural Revolution should be continued.

AFGHANISTAN. The Soviet invasion of Afghanistan in late 1979 had a profound effect on Chinese foreign policy, especially in its relationship with the United States. Like the United States, China roundly condemned the Soviet action and interpreted it as part of the USSR's broad offensive into various strategic areas of the world, including the Middle East, Africa, and Southeast Asia. The immediate impact of the invasion was to bring China into a closer strategic relationship with the United States to oppose the Soviet Union. Whereas before the Afghanistan invasion the United States under the Carter administration (1976–1980) had been reluctant as part of the political fallout over China's invasion of Vietnam (q.v.) in 1979 to elevate dramatically the level of U.S.–China cooperation, especially in the military arena, after the Soviet incursion into Afghanistan the U.S. quickly assented to significantly broad bilateral military ties. By the early 1980s, the U.S. government, under President Ronald Reagan (1981–1988), supported a coordinated policy with the Chinese to provide weapons and other material to the Afghan rebels known as the *Mujahideen*. Throughout the 1980s, China cited the Soviet occupation of Afghanistan as one of the three major obstacles preventing an improvement in Sino-Soviet ties. Soviet president Mikhail Gorbachev's decision in 1988 to remove all Soviet forces from Afghanistan removed this obstacle. The Soviet decision at about the same time to press for the Vietnamese withdrawal from Cambodia (q.v.) and to reduce Soviet forces along the Mongolian border with China removed all remaining barriers to improved Sino-Soviet relations that throughout the late 1980s and 1990s generally prospered, especially on the commercial front. *See also* SINO-SOVIET CONFLICT.

AGRARIAN REFORM LAW. *See* LAND REFORM.

AGRICULTURAL PRODUCERS COOPERATIVES (APCs). Established in 1953 out of the Mutual Aid Teams (q.v.), the APCs emerged as the major organizational structure for China's vast agricultural areas until the late 1950s. The "early stage" APCs created in 1953 did not affect the fundamental property rights of the rural population, though they did introduce the principle of property amalgamation. By the mid-1950s about one-third of the rural population had been enlisted in such APCs, theoretically on a "voluntary" basis, but often through pressure and coercion sanctioned by the CCP (q.v.). Demobilized soldiers from the PLA (q.v.) and Party cadres (q.v.) in China's one million villages provided the organizational weapon for enticing villagers to enter the "early stage" APCs where labor and land were pooled into a common production effort. In July 1955, despite significant progress in APC formation, CCP Chairman Mao Zedong (q.v.) called for a dramatic increase in the pace of APC formation and demanded that the "early stage" APCs be quickly replaced by "higher stage" cooperatives (also known as brigades) in which land ownership was fully collectivized and amalgamated into one APC per "natural village" (*cun*), although some of the 700,000 plus APCs were expanded to cover the much larger "administrative villages" (*xiang*). This organizational transformation meant, in effect, the creation of a unified village economy, particularly for the production of basic grains (wet rice in the south, and wheat/millet in the north). On average, one APC united about 250 families into a single unit led by a village CCP member where decisions on the allocation of labor and land were under the direct authority of the Party. The old landlord class that had been disposed of its property by the 1946–1953 Land Reform (q.v.) and rich peasants became part of the APCs, contributing labor, land, and capital. According to model "higher stage" APC regulations, "all privately owned land, draft animals, major production materials, such as large-scale farm implements were to be turned over to the APC as collective property" (Article 13, APC Regulations). Peasants could retain as private property what they needed for their own livelihood, along with domestic animals and small-scale tools that were needed for individual enterprise. In 1958, the "higher stage" APCs were replaced by the people's communes (q.v.) during the 1958–1960 Great Leap Forward (q.v.).

"AGRICULTURAL RESPONSIBILITY SYSTEM" (*SHENGCHAN ZIRENZHI*). Instituted in 1978 at the watershed Third plenum of the Eleventh Party Congress (q.v.), this system of organizing agriculture replaced the outmoded and highly inefficient rural people's communes (q.v.). The heart of the "responsibility system" is household contracting, technically referred to as "household contracts with fixed levies" (*baogan daohu*) whereby land is parceled out in small plots to individual households on the basis of labor power, and output quotas of particular crops are fixed by contracts signed by Chinese farmers with state purchasing agents. Under this system land is not formally "owned" but leased from the state for a period of fifteen years; this was subsequently extended to thirty years. Surplus output above the contracted amount is retained by the individual household for sale on the open market. Initiated in the late 1970s in one of China's poorest provinces, Anhui, and later in Sichuan, the country's most populated province, this system has since spread to most of China's rural areas, though levels of implementation differ between provinces, with some more conservative areas, such as Guangxi and Heilongjiang provinces, retaining elements of the old socialist model of agricultural production and even going so far as to imprison farmers who dared to dismember the socialist agricultural system.

The impact of the agricultural responsibility system on agricultural production in China was dramatic, especially in the early 1980s. From 1978 to 1983, per capita income more than doubled in the countryside from 133 *yuan* (approximately $67) to 310 yuan ($105) [2 *yuan* = $1, prior to late 1980s; 8 *yuan* = $1 in 1990s]. At the same time, China's rural areas experienced a major boom in housing construction, as farmers invested their newfound wealth in new houses, and a dramatic increase in small-scale rural industries that sopped up some of the surplus labor freed by the household contract system. Production of basic grains, cotton, and cash crops also increased during the 1978–1983 period, though since 1983 production increases have generally leveled off. In 1994, China's total grain yield was 444.6 million tons, 12 million tons below the previous year due to loss of acreage to industry and construction. The per-unit yield in China is still rising, but this may decline in the near future due to loss of fertility and general degradation of the quality of farmland. In 1994, China imported 12 million tons of grain and is expected to meet future shortfalls by additional imports.

The shift to the agricultural responsibility system is generally associated with the policy preferences of China's paramount leader, Deng Xiaoping (q.v.), and Zhao Ziyang (q.v.), the CCP general secretary from 1987 to 1989. Zhao experimented with the policy during his tenure as Party secretary in Sichuan province from 1976 to 1980. Deng Xiaoping supported such a policy even earlier, during the early 1960s after the disastrous Great Leap Forward (q.v.). Concerned with the lack of material incentives among China's suffering peasantry, Deng and other economically liberal-minded leaders in 1962 advocated a similar policy, known as "assigning farm output quotas for individual households" (*baochan daohu*). This policy initiative was quickly vetoed, however, by then CCP Chairman Mao Zedong (q.v.), who called for reinstituting socialist agriculture in the wake of the

Great Leap disaster. *Baochan daohu* was thus condemned during the Cultural Revolution (1966–1976) (q.v.) as a "right-opportunist" concept and "another disguised form of individual undertakings." Not until Mao's death in 1976 did a CCP leader dare revise this judgment and that leader was Deng Xiaoping. *See also* FLOATING POPULATION.

AIDS. About 1,700 cases of HIV infection were reported in China in 1995, a 27 percent increase over 1992. Fewer than 100 people were reported as having developed AIDS, yet only two million people in China have been tested for the virus. In 1992, it was estimated by the World Health Organization that, in fact, more than 10,000 people in China are HIV-positive. The spread of the disease to twenty-four provinces reflects the increase in intravenous drug use since the 1980s, especially in the southwestern province of Yunnan where most AIDS cases have been reported. Sexual transmission is also a problem because of the growth in recent years of prostitution.

The incidence of AIDS in China, as in much of Asia and elsewhere, has been surrounded by social and political controversy. Initially, the Chinese government blamed foreigners for the outbreak of AIDS, as conservative, anti-Western elements in the Chinese government linked the disease to China's Open-Door Policy (q.v.). AIDS has also been associated with the small but growing population of homosexuals in China. The first openly gay bar in Beijing was closed down in 1993 because, the government claimed, it posed health risks, particularly the spread of AIDS. Rigorous testing procedures for anyone entering China—including Chinese-returned students—were also imposed, provoking protests from frequent travelers (especially Overseas Chinese from Hong Kong) after it was discovered that the needles used to draw blood were being reused. Yet many Chinese doctors and medical professionals realize that AIDS is not just a foreign import and thus they support rational responses to the disease, including an education campaign and the construction of the first AIDS hospital in Yunnan. Unfortunately, ignorance of the disease and its transmission are widespread in China: the newly constructed Yunnan hospital has had trouble recruiting nurses and other personnel who fear that the disease can be casually transmitted. At the same time, many Chinese still associate the disease with foreigners and continue to believe that merely touching an infected person or object can cause infection. Chinese students traveling abroad are told by worrisome parents to wear rubber gloves when touching objects, such as doorknobs. The term for AIDS in Chinese has also been politically charged: *aizibing*—the Chinese transliteration of "AIDS"—is similar in pronunciation to a term that means "loving capitalism disease." The Chinese medical system has lagged behind in introducing safety controls: the development of a nationwide blood-testing system was only begun in 1996, and some hospitals reportedly reuse needles to save money. China has participated in several international conferences dealing with AIDS, including the 1994 conference in Japan where, it was warned, Asia will see the largest growth in AIDS cases over the next decade.

ALBANIA. *See* SINO-SOVIET CONFLICT.

ALL-CHINA FEDERATION OF TRADE UNIONS. *See* TRADE UNIONS.

ALL-CHINA FEDERATION OF WOMEN. Established shortly before the Communist takeover in 1949 as the All-China Democratic Women's Federation, it adopted its present name in September 1957. This organization is one of many "mass" organizations used by the CCP (q.v.) to maintain administrative and political control over various social groups. It is one of the three largest such organizations, the other two being the All-China Federation of Trade Unions and the Communist Youth League (q.v.). Other smaller "mass" organizations include the All-China Federation of Students, the All-China Federation of Industry and Commerce, and the All-China Youth Federation. Although formally "autonomous," these "mass" organizations are, in reality, under central control, intimately tied to the state and Communist Party apparatus. Based on the original Leninist-Stalinist model of administrative "transmission belts," their primary function is to mobilize their respective social groups behind policies decided on by Communist Party elites and to promote the political education of their members. Policies supported by the Women's Federation include guaranteeing equal pay for equal work, turning "petty housekeeping" into productive work, developing better education for women and children, and supporting the state's family planning policies. In helping to enforce the one-child policy (q.v.), the Women's Federation has been accused of contributing to the continuing oppression of women in Chinese society.

With more than 100 million members, the Women's Federation is represented in the CPPCC (q.v) and holds annual conferences. During the Cultural Revolution (1966–1976) (q.v.), however, the work of the Women's Federation, as that of all "mass" organizations, was severely disrupted. After 1978, the Women's Federation was reconstituted and headed by Kang Keqing, wife of Communist revolutionary Zhu De (q.v.). The federation's executive committee consists of more than 200 members and includes model workers and nationally prominent women from various fields, such as medicine, health services, culture, and sports.

ALLEY, REWI (1897–1987). A New Zealand–born writer and sympathizer of the CCP (q.v.), Rewi Alley lived in China from 1927 to his death in 1987. As a relief worker for famine and flood victims in the 1930s, Rewi Alley developed a profound compassion for China's poor and indigent population. Along with a group of other foreigners, Alley founded the Industrial Cooperative Movement in rural China that established more than three thousand light industrial cooperatives in villages outside Japanese control during the Sino-Japanese War (1937–1945) (q.v.). He also assisted in training Chinese workers in industrial and agricultural technology in the northwestern province of Gansu, one of China's poorest regions. Although not very political, Rewi Alley protected Communist underground organizers in his Shanghai (q.v.) home from Japanese and KMT (q.v.) persecution. After the Communist takeover in 1949, Alley worked for the Asian Pacific Peace Liaison Committee, a CCP front organization opposed to U.S. policies in Asia. Rewi Alley was a prolific writer and also translated Chinese poetry.

"ALWAYS THINKING OF MONEY" (*YIQIE XIANG QIAN KAN*). Phrase popular during the reform era in the 1980s and 1990s that was often used by political and economic conservatives to attack China's increasingly commercial economy and its social consequences. In orthodox Communist ideology, people should not work for money but to "serve the people" and build the socialist state. During the campaign to build "Socialist Spiritual Civilization" (q.v.), material values were roundly criticized for eroding the social fabric of the country and undermining the "selfless" integrity of the Chinese people. "Always thinking of money" was prima facie evidence that capitalism had penetrated the heart and soul of Chinese society since 1978. Political opponents of Deng Xiaoping (q.v.) used the phrase to attack Deng's ideological position that had replaced "distribution according to need" with the less socialist notion of "distribution according to work" (i.e., material incentives).

ANSHAN IRON AND STEEL CORPORATION. A major steel production facility in the northeastern province of Liaoning in Manchuria (q.v.), the Anshan Iron and Steel Corporation has for many years been China's largest industrial organization. Currently it employs 220,000 workers and produces one quarter of China's entire steel output, estimated at 92 million tons in 1991. Like most factories in China after 1949, Anshan became a center of conflicts among CCP leaders over the proper structure of management and authority. During the early to mid-1950s, the Anshan plant adopted the Soviet model of one-man management in which decision-making authority was vested in a single plant director. This highly centralized authority structure led to the creation of large administrative organs within the facility with direct ties to the Ministry of Metallurgy and other relevant ministries in Beijing (q.v.). This placed the Anshan Party Committee and the facility's workers in an early subordinate position, a situation that provoked a radical effort for industrial reorganization in the late 1950s. Led by the Anshan Party Committee and purportedly supported by the factory's workers, in 1960 the new "charter" of the Anshan Iron and Steel Corporation overturned the Soviet model and instituted a radically new and more decentralized structure of authority that was idealized by Mao Zedong. The charter of the Anshan Corporation has never been published, but according to Mao Zedong it contained the five following principles: give prominence to politics; strengthen the leadership of the Party; unfold mass movements in a big way; promote participation by the proletariat; and carry out technical reform. During the Great Leap Forward (1958–1960) (q.v.), leaders of the Anshan plant were major advocates of the rapid expansion of China's steel production, which led to excessively high targets and ultimately to damage to the country's industrial infrastructure.

ANTI-COUNTERREVOLUTIONARY CAMPAIGNS. From 1949 to the early 1980s, campaigns of mass mobilization and propaganda that targeted individuals and groups with heavy doses of coercion were a stable feature of Chinese society. Two of these campaigns, the first from 1950–1951 and known as the *zhengfan* campaign, and the second from 1955–1957 and known as the *sufan* campaign, targeted so-called counterrevolutionaries (*fangeming*). This label was frequently and arbitrarily attached to any opponent of the Communist regime. The purpose of the first *zhengfan* campaign was, according to CCP chairman Mao Zedong (q.v.), to "wipe out all the bandits, special agents, local tyrants, and other counterrevolutionary elements that bring harm to the people." This included KMT (q.v.) officials who had not fled to Taiwan (q.v.), and also included local landowners and landlords, critics of the new regime, and even businessmen and merchants in China's cities. Altogether, the campaign resulted in the execution of 700,000 to 800,000 people and the imprisonment of several million without the benefit of any legal protection or judicial procedures.

The second campaign, which extended from June 1955 to October 1957, largely spared the general population. This *sufan* campaign began ostensibly as an attack on the Marxist literary critic Hu Feng (q.v.) and his purported counterrevolutionary clique of writers and intellectuals who in 1953 had criticized CCP policies on literature and who had advocated greater freedom of expression. Ultimately, 81,000 intellectuals were implicated and persecuted. In the wake of the purge of top Party leaders Gao Gang and Rao Shushi—the Gao Gang–Rao Shushi Affair (q.v.)—the campaign rapidly expanded into an attack on their alleged supporters in the Party and government. Party members and government personnel under suspicion were detained, interrogated, and often obliged to "confess" their past and present political views. Many were sent for reform through labor (q.v.) without the benefit of any judicial proceedings, though some were released in 1956 and received official CCP apologies for having been falsely accused. By the time the campaign came to a close in October 1957, more than 18 million personnel had been pulled into the intense political struggle and 100,000 purported counterrevolutionaries were exposed inside the CCP the PLA (q.v.), government organizations and schools, and other public organizations. The public security bureaus were prime targets of the campaign as the CCP reasserted control over these potentially politically powerful bodies.

The announced goal of this campaign was to undermine "bureaucratism" (q.v.) among government personnel, to generate greater revolutionary fervor, and to eliminate opponents of the regime within each administrative apparatus. Advocates of the Soviet model of a planned economy and of an elaborate administrative bureaucracy were primary targets. Thus the power of the State Planning Commission, with its many pro-Soviet professionals, was circumscribed, along with the power of industrial managers in state enterprises. The number of deaths, injuries, and disappearances during the campaign has never been ascertained. But during the June 1957 Hundred Flowers (q.v.), liberal intellectuals proposed that committees be established to review the excesses of such anti-counterrevolutionary campaigns, a proposal that Mao Zedong at times reportedly supported. These committees never became a reality, however, as the relatively open Hundred Flowers was quickly followed by the repressive Anti-Rightist campaign (q.v.).

ANTI-LIN [BIAO], ANTI-CONFUCIUS CAMPAIGN (1973–1975). One of many mass study campaigns in China that employed contemporary political criticism and historiographic analogy. Following the death of Lin Biao (q.v.) in 1971 and the failure of his purported Project 571 (q.v.) plan to assassinate CCP Chairman Mao Zedong (q.v.), Lin Biao was one of the major targets of this campaign that was largely carried out in the official Chinese press. The other target was the ancient sage Confucius whose classical writings were subject to scurrilous attacks. In dubbing Lin Biao a "reactionary," one goal of the CCP leadership at this time was obvious: to discredit Lin, who in 1969 had been promoted as Mao Zedong's "closest comrade in arms." Despite Lin Biao's intimate ties with Mao and the radical faction led by Jiang Qing (q.v.) during the early years of the Cultural Revolution (1966–1971) (q.v.), it was claimed that Lin Biao had all along been a "capitalist roader" (q.v.). He was not progressive but retrogressive, a "reactionary" no different from Liu Shaoqi (q.v.) and other victims of the Cultural Revolution whom he himself had persecuted.

The same line of criticism was directed at Confucius (551 B.C.–479 B.C.), though any real similarity between the great classical Chinese philosopher and the former Chinese minister of defense requires a great stretch of the imagination. Writing near the end of China's "feudal" period, before the great transformation of China during the Qin dynasty into a single empire, Confucius, it was claimed, resisted historical progress and idealized the past. According to the propaganda line of the 1973–1975 campaign, Confucius defended the "slave system" in China, opposed the emerging "landlord class," and even denigrated the role of women. The ancient sage was made into a "reactionary" who, along with Lin Biao, was pummeled in China's daily press for almost two years.

Historiographic analogy is a frequent tool of ideological and political struggle in China. Each major faction at this time used the Anti-Lin, Anti-Confucius Campaign to advance its own position. The radical faction, fearing its declining power as Mao Zedong's health in 1973–1974 worsened, surreptitiously turned the campaign against Zhou Enlai (q.v.), with frequent criticism of the Duke of Zhou, a twelfth century B.C. political figure whose book on rituals Confucius had canonized. The moderate faction, led by Deng Xiaoping (q.v.), who was returned to power in 1973, turned the campaign back against the radicals by claiming that Confucius had resisted promoting scientific research and training intellectuals. Deng's foray back into Chinese politics at this time began with his effort to modernize Chinese science and technology and to improve the education system, efforts that the radicals opposed.

The Anti-Lin, Anti-Confucius Campaign was supposed to involve the Chinese people in a great study campaign. Photographs released by the Chinese government showed poor Chinese peasants engaged in "intense debates" about the historical role of Confucius and factory workers "spontaneously" condemning Lin Biao. In reality, by the mid-1970s the Chinese population, and even its political leadership, was exhausted by political campaigns and there was little popular enthusiasm for it. In early 1975, the Anti-Lin, Anti-Confucius Campaign petered out as the last mass campaign of the late Maoist era.

ANTI-RIGHTIST CAMPAIGN (1957–1958). Aside from the Cultural Revolution (1966–1976) (q.v.), this was the most destructive political campaign in the history of Communist China. The targets, who were labeled "rightists" (*youpai*), included intellectuals, members of China's democratic parties (q.v.), and some CCP (q.v.) members who had dared to speak out during the earlier Hundred Flowers campaign (q.v.). Although in June 1957 CCP Chairman Mao Zedong (q.v.) had called on the people to "rectify the Party" and to "express views and speak out freely," those who took Mao up on his offer were quickly subject to persecution in the Anti-Rightist campaign that lasted for more than a year. Contrary to Mao's expectation that Chinese intellectuals and non-Communist political figures would, if given the chance, freely praise the CCP, these highly articulate groups used their brief period of free expression to excoriate the CCP for its mismanagement of Chinese society and especially for promoting people into prominent positions on the basis of political loyalty rather than merit. After June 1957, such criticism was labeled as "counterrevolutionary" and more than 500,000 people were punished, ranging from the rather mild penalty of a reduction in pay and rank for "ordinary rightists" (*yiban youpai*) and "middle rightists" (*zhong youpai*), to more severe retributions of dismissal from the Party and from employment and/or sentencing to labor camps to undergo "thought reform" (q.v.) and manual labor for "extreme rightists" (*ji youpai*). Some of those accused committed suicide and others went mad. In 1959, the State Council and the CPPCC (q.v.) "reversed the verdicts" (*pingfan*) (q.v.) of many "rightists" who had been wrongly accused, though most still retained the "rightist" label (also referred to as a "hat"). Attacks on these individuals were renewed during the Cultural Revolution (1966–1976) when even more severe punishments were meted out by Red Guards (q.v.) and other political thugs against former "rightists." Beginning in 1978, the future CCP Chairman Hu Yaobang (q.v.) led an effort to rehabilitate the "rightists" once and for all. Most elderly "rightists" had their labels permanently removed as their personnel dossiers (q.v.) containing political accusations were returned to their person. But some "rightists," such as the journalist Chu Anping, had not, as of 1996, been officially "rehabilitated," evidently out of deference to CCP patriarch Deng Xiaoping (q.v.) who had been the chief prosecutor of the "rightists" in 1957 at the behest of Mao Zedong and who insisted that the campaign not be fully discredited.

ANTI-SPIRITUAL POLLUTION CAMPAIGN (1983–1984). A very brief campaign that began in October 1983 during which leftist CCP (q.v.) leaders tried unsuccessfully to repress certain social trends that they found offensive. Even as the Communist leadership pursued pro-market policies in the economic sector, leftist influence in the Party was evident in this propaganda campaign that stressed ideological orthodoxy in the face of growing foreign social and cultural influence stemming from China's Open-Door Policy (q.v.). Everything from the Agricultural Responsibility System (q.v.) to Western-style dress to rock music was targeted for criticism in the Chinese media. As part of the campaign, local cadres (q.v.) froze the bank accounts of rich peasants and budding entrepreneurs as peasants were condemned for being influenced by "decadent capitalist ideas and remnant feudal ideas," such as "always thinking of money" (q.v.) and "disregarding the interests of the state and collective." Almost immediately, however, the campaign provoked the united opposition of the then CCP general secretary Hu Yaobang (q.v.), Premier Zhao Ziyang (q.v.), and other committed reformers in the CCP leadership who also feared a repeat of the mass mobilization and mass frenzy of the Cultural Revolution (1966–1976) (q.v.). Although sympathetic to the campaign's denunciation of democracy and its call for ideological orthodoxy, Deng Xiaoping (q.v.) bristled at its attack on the Special Economic Zones (q.v.), the centerpiece of his economic reform program. Concern was also expressed by foreign investors and businessmen that China was reverting to its Maoist past which was fundamentally antagonistic to the Open-Door trade policy and its integration into the world economy. Thus, after only 28 days, in November 1983 the campaign was effectively restricted to the ideological realm, despite protestations from leftist and conservative elements in the Chinese leadership, such as Deng Liqun (q.v.) and Chen Yun (q.v.), who supported the campaign's basic goals.

APRIL 5TH MOVEMENT (1976). This crucial political event, also known as the first "Tiananmen Incident," marked the beginning of the end for the radical policies of the Maoist dictatorship and the turn to the economic reforms that were inaugurated in 1978. April 5 is the traditional festival day for "sweeping the graves" (*qingming*) when Chinese people pay homage to their ancestors. On this day in 1976, thousands of Beijing (q.v.) residents showed up in the massive Tiananmen Square at the city center to honor the recently deceased and highly revered premier of China, Zhou Enlai (q.v.), whose death in January earlier that year had been largely ignored by the press, which at the time was under the tight control of Jiang Qing (q.v.) and her radical supporters. Wreaths, banners, and slogans were raised to commemorate the beloved Zhou by crowds that on April 5 grew to more than 100,000 people. Attacks on radical political leaders and even Mao Zedong (q.v.) were also voiced by demonstrators who chanted "Long Live the People" as a comeback to the Cultural Revolution (q.v.) era chant of "Long Live Chairman Mao." These attacks on Mao and his personality cult (q.v.) and the radical program provoked the mayor of Beijing, Wu De (q.v.), to order the crowds to be dispersed. In the melee that followed, hundreds of people were injured and many were arrested and reportedly later executed. The demonstrations were immediately labeled "counterrevolutionary" by the CCP (q.v.) leadership which quickly moved to oust Deng Xiaoping (q.v.), whom many of the demonstrators had supported. Hua Guofeng (q.v.) was named premier and first vice chairman of the CCP, which put him in a clear position to succeed the then ailing Mao Zedong.

After the death of Mao Zedong in September 1976, and the subsequent arrest of radical leaders headed by the Gang of Four (q.v.), in November 1978 the CCP reversed its official position on the April 5th Movement. Demonstrators arrested in 1976 were released and calls were made to punish those remaining Party leaders who had authorized the post–April 5 executions, though this was never done. The April 5th Movement is considered the precursor to the 1978–1979 and 1989 Democracy Movements (q.v.) since it marked the first time average Chinese people directly challenged state authority.

ATOMIC BOMB. On October 16, 1964, China exploded its first nuclear weapon in a desert region of Xinjiang, an autonomous region in the country's northwest. This successful experiment culminated a decade-long effort by the Chinese government to achieve nuclear power status with the other nuclear powers, particularly the United States. The day after the explosion, Premier Zhou Enlai (q.v.) pressed for the "complete prohibition and thorough destruction of nuclear weapons," claiming that China's entry into the nuclear club had been "compelled" by the actions of the United States and other nuclear powers in the West. From 1964 to 1978, China carried out 25 separate nuclear tests underground and in the atmosphere involving a variety of weapons for use on bombers and missiles. In the 1990s, China still conducted periodic underground tests, despite a moratorium on similar tests by the United States and Russia. Currently, China is a major nuclear power possessing an inventory of nuclear weapons greater in number than Britain and France combined.

China's decision to join the nuclear club came in reaction to its participation in the 1950–1953 Korean War (q.v.). Although Mao Zedong (q.v.) dubbed the atomic bomb as a "paper tiger," he and other top CCP (q.v.) leaders, such as Nie Rongzhen (q.v.), believed that China could survive in the modern-day world of power politics only by developing and deploying the most advanced weaponry. The American threat near the end of the Korean conflict to use nuclear devices against Chinese targets in Manchuria (q.v.) convinced China's leaders that never again should the country be forced to submit to "nuclear blackmail." In 1958, during the Taiwan Straits Crisis (q.v.), the Chinese commitment to develop its own nuclear program was further spurred on by the decision of the Soviet Union, under the leadership of Nikita Khrushchev, not to provide China with nuclear secrets. Key scientists involved in China's nuclear program included many trained in the West, such as Qian Sanqiang and his wife, He Zehui, and Deng Jiaxian, who had studied in France and the United States, respectively. In its early stage of development, China was also assisted by the French couple, Frédéric and Irène Joliot-Curie, who helped Qian Sanqiang to purchase nuclear instruments in Europe and provided the Chinese physicist with samples of radium salt. During the 1980s and 1990s, China has been periodically accused, primarily by the United States, of attempting to assist other nations, such as Pakistan, in developing nuclear weapons in violation of the Nuclear Non-Proliferation Pact to which China is a signatory.

B

BA JIN (1904–   ). A major literary figure in China since the 1930s and a longtime anarchist, Ba Jin is the author of such famous novels as *Family* (*Jia*) and translator of the Russian writer Turgenev's *Fathers and Sons*. Since 1949 he has served in the NPC (q.v.) and as vice chairman of the All-China Writers' Association. During the Cultural Revolution (1966–1976) (q.v.) he was branded a "counterrevolutionary" and purged. He reappeared in 1977 and resumed his illustrious literary career, becoming president of the Chinese PEN Center and acting chairman of the All-China Writers' Association. In 1985 he was inducted as a foreign honorary member of the U.S. National Academy of Arts and Letters and in 1988 was reelected vice chairman of the CPPCC (q.v.). A supporter of the 1989 pro-democracy movement, Ba Jin was criticized by the Chinese government, but was left unharmed.

"BACKYARD STEEL FURNACES" (*XIAO GAOLU*). Along with the people's communes (q.v.), backyard steel furnaces were the most significant product (and one of the biggest disasters) of the 1958–1960 Great Leap Forward (q.v.). The furnaces were a central feature of the Chinese concept of "walking on two legs," that is, of carrying out economic and technological modernization by promoting both relatively capital-intensive, large-scale production units, and relatively labor-intensive, small-scale, and technologically backward production facilities.

The backyard steel furnaces originated in August 1958 when CCP (q.v.) Chairman and prime designer of the Great Leap, Mao Zedong (q.v.), plunged China into an all-out steel production campaign. This campaign was to increase the country's steel output dramatically to a level of 10 million tons, thus putting China well on the road to Mao's declared goal of surpassing British steel production in 15 years. Small, puddling-style furnaces were set up throughout the Chinese countryside and in cities, with the "steel" often smelted out of broken pots, kettles, and other iron implements contributed by the local population. At the height of the Great Leap, it was claimed that 49 percent of China's total steel production came from the backyard furnaces, with the rest supplied by more conventional plants in China's industrial centers in the northeast and Shanghai (q.v.). With tens of millions of peasants and urban residents contributing to the steel campaign, the target of 10 million tons was reached. Yet the costs were enormous since much of the steel from the backyard furnaces proved useless. More importantly, peasants ignored the more mundane, and less "heroic," tasks of harvesting bumper crops that were left to rot in the fields.

During the frenzy of the Great Leap, no one among the top CCP leadership dared criticize the backyard furnaces, except for Peng Dehuai (q.v.), who after visiting the countryside during the Leap, questioned Mao Zedong about the strategy and was thereafter purged for his impudence. Other leaders, such as Chen Yun (q.v.), had lingering doubts, but were unwilling to risk their political (and physical) lives by questioning Chairman Mao. Yet in the face of the cold realities, even Mao had to back down and thus the backyard furnaces were finally shut down in late 1959. By draining critical labor supplies in the countryside, the furnaces contributed to the devastating famine that occurred in the early 1960s, which cost perhaps more than 30 million lives. The furnaces were roundly criticized after Mao's death in 1976, as were many aspects of the ill-fated Great Leap Forward. *See also* GREAT LEAP FORWARD and TIAN JIAYING.

BAI HUA (1930–   ). A member of the PLA (q.v.), Bai Hua was labeled an "anti-socialist element" during the 1957 Anti-Rightist campaign (q.v.) and attacked during the 1966–1976 Cultural Revolution (q.v.). After returning to the army in 1977, he became famous in 1979 at a National Congress of Literature and Art by declaring: "No courage, no breakthrough, no breakthrough, no literature." Bai earned additional distinction by supporting the 1979 Democracy Wall Movement (q.v.) and by proclaiming that "Never again should we sing the praises of any savior." In 1981, Bai Hua's screenplay *Unrequited Love* was criticized for its portrayal of a patriotic artist who returns to China only to be savagely attacked by Maoist political officials. Accused of violating the Four Cardinal Principles (q.v.) and of being unpatriotic, this script set off a major political controversy between reformers and opponents of reform in the Chinese government over political control of the arts. Labeled the "Bai Hua Incident," the attack on Bai Hua brought to an end the relatively unrestricted literary freedom of the 1979–1980 period. The CCP's (q.v.) promulgation of Central Directive No. 7 in 1981 ordered, inter alia, that "artists must support the Four Cardinal Principles" and not "leave people sick at heart when dealing with the Anti-Rightist campaign or the Cultural Revolution." This created a chill in Chinese literary and artistic circles, though dissident writers and artists were generally treated with a lighter hand than they had been in the 1950s and 1960s. Bai Hua is a member of the All-China Writers' Association and works for the Wuhan Military Region in central China. In 1988, he visited France and the United States.

BANDUNG CONFERENCE (1955). At this conference of twenty-nine African and Asian nations held in Bandung, Indonesia, China's Foreign Minister, Zhou Enlai (q.v.), articulated Chinese policies stressing peaceful coexistence and neutrality toward other Third World nations. Despite China's association with the Soviet Union in the Communist bloc, Zhou emphasized China's solidarity with African and Asian nations that were trying to escape the pressures of the different power blocs and to forge an independent, third path to national development and independence. This "spirit" of Bandung led Zhou to propose opening negotiations with the United States and to express gestures of friendship to small, non-Communist Asian nations, such as the Philippines and Thailand, which feared Chinese support for domestic Communist insurgents. China embraced the Five Principles of Coexistence as it tried to appear as first an underdeveloped nation, rather than a Communist state. China also used this opportunity to develop increasingly cordial relations with African nations and with the host country of Indonesia until the 1965 anti-Communist and anti-Chinese coup there effectively terminated the two countries' relations for 25 years. In the 1960s, China's support for peaceful coexistence and neutrality gradually gave way to a more militant and aggressive foreign policy articulated by Mao Zedong (q.v.) and Lin Biao (q.v.), bringing to an end China's embrace of the Bandung "spirit." *See also* VIETNAM and LIN BIAO.

BANK OF CHINA. In 1979, the Bank of China was split off from the People's Bank of China (q.v.) and granted authority as the Chinese government's foreign exchange bank. Its main operations are to manage international settlements relating to trade and nontrade transactions with foreign countries and to handle export and import loans and foreign exchange loans. The bank can also issue stocks in foreign currencies and marketable securities. The power of the bank has been reduced as economic reforms initiated since 1978 provide for decentralized control over foreign exchange. *See also* PEOPLE'S BANK OF CHINA.

BAO TONG (1934–   ). A close adviser to CCP (q.v.) General Secretary Zhao Ziyang (q.v.), Bao Tong rose to political prominence in the late 1970s when, as director of the State Science and Technology Commission, he drafted speeches for Deng Xiaoping (q.v.) on political reform, including proposals for the separation of Party and government. Bao became a member of the CCP Central Committee at the 1987 Thirteenth Party Congress and beginning in 1988 headed the Research Center to Reform the Political Structure. Bao Tong was also the personal secretary to Zhao Ziyang, political secretary of the Politburo (q.v.), and a vice minister of the State Economic Reform Commission. Accused of conspiring with students against the Chinese state, Bao was arrested after the 1989 Beijing massacre and sentenced to seven years in prison. He was released in May 1996 but kept under house arrest.

BAOSHAN IRON AND STEEL COMPLEX. Located outside Shanghai (q.v.), this huge production facility is one of China's largest steel plants, along with the Anshan Iron and Steel Corporation (q.v.). Baoshan was begun in the late 1970s as a central component of then CCP (q.v.) Chairman Hua Guofeng's (q.v.) grandiose design for a "foreign leap forward" in which plans called for completion of several major industrial facilities financed by foreign loans and investment, especially from Japan. In 1978, in the midst of an overheated economy and an impending state budget deficit, and in a political climate in which Hua Guofeng's position was being seriously challenged by the reemergence of Deng Xiaoping (q.v.), one thousand joint ventures, including the Baoshan plant, were terminated or put on hold. Not until Japan agreed to provide an extra 300 billion yuan in commodity loans was the plant completed. More than 200,000 workers are employed at the plant, which like most state-owned enterprises, operated at a loss throughout the 1980s and 1990s. Production at the plant in 1992 was more than 3.5 million tons. In 1994, China's nationwide production of

92 million tons of steel was the largest in the world, though it is very costly and often of poor quality.

"BAREFOOT DOCTORS" (*CHIJIAO YISHENG*). This is an affectionate appellation purportedly used by peasants during the 1960s and early 1970s to refer to health workers who were given rudimentary training in order to bring basic public health care to China's hinterland. The "barefoot doctors" originated with Mao Zedong's (q.v.) "Instructions Concerning Health Work" in June 1965, which advocated bringing medical and health work to the neglected rural areas. The Soviet model of economic and social development adopted by China since 1949 had, in Mao's view, concentrated China's limited resources on the urban areas as policy realms such as health care were dominated by professionals in the Ministry of Public Health who paid inadequate attention to the health needs of China's vast rural population. In August 1965, Mao's instruction was picked up by the Hebei Provincial Committee, which proposed training part-peasant, part-medical doctors and one health worker and one midwife for each production brigade (q.v.) in the province. These individuals were to be prepared by medical and health personnel from hospitals at the county (*xian*) level. This policy was quickly endorsed by the Ministry of Public Health but was later dropped after the initiation of the economic reforms in 1978.

BASIC LAW FOR HONG KONG. This is the constitutional political structure under which Hong Kong is governed since the British colony reverted to Chinese sovereignty in July 1997. The Basic Law was passed by the Seventh NPC in April 1990, six years after negotiations were completed between China and the government of Great Britain in 1984 on the future status of Hong Kong. Under the terms of the Chinese state constitution passed by the NPC, Hong Kong and the Portuguese colony of Macao which reverts to China in 1999 assume the status of Special Administrative Regions (SAR) upon their reversion to China. This provision allows for particular regions in China to establish their own social-economic systems in accord with Deng Xiaoping's concept of "one country, two systems" (q.v.). The Basic Law is the implementing instrument of the SAR and carries the force of law. Institutionally, the Basic Law called for the creation of a powerful chief executive—Tung Chee-hwa (q.v.)—who both enforces the laws passed by the Hong Kong legislature and implements directives issued by the Chinese central government in Beijing (q.v.). Although Article 45 of the Basic Law indicates that the chief executive will be elected by universal suffrage, the Chinese government retains the power of veto, thereby ensuring that the chief executive will be subservient to Beijing's policies. A Legislative Council will also be established consisting of sixty members to be elected by geographical and functional constituencies, but with only limited direct election. The judiciary will consist of a Court of Final Appeal, a High Court, and district courts with judges appointed by the SAR chief executive. Originally, it was agreed that a judge from another common law jurisdiction would sit on the Final Court of Appeal for the entire judicial term, but this was later reduced to one half-term per year, a decision made over the objections of the pre-July 1997 Legislative Council in Hong Kong. The establishment of the Hong Kong Court of Final Appeal is regarded as a vital legal measure to ensure the colony's freedom after 1997.

"BASIC LINE OF THE PARTY" (*DANGDE JIBEN LUXIAN*). The fundamental parameters for policy in China are set by the "basic line of the Party" as enumerated by the CCP (q.v.) top leadership. From 1949 to 1976, it was Chairman Mao Zedong (q.v.) whose speeches and proclamations constituted the Party's basic line. Since 1976, this task has fallen to Deng Xiaoping (q.v.) whose "Four Cardinal Principles" (q.v.) have constituted the basic line since their enunciation in March 1979. Specific policies, speeches by other leaders, and general work pursued by CCP cadres (q.v.) must conform with the basic line. To do otherwise is to risk ouster from positions of authority. During the Maoist era deviance from the Party line could even mean purge or possibly physical elimination. Terms of the basic line are expressed in general language and thus can often be used as license to carry out major political struggles. This occurred in the case of Mao Zedong's 1962 statement that ". . . Socialist society covers a considerably long historical period. In the historical period of socialism, there are still classes, class contradictions, and class struggle (q.v.). There is the struggle between the socialist road and the capitalist road, and there is the danger of capitalist restoration." This and other general statements on the Communist Party's basic line became the foundation for the political struggles and attacks on top Party leaders, such as Liu Shaoqi (q.v.), during the Cultural Revolution (1966–1976) (q.v.). Deng Xiaoping's March 1979 "Four Cardinal Principles" were also the basis thereafter for opposing any efforts at substantial political reform in the PRC.

"BASIC UNIT" (*JIBEN DANWEI*). The matrix of basic-level organization in China into which all work and most residential units are structured, the basic unit is a self-sustaining, relatively closed, microsocial system with substantial political, personnel, financial, and social power. Organized geographically and functionally, the basic unit maintains comprehensive control over its members through regulation of basic necessities (housing, food distribution, jobs, and medical care), allocation of rewards (job promotions, permission to marry, bear children, and to divorce), and discharge of punishments (reductions in salary and housing privileges). Basic units are headed by a unit leader or administrator who, prior to the 1980s, was also the secretary of the Party committee that exists within all basic units. As a result of the preliminary political reforms of the 1980s, non-Party members were allowed to serve as unit leaders. Basic units also hold the personnel dossiers (q.v.) that are kept on every urban resident. During the Maoist period (1949–1976), the basic unit was a critical component of China's totalitarian system by monitoring the population through the CCP's (q.v.) elaborate vertical structure and effectively preventing lateral social organization among the population. Transfer out of a basic unit was rare; for most urbanites their work in the unit was for a lifetime. This not only created enormous tensions among the members of these small societies, but also serious rigidities in the allocation of labor, as some units would have oversupplies and other units deficits, without any method to share labor. But since the economic reforms and market system of the 1980s created greater labor mobility and lateral social organization, it is generally believed that the basic-unit system has weakened somewhat. During the 1989 Tiananmen massacre, many basic units in Beijing protected their members from arrest and surreptitiously documented the deaths and injuries caused by the military crackdown.

"BEATING, SMASHING, LOOTING, RANSACKING, AND KID-NAPPING" (*DA, ZA, QIANG, CHAO, ZHUA*). This phrase captures the random violence and outright thuggery that was committed by Red Guards (q.v.) and others during the most violent phases of the Cultural Revolution (1966–1976) (q.v.). Although Red Guards had been admonished by Mao Zedong (q.v.) to "struggle by reason," the attacks on Party cadres (q.v.) and CCP (q.v.) leaders, teachers, writers, and artists, and other targets singled out for persecution, quickly degenerated into wanton acts of violence. Top leaders, such as Liu Shaoqi (q.v.), were placed in cold, dark, isolated cells and submitted to hours of endless interrogation, after which they often collapsed from exhaustion and died. Writers and artists had their hands broken (to insure they could no longer produce "bourgeois art") and in some cases were then murdered or driven to suicide. Heavy doses of violence—including cannibalism—were meted out either by small groups of Red Guards or at mass rallies often attended by top leaders within the radical faction, such as Ye Qun (q.v.), Lin Biao's (q.v.) wife. In the countryside, the targets of Red Guard abuse were incarcerated in the notorious "cow sheds" where unsanitary conditions, limited food, and days-into-months of isolation also resulted in death or suicide. Jiang Qing (q.v.) and other radical leaders generally encouraged the violence and ordered the Public Security (q.v.) Bureau and the PLA (q.v.) not to intervene. By 1968, Mao Zedong and other top leaders put a stop to the worst violence, at least in the cities, by sending youth to the countryside and ordering the army to restrain Red Guard rampages.

BEIDA (PEKING UNIVERSITY). The premier university in China, Peking University was established in 1898 as the Imperial University and was renamed Peking University in 1912 after the downfall of the Qing dynasty (1644–1911) and the establishment of the ROC. The May Fourth Movement (1919–1923) (q.v.), ushering in modern Chinese nationalism, began at the university under the leadership of university professors led by Chen Duxiu (the founder in 1921 of the CCP) and many students. After the Communist seizure of power in 1949, the university was reorganized as part of the nationwide campaign of restructuring higher education. It was moved to its current site on the campus of former Yenching University in the western suburbs of China's capital city of Beijing (q.v.). The university was expanded into multidisciplinary programs of sciences, technology, humanities, social sciences, management, and education; Ma Yinchu, a renowned professor of economics, was chancellor until his purge in the 1960s. In 1989, the university had more than 9,000 undergraduates, 3,000 postgraduates, and in excess of 2,000 faculty members. The university has a Modern Physics Research Center headed by the world-renowned Nobel laureate physicist Li Zhengdao. Like all Chinese universities, Beida operates under the authority of the State Education Commission and is subject to political control by the Chinese state. Following the 1989 prodemocracy movement, the university's president, Ding Shisun, was replaced and the entering freshman class in fall 1989 was required to undergo one year of military training before matriculation.

BEIDAIHE CONFERENCE (1958). A critical meeting of the Communist Party leadership in August 1958 that committed the country to the ill-fated Great Leap Forward (1958–1960) (q.v.). Beidaihe is a summer resort on China's northeast coast where top CCP leaders from the Politburo (q.v.) retreat every summer in late August for high-level discussions and decisions. At this particular meeting held in mid-August 1958, Mao Zedong (q.v.) pushed through his plan to set up people's communes (q.v.) in the Chinese countryside and advocated major increases in domestic steel production through the resmelting of scrap steel and the infamous backyard steel furnaces (q.v.). In his major speech at the conference, Mao declared that the people's communes contained the "sprouts of communism" and he predicted that this new form of agricultural organization would provide China with a substantial grain surplus. Mao also extravagantly predicted that steel production would increase by millions of tons, such that every village in the country (there are more than one million) could build an airport. A substantial expansion of the People's Militia (q.v.) was also proposed. The Beidaihe conference represented the peak of Mao's utopian vision.

BEIJING. The capital of the PRC since 1949, Beijing in Chinese means "northern capital." The city became China's relatively permanent capital in 1271 during the Yuan dynasty (1264–1368) and remained so until 1928 when the KMT (q.v.) government under Chiang Kai-shek named Nanjing (Nanking), "southern capital," as the official capital of the ROC. (Nanjing had briefly served as the Chinese capital during the early phases of the Ming dynasty in the late fourteenth century). During the Nationalist interregnum (1928–1949), Beijing was renamed Beiping, "northern peace" (in Wade-Giles, Pei-p'ing), until the city was restored as the traditional seat of government in 1949 by the Communists who renamed it Beijing. (Nationalist authorities on Taiwan, however, still refer to the city as Pei-p'ing). The layout of the city on a north-south and east-west axis and its checkerboard streets reflect the traditional cosmology of the Chinese dynastic system. Central Beijing is dominated by the ancient Forbidden City (which is now a museum open to the public) and the giant 100 acre Tiananmen Square, which was quadrupled in size in 1958. Beijing was once surrounded, like all Chinese cities, by high city walls, but they were destroyed by the Communist authorities in the 1950s, much to the chagrin of local residents and city preservationists.

Beijing municipality (*Beijing shi*) is more than 16,000 square kilometers in size, and includes both urban and rural areas. The latter are broken down administratively into counties (*xian*) and the former into districts (*qu*) and subdistricts (*fenqu*). Total population of the municipality in 1993 was 11.12 million. In addition to serving as the site of the central Chinese government, Beijing is a major center of industry including electronics, textiles, chemicals, and steel production. The Capital Iron and Steel Corporation is located in the western part of the city and is one of China's largest such facilities. In June 1989, Beijing was one of the major sites of the pro-democracy movement and the military crackdown on June 3–4. *See also* BEIJING SPRING.

BEIJING OPERA. *See* PEKING OPERA.

BEIJING SPRING. This term is used to refer to two movements for democracy in recent Chinese history: the 1978–1979 Democracy Wall Movement (q.v.) and the pro-democracy movement from April to June 1989. *Beijing Spring (Beijing zhi chun)* is also the title of one of the major underground periodicals published in the 1978–1979 period.

The second Beijing Spring occurred in April-June 1989 when pro-democracy demonstrations broke out in China's capital city and in about one hundred other urban areas. It ended with a massacre around Beijing's (q.v.) Tiananmen Square on June 3–4, 1989. The immediate cause of this movement was the sudden death of the reformist CCP (q.v.) leader Hu Yaobang (q.v.) who had lost his position as general secretary of the Communist Party in 1987 but had remained a beacon of hope for students, intellectuals, and other social groups committed to substantial political reform. Hu's death in April 1989 and the rising power of hard-line conservatives led by premier Li Peng (q.v.) seemed to spell an end to China's ten years of reform that had begun in December 1978. Other festering social and economic problems helped generate the outburst of protests during the six-week Beijing Spring, including uncontrolled inflation, growing unemployment, corruption (q.v.) among Party leaders, and deteriorating conditions on China's college campuses.

At the height of the pro-democracy movement in late April and early May 1989, more than one million people filled the streets of the capital in peaceful demonstrations. The demonstrations were initiated largely by college students. But following a stern warning to the demonstrators in an April 26 editorial in the Party mouthpiece, *People's Daily* (q.v.), and especially after the declaration of a hunger strike by students on May 13, support quickly mushroomed among a variety of social groups, including intellectuals, newspaper reporters, government employees, urban residents (*shimin*), workers, peasants, and even some military and CCP personnel. Demands ranged from calls for more money for education to government recognition of the movement as "patriotic." Students also demanded that a dialogue be held with the government (which in fact occurred on nationwide TV), that Deng Xiaoping (q.v.) and Li Peng (q.v.) retire, and that there be fundamental institutional changes in the direction of greater democracy, legality, and individual freedoms. Just as the demonstrations seemed to be winding down and the hunger strike was called off, the government summarily declared martial law on the night of May 19, opening the way for the PLA (q.v.) to enter the capital, the first time army units had entered the city since its "liberation" (q.v.) in 1949.

Yet even the entry of overwhelming military force from the local garrison command in Beijing did not stifle the movement so much as reenergize it, as huge demonstrations occurred on May 21 and May 23. Urban residents and students joined in blocking military vehicles and established a defensive cordon around Tiananmen Square. For over two weeks a stalemate ensued as students refused to budge from Tiananmen (though the numbers occupying the increasingly fetid square diminished substantially) and the government apparently refused to authorize the use of lethal force against the Beijing citizenry. But after the purge of CCP general secretary Zhao Ziyang (q.v.) (who vehemently opposed the use of force), and an apparent nod from Party patriarch Deng Xiaoping, the way was open for using force to clear the square and to put down the democracy movement. Moving swiftly with coordinated actions throughout the city on the night of June 3 and the early morning hours of June 4, elements of Chinese army units opened fire in and around Tiananmen and in outlying parts of the city where the most number of casualties apparently occurred. Upwards of 2,000 people were killed in the military assault, though a final count is still unavailable. (Immediately after the crackdown the Chinese government admitted to only 300 dead, with many of the casualties occurring among PLA soldiers.) By the morning of June 4, Tiananmen was "recaptured" by the PLA and the city was put under virtual military occupation that lasted for several weeks. With student leaders either killed or on the run—several, including Wu'er Kaixi (q.v.), made it out of the country—this second Beijing Spring came to a rapid halt. *See also* DEMOCRACY WALL MOVEMENT.

BETHUNE, NORMAN (1890–1939). A Canadian doctor and prominent surgeon in Montreal, Norman Bethune traveled to China in 1937 after having served the Republican forces in the Spanish Civil War. Working behind Japanese enemy lines, Bethune brought rudimentary health care to many Chinese villages and to Communist soldiers wounded in battle. With very little available medicine, Bethune traveled throughout the Chinese countryside where he set up mobile medical care units and tended night and day to the sick and wounded. After incurring a self-inflicted cut while operating, Bethune developed septicemia, but lacked the necessary antibiotics to cure the disease from which he died in 1939. "In Memory of Norman Bethune," written by Mao Zedong (q.v.), lauds the doctor's selfless contributions to the Chinese people and was standard reading for Chinese children who were encouraged to put aside self-interest so as to "serve the people" (*weirenmin fuwu*).

"BIG-CHARACTER POSTERS" (*DAZIBAO*). A primary form of mass communication in China, big-character posters have been generally used for political purposes. First introduced in the Rectification Campaign (q.v.) of 1942–1944, they were a staple feature during the 1957–1958 rectification and especially during the Cultural Revolution (1966–1976) (q.v.) and the 1978–1979 Democracy Wall Movement (q.v.). In 1980, the NPC (q.v.) outlawed "big-character posters" as part of its deletion of the "Four Big Freedoms" (q.v.) from the state constitution in reaction to the growth of democratic forces in Chinese society. Nevertheless, during subsequent periods of political conflict involving the general population "big-character posters" criticizing the regime appeared on university campuses and at other sites of political protest. Thousands of such posters were mounted during the Beijing Spring (q.v.) from April to June 1989 and have been preserved in a series of volumes on the 1989 Democracy Movement in China. *See* the bibliography.

The popularity of "big-character posters" is in their direct appeal to the general population. Posters are written with Chinese ink brushes that produce large easy-to-read Chinese-language characters and then are pasted on walls that dominate the landscape in most Chinese cities and villages. During the mass mobilization campaigns directed by the government, such as that in 1957–1958, they served the interests of the CCP (q.v.) political leadership by directly communicating with the general populace, thereby circumventing the official press that at the popular level is often ignored or difficult to understand for many Chinese with limited literacy. During the initial stages of the Cultural Revolution, Mao Zedong authored his own "big-character poster" (titled "Bombard the Headquarters") to attack his main political rival, Liu Shaoqi (q.v.). In this way Mao could circumvent the CCP Propaganda Department whose control over the regular channels of communication (newspapers, radio, and TV) was purportedly in the hands of Liu's supporters. Mao's action legitimated the use of posters, which quickly became the major tool by which various Red Guard (q.v.) factions attacked government officials, intellectuals, and one another.

The appearance of "big-character posters" in the 1978–1979 Democracy Wall Movement was initially praised by Deng Xiaoping (q.v.) in his struggle at that time with Hua Guofeng (q.v.) and members of the "Two Whatevers" faction (q.v.). After Deng consolidated power in 1979–1980, however, he quickly turned against the Democracy Wall Movement and persecuted its leaders, such as Wei Jingsheng (q.v.), who was arrested in March 1979 for authoring perhaps one of the most famous "big-character posters" in China's recent history on the subject of democracy. In 1980, Deng thus supported abolishing the legal use of the posters that had been recognized in Article 45 of the PRC state constitution. Nine years later, during the Beijing Spring Democracy Movement, thousands of "big-character posters" appeared in Beijing and many other Chinese cities, some calling for Deng's resignation and quoting his own words on the need for reform. But since the Democracy Movement was crushed in June 1989, few posters have appeared publicly as the strong arm of state control prevents spontaneous political expression.

BIRTH CONTROL. *See* ONE-CHILD POLICY.

BO YIBO (1908–). Bo Yibo became a member of the CCP (q.v.) Central Committee in 1945 and of the Politburo (q.v.) in 1956. Throughout the 1950s and early 1960s, he served in various posts dealing with the economy, such as minister of finance and the vice chairman of the State Planning Commission. After his purge during the Cultural Revolution (1966–1976) (q.v.), Bo was rehabilitated in 1978 and assumed key positions in the government overseeing the economy and in the Party. In 1982 he joined the Central Advisory Commission (q.v.) as one of its vice chairmen in nominal "retire-ment," but he reportedly approved of the military crackdown in Beijing in June 1989.

"BOURGEOIS LIBERALIZATION" (*ZICHANJIEJI ZIYOUHUA*). The catchall term used by the CCP (q.v.) leadership to criticize the political, social, and cultural values of Western liberalism that Chi-nese intellectuals and young people have found attractive in the 1980s and 1990s and that clash with socialist orthodoxy. Despite the greater openness in China since the beginning of the reforms in 1978, ele-ments in the Communist regime fear the inherent attraction of West-ern notions of individual freedom and democracy that have been de-cried as "decadent capitalist ideology" and "money worshipping." For many relatively liberal Chinese intellectuals and artists, "bour-geois" ideas involve more profound values, such as respect for scien-tific knowledge over dogma, greater attention to talent instead of po-litical and personal favoritism, and more independence for academic research and artistic creation—realms that the CCP has controlled since the 1940s. Chinese intellectuals would also like to see greater freedom to explore the verities of the official orthodoxy of Marxism-Leninism-Mao Zedong Thought (q.v.), instead of unquestioned obe-dience.

The regime's opposition to "bourgeois liberalization" peaked in 1986–1987 when a nationwide "anti-bourgeois liberalization" cam-paign was inaugurated in the wake of the ouster of then CCP general secretary Hu Yaobang (q.v.). Although official media, such as the *People's Daily* (q.v.), were full of vitriolic denunciations of Western ideas and cultural values, at schools and universities the campaign was essentially ignored, even by local CCP personnel who themselves often found "bourgeois liberal" ideas attractive. Following the Tiananmen crackdown in June 1989, criticism of "bourgeois liberalization" was renewed in the media and at schools and colleges, but many intellectuals and students boycotted the campaign. In the early 1990s the campaign degenerated into an effort by the authorities to punish individuals with foreign friends and contacts. By 1993, however, the regime largely dropped the "anti-bourgeois liberalization" rhetoric and concentrated on the promotion of market socialism and other official slogans.

"BUREAUCRATISM" (*GUANLIAOZHUYI*). During the Maoist era (1949–1976), this term was used to characterize the insensitivity and detachment of Party and government personnel from the general population. The unwillingness of cadres (q.v.) to carry out investigations of practical conditions and to explain the policies of the government was a sign of being "divorced from the masses." "Bureaucratism" violated the "mass line" (q.v.) and was one of the major targets in Mao Zedong's (q.v.) support for a policy of transferring cadres to lower levels (q.v.) and for the Cultural Revolution (1966–1976) (q.v.) during which cadres were purged and spent years in May Seventh Cadre Schools (q.v.) in the countryside. Democratic critics of the communist system in China see "bureaucratism" as a major outgrowth of totalitarianism and believe that democratic procedures are the only mechanisms for insuring that "bureaucratism" is kept in check.

"BURNING BOOKS AND BURYING SCHOLARS ALIVE" (*FEN-SHU KENGRU*). This phrase originated with the tyrannical acts of China's first emperor, Qin Shihuang (221–207 B.C.), who destroyed the original Confucian texts and killed the scholars who had kept alive the ancient sage's teachings. Historically, Emperor Qin was vilified for attempting to destroy the Confucian canon. But during the 1973–1975 Anti-Lin [Biao], Anti-Confucian campaign (q.v.), the radical leftist faction behind the ideological and political struggle that was aimed at Zhou Enlai reversed this traditional historiographic judgment. They praised Qin Shihuang for playing a progressive role in history by "burning" the Confucian texts that had only confused people and prevented the unification of thought. A practitioner of Legalism (q.v.), Emperor Qin acted properly in eliminating contrary political principles and thereby was able to unify the country into an empire. "Burying the scholars" was also justified by the radicals in that it eliminated a backward-looking intellectual class who stood for restoring the old order. The Confucian scholars represented "feudalism" (q.v.) while Qin promoted "centralism"; in this struggle, defenders of the former had to be destroyed.

Politically, this phrase and the entire Anti-Lin and Anti-Confucian campaign aimed at justifying in historical terms the radicals' assault on Zhou Enlai and CCP (q.v.) leaders who were returning to power after many years in exile and who were intent on "restoring" the CCP to the status quo ante prior to the Cultural Revolution. This is an example of how historical allusions are used as frequent tools of debate by various political groups.

C

"CADRE" (*GANBU*). This is a generic term that refers to all government personnel in China. Party cadres belong to the CCP (q.v.) and may also hold positions in the government structure (q.v.) or the army. Non-Party cadres hold positions in the government or army without any responsibilities in the CCP. Cadres have official duties and are paid by the state; not all Party members are cadres since most rank-and-file Party members do not have official positions in either the CCP or the government. Cadres work in both urban and rural areas, though positions in the cities are most prized.

During the Cultural Revolution (1966–1976) (q.v.), cadres were divided into four categories: 1) good; 2) comparatively good; 3) those who had committed serious mistakes but who were not anti-Party, anti-socialist rightists, and 4) a small number of anti-Party, anti-socialist rightists. This categorization was based on whether one a) supported Chairman Mao (q.v.) and his policies; b) gave prominence to politics; and c) had a revolutionary will. Although cadres are afforded considerable privileges in Chinese society—cheap housing, relatively high wages, and job security—they have been frequent targets of political campaigns. Since the beginning of the economic reforms in 1978, cadres have been more secure from political attack, but their economic security has been threatened by wages that are relatively low in comparison to the private sector, and by the wage stagnation that has accompanied the periods of intense inflation throughout the 1980s and 1990s.

CAMBODIA. Although influenced culturally and religiously primarily by India, Cambodia has been the target of Chinese political interests for more than two millennia. During the Yuan dynasty (A.D. 1260–1368), Mongol invaders from China sought to split up the powerful state of Champa that encompassed modern-day Cambodia and South Vietnam. In the modern era, China has been deeply involved in international conferences and United Nations' (q.v.) actions affecting the country. During the 1954 Geneva Conference that ended the first Indochina War between France and the Vietminh, China played an active role in ensuring a successful conclusion to the conference by pressuring its Communist allies in Cambodia (the Khmers-Issaraks) to accept the agreement. During the late 1950s and throughout the 1960s China pursued a policy of strict neutrality on Cambodia and courted its non-Communist head of state, Prince Norodom Sihanouk, with frequent reciprocal state visits and generous economic assistance. The presence of a large Chinese colony in Cambodia reinforced China's attention to its relations with the Southeast Asian nation, and in 1958 led to the establishment of formal diplomatic relations between the two countries and in 1960 to the signing of a treaty of friendship and nonaggression, along with several economic agreements. From 1963 onward, Prince Sihanouk visited China almost every year to seek help in convening an international conference that, in the wake of the growing tension between South and North Vietnam and increased U.S. involvement in the region, would guarantee Cambodia's boundaries and neutrality and replace American aid, which the Prince had rejected in November 1963. China's own increasing involvement in the Vietnam conflict and the advent of the Cultural Revolution (1966–1976) (q.v.), however, created severe tensions in Sino-Cambodian relations that by the late 1960s verged on a breakdown.

The coup d'état in Cambodia in March 1970 that ousted Prince Sihanouk and installed General Lon Nol, an American ally, fundamentally altered Sino-Cambodian relations. Up to this point China had differentiated its relations with Cambodia, Laos, and Vietnam, pursuing formal neutrality with the former two and a tenuous alliance with the latter. From 1970 onward, China spoke of a single, unified "Indochinese war" and increased its influence in all three countries to the detriment of the Soviet Union and the United States, though China refrained from providing direct military assistance to Cambodia's Communist rebels. By 1973, however, after China signed the 1973 Paris Accord ending the American role in the Vietnam war, it returned to themes of peaceful coexistence in the region by renewing its support for Prince Sihanouk and opposing rising Vietnamese "hegemony" in the region. Sihanouk was welcomed back to Beijing (q.v.) where a National United Front of Kampuchea (FUNK) was established in exile and efforts were made on China's part to bring about a reconciliation between Sihanouk and the increasingly powerful Cambodian guerrilla forces known as the Khmer Rouge (Red Khmers).

Following the Communist Vietnamese conquest of the South in

1975, China reoriented its policy toward Cambodia to fit, ironically enough, its policy with the United States. As China acknowledged the desirability of a continuing American presence in Asia, the two countries coordinated their policies vis-à-vis Cambodia, agreeing on the maintenance of a neutral coalition government under Sihanouk, as opposed to a government headed by Lon Nol, the Khmer Rouge, or forces aligned with Vietnam. The triumph of the Khmer Rouge forces in Cambodia and their rapid defeat in 1978 at the hands of invading Vietnamese forces led to closer U.S.-China coordination in denying the pro-Vietnamese government in Phnom Penh a UN seat in favor of the anti-Vietnamese coalition headed by Prince Sihanouk (known as the Coalition Government of Democratic Kampuchea) and in seeking assistance for anti-Vietnamese forces in the Cambodian bush, including the Khmer Rouge. Throughout the 1980s, however, divisions developed in Sino-U.S. strategy toward Cambodia as China showed greater inclination to support the leftist faction in the coalition government consisting of the Khmer Rouge, led by the notorious leader Pol Pot (who is considered responsible for the genocidal killings carried out by the Khmer Rouge following their takeover in the 1970s) and Khieu Samphan. Meanwhile, the U.S. favored the non-Communist factions of Prince Sihanouk and Son Sann. In 1988, China agreed to change its position on Cambodia, reducing its support for the Khmer Rouge and embracing a plan that called for a Vietnamese withdrawal and the establishment of a coalition government, including but not dominated by, the Khmer Rouge, until elections could be held. In 1991 a negotiated settlement on Cambodia was reached as China reduced its commitment to the Khmer Rouge and participated in overseeing UN–sponsored elections that brought an end to the country's long civil war. In June 1997, reports of the capture of Khmer Rouge leader Pol Pot raised the possibility of placing the notorious leader on trial under United Nations auspices for crimes against humanity, an action that is opposed by the PRC (a member of the Security Council).

"CAPITALIST ROADER" (*ZOUZIPAI*). A term of opprobrium used in the 1960s by Mao Zedong (q.v.) and his supporters among radical CCP (q.v.) factions to label the Chairman's opponents. Liu Shaoqi (q.v.), Mao's first designated successor and target of his ideological ire in the Cultural Revolution (1966–1976) (q.v.), was labeled "the number one capitalist roader in the Party," even though it is clear that as committed Communists neither Liu nor Deng Xiaoping (q.v.) (the purported "number two capitalist roader") actually advocated capitalism. "Capitalist roader" became Mao's ideological cudgel for elevating genuine policy differences over the proper role of the state in agricultural policy into highly-charged ideological battles. In this Chinese version of political McCarthyism, Liu Shaoqi and thousands of others in the CCP found it difficult to defend themselves against such hot-button labels, particularly in a society that lacked institutions for rational dialogue. Accusations were equated with the truth as Mao's imprimatur became the ultimate sanction for the spurious claims that in advocating a slower pace of agricultural collectivization in the 1950s and foreseeing at least a limited role for the market, Liu and other CCP leaders were advocating "capitalism."

Mao Zedong first hinted in 1965 that the CCP—the purported vanguard of proletarian class consciousness—was itself infected with "capitalist roaders." At that time, the Central Committee of the CCP issued the document inspired by Mao on "Some Current Problems Raised in the Socialist Education Movement (q.v.) in the Rural Areas." Here it was explicitly noted that "the crux of the Socialist Education Movement is to purge the capitalist roaders in authority within the Party." These purported "capitalist roaders" were, according to the document, not only found among ex-landlords, rich peasants, and other social groups, but also in CCP provincial organizations and even central CCP departments. In organic metaphors so prevalent in ideologically charged CCP documents, these individuals were accused of having "wormed their way into the Party."

"Capitalist roader" was generally dropped from CCP ideological proclamations after the Cultural Revolution and especially after the rise of Deng Xiaoping in 1978. Yet such terminology still finds its way into statements and proclamations by remnant leftist forces in the CCP, such as Deng Liqun (q.v.).

CENSORSHIP. Control of the press and its content has been a central component of the CCP (q.v.) dictatorship. Beginning in the 1940s and continuing to the 1990s, the editorials and news reports of the press, especially the *People's Daily* (q.v.), books and magazines, and the electronic media have been subject to political control. From the center to the localities, the CCP exercises strict management of the media through its Propaganda Department and other agencies.

Three kinds of censorship exist in China. The first is self-censorship, representing conscious efforts by news reporters and writers to remain within the guidelines established by the CCP and to express views consistent with CCP policies. Since policies are subject to sudden and arbitrary change, self-censorship requires constant attention to even the most subtle shift in the Party line. The second form of censorship is formal, pre-publication censorship. Newspapers, such as the *People's Daily*, have set up an elaborate system involving review of draft editorials prior to publication by the chief and vice editors as well as by the director of the paper. Editorials and articles by official "commentators" undergo a continuous process of revision before they are sent to Party and state leaders for final review. Party leaders assigned responsibility for a certain field, such as foreign affairs, will review all editorials dealing with the area under their purview. In addition, the central leader in charge of propaganda reviews virtually all editorials and commentaries, while especially important pieces are sent to the CCP general secretary for his final imprimatur. Revisions by the top leader become the standard that all reporters must follow. Editorials, commentators, and straight news items from the *People's Daily* are often republished in other central and lower-level newspapers, creating an enormous uniformity of opinion and message. During the 1980s, some newspapers, most notably the Shanghai-based *World Economic Herald* (q.v.), were able to avoid, to a certain degree, this censorial system.

The third form of censorship is post-publication review. Authors of editorials or news items that are published and then singled out for criticism by top leaders will usually encounter severe repercussions. Books, magazine articles, and films that are initially approved for publication, or somehow get by the censors, are often subject to post-publication censorship by being banned, confiscated, and destroyed. This proved to be the fate of the *World Economic Herald* during the 1989 Tiananmen Square crisis.

Opposition to CCP censorship has been a constant theme in political protests in post-1949 China from the 1957 Hundred Flowers (q.v.) campaign to the 1989 Tiananmen Square pro-democracy movement. During the latter movement, reporters joined the demonstrations carrying banners reading "Don't Force Us to Lie" and, prompted by liberal head of the Propaganda and Ideological Work Leading Group under the CCP, Hu Qili (q.v.), they engaged in open reporting throughout the Spring pro-democracy movement. A large group of reporters, led by veteran *People's Daily* director Hu Jiwei (q.v.), also issued a statement during the movement calling for radical changes in CCP press controls. Following the military crackdown on June 4, TV news broadcasters exhibited their disgust with the government by dressing in black while reporting the news. All these efforts came to naught, however, as protesting newsmen were fired from their positions and the censorship system was reestablished, first under strict control of the military, and then under the authority of a rebuilt CCP propaganda apparatus headed by more conservative leaders, such as Wang Renzhi (q.v.). *See also* INTERNAL MATERIALS and THREE GORGES DAM PROJECT.

CENTRAL ADVISORY COMMISSION (CAC). Established in 1982 and abolished ten years later at the October 1992 Fourteenth Party

Congress, the Central Advisory Commission (*Zhongyang guwen wei-yuanhui*) was intended as a kind of "halfway" house between full retirement and active service for elderly CCP (q.v.) leaders. With the advent of the economic and political reforms in the early 1980s, the CAC was devised by Deng Xiaoping (q.v.) as an institutional arrangement to encourage senior Party and military leaders to give up their positions of authority without a total loss of influence or prestige. Initially, the CAC was composed of more than 170 aged leaders, including Deng Xiaoping as its chair. Commissions were also set up at the provincial level and below to receive elderly local leaders. Although all leaders with more than forty years of service to the CCP were "qualified" to join the CAC, the intention of Deng Xiaoping was to encourage those older leaders, such as Chen Yun (q.v.), who often opposed reform efforts, to join its ranks. The CAC was designed to end lifelong tenure for Party and government positions in China, a tradition that effectively prevented younger (and presumably more pro-reform) CCP leaders to move up the ranks into positions of authority. Commission members were given the right to "consult" with formal Party and government leaders, and they could even attend Central Committee and Politburo (q.v.) meetings, but without a formal vote. In reality, CAC members intervened in a decisive manner during the high-level decision in January 1987 forcing CCP general secretary and political reformer Hu Yaobang (q.v.) to step down after student demonstrations broke out in a number of cities. The role of these nominally "retired" elders was also critical during the 1989 Beijing Spring (q.v.) to produce a consensus among the top leadership to use military force against pro-democracy demonstrators and to force the ouster of then CCP General Secretary Zhao Ziyang (q.v.). For critics of China's authoritarian government structure, the experience of the CAC is another example of the weakness of political institutions and rules in a country where "rule by man" prevails over "rule by law."

CENTRAL COMMITTEE OF THE CHINESE COMMUNIST PARTY. *See* CHINESE COMMUNIST PARTY.

CENTRAL DISCIPLINE INSPECTION COMMISSION (CDIC). The internal disciplinary organization of the CCP (q.v.), the CDIC (*Zhongyang jilu jiancha weiyuanhui*) was established in 1977 soon after the death of Mao Zedong (q.v.) and the purge of the radical faction led by Mao's widow, Jiang Qing (q.v.). The original purpose of the commission was to ferret out CCP members who had risen through the ranks during the Cultural Revolution (1966–1976) (q.v.) and, theoretically, to control abuses by Party members of their subordinates and the general population. In 1982, the power of the CDIC was expanded to include monitoring adherence to Party rules and regulations, the reporting of violations of Party discipline to Party committees, including to the Central Committee, and the ensuring of implementation of Party policies. The reining in of increased corruption (q.v.) by Party members evidently brought on by the economic reforms and open-door policy (q.v.) was also a major charge of the CDIC. Headed by the relatively conservative Party leader Chen Yun, the CDIC quickly degenerated into an instrument used by Chen and other opponents of economic reforms to persecute pro-reform Party members at the provincial level and below. Charges of embezzlement, corruption, bribery, smuggling, and other serious crimes were brought against noted Party reformers who generally regarded the accusations as fabrications. Party members lived in constant fear that CDIC investigators would seize their personal property, calculate its value, and compare this figure to one's salary. Any discrepancy could lead to formal charges of corruption and disciplinary action by the relevant Party committee. Although the CDIC and its subordinate organs at the provincial level and below theoretically can bring charges against the highest officials in the CCP, regular Party members are extremely reluctant to report abuses by their superiors out of fear of retribution. As an internal disciplinary organization, the CDIC often protects Party members, especially top officials, from prosecution and punishment by the legal system. In that sense, it is widely perceived in China as yet another "special privilege" enjoyed by CCP members.

A system of control was employed during the 1950s and early 1960s modeled after a similar structure in the Communist Party of the Soviet Union. During the Cultural Revolution (1966–1976), however, these organs were abolished and replaced by the "mass" criticism and supervision advocated by Mao Zedong that often degenerated into political persecution and wanton violence against CCP members and any and all political "enemies." After Mao's death, the CDIC was established to reinstitutionalize the disciplinary function firmly within the CCP hierarchy.

CENTRAL PARTY SCHOOL. Located in Beijing's northwestern suburbs, the "Central Party School" (*Zhongyang dangxiao*) provides political training and ideological indoctrination for the CCP's (q.v.) leadership personnel, primarily from Party organs below the central level. "Students" at the Central Party School come from all over the country for lectures and discussion groups that deal with major policy initiatives, such as the economic reform instituted in 1978, and to improve Party members' basic knowledge of CCP history and Party norms. The system of Party schools was established in the 1940s during the CCP's Yan'an period as institutes to indoctrinate the membership in Marxist-Leninist and Maoist ideology. After 1949, Party schools were not only established at the central level, but also at the provincial level and below. In recent years, the curriculum of the Party schools has been depoliticized somewhat with the introduction of course work in such fields as Western theories of economics and personnel management. The fundamental ideological purpose of the Central Party School is still very important, however, as every shift in political line at the Party Center brings a concomitant change in the curriculum at the Party schools. A center of relatively "liberal" opinion in the CCP, the Central Party School has been subject to frequent purges and rectifications of its most outspoken members, such as the theoretician Ruan Ming.

CHAIRMAN OF THE CHINESE COMMUNIST PARTY. *See* CHINESE COMMUNIST PARTY.

CHEN BODA (1904–1989). Chen Boda served as political secretary and ghost writer to Mao Zedong (q.v.) during the Yan'an period (1936–1945). In the early 1950s he was involved in CCP propaganda work and was vice president of the Institute of Marxism-Leninism in Beijing. In 1956 he was appointed to the Politburo (q.v.) and became vice director of the CCP Propaganda Department. In 1968 he became editor-in-chief of *Red Flag* (*Hongqi*) (q.v.). A radical during the Cultural Revolution (1966–1976) (q.v.), he headed the Central Cultural Revolution Small Group (q.v.), with Jiang Qing (q.v.) as deputy head, until he was purged in 1970.

CHEN JINHUA (1929–). From 1952–1971, Chen worked in the Ministry of Textile Industry. From 1976 to 1983, he was vice secretary of the Shanghai (q.v.) Municipal Party Committee and vice mayor of Shanghai. From 1983 to 1990 he served as minister in charge of the State Commission for Restructuring the Economic System and from 1993 as minister in charge of the State Planning Commission.

CHEN JUNSHENG (1927–). A native of China's northeastern province of Heilongjiang, Chen Junsheng served from 1949 to 1973 in various county-level and provincial posts. From 1974 to 1979 he was the deputy director of the Policy Research Center under the Heilongjiang Provincial Party Committee and in 1980 became Party secretary in Qiqihar city. In 1982 he was identified as a secretary of the Heilongjiang Party Committee and in 1984 became vice chairman of the All-China Federation of Trade Unions (q.v.). In 1988 Chen was appointed a state councilor.

CHEN KAIGE (1952–   ). A prominent member of China's "fifth generation" of filmmakers (so named for their exposure to international cinema), Chen Kaige has produced such sterling classics as *Yellow Earth*—in conjunction with Zhang Yimou (q.v.)—and *Farewell My Concubine*. The former tells the 1939 story of a soldier who goes to a village in the poverty-stricken area of northern Shaanxi province to collect folk songs. He describes to the local peasants how women have been liberated in the nearby Communist redoubt of Yan'an. A local peasant girl, married at the age of thirteen to an older man to whom she had been betrothed since infancy, sets out in search of Yan'an, only to be drowned in the process. Ultimately, the local peasants continue to seek salvation from the local gods, rather than Mao Zedong (q.v.), the PLA (q.v.), or themselves. *Farewell My Concubine* covers a vast swath of Chinese history from the Republican era (1912–1949) to the Cultural Revolution (1966–1976) (q.v.) to the post-Mao period through the eyes of two Peking opera singers. As in the opera, the film is filled with tragedies—of Republican-era corruption, the Japanese invasion, Communist oppression, and, lastly, the loss of Peking opera traditions in the midst of overcommercialization. The film also contains the first explicit treatment of homosexuality in China in this medium.

CHEN WEIHUA. Daughter of Chen Yun (q.v.), China's venerable economic planning czar, Chen Weihua is an ordinary cadre in a Beijing unit.

CHEN XILIAN (1913–   ). Chen Xilian rose to prominence in the Communist armies in the 1920s and 1930s where he was closely associated with Lin Biao (q.v.) and Liu Bocheng (q.v.). Chen became commander of the Beijing (q.v.) Military Region in 1974 and a member of the Central Military Commission in 1977. He was removed from his post as a Politburo (q.v.) member at the 1980 Fifth Plenum of the Eleventh Party Congress and was appointed to the CAC (q.v.) in 1982.

CHEN YIZI (1940–   ). In 1987 Chen Yizi became the director of the Institute for Reform of China's Economic Structure (*Zhongguo jingji tizhi gaige yanjiusuo*, abbreviated as *tigaisuo*) under the State Commission for Restructuring the Economy. He also served as the secretary in charge of daily operations of the Political Reform Office (*Zhengzhi tizhi gaige bangongshi*, abbreviated as *Zhenggaiban*) established by Zhao Ziyang in 1986. He has been accused by the Chinese government of fomenting student unrest. He fled China in the aftermath of the 1989 demonstrations and thereafter took part in Paris in the formation of the Front for a Democratic China (q.v.).

CHEN YONGGUI (1913–1986). After eking out an existence in Dazhai, Shanxi province in the 1940s, Chen Yonggui began his rise to prominence in 1950 by organizing a Mutual Aid Team (q.v.) composed of poor peasants. In 1953 during the establishment of APCs (q.v.), Chen was criticized for his own radical initiatives as a "supporter of utopian agrarian socialism." In 1963, Chen became Party secretary of the Dazhai Production Brigade (q.v.), which in 1965 was given national prominence as an example of "self-reliance" (*zili gengsheng*) (q.v.). "In Agriculture learn from Dazhai" became a slogan issued by Mao Zedong (q.v.) to idealize his vision of socialist agriculture in contrast to the more liberal, market-oriented approach of Deng Xiaoping (q.v.) and Liu Shaoqi (q.v.).

During the Cultural Revolution (1966–1976) (q.v.), Chen Yonggui came under renewed attack, yet he ended up playing a critical role assisted by Red Guards (q.v.) in establishing the Revolutionary Committee (q.v.) for Shanxi province. In April 1969, Chen was elected to the CCP (q.v.) Central Committee at the Ninth Party Congress and in 1971 he became first Party secretary of Xiyang county, Shanxi. In 1973, he was promoted to the CCP Politburo (q.v.) and traveled widely throughout China to propagate the Dazhai model. Following the inauguration of the economic reforms in 1978 at the CCP Third Plenum (q.v.), Chen's political star faded quickly, and in 1980 and 1982 he was dropped from all central leadership posts.

CHEN YUAN (1945–). Son of Chen Yun (q.v.), China's economic czar and perennial conservative, Chen Yuan was trained as an engineer in the Automatic Control Department at Qinghua University (q.v.). In 1983 he was appointed Party secretary of a West Beijing (q.v.) district and in 1984 to the Standing Committee of the Beijing Municipal Committee. He became a vice governor of the People's Bank (q.v.) in 1988. In September 1991, Chen Yuan reportedly joined other members of China's so-called "prince's faction" (*taizidang*) (q.v.) (the adult offspring of senior CCP [q.v.] officials) in composing a neoconservative document entitled "Realistic Responses and Strategic Choices for China after the Soviet Union Upheaval."

CHEN YUN (1905–1995). Born Liao Chenyun in a rural county outside Shanghai (q.v.), Chen Yun became active in the early 1920s in the trade union (q.v.) movement, along with Liu Shaoqi (q.v.), and joined the CCP (q.v.) in 1925. He became a member of the CCP Central Committee in 1934 and worked in the Party Organization Department. In the mid-1930s he was in the Soviet Union and in 1937 he returned to China, accompanying Wang Ming and Kang Sheng (q.v.). In 1940 he became active in economic issues and worked in Manchuria (q.v.). Throughout the 1950s and early 1960s he served on the Politburo (q.v.) and as a vice premier in charge of financial and economic affairs. From the mid-1960s to 1976, Chen was a member of the Central Committee but lived in self-imposed exile to avoid the radicalism of Mao Zedong. In the late 1970s, Chen opposed remnant pro-Mao radicals and endorsed Deng Xiaoping's (q.v.) proposals for limited reforms in the economy. Throughout the 1980s, however, Chen led the CCP faction that was opposed to wholesale economic liberalization, calling instead for limitations to the market reforms in rural and urban areas and for maintaining a strong role for economic planning. Chen nominally retired in 1987, but despite ill health he nevertheless remained the leading opponent of radical economic reform and a staunch critic of any and all political reform measures that would undermine the CCP's political power. Yet Chen also opposed the arrest of the dissident Wei Jingsheng (q.v.) and reportedly was against the decision in June 1989 to employ military force during the Beijing Spring (q.v.). Chen Yun died in 1995 at the age of 89.

CHI HAOTIAN (1928–   ). A full general in the PLA (q.v.), Chi Haotian ranks as one of China's most important military figures. Purged during the Cultural Revolution (1966–1976) (q.v.), Chi Haotian returned to political life in 1975 and became the deputy political commissar (q.v.) of the Beijing Military Region. From 1977 to 1982 he served as deputy chief of staff of the PLA and in 1987 became head of the PLA General Staff. Since 1988 he has been a member of the Central Military Commission. During the military crackdown on pro-democracy demonstrators in Beijing on June 3–4, 1989, Chi Haotian commanded PLA troops involved in the operation.

"*CHICU*." Chinese phrase literally meaning "to eat vinegar" refers to jealousy in affairs of the heart. "You eat vinegar!" is what the comely but innocent bride cries out to her poor husband, racked with jealousy, when he accuses her of flirting with the man in the bicycle shop the day after their wedding. This venerable expression can be traced back to the Tang dynasty (A.D. 618–904). Emperor Li Shimin, it seems, granted his assistant, a certain Fang Xuanliang, king in a territory known as Liang, a selection of unusually beautiful women for his personal disposition. This put Fang in a tricky spot. He was quite sure his wife would look askance at a gift of this kind, so he turned down the offer. But Emperor Li, for reasons of his own, was determined to force the issue. He insisted on pressing these beautiful concubines on his reluctant chief of staff. When Fang Xuanliang once again respectfully declined his offer, the Emperor asked his own wife if she would have a word with Fang's wife to get her to go along with the idea. Fang's wife, however, was not amused. "Absolutely not!" she cried. The Emperor, still unwilling to take no for an answer, tried to "persuade" Madame Fang more directly. He arranged to have a bottle of dark liquid sent to the Fang household, along with a minatory note addressed to Fang's wife. "If you reject my final offer," he warned her, "you might as well drink the 'poisonous' liquid inside this bottle and kill yourself." Fang's wife didn't budge. She was as resolute as ever. Instead, she drank every last drop of the liquid. It turned out not to be "poisonous" at all. It was merely an acid test—of vinegar.

CHINA INTERNATIONAL TRUST AND INVESTMENT CORPORATION (CITIC). A central component of China's open-door policy (q.v.), CITIC was established in 1979 as a state corporation to coordinate national planning and economic goals and to assist foreigners seeking to do business in China. It is a comprehensive conglomerate comprised of production, technology, financing, trade, and service businesses. CITIC has set for itself the task of absorbing and utilizing foreign and domestic capital, introducing foreign technology, equipment and managerial expertise, and investing in China's construction. Immediate priority has been given to developing the raw and semifinished materials industries, transforming the obsolete techniques of domestic enterprises, and fostering overseas investments mainly in the exploitation of those natural resources that China is lacking. Numerous new laws, codes, and regulations affecting foreign corporations and employees in China have also been enacted. In the bureaucratic organization of the Chinese government, CITIC operates under the direct authority of the State Council and is of the same rank as a state ministry. From this strategic position, CITIC has consistently acted as a powerful force to support the country's opening to the international economy. Yet like many state-run entities in China, CITIC has suffered from financial mismanagement. In 1994 it defaulted on a $30 million loan to foreign interests.

CHINESE ACADEMY OF SOCIAL SCIENCES (CASS). This research center for social sciences was founded in 1977, comprised of thirty-two separate institutes. These include philosophy, Marxism-Leninism-Mao Zedong Thought, world religions, industrial economics, finance and trade, minority literature, foreign literature, modern history, world economics, politics, and others. In 1982, over 5,000 researchers, assistants, and translators were employed in the Academy, which also published in excess of 50 journals, including *Social Sciences in China* (*Zhongguo shehui kexue*). CASS initially emerged from the Philosophy and Sociology Department of the Chinese Academy of Sciences, which was established after the Communist seizure of power in 1949. Previous presidents and vice presidents of CASS include Hu Qiaomu (q.v.), Ma Hong, Deng Liqun (q.v.), and Yu Guangyuan, all of whom took part in the intellectual and ideological controversies in the late 1970s and 1980s involving the direction of Chinese economic and political reforms. During the 1989 pro-democracy movement, CASS members joined in calling for the ouster of Chinese premier Li Peng (q.v.). After the June 4 military crackdown, key figures in CASS, such Su Shaozhi, director of the Institute of Marxism-Leninism-Mao Zedong Thought, were forced to resign and/ or flee the country. Offices of CASS were occupied by martial law troops for a time and the academy was thereafter reorganized.

CHINESE COMMUNIST PARTY (CCP). The CCP is the "vanguard" of the Chinese Communist movement that began in 1921 and since 1949 has been the ruling party of the PRC (q.v.).

HISTORY, 1921–1949: The CCP was founded in July 1921 in Shanghai in a French-run girls' school. The decision to form a communist party in China was a response to domestic and international developments. Among these were the failure of the Chinese Republic, founded in 1912, to solve the internal political crisis fomented by powerful warlords and the Republican government's inability to prevent the post–World War I Versailles Conference, held outside Paris, from transferring Chinese national territory in Shandong province (the birthplace of Confucius) from German to Japanese control. The 1917 Bolshevik Revolution in Russia also had a profound effect on Chinese intellectuals, led by Chen Duxiu and Li Dazhao, who gathered in 1921 to create an alternative model of political and state power.

The Leninist-party model was considered a "modern" institutional structure with the capacity to mobilize society's resources, but without the debilitating weaknesses of Western parliamentary democracy. What began as a small and rather ineffectual group of intellectuals and a few workers rapidly expanded in 1925–1926 to an organization with a membership of 18,000. This stemmed in part from the First United Front (1924–1927) that was established by the CCP, under Soviet pressure, with the KMT (q.v.) under the leadership of Chiang Kai-shek. In April 1927, however, Chiang turned on his erstwhile Communist allies and effectively destroyed the urban apparatus of the CCP, forcing remnant CCP forces to shift operations to the countryside. Although the Party retained the basic organizational structure established in the 1920s, changes were instituted to reflect the Communists' new rural environment and its military orientation. The system of "Party core groups" (*dang hexin xiaozu*) was set up to ensure tight Party control of the military and various "mass" organizations. In the Communists' main redoubt in rural Jiangxi province, a Soviet form of political organization was adopted and land reform policies were vigorously pursued. During the Long March (q.v.), at an enlarged Politburo (q.v.) meeting in 1935, it was decided to "establish Mao Zedong in the leading position of the Red Army and the Party Center." Steps were also taken to avoid independent power bailiwicks from emerging in the Red Army as a hierarchical structure of military-political committees and CCP political departments were established to ensure Party control over the military.

By 1938 the Communist Party structure of the war years was completed at the Sixth Plenum of the Sixth Party Congress held in the new Communist stronghold in Yan'an in rural Shaanxi province. Ad hoc decision making was formally ended as Party rules established clear lines of authority. The Central Committee was reaffirmed as the highest organ in political and organizational matters (except during periodic Party congresses), and standing committees were subordinated to their respective Party committees, reversing a decision made in 1927 during the height of the CCP's fight for survival. The apex of the CCP was the Politburo (q.v.), the Secretariat, and a Central Bureau and central sub bureaus. The latter two directed Party activities through a vertically-organized structure of Party committees established at the region, prefecture, county, city, district, and branch (*zhibu*) levels. Six departments—organization, propaganda, war mobilization, popular movements, united front, and the Secretariat—were established at the central level with branches of each extending below. Overall, the Organization Department (*Zuzhibu*) and Secretariat (*Shujichu*) emerged as the most powerful apparatus for directing a membership that by 1942 had grown to more than 800,000.

During the 1942–1944 Party Rectification (q.v.), an even more elaborate organizational structure was created. This included a Central Committee Office, a Party Committee for Managing Organs Directly Subordinate to the Central Committee, and the highly secretive Central Investigation Department and the Social Affairs Department. These were charged with investigating cadre loyalty and ferreting out purported Nationalist "spies." Under the influence of Kang Sheng (q.v.), this internal security apparatus effected the first major internal Party purge, which Mao Zedong ultimately terminated because of excessive killings and cadre suicides. Finally, Mao Zedong's position as Party chairman (which he had assumed at the 1938 Sixth Party Plenum) was further enhanced by a March 1943 decision giving him the authority to "make final decisions regarding all problems discussed by the [three member] Central Secretariat." With the promulgation of the Mao personality cult (q.v.), the CCP and the great leader were now virtually indistinguishable. Yet in upholding the supremacy of the Party committees over individual leaders in a 1948 speech, Mao presaged the forthcoming clash between charismatic and institutional authority that would evidently divide the CCP.

THE CHINESE COMMUNIST PARTY IN POWER, 1949–1996: The CCP emerged from the 1946–1949 Civil War (q.v.) with an elaborate organization that quickly imposed its control over the entire country. From the central to the county level, there were six central and four subcentral bureaus, 24 provincial committees, 17 regional committees, and 134 city and 218 area committees. Total Party membership in 1950 was 4.5 million (up from 3 million in 1948), with 80,000 full-time cadres forming the CCP's organizational core. As the CCP's role rapidly shifted from wartime mobilization (during both the Civil and Korean wars [q.v.]), the need for professionally trained cadres increased dramatically. Meanwhile, the illiterate Party veterans of the wars against the Japanese and Nationalists were now confronted with their own political obsolescence. Party rectifications in the early 1950s thus squeezed out 670,000 rural uneducated members, while 910,000 more well-educated members were recruited into a Party whose membership continued to expand to 6.2 million by 1953.

Party organization also reflected the imperatives of economic growth and control over the burgeoning state bureaucracy. In 1953, the CCP Central Committee ordered that all laws and regulations dealing with state and government affairs be initiated and drafted by the Central Committee and then implemented by the State Council. Party secretaries were also empowered to take charge of directing and supervising their counterparts in the state apparatus. Leading Party figures also assumed the top positions in the government in order to ensure CCP domination. In 1955 five new Central Committee departments—industry, finance and trade, communication and transportation, political-legal, and agriculture—were also established. In the mid-1950s "Party core groups" made up of four or five Party members who held senior posts in the government were extended throughout the administrative system (down to the bureau level) as the real center of decision-making authority in the government. This was in addition to the Party unit affairs committees (*jiguan dangwei*) which were elected by CCP members working in the relevant government bodies, but which exercised little decision-making authority, focusing instead on such tasks as Party recruitment and directing ideological study. Control over government appointments and the training of technical cadres, however, was decentralized, with a concomitant reduction in the authority of the Organization Department. While Mao Zedong evidently supported such changes, he showed increasing impatience with the deliberative process of decision making that emerged with the CCP's shift to economic management. In July 1955 Mao thus upset the gradualist approach to organizing APCs (q.v.) by announcing a "socialist upsurge" in the Chinese countryside.

From 1955 onward, the issue of procedural and "collective leadership" versus Mao's impulsive and individualistic leadership style increasingly divided the CCP. While Mao's enormous charisma allowed him to prevail in most political standoffs, elliptical criticism of the chairman was expressed by relatively liberal CCP leaders, such as An Ziwen, who extolled the Party committees, including the Central Committee, as the final sovereign body. Strengthened by the emphasis on collective leadership in the Soviet Union following the death of Stalin (q.v.), Chinese proponents of the institutionalization of authority in the CCP won significant concessions from the chairman at the pivotal 1956 Eighth Party Congress (q.v.). In addition to deleting "Mao Zedong Thought" from the Party constitution, a more collective top leadership was created with the appointment of five vice chairmen, the formal prohibition against leader cults, and a renewed emphasis in CCP decision making on such procedures as periodic congresses with utilization of formal agenda.

Yet, Mao was still able to circumvent the formal Party apparatus with his personal charisma and the support of local Party secretaries—the "little Maos"—who evidently admired his decisive leadership. Thus, without formal Central Committee or Politburo approval, Mao personally ordered the wide-open Hundred Flowers campaign (q.v.). Speaking prior to a planned Party plenum, Mao exhorted subordinates to "relay and implement" his proposals without formal authorization. "Being the first secretary, I will take charge of ideological work," Mao arrogantly asserted. Then during the debate over the proposed Great Leap Forward (1958–1960) (q.v.), Mao showed his contempt for institutional procedure by authorizing the formation of the people's communes (q.v.) before formal Politburo approval. Mao also personally countermanded central decisions on grain deliveries and production quotas. When Peng Dehuai (q.v.) responded at the 1959 Lushan conference (q.v.) by voicing surprisingly mild criticisms of the chairman's leadership style during the Leap, Mao countered by purging Peng and launching a campaign against "rightist opportunism." This action effectively silenced the entire organization and evidently created a basis for Mao's later decision to launch the Cultural

Revolution (1966–1976) (q.v.). The relatively open and semilegal model of the Party's decision-making structure outlined at the 1956 Eighth Congress was now effectively defunct.

Following the collapse of the Leap and Mao's retreat to the second front of decision making, CCP propaganda organs revived the Eighth Party Congress model. Throughout the early 1960s, "regularization" of Party decision making through majority rule in Party committees was reemphasized. A "moderate" leadership style was also advocated in place of the "tyrannical way" (*badao*) that the Party intellectual Deng Tuo (q.v.) had criticized in a Beijing newspaper. In an obvious reference to the cavalier purge of Peng Dehuai, the right of every Party member to voice his or her views was defended, and Mao's tendency to rely on oral orders was indirectly criticized. With Party membership at 17 million, central authorities also emphasized the recruitment of educated cadres. The increasingly leftward trend of the rural Socialist Education Movement (1962–1966) (q.v.), however, effectively prevented the full substitution of expertise over "redness" in CCP ranks.

In the early to mid-1960s, Mao entered the political fray intent on eliminating political obstruction of his renewed effort to attempt yet another Great Leap Forward. Detaching himself from central Party leaders, the chairman mobilized youthful Red Guards (q.v.) to attack veteran cadres whom Mao accused of "taking the capitalist road" (q.v.). As Party ranks were decimated at all organizational levels, Mao supported the establishment of alternative political bodies to replace the Leninist structures of the CCP. Revolutionary Committees (q.v.) and Party "groups" (*zu*) replaced the regular structure of Party committees throughout the Cultural Revolution. At the April 1969 Ninth Party Congress, the unprecedented action was taken of naming Mao's successor—Lin Biao (q.v.)—in the new Party constitution. Yet, even as the last Revolutionary Committees were established in the provinces, Mao was already convinced that "rebuilding the Party" was necessary to avoid civil war and chaos, and so throughout the early 1970s the CCP's conventional structure of Party committees was gradually reestablished. Veteran cadres vilified during the Cultural Revolution were rehabilitated (q.v.) and Party members recruited during the mass campaigns were gradually ferreted out.

Mao's death in 1976 brought an end to mass campaigns and in 1978 Deng Xiaoping (q.v.) called for bringing about further Party reform. In August 1980, Deng Xiaoping promised to "institutionalize democracy" by strengthening the legal system and restraining political leaders from exercising absolutist authority. Criticizing the "patriarchal system" in the CCP and the influence of "feudalism" on Party leaders, Deng promised a more open and responsible CCP that would never again make the errors of the Maoist era. Yet as criticism of Deng's own leadership by democratic dissidents mounted in the early 1980s and problems emerged in China's economic reforms, major political reform of the CCP was effectively tabled as Deng Xiaoping exercised effective leadership over the CCP, despite the absence of a formal position of authority.

ORGANIZATIONAL STRUCTURE: The organizational structure of the CCP is based on the fundamental Leninist principles of democratic-centralism (q.v.). Theoretically, authority inheres in the National Party Congress (q.v.) (held every five years and composed of almost two thousand delegates) and, when not in session, the Central Committee (188 members), which, in turn, selects as its executive organ the Politburo (nineteen full and two alternate members). In reality, the Politburo and its executive organ of a Standing Committee usually exercise final decision-making authority. Since the abolition of the position of chairman at the Twelfth Party Congress in 1982, the top executive position in the CCP is the general secretary; from 1989 the position has been filled by Jiang Zemin (q.v.), whom Deng Xiaoping appointed as the "core" of the "third generation of leadership." Other key central bodies include the Central MAC (which ensures CCP control of the PLA [q.v.]), the Central Discipline Inspection Commission (q.v.), the Central Advisory Commission (q.v.), a body established in 1982 (and abolished in 1992) for semiretired leaders, and the all-powerful Secretariat which prepares reports for top leaders and controls key appointments. Formal departments of the CCP include: the United Front (q.v.) (for work with non-Communist groups); International Liaison Department (for maintaining ties with foreign communist parties); Propaganda Department; General Office; Central Policy Research Office; and the Central Party School (q.v.). Several informal "central leading groups" to deal with problems of finance, Party building, propaganda and thought, and so on have also been established under the direct authority of the Politburo.

The CCP structure at the provincial, municipal, prefectural, and local levels is similar to its central organization. A vast organizational web of various Party "core groups" (*hexin xiaozu*) are also maintained in mass organizations, government bodies, and army units to ensure CCP control of Chinese society. Party reforms inaugurated by Zhao Ziyang (q.v.) in the mid-1980s called for the abolition of the core groups and the Party departments in government organizations and a concomitant reduction in the authority of Party secretaries in state-run industries and universities. After the military crackdown in 1989, however, the role of both the "core groups" and the Party secretaries was reinvigorated, returning the CCP to a more dominant role in social and political life. In the mid 1990s, Party membership stood at 57 million, while the level of education among Party members has increased correspondingly in the last few years. The 188 members of the Central Committee of the CCP chosen at the October 1992 Fourteenth Party Congress had an average age of 57 years, 8 percent of whom were female, 11 percent were of minority nationalities, and 84 percent consisted of college graduates. *See also* ENTERPRISE REFORM, PEOPLE'S LIBERATION ARMY, and EDUCATION.

CHINESE PEOPLE'S POLITICAL CONSULTATIVE CONFERENCE (CPPCC). This is a "consultative" body established by the CCP (q.v.) in 1949 and composed of both Communist and non-Communist members. A "United Front" organization, the CPPCC (*Zhongguo renmin zhengzhi xieshang huiyi*) united all "patriotic" forces in China that opposed the KMT (q.v.). From 1949 to September 1954, it functioned as the parliamentary body of the PRC (q.v.), which the CPPCC had formally proclaimed in October 1949. With representatives from many of China's democratic parties (q.v.), the CPPCC was originally considered a critical institution in Mao Zedong's (q.v.) plan for a New Democracy (q.v.) in China. The establishment of the NPC (q.v.) in 1954, however, eliminated the official role of the CPPCC as an organ of national power and reduced its function to "rallying" the various nationalities and satellite parties behind the CCP cause. This, in effect, transformed the CPPCC into a transmission belt of the CCP, denying it any real political autonomy.

During periods of political relaxation in China, however, non-Communist CPPCC members have been relatively outspoken in their criticisms of Communist policies. This occurred during the 1957 Hundred Flowers campaign (q.v.) and in the more tolerant political atmosphere of the early 1980s when CPPCC meetings involved real debates over issues of the national economy, education, and corruption. Since the 1989 crackdown against the Beijing Spring (q.v.) democracy movement, however, the CPPCC has ceased to be a source of policy opposition and has obediently complied with CCP decisions, such as the 1992 NPC resolution authorizing final construction of the Three Gorges dam project (q.v.).

CIVIL WAR (1946–1949). This four-year conflict led to the defeat of KMT (q.v.) military forces by the Chinese Communist armies and the establishment of the PRC (q.v.) in 1949. Following the defeat of the Japanese in the Asian-Pacific War in 1945, the KMT and CCP (q.v.) engaged in peace talks but also carried out an undeclared war. From August 1945 to June 1946, KMT military units (which outnumbered Communist forces three to one) were transported by U.S. aircraft and retook strategic cities in central, south, and east China, while the Communist forces entered Manchuria (q.v.), where they were provided with substantial stocks of Japanese weapons by the occupying Soviet forces. During this period, American negotiators led by General George C. Marshall, attempted to mediate the KMT-CCP conflict, but to no avail as neither the Communists nor the KMT invested much trust in the United States. From late 1946 to mid-1947, fighting became more intense as the KMT captured the Communist wartime capital of Yan'an, while Communist forces engaged in mobile warfare and mobilized student and intellectual sympathizers in Chinese cities where KMT corruption was rampant and its political repression was growing. In July 1947, the Communists launched a counteroffensive that lasted a year and led to a virtual Communist encirclement of KMT forces in the northeast and in central China. At this point, CCP and KMT forces were basically equal in terms of manpower and weaponry. Hyperinflation in Chinese cities continued to alienate the urban population, while CCP underground organizers promoted the CCP line of "peace, democracy, and unity." By late 1948, KMT troops were defeated in two significant battles in Manchuria and central China, as more and more KMT units led by their officers defected to the Communist side. A last-ditch peace initiative by the KMT was turned down by the Communists, and in December 1949 remnant KMT forces fled to the island of Taiwan (q.v.). Throughout the war, the KMT was hampered by its corruption, economic mismanagement, and the unwillingness of its leader, Chiang Kai-shek, to delegate authority to military commanders, many of whom worked at cross purposes.

"CLASS LABELS" (*JIEJI CHENGFEN*). A politically and ideologically defined label that all Chinese are given based on their family lineage prior to the Communist takeover in 1949. Several categories or labels are widely employed: "bad" labels include "capitalist," "landlord," and "rich peasant"; "good" labels are "cadre" (q.v.), "worker," "revolutionary soldier," "revolutionary martyr," and "poor and lower middle peasant." The category of "intellectual" has, at different times in the history of the PRC (q.v.), been "bad," especially during the Cultural Revolution (1966–1976) (q.v.), but at other times "good," namely since 1978 when, it was officially declared, intellectuals were part of the working class. One's class label can affect opportunities such as school, employment, and promotions, plus the possibility of joining the CCP (q.v.). Most importantly, class labels were instrumental in determining whether an individual became a target in the many political campaigns that occurred in China during the Maoist period (1949–1976). Class labels can only be changed across generations. Offspring from a family with a mixture of "good" and "bad" class labels—to wit, the father is a "worker" and the mother is a "capitalist"—are generally assigned the latter.

"CLASS STRUGGLE" (*JIEJI DOUZHENG*). The core of Chinese Communist ideology is composed of Marxist-Leninist and indigenous Maoist beliefs in which class struggle is a central value. The goal of class struggle in China has been the proletarianization of the entire society and the creation of a modern industrial society that would create the basis for the Marxist utopia of a classless social order. Class struggle occurred domestically between capitalists and the workers and peasants, and internationally between imperialism and socialism. In the early stages of CCP (q.v.) rule in the 1950s, the domestic class struggle led by the Party was directed at landlords and other so-called bad elements and counterrevolutionaries opposed to the establishment of the socialist state. The leading force of international imperialism, the United States was also the target of the international class struggle that the Chinese government promoted throughout the 1950s and 1960s until the rapprochement between China and the U.S. in the early 1970s. In the Maoist perspective, class struggle in China was a perpetual feature of Chinese society after the completion of the socialist revolution and even occurred within the CCP—the vanguard of the proletariat. It is for this reason that in the early 1960s Mao warned "never to forget class struggle" and went so far as to sanction attacks against so-called capitalist roaders (q.v.) in the CCP during the Cultural Revolution (1966–1976) (q.v.) when "class struggle" degenerated into factional infighting and power struggles among contending leadership groups. Yet even Mao adjusted his views regarding the intensity of class struggle depending on the political situation. Thus during the Sino-Japanese War (q.v.) Mao called for limiting class struggle to "big bourgeoisie" and "compradors" opposed to China's independence, while forming alliances with national bourgeoisie and other nonproletarian class elements who were willing to fight Japanese imperialism. From the perspective of less radical leaders in the CCP, class struggle should have ended with the completion of Land Reform (q.v.) and the socialist transformation of the economy in the late 1950s and early 1960s. In the absence of a "capitalist" class, the regime should have concentrated solely on developing the economy and the notion of "class struggle" in the CCP should have been regarded as heretical. Although this perspective lost out to Maoist radicalism during the Cultural Revolution, it regained prominence after Mao's death in 1976 as references to "class struggle" in China nearly disappeared from official propaganda. Hard-line ideologues in the CCP, however, still periodically raise the issue of "class struggle" against a reemergent capitalist class that has been fostered by the economic reforms pursued since 1978 and against "bourgeois liberal" ideas imported from the West. *See also* "BOURGEOIS LIBERALIZATION."

CLEANSING OF THE CLASS RANKS. This was one of the many movements launched during the Cultural Revolution (1966–1976) (q.v.) that aimed at purging the CCP (q.v.) and Red Guard (q.v.) organizations of purported "class enemies." The campaign officially targeted "stubborn bourgeois power holders" (i.e., still unrepentant and perhaps silent supporters of Liu Shaoqi [q.v.], the primary target of the Cultural Revolution); "renegades and spies" (a catchall category of individuals who were accused of being in the service of the KMT [q.v.] and/or American "imperialists"); and "landlords, rich peasants, reactionaries, bad elements, and rightists who had not been well reformed" (i.e., individuals who were accused of not yet embracing the Maoist cause). Both class origin and political performance were the criteria for being targeted in this campaign. Overall, the campaign aimed at "cleansing" the newly formed Revolutionary Committees (q.v.) and other "mass organizations" of people who did not fit the radical prescriptions for political allegiance offered by Jiang Qing (q.v.) and the radicals. These various organizations had emerged in the political vacuum created during the Cultural Revolution due to the organizational disintegration of the CCP, but were often staffed with individuals of various political stripes, ideological persuasions, and factional allegiances, in addition to administrative incompetents and opportunists. The entire movement quickly degenerated into political retributions and mutual recriminations by one faction against another in the turmoil and chaos of the period.

COLLECTIVIZATION OF AGRICULTURE. *See* AGRICULTURAL PRODUCER COOPERATIVES and PEOPLE'S COMMUNES.

"COMMON PROGRAM" (*GONGTONG GANGLING*). Inaugurated in September 1949, the Common Program was passed by the first session of the CPPCC (q.v.). This meeting was held in Beiping (soon thereafter to be renamed Beijing [q.v.]) on the eve of the PLA's (q.v.) victory in the Civil War (q.v.) against the KMT (q.v.). With more than 600 delegates, including many non-Communists, the conference was considered more broadly "representative" of the Chinese nation than the CCP (q.v.). According to an official CCP chronology, the meeting "acted on behalf of the NPC" (q.v.), which did not formally convene until late 1954.

The full title of the approved document was the "Common Program of the Chinese People's Consultative Conference" (*Zhongguo renmin zhengzhi xieshang huiyi gongtong gangling*). The document was drafted by the CCP and presented to the conference by Zhou Enlai (q.v.). Although various non-Communist "democratic parties (q.v.) and people's organizations" purportedly contributed to its drafting, the document was clearly based on the CCP's basic policy line for the "transition period," which had been decided at the March 1949 Second Plenum of the Seventh Central Committee. The Common Program contained seven chapters and sixty articles that evidently were not significantly amended or altered by the rubber-stamp CPPCC.

The basic purpose of the Common Program was to lay out the broad national goals of the new government consistent with Mao Zedong's (q.v.) doctrine of New Democracy (q.v.). Specifically, it "summarized the experiences of China's new democratic revolution and clearly stipulated that the PRC (q.v.) was a country led by the working class." It also declared China to be a "people's democratic dictatorship founded on the worker-peasant alliance." In the spirit of the New Democracy's United Front (q.v.) policies, the program emphasized unifying China's various classes and nationalities and "stipulated the election rights and powers of citizens and their political freedoms." Yet, as a harbinger of the harsh persecution of intellectuals and other social groups that would soon follow, the program singled out "reactionary elements, feudal landlords, and bureaucratic capitalists"—catchall categories in which almost anyone could be arbitrarily placed—as targets of the new dictatorship. Despite the "moderate" tone of the Common Program—especially in comparison to later CCP policies—this document marked the PRC's inexorable path to class warfare and political persecution that would peak in the 1957–1958 Anti-Rightist campaign (q.v.) and the 1966–1976 Cultural Revolution (q.v.).

The program also signaled the Chinese Communists' clear intention to create a unified and powerful state structure. After years of warlordism and civil war, the program promised a "unified military force, composed of the PLA and the People's Public Security Bureau" (q.v.). It also committed the new government to establishing state control over the economy and "integrating" different sectors of the economy, such as agriculture, industry, and transportation. During the first five years of the PRC, the Common Program served as a "temporary constitution" until it was formally replaced by the PRC State Constitution adopted in 1954.

COMMUNE. *See* PEOPLE'S COMMUNES.

COMMUNIST YOUTH LEAGUE. *See* YOUTH LEAGUE.

CONSTITUTIONS. *See* CHINESE COMMUNIST PARTY and GOVERNMENT STRUCTURE.

CONTINUING REVOLUTION. *See* UNINTERRUPTED REVOLU-
TION.

CORRUPTION. A by-product of the economic reforms introduced in
China from 1978 onward, corruption emerged as a major issue in the
1989 pro-democracy movement. The CCP (q.v.) had won power in
1949 in part because of its opposition to, and political exploitation
of, the enormous corruption of the ruling KMT (q.v.). Yet by the
1980s, official corruption in China probably surpassed that of the Nationalist predecessors and was a target of popular ire. Bribery, smuggling, nepotism, eating and drinking at public expense, and outright
embezzlement are the primary forms of corruption that span from
local policemen and clerks in government offices to the highest leaders (and their offspring) in the CCP. "Official profiteering" (*guandao*)
is undoubtedly the worst form of such corruption in which an official
and/or his/her family members buy scarce commodities or raw materials at low, state-fixed prices and then sell them on the open, private
market at huge markups. Such corruption is made possible by the
existence of a dual-price system, that is, low official state prices (for
raw materials, such as coal and food) and high free-market prices for
the same items. Lavish lifestyles by high officials result from such
corruption: the import of Mercedes-Benz automobiles, the construction of expensive apartments and hotels in major cities for exclusive
use by officials, and the sending of their offspring abroad ostensibly
for education. The buying and selling of official "receipts" to pad
expense accounts and the scalping of tickets for transportation and
entertainment events are smaller, yet no less virulent aspects of this
corruption.

During the 1989 pro-democracy movement, popular discontent was
directed at the corruption of the political leaders and their families,
including the sons of then CCP general secretary Zhao Ziyang (q.v.).
One of the reasons that CCP general secretary Hu Yaobang (q.v.) lost
his position in 1987 was because of his insistence that all top political
leaders, such as Hu Qiaomu (q.v.) (whose son was accused of embezzlement), take a strong stand against corruption among family members. After 1989, major anticorruption campaigns were launched by
CCP political leaders, and several officials were executed on charges
of corruption. Yet corruption still remains a major problem. In 1993,
for example, fraud almost cost the Agricultural Bank of China a loss
of $10 billion. Corruption is also linked to the growth of mafia-style
organized crime, led by traditional Chinese gangs such as the Triads.
In some places, these gangs have taken over local Chinese government and police organs and have even directed organized crime activities abroad, including in New York's Chinatown, and on the high
seas where Chinese pirates raid commercial shipping. The smuggling

of stolen cars from Hong Kong and even New York to clients within the Chinese government and the police is now part of the pervasive system of corruption in China. Warnings that corruption might bring down the Communist Party have been voiced by the press and even by Deng Xiaoping (q.v.) himself. In 1995, yet another anticorruption drive was launched to eliminate widespread graft in the CCP; it resulted in the reported suicide of Wang Baosen, a vice mayor of Beijing (q.v.) who was under official investigation. His "suicide" was seen as an indication of the extent and seriousness of the investigation. But some in China saw this as an example of "sacrificing the pawn to save the general," that is, as an attempt to protect more senior officials in the Beijing municipal government.

COUNTERREVOLUTIONARY. *See also* ANTI-COUNTERREVOLU-TIONARY CAMPAIGNS.

CRITERION OF TRUTH. *See* PRACTICE IS THE SOLE CRITERION OF TRUTH.

"CRITICISM AND SELF-CRITICISM" (*PIPING YU ZIWOPIPING*). This was originally a Leninist concept introduced into the Bolshevik Party organization to ensure that members abide by the policies of the leadership. Individuals on the wrong side of policy and/or power struggles were forced to submit to criticism from others and to criticize themselves. During the 1930s and 1940s in China, the CCP (q.v.) adopted the same method to impose control over Party members who wavered from the center. Criticism and self-criticism were harsh and often resulted in purges and even executions. While in theory criticism and self-criticism were to be comprehensive within the Party and to involve even top leaders, the focus was on Party members who support the wrong side in the interminable ideological and power struggles that have marked CCP history.

CULT OF MAO. *See* PERSONALITY CULT.

CULTURAL REVOLUTION (1966–1976). Perhaps the seminal event of post-1949 Chinese Communist history, the Great Proletarian Cultural Revolution (*wuchanjieji wenhua dageming*), as it was officially called, represents Mao Zedong's (q.v.) personal crusade to purge the CCP (q.v.) of his political opponents. The primary target of this power struggle was Mao's first successor, Liu Shaoqi (q.v.), whom Mao accused of "revisionism" (q.v.) and of being a "capitalist roader" (q.v.). The ensuing battle between the Maoist-radical faction in the CCP, which included the chairman's wife, Jiang Qing (q.v.), and the moderate faction led by Liu and composed of Deng Xiaoping (q.v.), Beijing mayor Peng Zhen (q.v.), and many other top CCP leaders, brought China to the brink of civil war.

The Cultural Revolution officially began in August 1966 when the CCP Central Committee narrowly approved a resolution calling for a complete revolution in Chinese society, politics, and culture. Mao Zedong's cudgel in this political struggle was the Red Guards (q.v.) whose organization Mao sanctioned at a mass rally on August 18, 1966. For Mao, the Cultural Revolution was an ideological crusade to reinvigorate the Chinese revolution, train a new generation of "revolutionary fighters," and radically alter Chinese culture by Red Guard attacks on the "four olds" (q.v.). From late 1966 to early 1967, Chinese cities, factories, and university campuses were in turmoil as the Red Guards engaged in open-pitched battles. By mid-1967, Mao ordered in the PLA (q.v.) to stabilize production and social order. In 1968 the chairman ordered that the rambunctious Red Guards be sent to the countryside. During the last years of the Cultural Revolution and during the period of Late Maoism (1976–1977), China was effectively under military rule.

Mao Zedong's goal of cleansing the CCP was successful, at least temporarily. Liu Shaoqi was purged from the Party and in 1969 died in a small prison cell. Deng Xiaoping—the "second capitalist roader"—lost his positions of power, but was protected from physical harm by sympathetic military commanders. Other targets of Mao's ire were hounded and criticized, but most top leaders, such as Yang Shangkun (q.v.), Bo Yibo (q.v.), and others, survived the ordeal and returned to power after Mao Zedong's death in 1976. Besides enormous economic disruption in China's factories and some agricultural areas, the Cultural Revolution also caused the deaths of more than 2 million people, including many scholars, teachers, scientists, and artists who were sometimes killed by their own students. Since 1978, the Cultural Revolution has been roundly condemned by the CCP leadership and Cultural Revolution changes in education and political institutions, such as the Revolutionary Committees (q.v.), have been abandoned. *See also* CLEANSING OF THE CLASS RANKS, CULTURAL REVOLUTION SMALL GROUP, JIANG QING, PEOPLE'S LIBERATION ARMY, and MAO ZEDONG.

CULTURAL REVOLUTION SMALL GROUP. There were two such "Cultural Revolution Small Groups" during the Cultural Revolution (1966–1976) (q.v.). The first was headed by Beijing mayor Peng Zhen (q.v.) and was disbanded on May 16, 1966 for its refusal to engage in the political struggle promoted by Mao against Liu Shaoqi (q.v.) and other top CCP (q.v.) leaders. A second Cultural Revolution

Small Group was then established and headed by Mao confidant Chen Boda (q.v.) and included major radical leaders such as Jiang Qing (q.v.), Kang Sheng (q.v.), Yao Wenyuan (q.v.), and others. The group operated directly under the Standing Committee of the Politburo (q.v.) and was responsible for leading the Cultural Revolution. It was abolished in the 1970s as the Cultural Revolution came to an end.

D

DAI QING (1941–). Trained as a missile engineer, the adopted daughter of Ye Jianying (q.v.), Dai Qing, became a Red Guard (q.v.) activist during the Cultural Revolution (1966–1976) (q.v.) and underwent secret service training in the military. In the early 1980s, she became a journalist at the *Enlightenment Daily* and became known for her investigative reporting of intellectual persecution in the history of the CCP (q.v.), including the cases of Wang Shiwei (q.v.), Liang Shuming, and Chu Anping. She is a strong advocate of press freedom and environmental protection and has collected documents from many scientists and economists opposed to the Three Gorges Dam project (q.v.). In 1989 Dai Qing was imprisoned after the June 4, 1989, crackdown; her book on the Three Gorges Dam, *Yangtze! Yangtze!* was banned for allegedly contributing to the political "turmoil." Subsequently released, Dai Qing has traveled extensively abroad and has been a Nieman Fellow at Harvard University and a fellow at the Freedom Forum, School of Journalism, Columbia University. She is a recipient of the Goldman Environmental Foundation Award.

DALAI LAMA (1935–). The spiritual and temporal leader of Lamaism in Tibet (q.v.), the current Dalai Lama is the fourteenth reincarnation of the first Dalai Lama who was initially proclaimed during the Ming dynasty (1368–1644) by the Mongolian ruler Altan Khan. Dalai is Mongolian for "sea" and Lama is Tibetan for "wise master." Beginning in the eighteenth century, China began to intervene in Tibetan affairs by installing the Dalai Lama. The Dalai Lama is the religious and temporal leader of Tibet.

Born at Amdo to a Tibetan peasant family, the current Dalai Lama (also known as Tenzin Gyatso) was installed in 1940, when at the age of five he identified the previous Dalai Lama's possessions "as his own." Since 1959 the fourteenth Dalai Lama has been in exile in northern India where he fled following an uprising against Chinese rule by Tibetan monks and the general populace. While China has tried to persuade the Dalai Lama to return to Tibet, the Dalai Lama continues to speak out against Chinese policies toward his people in various international forums. In 1987, the Dalai Lama proposed a five-point peace plan to the Chinese government: 1) demilitarization of Tibet; 2) an end to Chinese (Han) (q.v.) immigration into Tibet; 3) respect for human rights in Tibet; 4) a halt to the production and testing of nuclear weapons in Tibet; and 5) negotiations on the future status of Tibet. In 1989 the Dalai Lama received the Nobel Peace Prize over objections from the Chinese government, and in 1993 he was given an official reception by U.S. President Bill Clinton. In July 1993, the Dalai Lama sent an official delegation led by his brother to Beijing (q.v.) to push for negotiations. *See also* TIBET.

DAQING OIL FIELD. Located in China's northeastern province of Heilongjiang (Black Dragon River), the Daqing oil field has been a major petroleum producer and a subject of considerable political adulation and controversy. The development of the field began in the early 1960s—reportedly against the advice of Soviet oil specialists then in China—and production was rapidly increased to replace diminishing oil reserves in other parts of China and the loss of oil imports from the Soviet Union. By 1963, 68 percent of all oil being pumped in China came from Daqing, a situation that prompted CCP (q.v.) Chairman Mao Zedong (q.v.) to inaugurate a campaign glorifying the achievements of the field's oil workers and the egalitarian political line of the local Party leadership that, Mao argued, explained Daqing's enormous successes. Daqing was held up as a model of "more, faster, better, and more economical," a phrase that had been used in the late 1950s to promote the ill-fated Great Leap Forward (1958–1960) (q.v.). Along with the Dazhai Brigade (q.v.) that Mao also idealized, Daqing became the subject of a propaganda campaign promulgating "self reliance" (*zili gengsheng*) (q.v.) and the role of ideology in motivating workers to produce. Under the banner of "in industry learn from Daqing," it was said that the "Daqing spirit is the revolutionary spirit of the proletariat" and that the "Daqing people know profoundly the great significance of developing the revolutionary tradition of hard struggle and self-reliance." As a result, the oil field became a favorite site for visits and junkets by government personnel. In the meantime, Daqing Party leaders Yu Qiuli, Kang Shien, and Gu Mu, rose to prominence as key economic advisers to Mao Zedong throughout the Cultural Revolution (1966–1976) (q.v.).

Unfortunately, Daqing's rapid increases in production probably stemmed less from politics and revolutionary zeal and more from the utilization of a water extraction technique that maximized recovery at the early stages of production, but led to later dramatic reductions. By the late 1970s, with the move to economic reform and an emphasis on material incentives, the Daqing model was eclipsed as China opened new and more productive oil fields offshore and in the Central Asian interior. In 1995, China announced plans to invest 100 billion yuan ($11.7 billion) in the petroleum sector by the year 2000, a substantial portion of which will come from abroad. *See also* ENTERPRISE REFORM.

DAZHAI BRIGADE. Located in the poor mountainous region of Shanxi province, the Dazhai Brigade was hailed by Mao Zedong (q.v.) as a model of socialist production in the countryside. Like the Daqing oil field (q.v.), Dazhai was the subject of a nationwide campaign in the 1960s promoting the concept of "self-reliance" (q.v.) and the role of socialist ideology and egalitarianism in "transforming nature" and dramatically increasing production. "In agriculture, learn from Dazhai" became the guiding nationwide slogan that hailed the brigade as a "new socialist village." Dazhai reportedly doubled per unit yield and gross output and at the same time made considerable progress in forestry and animal husbandry. "Revolutionary spirit" and "revolutionary vigor," it was claimed, were the deciding factors in leading the peasants to "give priority to the interests of the whole" and to adhere to "socialist principles of distribution" in which work points (q.v.) and income were allocated on a basis that, while not strictly egalitarian, allowed for only small differentials in compensation. Self-assessment and public discussion, it was said, were the means for determining the allocation of work points that ultimately determined income in the Chinese countryside. Brigade members who worked overtime did receive additional points, but not enough to lead to dramatic differences in wealth. Collective labor gangs in Dazhai were touted for digging a vast array of irrigation ditches and for terracing fields up steep mountainsides that made possible the dramatic increases in agricultural production.

The leader of Dazhai, a nearly illiterate peasant named Chen Yonggui (q.v.), was elevated to national prominence and ultimately became a member of the CCP (q.v.), Politburo (q.v.), and a vice premier until his rude dismissal from these posts in 1980 and 1982, respectively. Mao Zedong's purpose in promoting Dazhai was clear. After the disastrous Great Leap Forward (1958–1960) (q.v.), the commune (q.v.) and brigade as the highest forms of "socialist" organization in the countryside yielded their decision-making authority to the lower level and less socialized production team (q.v.). In championing Dazhai in the early 1960s, Mao made a concerted effort to overturn the reversions to the production team and to renew the advance to a more socialist system in the countryside that, he believed, Party leaders such as Deng Xiaoping (q.v.) and Liu Shaoqi (q.v.) firmly opposed.

Once the Cultural Revolution (1966–1976) (q.v.) broke out, however, Dazhai receded into the background, though in the mid-1970s a Dazhai-type commune was briefly touted as another agricultural model. By 1978, the introduction of the Agricultural Responsibility System (q.v.)—the polar opposite of the Dazhai model—buried any memory of Dazhai, while recent government studies show that, contrary to its assertions of self-reliance, the Dazhai Brigade had actually received large infusions of state funds, thereby assisting its reputed increases in production.

DEMOCRACY WALL MOVEMENT (1978–1979). The first of the post-Mao movements for democracy in China, this short-lived but intensely popular movement centered around a high brick wall located on Chang'an Avenue in Beijing's (q.v.) Xidan district. For more than a year big-character posters (*dazibao*) (q.v.) were plastered on the wall, evidently with the support of key CCP (q.v.) leaders who were committed to changing the political leadership in China. The first posters appeared in March 1978 and focused their attacks on the leftist mayor of Beijing and Politburo (q.v.) member Wu De (q.v.), who was summarily dismissed as first secretary of the Beijing Party Committee in October 1978. Other themes in the wall posters included calls for reversing the official CCP verdict on the April 1976 Tiananmen movement, which had led to the purge of Deng Xiaoping (q.v.) and the rise of Jiang Qing (q.v.) and the Gang of Four (q.v.). Condemnation of Mao Zedong (q.v.) for his purge of popular political leaders, such as Peng Dehuai (q.v.), attacks on ideological orthodoxy, and advocacy of democracy, human rights (q.v.), and rule by law were all central themes on Democracy Wall posters.

The Democracy Wall movement peaked in late 1978 at the time Deng Xiaoping was making his political comeback at the important Third Plenum of the Eleventh CCP Central Committee (q.v.). Locked in a titanic political struggle for control of the Chinese state with the leftist "Whatever" Faction (q.v.), Deng, it is widely believed, countenanced and even encouraged the proliferation of wall posters that largely supported his political position. At the same time, activists in the poster campaign, such as Wei Jingsheng (q.v.), began to expand their activities to include organization of study groups and dissident organizations such as the Enlightenment Society and the China Human Rights Alliance. After Deng Xiaoping consolidated his political position at the December 1978 Third Plenum, his need for the Democracy Wall movement quickly evaporated, and so the screws were gradually tightened against the wall and the democratic activists. A ban was placed on activities at the wall (which since 1979 has been covered with commercial advertisements), and Wei Jingsheng and other prominent leaders were arrested, tried, and imprisoned. In December 1982, the possibility of another such movement was quashed as the CCP eliminated from the state constitution the so-called Four Freedoms (*sida*) (q.v.) that had guaranteed Chinese citizens the right to speak out, air views fully, hold great debates, and put up wall posters. Now the leadership, firmly under control of Deng Xiaoping, stressed "stability" and "unity" and opposed any further expression of democratic ideas.

"DEMOCRATIC CENTRALISM" (*MINZHU JIZHONGZHI*). Democratic centralism is a model of organizational structure and decision making employed by Communist parties throughout the world. In the CCP (q.v.), it is described as the "basic principle of the proletarian party," providing a "dialectical unity of democracy and centralism." In theory, it ensures both widespread participation of all Party members in decision making and "iron discipline," that is, obedience to central commands.

Lenin developed democratic centralism during the early years of the underground Bolshevik Party in Russia. It figured prominently in Lenin's major writings on Party organization where he contrasted this principle of decision making and discipline to the opposite extremes of "bureaucratic centralism" and "anarchism" that purportedly infected other opposition political movements. Democratic centralism reflected Lenin's deep fear of "spontaneity" in Russian political life, while promising the organization and planning necessary to seize and maintain political power. Democratic centralism has four essential features as outlined in the rules of the former Communist Party of the Soviet Union and the CCP: 1) all leading bodies are elected; 2) Party bodies must report periodically to their organizations and to higher bodies; 3) the minority is subordinate to the majority; and 4) decisions of higher bodies are obligatory for lower bodies. In theory, democratic centralism allows for substantial debate on policy issues (though within the general guidelines of the official ideology and the Party program) before formal decisions are taken. After decisions are reached, however, strict discipline (what Lenin called "iron discipline") must be followed by all Party members in implementing the decisions of the "majority." *See also* CHINESE COMMUNIST PARTY.

DEMOCRATIC PARTIES. Also known as satellite parties, the democratic parties (*Minzhu dangpai*) in China have existed since 1949, reflecting the united-front strategy pursued by the CCP (q.v.) in its rise to power. As part of his 1940 theory of New Democracy (q.v.), Mao Zedong (q.v.) promised that China would be a multiparty state reflecting its multi-class character. As an underdeveloped nation making the transition, in Marxist terminology, from feudalism (q.v.) to capitalism, there were a number of classes that existed, besides the minuscule proletariat class, that were potential allies of the CCP. Besides the peasantry, the largest potential ally was among the bourgeoisie, a class Mao divided into two component parts: "big bourgeoisie" and "national bourgeoisie." Many, in this bifurcated bourgeoisie, were considered allies of the Communists, especially in the nationalist cause to defeat the Japanese and oust the KMT (q.v.), though their political influence even before 1949 was minimal. From 1949 onward, China, like some Eastern European Communist nations, such as Czechoslovakia, permitted the continued existence of non-Communist parties, at least in name.

The major democratic parties in China are: Democratic League, Revolutionary Kuomintang, National Construction Association, Jiusan (literally "nine-three"), Association for Promoting Democracy, and the Peasants' and Workers' Democratic Party. Altogether their membership is no more than a few hundred thousand in a country of over one billion people. In reality, these organizations are not political parties in the conventional sense, but closer to interest groups and professional associations. Their major role in contemporary China is educational, as many such parties run schools and do consulting work for enterprises. Fielding candidates in elections for people's congresses (q.v.) is but a minor function.

The Democratic League is the largest democratic party, composed of approximately 50,000 members, mostly intellectuals. In the 1940s, it was ostensibly a middle-of-the-road party that largely inclined toward the Communists out of disgust with the corruption (q.v.) and repression of the KMT. (In 1946, after a Democratic League press conference, the poet and KMT critic Wen Yiduo was gunned down after criticizing KMT corruption.) The League was formally dissolved by the Nationalist government, but reconstituted itself in Hong Kong in 1948 and then was reestablished as a political party in the mainland after the CCP seized power in October 1949. The Revolutionary Kuomintang began with disaffected elements of the KMT, particularly individuals opposed to Chiang Kai-shek. From 1927 to 1949, it existed as an underground organization, with its agents working in the KMT apparatus where they engaged in intelligence work and sabotage. In Hong Kong, Song Qingling (q.v.) was honorary chairman and chairman was Li Jishen, a man who in 1927 had brutally crushed a Communist uprising in Canton, but who in the 1940s was courted by the CCP. After 1949, Li became a leading figure of the democratic parties, constantly luring KMT defectors from Taiwan (q.v.). The National Construction Association was formed in the mid-

1940s to serve as a mediating force between the CCP and the KMT in the run-up to the 1946–1949 civil war (q.v.). Its major constituency was the business community that was disaffected with KMT policies. The Jiusan Society formed from a tiny leftist academic group in 1945 and is composed solely of intellectuals. The Association for Promoting Democracy was formed in 1946 and consists primarily of school teachers. Finally, the Peasants' and Workers' Party was formerly known as the Third Party, an organization that tried to effect a cease-fire between the CCP and the KMT in the civil war. Despite its name, its primary constituency is health professionals.

After the Chinese Communist seizure of power in 1949, the democratic parties were put under the United Front Department of the CCP which was maintained as a bridge to non-CCP groups. Financed by the Chinese government, these "parties" were immediately purged of members considered antagonistic to the Communist government and reorganized in a fashion to ensure their subservience to the CCP. They were represented in the CPPCC (q.v.), which itself lacked any real decision-making authority. Democratic party members were obliged to participate in many early CCP propaganda campaigns, such as the Resist America, Aid Korea campaign and often became victims of CCP-led purges, such as the Five Antis (q.v.).

In 1957, however, the role of the democratic parties changed fundamentally as Mao Zedong and other Party leaders encouraged the democratic parties to join in the Hundred Flowers (q.v.) and voice criticism of the CCP. Through newspapers still controlled by the democratic parties (such as the *Enlightenment Daily*, which at the time was an organ of the Democratic League), a bevy of criticism was directed at the CCP and proposals were aired for radical political change. Accusations were directed at the Communists for trying to control the entire society through their systematic apparatus of "Party core groups" (*hexin dangxiaozu*), to carrying out "thought reform" (q.v.) against the bourgeoisie and intellectuals, for preventing the creation of a true independent legal system, and for being arrogant and never listening to advice. Universities, it was proposed, should be freed from CCP control; the CPPCC should be given real power in the state; and, political decision making should be more open. After a few weeks of such criticism, Mao Zedong and more conservative elements in the CCP had had enough and many democratic party members were forced to recant, while others suffered greater humiliations.

From 1958 to 1978 the democratic parties were effectively suffocated as their independent newspapers, such as the *Enlightenment Daily*, were put under direct CCP control. During the Cultural Revolution (1966–1976) (q.v.), many members of the democratic parties suffered, though, ironically, membership in these organizations acted as political cover as Red Guards (q.v.) directed their ire at the CCP apparatus. Following Mao Zedong's (q.v.) death in 1976, an effort was made to revive the democratic parties, though much of the membership by then consisted of the elderly who were fearful of again voicing independent views. Nevertheless, at the height of the political reform in the mid- to late-1980s, some democratic party members once again took up social causes, such as opposition to the massive Three Gorges Dam project (q.v.), which was led by Jiusan member Qian Jiaju (q.v.). Still, these parties are largely window dressing to CCP's claims that China has a multiparty system allowing for political pluralism, a claim that is blatantly false since the democratic parties are still virtually powerless.

DENG LIQUN (1914–   ). From Mao Zedong's (q.v.) native province of Hunan, Deng Liqun worked in the early 1950s in Xinjiang province where he assisted in putting down Muslim resistance to communist rule. Serving as secretary to Liu Shaoqi (q.v.), Deng was purged in the Cultural Revolution (1966–1976) (q.v.), but returned in 1975 to serve on the State Council and in 1978 as vice president of the Chinese Academy of Social Sciences (q.v.). In the early 1980s, he headed the Policy Research Office of the Central Party Secretariat (*Zhongyang shujichu yanjiushi*), from where he mobilized internal CCP (q.v.) opposition to market reforms. He was also a member of the Central Commission for Guiding Party Consolidation. From 1982 to 1985 he was director of the CCP Department of Propaganda. Following the June 1989 Beijing massacre, Deng Liqun emerged as a major "leftist" opponent of political reform and as an outspoken critic of "bourgeois liberalization" in the CCP among intellectuals (q.v.).

DENG PUFANG (1943–   ). The son of China's former paramount leader, Deng Xiaoping (q.v.), Deng Pufang is a graduate from the Physics Department at Beida (Peking University) (q.v.). In 1968, reportedly thrown from a window, he was crippled by Red Guards (q.v.). Throughout the 1980s and early 1990s he has served in various national and international organizations for disabled persons.

DENG RONG (1950–   ). The third daughter of Deng Xiaoping (q.v.) and his wife Zhuo Lin, Deng Rong (nicknamed "Mao Mao") entered Jiangxi Medical School in 1972 as a "worker-peasant-soldier student" while her father was still in exile. When her father returned to power she transferred to Beijing Medical College and graduated in 1977 and was assigned to work in the PLA's (q.v.) General Political

Department. She was posted to the Chinese Embassy in Washington for four years. Thereafter, she became her father's secretary and as his health declined and his hearing and speaking became difficult for him prior to his death in 1997, she served as both his ears and mouth.

DENG TUO (1912–1966). One of the premier journalists in the CCP (q.v.) along with Hu Jiwei (q.v.) and Liu Binyan (q.v.), Deng Tuo was a veteran Communist who during the Sino-Japanese War (q.v.) in the late 1930s and 1940s was editor of *Resistance News* (*Kangdi bao*), a major CCP-run newspaper, established in the "white" areas behind Japanese lines. After 1949, Deng Tuo was quickly promoted to editor in chief of *People's Daily* (q.v.), under the CCP Central Committee, and was a major contributor to *Study* (*Xuexi*), the CCP's primary theoretical journal from 1950 to 1958. Deng also served as head of the Propaganda Department of the Beijing Municipal Committee and was a close associate of Peng Zhen (q.v.). A polymath, polished poet, and traditional calligrapher, in the late 1950s Deng wrote such scathing essays as "Discard 'The Politics of Simpletons.' " Using the pseudonym Ma Nancun, Deng Tuo also wrote two columns, under the general title of "Evening Chats at Yanshan" and "Notes from a Three Family Village," that were later criticized by Jiang Qing (q.v.), Yao Wenyuan (q.v.), and other leftist leaders in the CCP as an attack on Mao Zedong (q.v.) and the policies of the Great Leap Forward (1958–1960) (q.v.). Mao criticized Deng Tuo for running a "dead" newspaper at the *People's Daily* because of his apparent refusal to support Mao's grandiose plans during the Great Leap. Relieved from his post at *People's Daily*, Deng Tuo edited the journal *Frontline* (*Qianxian*) until he was purged during the Cultural Revolution (1966–1976) (q.v.). Persecuted by Red Guards (q.v.), Deng committed suicide in May 1966. He was officially "rehabilitated" (*pingfan*) in 1979.

DENG XIAOPING (1904–1997). Born in Sichuan province, Deng Xiaoping was the eldest son of a landowner. In 1920 he traveled as a work-study student to France where he joined a Chinese socialist youth organization. Upon returning to China, he entered the CCP (q.v.) in 1924 and assumed his first position as an instructor at the Xi'an Military and Political Academy, established under the auspices of the warlord Feng Yuxiang. In 1929 he helped organize Communist military forces in the southwestern province of Guangxi and became a political commissar (q.v.). During the 1946–1949 civil war (q.v.), Deng was a member of the Second Field Army in the Crossing the Yangtze River and Huaihai battles. In 1952 he was appointed a vice premier and in 1956 became a member of the Politburo (q.v.) Standing Committee and head of the Party Secretariat. He was condemned in the Cultural Revolution (1966–1976) (q.v.) for having previously criticized the personality cult (q.v.) of Mao Zedong (q.v.) and for advocating relatively "liberal" agricultural policies. He first appeared after the Cultural Revolution in 1973 as a vice premier. In 1975 he was reappointed to the Politburo Standing Committee, only to be dropped again in 1976 following the April Tiananmen demonstrations. Deng reappeared in July 1977 and assumed all previous posts, plus that of PLA (q.v.) chief of staff, and in 1981 he became chairman of the Central Military Commission. In November 1987 he "retired" from all posts, except the chairmanship of the Central Military Commission, a post that he finally relinquished in 1989. Yet, Deng remained the paramount leader of the CCP as indicated by his key role in sanctioning the crackdown on prodemocracy demonstrators in June 1989 and in making his historic "southern tour" in 1992 to stave off conservative attempts to reverse his economic reforms. In 1993, Deng again defended his economic reform program in a "Five-Point Opinion on Reform" that called for further "emancipating the mind" (q.v.), "speeding up the pace of reform," "strengthening the unity of leading bodies," "eliminating bureaucratism (q.v.) and corruption" (q.v.) and bringing about "the integration between political reform and economic reform." In 1995, rumors spread inside and outside of China that Deng Xiaoping was gravely ill, provoking speculation of a succession crisis. Deng was noted for his love of playing bridge. Deng Xiaoping died on February 20, 1997, at the age of 92.

DENG YINGCHAO (1903–1992). Wife of Zhou Enlai (q.v.), Deng Yingchao joined the Communist movement in China very early in life and became quite active in CCP (q.v.) policy on women. Her political role preceded her marriage to Zhou Enlai, though undoubtedly this union facilitated her position in the CCP hierarchy. Deng Yingchao was drawn to political involvement during the 1919 May Fourth Movement (q.v.) and joined the CCP in 1925, heading the Party's Women's Department in the city of Tianjin where in the same year she married Zhou Enlai. After serving in the Jiangxi Soviet, Deng was one of the few women to participate in the epic Long March (1934–1935) (q.v.). During the period of the Second United Front (1937–1945) with the KMT (q.v.), she joined her husband in carrying out a liaison role with Nationalist leaders in Chungking (Chongqing), the Nationalists' wartime base in Sichuan province. In 1949, she was appointed to head the All-China Federation of Women (q.v.), a post she would hold until the 1970s, and she participated in drafting the Marriage Law (q.v.) that was adopted in 1950. In the mid-1950s she became a member of the Standing Committee of the NPC (q.v.) and was appointed to the CCP Central Committee where she played a crucial role in formulating Party policy on women. Following her husband's death in 1976, she was elected to the CCP Politburo (q.v.) in December 1978 and then in 1985 resigned from her Politburo and Central Committee positions. One of the revered Party "revolutionary elders" (q.v.), Deng reportedly agreed to the use of force in June 1989 to put down the Beijing Spring (q.v.) pro-democracy movement.

"DICTATORSHIP OF THE PROLETARIAT" (*WUCHAN JIEJI ZHUANZHENG*). In the Marxist-Leninist system that governs China's post-1949 politics, the Communist Party maintains its dictatorship in the name of the proletariat over other "classes" (bourgeoisie, landlords, rentiers) in the period of "socialism" (q.v.) that in theory precedes the "final" historical stage of "communism." Marx had originally foreseen a very short, transitional socialist period, in which such a dictatorship by the proletariat was necessary to eliminate from the state and society the remnant capitalist influence in politics, economics, and culture. In the relatively "backward" conditions confronting the Bolsheviks in Russia after the 1917 October Revolution, Lenin then expanded "socialism" and the period of the dictatorship of the proletariat into a much longer historical stage, during which the proletariat's struggle with the still vibrant bourgeoisie would require a more intense struggle with the full weight of state power under Communist Party control being directed at the capitalist classes. Throughout this period, the restoration of capitalism would be a constant threat and the Communist Party could use any means necessary to destroy the capitalists' social, economic, and political power. In effect, Lenin's elaboration of Marx laid the ideological foundations for the extended period of the Soviet state dictatorship that did not end until the collapse of Soviet communism in 1991.

China fully adopted this Leninist perspective after 1949. Although the degree of dictatorship exercised against the "capitalist classes" in China varied in intensity, China's merchants, businessmen, and incipient entrepreneurs have been frequent targets of political persecution in Marxist-Leninist garb since 1949. In the early 1950s, indigenous capitalists had their industrial/commercial and personal property seized with little or no compensation, and, along with their family members, they were frequently killed or driven to suicide, all in the name of promoting "socialism." The same was true for rural landlords and peasants. During the mid-1960s attacks against virtually all forms of private property were intensified by the Red Guards (q.v.), acting on edicts and instructions from Mao Zedong (q.v.) and the radical faction led by Jiang Qing (q.v.). Mao, in particular, emphasized the interminable struggle between "the two roads of capitalism and socialism" and used this to justify the harshest measures against private interests in the society. Following the Chairman's death in 1976, radical faction leaders such as Zhang Chunqiao (q.v.) took up the cause of the "dictatorship of the proletariat" to block the reappearance of Party leaders, such as Deng Xiaoping (q.v.), who opposed the radical and antidevelopment policies of the Jiang Qing group. In this formulation, the "dictatorship of the proletariat" was no longer directed at "capitalist classes" in Chinese society, as they had largely disappeared years earlier, but rather at proponents of economic reform within the CCP (q.v.) who, following Mao's death, were now poised to return to positions of political leadership. With Deng Xiaoping's return to power in 1978, the "dictatorship of the proletariat" was no longer used in attacks against senior Party leaders. Yet the term is still employed to justify the suppression of social democratic forces, such as those that promoted the 1989 Beijing Spring (q.v.) prodemocracy movement. *See also* LAND REFORM.

DING GUAN'GEN (1929–). Trained as a railway engineer in the early 1950s, Ding Guan'gen served from 1952 to 1983 as a technician in various bureaus of the Ministry of Communication and the Ministry of Railways. In 1983, he was appointed deputy secretary-general of the NPC (q.v.) Standing Committee and in 1985, he became minister of railways. In 1987, Deng was appointed to the CCP (q.v.) Central Committee and became an alternate member of the Politburo (q.v.). In 1988, he voluntarily resigned as minister of railways as a result of three major train accidents. In 1989 he became a member of the powerful Secretariat of the CCP Central Committee where he generally sided with conservative leaders on propaganda issues and against further economic and political reform.

DONG FURENG (1927–). Trained in the early 1950s in Marxist economics at the Moscow State Institute of Economics, Dong Fureng joined the Economics Institute under the Chinese Academy of Sciences and in 1978 became deputy director of the Economics Institute of the Academy of Social Sciences (q.v.). In 1982 he was identified as the vice president of the Graduate School under the Chinese Academy of Social Sciences (q.v.) and in 1985 he became the director of the academy's Economics Institute and a consultant to the World Bank. In 1988 he was a delegate to the NPC (q.v.) from Zhejiang province and a member of the NPC Standing Committee.

E

ECONOMIC REFORM. *See* AGRICULTURAL RESPONSIBILITY SYSTEM, ENTERPRISE REFORM, and OPEN-DOOR POLICY.

EDUCATION. The commitment to education in post-1949 China by the CCP (q.v.) began in 1951 with the "Decision of the Reform of the Education System." During the First Five-Year Plan (1953–1957) (q.v.) the educational system in China was based on the Soviet model, emphasizing technical training, to fill the new positions created by the industrialization program. Primary schooling during this period was for six years in urban areas and three to four years in the countryside. Although primary schooling was not compulsory, national enrollments increased from around 25 million in 1953 to 86 million in 1958. Secondary schooling during the same period consisted of six-year junior and senior middle schools focusing on general academic training, though these schools were largely restricted to urban areas. There were also vocational schools and polytechnic schools. The latter were half-work, half-study schools that prepared students for work in industry and agriculture. Enrollment in secondary schools grew from 2 million in 1953 to more than 9 million in 1958. Higher education consisted of comprehensive universities with full-time students and polytechnic universities, such as Qinghua University (q.v.). Entrance to universities was based on demanding entrance examinations. Many Chinese university students also studied in the Soviet Union. Overall enrollment in higher education grew from 110,000 in 1950 to 800,000 in 1959.

During the Great Leap Forward (1958–1960) (q.v.) and the Cultural Revolution (1966–1976) (q.v.), various educational experiments were attempted, usually with dire results. During the Leap, vocational and polytechnic education was expanded at enormous rates, with an emphasis on half-work, half-study and heavy doses of political education. From 1966 to 1968, during the Cultural Revolution, just about all schools and universities in China were closed during the height of factional strife among Red Guards (q.v.) that plagued campuses. When the schools reopened, the average length for primary and secondary education was reduced from twelve to nine years in the cities and to seven years in the countryside. Most youth entered the workforce—urban and rural—at the ages of 15 or 16, while students planning to attend the universities that had reopened were required to engage in "practical" work for two to three years before admission. In 1970 all universities reopened as students were admitted on the basis of "nominations" from their work units that stressed political reliability and appropriate class background. Educational administration was given over to revolutionary committees (q.v.) at the expense of professional educators—which saved the central government money but produced poor-quality students.

After the death of Mao Zedong (q.v.) in 1976, the Chinese educational system underwent major revamping to fit the nation's goal of modernization in science and technology. In 1977, the government restored the system of competitive examinations for university admission, and at the primary and secondary levels in urban areas it revived so-called key-point schools (*zhongdian xuexiao*). Condemned by radical Maoists as "elitist," these schools receive special government funds and the best-trained teachers for the brightest students. Previously taboo subjects such as art, classical music, and philosophy were added to secondary and university curricula while the role of political-ideological studies has been significantly downgraded. In the mid-1980s, all school-age children were required to attend at least nine years of school and government funding for education was increased to over $40 billion per year. University admissions rose dramatically and Party-state control of curricula and student life was significantly reduced as university administrators under a "presidential responsibility system" were freed from direct political controls. University students were also required to contribute financially to their education. After the Tiananmen crisis in 1989, the flow of university students interested in studying abroad increased significantly while only about one quarter of the more than 65,000 Chinese students overseas had returned by 1990. At centers of student protest, such as Peking University (Beida) (q.v.), political education and controls were reestablished and curricula with "Western" biases were significantly altered. At the same time, the allure of opportunities in the economic realm drew increasing numbers of students and teachers away from education and into the market, raising questions about the future quality of Chinese education. State spending on education remained flat and, as a result, China's goal of achieving universal, compulsory education was not achieved. From 1949 to 1985, 4.73 million students graduated from colleges or universities, 22 times the number from 1912 to 1947. China currently ranks 60th among 122 nations in the proportion of people over 25 years of age who have received higher or secondary education. Only 2.5 percent of the Chinese GNP is invested in education and the illiteracy rate in the country is nearly 25 percent.

EIGHTH PARTY CONGRESS (1956). A watershed meeting of the CCP (q.v.), the First Session of the Eighth Congress held in September 1956 signaled dramatic changes in China's political and economic policies that set the stage for intra-elite conflicts that ultimately led to the Cultural Revolution (1966–1976). More than one thousand delegates attended the twelve-day congress, theoretically representing the 10 million members of the CCP. A new Party constitution was adopted and a new Central Committee was chosen. Forty-five reports were presented by top CCP leaders. The congress also decided on the contours of the Second Five-Year Plan (q.v.).

The congress took a conciliatory attitude toward "class struggle" (q.v.) and declared that "the question of who will win in the struggle between socialism (q.v.) and capitalism in our country has now been decided." In effect, this statement suggested that the mass movements and struggle campaigns that had marked the early 1950s would be phased out. During the congress, the Party leadership also suggested moderation in its treatment of intellectuals (q.v.) and in economic policies as the intensive drives in industry and agriculture launched in 1955 were slowed down. According to Chen Yun's (q.v.) report to the congress, CCP policies would be "prudent and practical," with an emphasis on gradual change. In this sense, the congress reflected Mao Zedong's (q.v.) concept of "balanced" development laid out in his 1956 speech "On the Ten Major Relationships" (q.v.). The congress also called for greater stress on "democracy," which was taken to mean more decentralization of authority in the elaborate administrative apparatus established by the CCP since 1949 and more tolerance for lower-level initiatives.

Organizationally, the Eighth Party Congress introduced several changes, some substantive and some merely cosmetic. The former included the creation of a Standing Committee (consisting of seven members) to the top decision-making body of the Politburo (q.v.) and the formation of a Secretariat (headed by the general secretary) to carry out the leadership's decisions. Five vice chairmen were also appointed to assist the Party chairman, Mao Zedong, in the formulation and execution of policy. In effect, these changes diluted the CCP's highly concentrated power structure, as decision-making authority was divided between the Secretariat and the Politburo (which Mao Zedong labeled the "first" and "second fronts," respectively). The size of the Central Committee was also expanded to almost one hundred members, thereby making it an even more unwieldy body. In a move to standardize the CCP's top policy-making bodies, the ad hoc commissions that reported to the Central Committee were also abolished.

During the Eighth Party Congress, Party Chairman Mao Zedong was generally on the political defensive. After presenting a short opening and closing address, Mao saw references to his "Thought" dropped from the Party constitution and his policies for "rapid advance" (*maojin*) in the economy replaced by the gradualist approach championed by Chen Yun. Criticisms of the "personality cult" (q.v.) were also written into Party documents. Whether Mao genuinely endorsed these policies is unknown. In his April 1956 speech "On the Ten Major Relationships," Mao had seemed to endorse this strategy.

But within six months of the congress Mao was to assert a more radical line claiming that development could not occur without "struggle."

In May 1958 an extraordinary Second Session of the Eighth Party Congress was held, which approved a fundamentally different policy line. Delivering five separate speeches, Mao Zedong dominated this second session that wholeheartedly endorsed his strategy of bringing about a Great Leap Forward (q.v.) in the Chinese economy and pursuing a more radical line in agricultural development. Unlike the moderate line of the first session which had declared the primary contradiction in China to be between "[economic] backwardness and development," this second session put a harder-edge spin on this formulation by announcing that "proletarian versus bourgeois, and socialist versus capitalist roads" were now the primary contradictions. Internationally, the hard line continued as Mao, prompted by the stress on international Communist unity at the November 1957 Moscow Conference, positively appraised the possible results of nuclear war. It is generally agreed that the Hungarian Uprising in 1956 helped shift the political landscape in China from the moderation of the September 1956 first session to the hard-line May 1958 second session.

"ELIMINATE THE FOUR PESTS" (*CHU SIHAI*). In the mid-1950s as part of its "National Program for the Development of Agriculture," the CCP (q.v.) took on the task of ridding urban and rural China of vermin and other threats to public health. Prior to the CCP takeover of power in 1949, the garbage and filth in China's cities and villages were breeding grounds for animals and insects that carried serious infectious diseases and brought illnesses and suffering to the general population. The "four pests" targeted for total extinction in a twelve-year period beginning in 1956 included rats, flies, mosquitoes, and sparrows, the latter apparently because they ate grain in the fields. (In 1960, sparrows were replaced by bedbugs as a target for extinction.) The mobilization of millions of people in the campaign succeeded over the years in virtually eliminating these creatures from much of the country. Young and old alike were trained in various procedures to rid their surroundings of these vermin. The unfortunate sparrows were targeted by the widespread use of slingshots by youngsters, resulting in an especially devastating impact on the bird population. Overall, however, there was a concomitant benefit to public health as rats, flies, and mosquitoes were generally eliminated, at least in the cities. Since 1978, however, the general increase in wealth has combined with less-stringent efforts at "pest control," thus bringing about a reappearance of vermin, though the public health system is better prepared today to deal with the problems of carriers of infectious diseases in more conventional manners.

"EMANCIPATION OF THE MIND." *See* **"PRACTICE IS THE SOLE CRITERION OF TRUTH."**

ENTERPRISE REFORM. The structural and economic reform of the approximately 400,000 Chinese state-owned industries, which employ 80 million workers, began in earnest in the early 1980s. Organized into vertically structured "systems" (*xitong*) controlled by central state ministries in Beijing (q.v.), industrial enterprises have been the focus of reforms aimed at decentralizing decision-making authority, reducing the role of the CCP (q.v.) in the economy, reforming the price system, and altering the tax system. These reforms proceeded from a 1978 report to the State Council by Hu Qiaomu (q.v.) titled "Act in Accord with Economic Laws, Step Up the Four Modernizations" in which the Daqing (q.v.) model of industrial organization and development was criticized and Chinese economists were encouraged to study management techniques of capitalist industry abroad. This report did not, however, challenge the fundamentals of the Chinese system of state planning, namely that planners rather than the market establish prices and economic goals.

At the Wuxi conference in April 1979, proposals were made to integrate the state economic plan and the market and to give greater decision-making authority to enterprises. Criticisms of the state planning system were also aired for its overconcentration of authority that effectively stifled managerial initiative and innovation and led to a one-sided emphasis by enterprises on output value and a neglect of costs and efficiency, resulting in huge wastes of resources and labor. Prices of processed goods were too high and those of basic industrial goods and energy were too low. Thus a new system was proposed to bring about an "organic" integration of plan and market and reliance on the "law of value" in establishing prices. Enterprises needed to have greater flexibility to establish horizontal ties with other producers and to break the limitations of vertical, ministerial branch systems and of local government controls, both of which kept enterprises in dependent positions. In this way, enterprises that had protected themselves from arbitrary outside controls by becoming totally self-sufficient (and highly inefficient) would establish networks of supplies and would contract work to make a more efficient state sector. The state plan would not be mandatory but serve only as a guide to production and pricing. Some Chinese economists even went so far as to suggest that ownership of enterprises be shifted from the state to collective (but not private) hands.

In 1981, the leadership structure in state enterprises was also adjusted, giving greater stress to the role of industrial managers over enterprise Party committees, but without fundamentally altering the CCP committee system. In 1984 a State Council decision advanced enterprise reform by authorizing experimental reforms in Guangdong and Shanghai (q.v.) where enterprises were given control over their profits and losses after paying various state taxes which were established through a contract between the enterprise and the state authorities. Wages were linked to profits, and enterprises were given authority to hire their own laborers, buy materials on the market, and set prices according to demand, while funds were established at the enterprise level for reinvestment purposes. A "factory responsibility system" was also adopted through which enterprises were allowed to retain profits above a certain quota. Small-scale state enterprises in the retail, service, and repair sectors were leased out and large-scale state-owned enterprises not engaged in vital production were allowed to form joint-stock companies.

As a result of these reforms, output rose dramatically in the mid-1980s, contributing to rapid inflation that ultimately led to government cutbacks and restrictions and the reinstitution of price controls in key sectors. Party cadres (q.v.) and bureaucrats also took advantage of the new two-tiered pricing system (low, subsidized state-set prices of goods and high market prices), thus leading to an explosion in official corruption (q.v.) and profiteering (*guandao*).

In October 1984, at the Third Plenum of the Twelfth Central Committee, the decision on the "Structural Reform of the Economy" fundamentally altered relations between the Party and enterprises by replacing the Party committee system in factories with a "managerial responsibility system" (*yichangzhizhang*). But such experimentation occurred on only a small scale in a few enterprises.

However, in 1986 there were proposals that the enterprise Party committees no longer be subordinate to Party committees in the relevant state ministries but, instead, be subordinate to territorial Party committees (city districts or residential Party committees), thereby breaking the longstanding vertical connection to Beijing. This change was more apparent than real, however, as Party secretaries familiar with production and exercising capable leadership were simply switched to the position of industrial manager. By 1989, the new managerial system was established in more than 400,000 large and medium state enterprises. In order to gain the support of labor, increases in salaries, bonuses, and wages were enacted, thereby dramatically fueling the inflation that contributed to the 1989 Tiananmen crisis and that after 1989 provoked the government to adopt severe austerity measures.

With state-run factories still reluctant to fire or lay off workers and with increasing overhead costs, losses and debts at these industrial facilities rose substantially, leading the central bank to issue loans and lines of credit to tide over the firms. Austerity measures were eased from 1993 onward, but the prospect of huge losses in the industrial sector and massive bankruptcies have prevented any further moves toward fundamental enterprise reform, especially reforms of state ownership. By 1995, despite huge losses, the state-owned sector in China was actually expanding. This apparently stiffened resistance to privatization measures that China must adopt in order to join the World Trade Organization.

ENVIRONMENT. The issue of environmental protection in China gained national attention in 1973 with the first "Environmental Protection National Conference," which was held in Beijing (q.v.). In 1979 the National People's Congress (q.v.) committed itself to annual reviews of China's environmental conditions, and throughout the 1980s a series of laws were passed to strengthen environmental regulation: Seas and Ocean Environmental Law (1982), Water Pollution and Control Law (1984), Air Pollution and Control Law (1987), Environmental Protection Law (1989), and Water and Soil Protection Act (1991). Enforcement was advanced in 1983 by the creation of a State Environmental Protection Commission (SEPC), with more than 70,000 local offices established throughout the country to monitor pollution problems. In 1995, this agency became popularly known as the "richest" government bureau due to its well-known inclination to impose heavy fines on violators, though overall enforcement remained weak. In 1994, China spent 0.8 percent of its GNP on environmental protection, which is barely half the 1.5 to 2.0 percent that is needed for a serious effort to control pollution. China's environment has continued to suffer deterioration in the wake of the rapid economic development and the general weakness of the SEPC enforcement mechanisms. Air pollution is perhaps China's most serious environmental problem, stemming from the large-scale burning of coal for domestic and industrial purposes and from the lack of widespread use of natural gas in most Chinese cities. In 1994, China ranked third in the world, and could soon be first, in carbon dioxide emissions. China is already the world's greatest contributor to methane greenhouse gas (largely from livestock and wet rice paddies), while two-thirds of the sulfur oxides emitted in Asia come from the PRC (q.v.). With its dramatic increase in production of refrigerators, China has also increased its contribution to worldwide emission of CFCs and halons. Chongqing, Sichuan province, is China's most polluted city because of high sulfur-content coal burned for fuel and highly acidic rain. Investment in industrial waste-water treatment plants has increased nationwide, but it still stands at less than one-half of 1 percent of GNP, as water quality of rivers passing through cities has either remained stagnant or declined. Hunan province and the Huai and Pearl river basins in southern China are also highly polluted because of the continued use of obsolete industrial equipment. Average per capita fresh water availability is about one-fifth the world average, while production of raw sewage continues to outpace the capacity of treatment plants. China also reports sharp decreases in marine fisheries, principally due to overfishing and the effects of ocean pollution near its shores. Land reduction and desertification have also intensified as industrial development zones and real estate speculation consume more and more farmland.

The willingness of the local authorities in China to sacrifice the environment for the sake of economic development is a major cause of the country's continued environmental degradation and increased rates in respiratory diseases and related cancers. At the international level, China has generally resisted the more stringent controls of developing nations. In the run up to the 1995 Berlin Climate-Control Conference, China sided with the mostly "southern" developing nations that demanded that more steps be taken by the "northern," developed nations to restrict carbon dioxide emissions into the atmosphere. In terms of pollution control equipment, China has, however, become a major producer, exhibiting its wares at recent international environmental meetings, such as the Rio Summit in 1992. *See also* THREE GORGES DAM PROJECT.

F

FAMINE. *See* GREAT LEAP FORWARD.

FANG LIZHI (1936–   ). An astrophysicist by training and one of China's most eminent scientists, Fang has been a constant critic of the CCP (q.v.) dictatorship. Fang was denounced by the Party leadership for allegedly instigating student demonstrations in late 1986 that resulted in the removal of Hu Yaobang (q.v.) as CCP general secretary. Purged from the CCP in January 1987, Fang wrote an open letter to Deng Xiaoping (q.v.) in January 1989 calling for an amnesty for all political prisoners, particularly Wei Jingsheng (q.v.), China's most famous dissident. After the June 1989 crackdown, Fang sought refuge in the American Embassy in Beijing (q.v.) and one year later was allowed to leave China for the West. He currently resides in the United States and teaches physics at the University of Arizona.

FANG YI (1916–   ). A deputy mayor of Shanghai (q.v.) and vice minister of finance in the 1950s, Fang Yi became a vice chairman of the State Planning Commission in the 1960s. Protected by Zhou Enlai (q.v.) during the Cultural Revolution (1966–1976) (q.v.), Fang was elected to the Central Committee in 1973 and in 1977 became a member of the Politburo (q.v.) and a vice president of the Academy of Sciences. In 1978 he became minister of the State Science and Technology Commission and a vice premier; from 1982 to 1988 he was also a state councillor.

"*FANSHEN.*" This Chinese term literally means to "turn over the body." During the 1946–1953 Land Reform campaign (q.v.), it came to mean to "shake off the feudal yoke"—that is, the willingness of the peasant and working classes to overthrow the ruling classes that exploited and suppressed them. In concrete terms, *fanshen* meant that previously landless or land-poor classes had gained land, livestock, farm implements, and even houses in a massive seizure of property that was later reversed by the CCP's (q.v.) socialization of the means of production in the countryside and cities. *Fanshen* also implies a change in worldview, an abolition of superstition, and empowerment of the poorest and most dispossessed elements in society, including women. This aspect of *fanshen*, however, may be more a product of CCP propaganda than representative of a real change in consciousness.

"FEBRUARY ADVERSE CURRENT" (1967). This phrase was concocted by the radical faction in the Cultural Revolution (1966–1976) (q.v.) to describe the conservative reaction against the "January Storm" in 1967 that was the most violent phase of Red Guard (q.v.) action against Party and government cadres (q.v.). Rebel factions of Red Guards, who in January "seized power" at provincial levels and below, not only physically abused Party and government officials, but also attempted to establish new political structures based on the Paris Commune as originally described by Karl Marx. Mao Zedong (q.v.) rejected these power seizures as a sham and, to the consternation of many Red Guards, vetoed the Paris Commune model, opting instead for the Revolutionary Committees (q.v.). Meeting in February 1967, top Party officials detected ambivalence on Mao's part and protested that the Cultural Revolution was targeting the entire Party membership irrespective of revolutionary experience or ideological purity. Fearing for their own lives, these same officials convinced Mao to restrict the targets of attack to only a "small handful of capitalist roaders" (q.v.) in the CCP (q.v.). The vast majority of cadres were declared to be "good or very good." Efforts to spare CCP leader Liu

Shaoqi (q.v.), whom Mao had designated the "number one authority in the Party taking the capitalist road," did not, however, succeed. Radical groups denounced the "February Adverse Current" but were never able to overcome the strictures against attacking virtually all government and Party cadres, many of whom joined the Revolutionary Committees (q.v.).

FEI XIAOTONG (1910–). China's most prominent anthropologist, Fei Xiaotong studied at London University and worked at Harvard University in the mid-1940s. He has been chairman of the China Democratic League, one of the small democratic parties (q.v.), and has published several books on Chinese rural life and minority groups. Fei accompanied Hu Yaobang (q.v.) on a 1986 trip to the West.

FENG WENBIN (1911–). A prominent member and leader of the Communist Youth League (q.v.) since 1925, in 1957 Feng Wenbin was replaced as head of the league by Hu Yaobang (q.v.). After dropping out of the national political limelight for more than twenty years, in 1979 Feng became a vice president of the Central Party School (q.v.) in Beijing (q.v.). In the early 1980s he was appointed first deputy director of the General Office of the CCP (q.v.) and head of the Party History Research Center.

"FEUDALISM" (*FENGJIANZHUYI*). One of the major historical stages in the Marxist view of history, "feudalism" has proved to be a difficult concept for the Chinese Communists to incorporate into their periodization of Chinese history. Marx's remarks on feudalism are scattered throughout his works as part of his overall analysis of capitalist development and are generally ambiguous in meaning. Engels, however, focused on the self-sufficient nature of the feudal economy, with its orientation to immediate consumption of "small commodity production" by the producer and the lord, without consideration for a market. For both Marx and Engels, the means of "exploitation" under feudalism combined economic and political instruments in an almost indistinguishable form to ensure expropriation of "surplus" production by the peasantry. But the political-military apparatus of the state was of a more limited and circumscribed form geographically and institutionally in comparison to the subsequent development of the state under capitalism.

In the history of the CCP (q.v.), the concept of feudalism and its political usage has varied. During the 1921–1949 period, the CCP was profoundly affected by the Leninist-Stalinist notion that political and economic power in China was in the hands of backward "feudal

forces" and "feudal remnants" personified by warlords and milita-
rists against whom the revolution was directed. The revolution, in
other words, was primarily an "anti-feudal" and "anti-imperialist"
struggle led by the working and peasant classes, in alliance with the
relatively "weak" Chinese bourgeoisie, against "feudal and medieval
methods of exploitation." This contrasted with the Trotskyist view
that downplayed the "feudal" character of China, emphasizing instead the role of a powerful bourgeoisie and the leading role of the
proletariat in destroying a fairly well-developed capitalist system that
relied on foreign imperialism.

Mao Zedong (q.v.) essentially adopted the Stalinist view of China
as "feudal" and "semi-feudal." In his speech "New Democracy"
(q.v.) Mao declared that China had been "feudal" from the Zhou
(1122 B.C.–256 B.C.) and Qin (221 B.C.–207 B.C.) dynasties until
the intrusion of capitalism and imperialism in the mid-nineteenth century, which transformed the country and culture into a "semi-feudal"
one. In 1949, Mao declared the Communist revolution to be a victory
over "imperialism, feudalism, and bureaucratic capitalism." As the
major social prop of "feudalism," the landed gentry were expropri-
ated during the 1946–1953 Land Reform campaigns (q.v.). Yet as
"feudal forces" were eliminated, Mao claimed that new capitalist
forces had arisen that increasingly emerged as the target of Mao's
political ire, especially during the Cultural Revolution (1966–1976)
(q.v.). "Feudalism" thus gradually waned in importance in Mao's
political-ideological discourse. In the post-Mao period, however,
"feudalism" once again became a catchall term that represented China's political and economic backwardness. The danger of "capitalism" in the CCP that had been stressed by Mao was now replaced by
the purported presence of "feudal" attitudes toward authority among
CCP leaders. Mao's patriarchal leadership style was considered a
"feudal remnant," and in calling for an amelioration of authority relationships in the CCP, Deng Xiaoping (q.v.) and other reform-minded
leaders attacked "feudalism." In this sense, Chinese feudalism refers
not to the economic formation defined by Marx to describe medieval
Europe, but to an imperial autocratic system in China that stretched
from the Qin dynasty to the Stalinist-Maoist state and to ideological
despotism of both thought and culture. Since 1978, feudalism has
also been used in economic terms to describe the small commodity
economy that the economic reforms have begun fundamentally to
transform. Politically, feudalism has been used by proponents of political reform to criticize the traditional leadership style among old-
line Communist cadres and outworn practices in the CCP, such as
life-long tenure for cadres (q.v.).

"FIELD ARMY" (*YEZHAN JUN*). The field army system was established as a basic organizing unit of the Chinese military forces in 1948, just prior to the Communist takeover of China in 1949. Organizationally, a field army consisted of several armies, corps, divisions, and regiments. Designation of field armies was by location and included the Northwest (First) Field Army, the Central Plains (Fourth) Field Army, the Eastern China (Third) Field Army, the Northeast (Fifth) Field Army, the Southwest (Second) Field Army, and the Northern China (Fifth) Field Army, all of which composed the PLA (q.v.). These were later given numerical designations as the First, Second, Third, and Fourth Field Armies, respectively, while the Northern China Field Army was put under the direct command of the General Headquarters of the PLA. The transfer of personnel, including officers, between field armies was very rare and loyalty in the military was primarily to one's particular field army. Leaders who rose to high military or political positions generally promoted associates from their respective field armies. Thus during his political ascendancy in the 1960s, Lin Biao (q.v.) promoted officers from his Fourth Field Army. When Lin Biao disappeared from the political scene in 1971, Fourth Field Army military personnel also lost many positions of influence. In this sense, the Chinese military is still not a fully unified military organization. Military regions (q.v.) differ organizationally from the field army system.

FIFTH MODERNIZATION. In addition to the four modernizations (q.v.) advocated by CCP (q.v.) leaders, a fifth modernization, namely democracy, was also proposed in the late 1970s by the political dissident Wei Jingsheng (q.v.), and even by political reformers in the CCP. In January 1979, for instance, the *People's Daily* (q.v.), the official organ of the CCP Central Committee, stated that "the four modernizations must be accompanied by political democratization." In a similar vein, Yu Haocheng stated that "without democracy there can be no modernization." The most forceful statement, however, came from the Democracy Wall (q.v.) dissident Wei Jingsheng, who used this phrase as the title of a big-character poster (q.v.) in which he asserted that the CCP's program for four modernizations was viable only when accompanied by necessary political reforms toward democracy. This poster spurred a torrent of criticism toward the CCP and its leadership that ultimately led to Wei's arrest in 1979 and the shutting down of Democracy Wall in 1980.

"FIVE-ANTIS CAMPAIGN" (*WUFAN YUNDONG*). This campaign of mass mobilization was launched in 1952 soon after the Three Antis movement (q.v.). It targeted the owners of private property and industrial capital that the CCP (q.v.) had not yet abolished. Ostensibly, the campaign aimed at eliminating bribery, tax evasion, theft of state property, cheating on government contracts, and theft of state economic intelligence. In reality, the campaign's purpose was to increase the government's taxes on the private sector, which had actually flourished in the first two years of Communist rule, with growth rates of over 11 percent per annum. The government also claimed that private business had sold useless products to Chinese military forces during the Korean War (1950–1953) (q.v.). As in the Three Antis and Land Reform campaigns (q.v.), the masses were mobilized to denounce purported offenders. Specially trained CCP cadres also extorted confessions from businessmen who were forced to engage in "criticism and self-criticism" (q.v.). For some, the pressure was too great and many suicides were reported and bankruptcies also mushroomed. Thus in mid-1952 the campaign was softened as the majority of private businessmen were declared to be "basically law-abiding." However, the campaign significantly weakened the urban private sector so that by 1957 it could be completely socialized. Not until the 1980s would the CCP allow for the existence of private enterprise.

"FIVE BLACK CATEGORIES" (*HEIWULEI*). Originally "Four Black Categories," this phrase refers to anyone from a family of "landlords, rich peasants, counterrevolutionaries, and/or bad elements," plus anyone fired from his job or disciplined by his organization. In the first two years of the Cultural Revolution (1966–1976) (q.v.), members of these groups were frequent targets of Red Guard (q.v.) violence and persecution. It was once said that people from the "Five Black Categories" were so evil they were not allowed to donate their blood because it lacked revolutionary character. Over the course of the Cultural Revolution, the radical leadership led by Mao Zedong (q.v.) and the Cultural Revolution Small Group (q.v.) mobilized support among these dispossessed groups and directed their animosity toward the regular CCP organization, which was the target of Mao's ire. By emphasizing that "political performance," not "class origin," determines one's class status, people from the Five Black Categories joined the most radical Red Guard faction of revolutionary rebels (*zaofanpai*) (q.v.) in their political movement. Ultimately, the designation itself was abolished.

"FIVE GOOD WOMEN" (*WUHAO FUNÜ*). Social models for behavior by individuals and groups in China is a staple of CCP (q.v.) propaganda that aims to mold the social order. These emerged in the absence of a well-developed legal system and as surrogates for the moral vacuum left by direct assaults on Confucianism, Christianity, and other moral norms because of their antagonism to Marxism-Leninism-Mao Zedong Thought (q.v.). In the early 1950s, Chinese women were urged to adhere to the model of the "five good women." These were women who "made good arrangements for the livelihood of the family, kept good relations with neighbors, brought up children well, did well at encouraging the workers in production, work, and studies, and were good in studies [themselves]." Despite the "revolutionary" goals of the CCP, these standards were socially conservative and envisioned a role for women squarely within the family and generally subservient to men, "the workers in production. . . ." In 1957, the strictures were changed to emphasize women's role in performing "cleaning and hygienic work" at home. Women living in China's rural areas were given a different spin on the "five goods" by also being encouraged to "cherish the [agricultural] cooperative" and to "show respect for one's mother-in-law." As mother-in-law–daughter-in-law relations in China are generally quite tense, the Party's propaganda on this matter aimed at achieving a measure of social peace within the rural family.

"FIVE RED CATEGORIES" (*HONGWULEI*). This phrase refers to children of "poor and lower middle peasants, workers, revolutionary armymen, revolutionary martyrs, and revolutionary cadres." These are the five "good" class labels (q.v.) in China. During the Cultural Revolution (1966–1976) (q.v.), students from these five categories, and especially the latter three, used their privileged positions to come to the defense of the established Party apparatus that increasingly was the target of Mao Zedong's (q.v.) purges. In this sense, "five red category" offspring served as a conservative force during the Cultural Revolution, thus making them a primary target of the leftist Maoist forces, which mobilized "five black category" (q.v.) offspring against the establishment CCP (q.v.). Throughout the Cultural Revolution, students from these "good" families argued that "class origin" (*chusheng*) should determine one's "class status" (*chengfen*), which, in turn, defined one's political standing in the Cultural Revolution and in Mao's revolutionary ranks of Red Guards. In line with this "theory of class origin," it was said "If one's father is revolutionary, then his son is a hero; and if one's father is reactionary, his son is a rotten egg." Initially, membership in Red Guard groups was restricted to students with "good" class backgrounds while students from five black category backgrounds were singled out for persecution and even murdered on the basis of information the Red Guards gleaned from personal dossiers (q.v.). But as Mao Zedong emphasized the role of "performance" and "thought" over "class background," Red Guard groups, known as revolutionary rebels (q.v.), mushroomed from all social groups, including the five black categories. Among the children from "bad" family backgrounds, Mao Zedong discovered a potent political force to mobilize against CCP leaders whom he was intent on purging. As it turned out, however, factional struggles between competing Red Guard groups led to the most violent phases of the Cultural Revolution in 1967–1968, leading to Mao's decision to "send down" (q.v.) Red Guards to the countryside.

FIVE-YEAR PLANS. Like the Soviet Union, China organized its planned economy around a series of five-year plans that began in 1953 and continue into the 1990s. The underlying theory of the planned economy is that, contrary to the free market forces of capitalism, a socialist economy plans the production of goods, prices, and distribution. The "irrationality" of capitalism whereby the market dictates production, prices, and distribution is replaced by a "rational," planned approach that in both the former Soviet Union and China emphasized rapid heavy industrial production, low agricultural prices, and few consumer goods. Expenditures on education, cultural activities, and the military were also part of the five-year plan's budgetary outlays.

The First Five-Year Plan extended from 1953 to 1957. During that period, total industrial output was planned to increase by 98 percent, agriculture by 24 percent, and retail sales by 80 percent. These targets were reportedly "overfulfilled," though the reliability of the statistics can be questioned. The Second Five-Year Plan, which began in 1958, originally aimed for modest increases in economic growth over the First Five-Year Plan. This generated considerable controversy within top levels of the CCP (q.v.) as Mao Zedong (q.v.) opposed the excessively "conservative" targets. The result was considerable revision of the Second Five-Year Plan in mid-stream, especially during the Great Leap Forward (1958–1960) (q.v.). This plan in effect was not completed until 1965, although from 1961–65 China shifted to yearly planning in order to deal with the economic disruptions brought on by the Great Leap.

The Third Five-Year Plan did not begin until 1966 and it too was disrupted during the Cultural Revolution (1966–1976) (q.v.) and never really completed. Following the death of Mao Zedong in 1976, the implementation of the five-year plans was afforded greater regularity with fewer mid-course corrections and disruptions. And despite China's move to economic reform since 1978, the five-year plans are still employed, though the degree of state control over the economy, especially over agriculture and light industry, has been reduced. Still, the continued ownership of heavy industrial facilities by the state allows for a significant, though not comprehensive, role for the economic plan. *See also* AGRICULTURAL RESPONSIBILITY SYSTEM and ENTERPRISE REFORM.

"FLOATING POPULATION" (*LIUDONG RENKOU*). A product of the agricultural reforms inaugurated since 1978, China's floating population of laborers and itinerants is now estimated between 20 and 100 million people. Since 1958 the people's communes (q.v.) had effectively tied people to their workplace with no chance for mobility. As the rural population expanded and agriculture was subjected to growing efficiencies and mechanization, significant surplus labor emerged in the countryside. After 1984, when the State Council gave them permission to leave the land, these surplus laborers moved into cities and towns and became the primary labor force in local industries. These transient workers have become vital to a variety of industries, especially construction, but have also placed enormous strains on China's still underdeveloped urban infrastructure. Because these laborers were assigned the household registration (*hukou*) (q.v.) of their rural parentage (inherited through the mother and which is extremely difficult to alter), they do not have access to the various amenities of urban *hukou*, such as education, free medical coverage, housing, and the right to be permanently employed in state-run industries with their "Iron Rice Bowl" (q.v.). Numbering more than 1 million in large cities such as Beijing (q.v.) and Shanghai (q.v.), transient workers have become something of a disruptive force as their movements have placed enormous pressure on China's antiquated transportation system while their ramshackle dwellings have become serious eyesores. Yet they are also a generally compliant and low-wage labor, valued by upstart industries and new entrepreneurs. The overwhelming percentage of the floating population is male and quite young; and many remit their earnings to family members still residing in rural villages. Only 5 percent or so of the floating population are vagrants, criminals, and prostitutes; yet it is feared by Chinese government authorities that the floating population could become a politically destabilizing force, as apparently occurred during the 1989 Tiananmen protests in Beijing. Fears that a vast army of floating laborers will descend on the area in and around the Three Gorges Dam project (q.v.) have prompted Chinese authorities to strengthen public security controls in the construction zone. *See also* THREE GORGES DAM PROJECT.

FOUR BIG FREEDOMS. Also known as the "four bigs" (*sida*), these "freedoms" refer to the writing of big-character posters (q.v.), holding great debates, airing one's views, and "contending in a big way." These "freedoms" were first mentioned in the late 1950s and were extensively employed during the Cultural Revolution (1966–1976) (q.v.) by Red Guards (q.v.) in their assaults on the CCP (q.v.) apparatus. In 1966, the "four big freedoms" allowed for open debate and enabled the general population to "clarify correct views, criticize wrong views, and expose all ghosts and monsters" (i.e., opponents of CCP Chairman Mao Zedong [q.v.]). In 1975, near the end of the Cultural Revolution, the "four bigs" were incorporated into the state constitution of China. According to the *People's Daily* (January 20, 1975), this was to allow for "new forms of carrying on socialist revolution created by the masses of the people . . . and [to] ensure the masses the right to use these forms." During the 1978–1979 Democracy Wall movement (q.v.), big-character posters and the open airing of views were extensively used by social reform forces in support of Deng Xiaoping's (q.v.) return to power and of political and economic reforms. But once Deng Xiaoping was securely installed in power, Democracy Wall was closed down and the "four big freedoms" were eliminated from the state constitution in 1982 and derided by Deng Xiaoping as a vestige of the Cultural Revolution and a threat to political "stability."

"FOUR CARDINAL PRINCIPLES" (*SIXIANG JIBEN YUANZE*). These "principles" of the CCP (q.v.) are aimed at rigidly defining the limits of dissent and protest in Chinese society in the post-Mao era. They were enunciated by Deng Xiaoping (q.v.) in March 1979 at a forum on the principles for the Party's theoretical work that followed the CCP's suppression of the Democracy Wall movement (q.v.) that had begun in 1978. They call on all Chinese to "uphold the socialist road; uphold the dictatorship of the proletariat; uphold the leadership of the CCP; and uphold Marxism-Leninism and Mao Zedong Thought." Overall, they provide hard-line, orthodox leaders in the Communist Party with an ideological carte blanche to persecute any individual, including Party members, who advocates significant political reform and human rights.

Since 1979, China's leaders have periodically invoked the Four Cardinal Principles to justify political repression and cultural conservatism. Although always cited in the press and cultural circles as official ideology even during times of great relaxation and openness, the government's reliance on these "principles" has been especially pronounced during periods of retreat from political reform. This was true during the "Anti-Spiritual Pollution Campaign" (q.v.) in 1983 and the subsequent attack on "bourgeois liberalization" following the dismissal of Hu Yaobang (q.v.) as CCP general secretary in 1987. The four "principles" were also a central feature of the Communist orthodoxy after the military crackdown against the prodemocracy movement in June 1989.

From the orthodox Chinese Communist point of view, "upholding socialism and the CCP's dictatorship" are essential to combat the penetration of Western pro-capitalist and democratic ideas into China. Similar to nineteenth-century Chinese conservatives who attempted to "use" Western technology (*yong*) while maintaining the essence, or "body" of traditional Chinese culture (*ti*), since 1978 Deng Xiaoping introduced modern economic principles and technology while trying to avoid the inevitable cultural and political influences of the outside world. The contradictions intensified when the Communist Party exhorted its members to "liberate their thought" (*jiefang sixiang*) from the "evil" leftist influences of the radical Gang of Four (q.v.). Contrary to the intention of orthodox leaders, such pronouncements seemingly encouraged learning from the democratic capitalist world, which is why Deng Xiaoping had a difficult time differentiating "bourgeois liberalization" from "liberation of thought."

Official CCP documents thus warn CCP members against being influenced by "the wave of capitalist ideas on freedom" and "capitalist standards of morality and literature and art." One document complained that "in the Party there are certain comrades who not only do not recognize the dangers of this wave, but even go so far as to encourage more of it." Such warnings were undoubtedly aimed at supporters of Hu Yaobang and the relatively liberal Party members at universities and research institutes, such as the Chinese Academy of Social Sciences (q.v.), where support for dramatic political change in the direction of democratic liberalism was strong. Even before the spring 1989 demonstrations, Chinese Communist leaders expressed alarm over the active role some Party members were taking in street demonstrations and other popular protests. Once Party members applied their considerable organizational skills to mobilizing the population for political change, it was obvious that the old guard's grip on power would be seriously threatened. *See also* the SOCIALIST EDUCATION MOVEMENT.

FOUR MODERNIZATIONS. The modernization of agriculture, industry, defense, and science and technology by the year 2000 have constituted the goal of CCP (q.v.) leaders since the Fourth NPC (q.v.) in January 1975 when the phrase was first put forth by Zhou Enlai (q.v.). It was not until the watershed Third Party Plenum (q.v.) in December 1978, however, that the leadership united fully behind these goals and introduced the economic reform policies, the open-door policy (q.v.), and changes in the educational system to make such a radical transformation of Chinese society and economy possible. A central element of the pursuit of the Four Modernizations has been a substantial turnover of CCP cadres (q.v.) from those skilled in politics and ideological struggle to a more professionally trained corps. This has been achieved through an elaborate process of cadre retirement throughout the 1980s and the recruitment of college-educated personnel into CCP ranks. Although slow in the beginning, by 1985 the CCP had carried out a substantial alteration of its ranks, creating a "third echelon" of younger leaders with training and professionalization necessary to achieve the Four Modernizations. On the national level, the average age of ministers and vice ministers dropped in 1985 from 65 to 59 years of age, while the number of ordinary cadres in the central state ministries with a college education grew from 38 percent to 50 percent. Similar changes were also effected at the provincial and local levels of the CCP in pursuit of modernization.

"FOUR OLDS" (*SIJIU*). This refers to old ideas, old culture, old customs, and old habits in China that were a target of the Red Guards (q.v.) during the Cultural Revolution (1966–1976) (q.v.). The so-called exploiting classes in China had, it was said, imposed cultural attitudes and customs on the consciousness of the common people that the radical leadership was seeking to eradicate. In the late 1960s, Red Guards attacked all aspects of the traditional cultural realm by destroying books by classical philosophers, such as Confucius and Mencius, trashing temples, and defacing artwork at traditional Buddhist and Taoist religious sites. Particularly hard hit were religious sites in minority areas, such as in Tibet (q.v.), where more than ten thousand temples were destroyed and many monks killed. Major historical sites in Beijing (q.v.), however, were largely spared as Zhou Enlai (q.v.) ordered the PLA (q.v.) to protect the ancient Forbidden City in the capital.

FRONT FOR A DEMOCRATIC CHINA. Following the military crackdown in June 1989 of the pro-democracy movement, exiled Chinese students and democratic leaders met in France and established the Front (or Federation) for a Democratic China. This marked the end of the belief by older intellectuals that the Communist Party (q.v.) could be reformed from within. Political change in China, it was now believed, could only be effected by the establishment of an organization independent of the Party. The establishment of the Front also marked the first time that older dissident intellectuals, such as Liu Binyan (q.v.), Su Shaozhi (q.v.), and Yan Jiaqi (q.v.), cooperated with younger students, such as Wu'er Kaixi (q.v.) and Shen Tong, whose actions until then had been relatively independent. The immediate goal of the Front is to establish a multiparty system in China, even though its founders have explicitly denied it is a political party. Violence has been abjured as a means of effecting political change; it sees economic growth and the emergence of a middle class as the path to democratization. Annual meetings of the Front have been held in Paris and it has consistently called for a dialogue with the Chinese government to resolve China's political problems. In 1995, the chairman of the Front was Wan Runnan (q.v.).

G

"GANG OF FOUR" (*SIREN BANG*). This group consisted of the major radical political leaders during the Cultural Revolution (1966–1976) (q.v.). They were Jiang Qing (q.v.) (the wife of CCP [q.v.] Chairman Mao Zedong [q.v.]), Zhang Chunqiao (q.v.), the Shanghai (q.v.) political leader, Wang Hongwen (q.v.), an industrial worker promoted to political prominence by Mao Zedong, and Yao Wenyuan (q.v.), a polemical literary critic and confidante of Madame Mao. They themselves never used the term "Gang of Four" during the Cultural Revolution, but it became popular after their arrest in October 1976 following the death of Mao. The appellation was reportedly first used by Mao when he warned his wife, Jiang Qing, not to form a "Gang of Four." After their arrest, the "Gang" was accused of usurping the leadership of the CCP and attempting to "seize power" through unlawful factional activities. Despite their promotion of radical politics, opponents of the "Gang of Four" claimed that they represented the "bourgeoisie" inside the CCP. A nationwide campaign to criticize the "Gang of Four" and their network of supporters began in 1977 and continued into the early 1980s. All four members of the so-called gang were tried in 1980 for "crimes" involving the innumerable deaths during the Cultural Revolution. Jiang Qing and Zhang Chunqiao were both sentenced to death (with a two-year reprieve) and Yao Wenyuan and Wang Hongwen were given lighter sentences because of their contrition. Political dissidents in China claim that by blaming the Cultural Revolution on the Gang and the now deceased Mao Zedong, CCP leaders have avoided confronting the systemic flaws in China's autocratic political system.

GAO DI (1927–). Beginning in the 1950s as a county Party secretary in Jilin province, by 1983 Gao Di had risen to Party secretary of the Jilin Provincial Party Committee. In 1985, he became a member of the CCP (q.v.) Central Committee and in 1988 he was appointed vice president of the Central Party School (q.v.) and visited North Korea.

In 1989 following the Beijing massacre, he became director of the *People's Daily* (q.v.) but was later replaced.

GAO GANG–RAO SHUSHI INCIDENT. This incident involved the first major factional struggle and purge in the post-1949 CCP (q.v.) leadership. As the major Party figure in northeast China, in 1953 Gao Gang proposed that the chairmanship of the CCP be rotated among the top leaders rather than held solely by Mao Zedong (q.v.). Rebuffed by Mao, Gao began to engage in clandestine appeals to potential supporters, including Zhu De (q.v.) and Peng Dehuai (q.v.), but to no avail. Despite the fact that Mao Zedong and Gao Gang were in agreement on many policies for China, and that Gao was one of the few upfront supporters of the chairman on the Korean War (q.v.) decision, Mao decided to move against Gao, ousting him from his leadership position in 1955. Gao subsequently committed suicide. Rao Shushi, a senior Party leader in Shanghai, was implicated in the affair, though very little evidence was ever publicized indicating that Rao Shushi had actively joined Gao Gang's "conspiracy." In all likelihood, the purge of Rao Shushi reflected fundamental differences among top CCP leaders over economic and financial issues that had emerged in the early 1950s. Following the purge of Gao and Rao, extensive criticism was launched against Party leaders who violated principles of "collective leadership" (*jiti lingdao*) and who prevented the normal operation of Party committees. Although aimed at Gao and Rao, some Western observers have suggested that these criticisms were directed at Mao for fostering his personality cult (q.v.) that would come to the fore over the next decade.

GENERAL LINE FOR THE TRANSITION PERIOD. This refers to the set of policies adopted by the CCP (q.v.) in the period from 1949 to the completion of the socialist transformation of the economy in the 1950s. In 1949, China's situation was similar to that of Russia in 1917 in that capitalism was underdeveloped; thus the transition to socialism would take much longer than Karl Marx had originally envisioned. This required a relatively long "transition period" that would entail the takeover of industry, agriculture, and commerce by the state (i.e., the so-called socialization of the means of production). In urban areas, according to official CCP decisions, this was to occur in a step-by-step manner and without coercion as China's captains of industry and commerce would, during the first stage of socialization, be "encouraged . . . to move toward the direction of state capitalism," that is, capitalism with considerable state intervention, but still capitalism, not socialism (i.e., outright state ownership). Industry and commerce would then, during the second stage, be transformed into a socialism of state-run and cooperative commerce. In rural areas, the "transition" would occur in three stages, as agriculture would move from Mutual Aid Teams (q.v.) to "semi-socialist" APCs (q.v.), and finally to state farms where the state would be the legal owner of the land. The moderate pace of "socialization" proposed under this policy rubric of the "transition" was generally abandoned in the mid-1950s as Chairman Mao Zedong (q.v.) pushed for rapid "socialization" of industrial and commercial property and an equally rapid pace of agricultural cooperativization that was then quickly followed in 1958 by the ill-fated people's communes (q.v.).

GENERAL SECRETARY. *See* CHINESE COMMUNIST PARTY.

GENG BIAO (1909–   ). A Long March (q.v.) veteran, in 1960 Geng Biao became a vice minister of foreign affairs and in 1969 was elected to the Central Committee at the Ninth Party Congress. In 1971 he became the director of the International Liaison Department of the CCP (q.v.) and in 1977 he was appointed to the Politburo (q.v.). In 1978 he became a vice premier and in 1981 minister of national defense. In 1982 he nominally "retired" by joining the Standing Committee of the Central Advisory Commission (q.v.).

"GOING THROUGH THE BACK DOOR" (*ZOU HOUMEN*). This means to seek certain personal gains or objectives by making use of "connections" (*guanxi*) with people in responsible positions. These "connections" are usually personal and are frequently used to get favorable treatment in the allocation of rationed goods and commodities to obtain an urban household registration (*hukou*) (q.v.), or to gain entry into prestigious schools and universities. "Going through the back door" is perhaps the most blatant form of corruption (q.v.) in China, though the growth of the market economy since 1978 has perhaps reduced its importance since "connections" have been replaced by "money" as the new grease of corruption. *See also* CORRUPTION.

GOVERNMENT STRUCTURE. The government or state structure of China is highly complex and since 1949 has undergone significant institutional revisions that have reflected CCP (q.v.) policies and changes. The state structure parallels and significantly overlaps with the organizational structure of the CCP, which retains ultimate authority in the Chinese political system. Under the principle of interlocking institutions, Party leaders serve in various state positions of authority at the central level and below. The highest organ of state power is the National People's Congress (NPC) (q.v.), a "legislative" body with a five-year term that authorizes all state laws and produces the state constitution (q.v.). The NPC elects as its executive body the NPC Standing Committee, headed by a chairman and several vice chairmen, which oversees the state Central Military Commission and the Legislative Affairs Commission. The NPC also elects a State Council composed of the premier (in 1996, Li Peng), vice premiers, state councillors, a secretary-general, and the various ministers. Below the NPC is a subordinate structure of people's congresses at the provincial level and below that theoretically are elected, the Supreme People's Court, and the Procuracy (q.v.). The State Council administers the economy and society through an elaborate structure of thirty ministries, ten commissions, thirteen bureaus and administrative organs, and several institutions and working organs of the State Council. Major ministries include: agriculture, coal, communications, culture, electronics industry, finance, foreign trade and economic cooperation, labor, machine-building industry, power industry, public security, railways, state security, and water resources. Several of these ministries, such as the Ministry of Railways, are organized and run along highly centralized and militarized lines. Among the most important commissions are: Science, Technology, and Industry for National Defense, State Education, State Family Planning, State Planning, State Restructuring of the Economic System, and People's Bank of China. Bureaus and administrative bureaus include: Administration for Industry and Commerce, Environmental Protection Bureau, and State Statistical Bureau. Other institutions and organs under the State Council are the Academy of Sciences and the Academy of Social Sciences, Xinhua News Agency, the Hong Kong and Macao Affairs Office, and the Special Economic Zones Office. Many of these organizations have subordinate offices at the provincial level and below. *See also* PRESIDENT OF THE PRC.

GREAT LEAP FORWARD (1958–1960). A radical attempt to overcome China's economic backwardness and achieve the stage of "communism" in one fell swoop through mass mobilization, the Great Leap Forward (*dayuejin*) was a bold plan concocted largely by Mao Zedong (q.v.) at the August 1958 Beidaihe Conference (q.v.) that ultimately produced a major economic and demographic disaster. The basic strategy of the leap was to rely on the creative enthusiasm of the masses and the country's nearly unlimited manpower to substitute for the severe lack of capital goods in bringing about dramatic increases in both agricultural and industrial production and thereby to free China from excessive dependence on the Soviet Union. The unemployed were to be put to work and the already employed were driven to work harder, all under military discipline, so that China could break out of the limitations of its economic backwardness. Both the modern sector of the economy—steel plants and other industries built over the past years by the KMT (q.v.), the Japanese, and the Communists—would join with the traditional sector of the economy composed of labor-intensive, small-scale production to make a gigantic leap in production. Referred to as "walking on two legs," this policy in the industrial sector was to lead to dramatic increases in steel production by conventional factories and to the "backyard steel furnaces" (q.v.) developed by the Chinese during the leap. In agriculture, the major mechanism for increasing production was organizational—that is, the elevation of the basic production and accounting unit in the countryside to the people's communes (q.v.). By 1959, 26,000 had been established, with an average of 2,000 households (approximately 10,000 peasants). In addition to radically altering the allocation of labor for agricultural production, the communes served as local government and Party organs that took over virtually all administrative functions in the countryside. As a labor-saving device some communes also set up canteens for collective eating and encouraged peasants to contribute their pots, pans, and other iron materials to the backyard steel furnace campaign.

The Great Leap Forward ultimately failed for a variety of reasons. Excessive demands on urban and rural laborers by Party cadres (q.v.) produced an exhausted labor force that was unable to keep up with the pace of work demanded by the production goals established by the CCP (q.v.) leadership. In addition, Maoist experiments in the countryside—the backyard steel furnaces, the close planting of rice, and deep plowing, which were designed to increase production dramatically—spawned massive reductions in food output that ultimately led to a rural famine that cost upward of 30 million deaths. These manmade disasters were exacerbated in 1959 by serious flooding and drought. Economically, the Three Bad Years (1960–1962) followed the Great Leap Forward, while politically it produced deep divisions in the CCP leadership that ultimately led to the Cultural Revolution (1966–1976) (q.v.). *See also* LUSHAN PLENUM and BEIDAIHE CONFERENCE.

GU MU (1914–   ). A member of the League of Left-Wing Writers in Beijing (q.v.) in the 1930s, Gu Mu was a vice minister of the State Economic Commission in the 1950s and in 1965 headed the State Capital Construction Commission. After disappearing during the Cultural Revolution (1966–1976) (q.v.), he was elected to the Central Committee in 1973, resumed his post at the Capital Construction Commission, and from 1982 to 1988 was a state councillor. In 1986 he headed the Leading Group in Charge of Foreign Investment and in 1988 he joined the CPPCC.

GUO MORUO (1892–1978). Trained in classical Chinese language and educated in Japan at Kyushu University, Guo Moruo emerged as one of China's leading Communist intellectuals (q.v.). Appointed a vice premier in 1949, Guo headed the Federation of Literary and Art Circles from 1949 to 1966 and was a member of the All-China Writers' Association from 1953 to 1966. In the late 1950s, Guo also served on the State Planning Commission. Author of many books on China's ancient history, he was a member of the CCP (q.v.) Central Committee from 1969 until his death in 1978.

H

"HAI RUI DISMISSED FROM OFFICE" (*HAI RUI BAGUAN*). A play written by Beijing vice mayor Wu Han (q.v.), it describes the role of a sixteenth-century Ming dynasty (1368–1644) official who remonstrated with the emperor for his harsh treatment and overtaxation of the peasantry. Hai Rui was described as a "good and upright" official who was "consistent in words" and "was respected and loved by the broad masses of people." For having "upbraided" the emperor, Hai Rui was summarily dismissed. Written soon after the disastrous 1958–1960 Great Leap Forward (q.v.) and the purge of Peng Dehuai (q.v.) who had criticized the leap for its devastating impact on China's peasantry, the play was attacked, beginning in 1965 by leftist leaders aligned with Jiang Qing (q.v.), the wife of CCP Chairman Mao Zedong (q.v.), as the opening shot in the Cultural Revolution (q.v.). *Hai Rui Dismissed from Office*, it was said, was an elliptical attack on Chairman Mao and his policies, and therefore counterrevolutionary. Wu Han was purged and along with him the entire Beijing Party Committee led by Peng Zhen (q.v.). Wu Han denied the charge and indeed intellectuals in China have maintained that the play was never interpreted as an elliptical attack on Mao.

HAN. This is the dominant ethnic group in China incorporating about 92 percent of the entire population. The Chinese people refer to themselves as Han (*Han minzu*) after the name of the highly esteemed Han dynasty (202 B.C.–A.D. 222) that followed the chaos of the Qin dynasty (221–207 B.C.) and created a stable, aristocratic social order that spread Chinese influence far and wide. Han people first distinguished themselves from the "barbarians" of Inner Asia. The Han were often weaker militarily than their "barbarian" neighbors and thus sought refuge in superior social institutions and feelings of cultural superiority. Those who most vigorously opposed assimilation by the Chinese (Han) migrated away and stubbornly developed their own autonomous civilizations, such as the Vietnamese. National minorities (q.v.) within China, such as the Zhuang, have been highly Sinicized, but still distinguish themselves from the Han. *See also* MINORITIES.

HAN DONGFANG (1963–). A railway worker in the Fengtai Locomotive Maintenance Section in Beijing (q.v.), Han Dongfang emerged as a prominent human rights and working-class activist in the wake of the 1989 pro-democracy movement. Along with other workers, Han Dongfang organized the Beijing Workers Autonomous Federation on the eve of the declaration of martial law in China's capital city. This was one of the few independent labor organizations established in China since the Communist takeover in 1949. Turning himself in to the police soon after the June 4, 1989, crackdown in Beijing, Han Dongfang was labeled a "counterrevolutionary" and in 1990 was incarcerated in a police hospital with a stomach ailment. He was subsequently released for medical reasons and was treated in the United States. Unable to return to China proper on orders of the central government he now resides in Hong Kong.

Han Dongfang's early life provides few clues to his later rebellion. His given name, Dongfang, translates as the "east," and is from the first line of China's martial tune, *The East is Red*, indicating his parents' initial devotion to the Communist cause. In the 1980s, Han was trained in the Public Security Soldiers Corps (*gong'an bing*) and was a guard at a prison labor camp near Beijing where he received positive evaluations until he challenged the corruption (q.v.) among the officer corps at the camp. This rebellious act cost Han his membership in the CCP (q.v.). Thereafter, Han became an assistant librarian at Beijing Teacher's College where he read Western and Chinese works voraciously. Han then joined the maintenance team at the Beijing railway yard, where he gradually evolved into a political and labor activist, protesting the compliant submission of the official trade unions (q.v.) to CCP (q.v.) dictates.

HAN XU (1924–1994). China's ambassador to the United States from 1985–1989, Han Xu was a central figure in the development of Sino-American relations from the 1970s onward. Han Xu was born in Beijing (q.v.) to an elite family and attended Yenching University in the 1940s. Despite the fact that his father was a judge in the Nationalist government, Han joined the Communist guerrillas and during World War II assisted downed American flyers in China. After 1949, he rose through the ranks of the Foreign Ministry where he worked very closely with Zhou Enlai (q.v.) and became head of the all-important protocol office in the ministry. Fluent in English, Han Xu was the first person to greet U.S. National Security Adviser Henry Kissinger during his first visit to China in 1971. From 1973 to 1979 Han served in the PRC Liaison Office in Washington. He became a vice foreign minister in the early 1980s. Han Xu also served on the CPPCC (q.v.) and was president of the Chinese People's Association for Friendship with Foreign Countries.

HAN ZHIXIONG. A young worker, in 1976 Han was arrested and imprisoned after giving a speech denouncing the Gang of Four (q.v.) during the April Fifth Qing Ming festival demonstrations on Tiananmen Square (q.v.). After the smashing of the Gang, Han was released and wrote an article memorializing the April Fifth Movement in the newly restored journal *China Youth*. This article provoked the rage of security chief Wang Dongxing (q.v.). Hu Yaobang met with Han soon thereafter and recommended him for membership on the Central Committee of the Communist Youth League (q.v.).

HE DONGCHANG (1923–). Trained as an aeronautical engineer, in the 1950s He Dongchang was the Party secretary of Qinghua University (q.v.) and director of the Department of Engineering Physics. Branded a "counterrevolutionary" in the Cultural Revolution (1966–1976) (q.v.), he returned to public life in 1978 and was appointed to the Central Discipline Inspection Commission (q.v.) and became a vice president of Qinghua University. In 1982 he was appointed minister of education and became a member of the CCP (q.v.) Central Committee. In 1986 he headed the State Education Commission and in 1987 was appointed to the presidium of the CCP Thirteenth Party Congress. In 1988 he became a member of the National Academic Degrees Committee. He is a frequent critic of excessive "westernization" in Chinese education (q.v.).

HE JINGZHI (1924–). A leftist writer, in 1945 He Jingzhi wrote the libretto for the revolutionary ballet-opera *The White-Haired Girl* (*Baimao nü*) for which he received the Stalin Literary and Art Award in 1951. In the early 1980s, He Jingzhi was a vice minister of culture and a vice chairman of the All-China Writers' Association. He was appointed acting minister of culture following the 1989 Beijing massacre, but was later replaced.

HE XIN (1949–). A college dropout, He Xin joined the Chinese Academy of Social Sciences (q.v.) and in 1982 became a research fellow at its Institute of Modern Chinese History. A constant critic of the excessive attraction to "westernization" among many Chinese intellectuals (q.v.), he has emerged as the intellectual darling of China's conservative leadership, especially since June 1989. He Xin is also a specialist in Chinese fine arts and has written several books on Chinese cultural history and western philosophers, such as Sir Francis Bacon.

HEALTH CARE. *See* BAREFOOT DOCTORS.

HONG KONG. *See* BASIC LAW FOR HONG KONG.

HU FENG AFFAIR. This refers to the attacks on the Marxist literary critic Hu Feng by the CCP (q.v.) in the mid-1950s. Hu Feng was a longtime supporter of the Communist movement in China who soon after 1949 challenged CCP and Maoist orthodoxy on the role of literature in a revolutionary society. A leader in many of the CCP's mass organizations established for writers and artists, Hu Feng argued that the Party should show greater tolerance for the independent views expressed in literature. In so doing, Hu Feng challenged the Maoist principle laid out in the 1942 Yan'an Talks on Literature and Art in which Mao Zedong (q.v.) asserted that literature and art should serve the interests of politics. "Art for art's sake" was denounced by Mao in favor of the socialist realist principle that writers and artists should portray the lives of workers and peasants in idealistic, utopian terms. Denouncing Hu Feng as anti-Marxist and anti-Party, the CCP launched a massive nationwide campaign that encompassed thousands of literary figures and led to systematic persecution of intellectuals (q.v.) in a fashion that anticipated the 1957 Anti-Rightist campaign (q.v.) and the 1966–1976 Cultural Revolution (q.v.). Hu Feng was arrested and incarcerated for many years. He died in 1985 in an insane asylum.

HU JIWEI (1916–   ). One of China's most prominent journalists, in 1954 Hu Jiwei became deputy editor and then in 1958 deputy editor in chief of the *People's Daily* (q.v.), the official organ of the CCP (q.v.) Central Committee. Hu disappeared during the Cultural Revolution (1966–1976) (q.v.), but returned as director of the *People's Daily* in 1982 as a staunch advocate of press reform and liberalization. Hu voluntarily resigned from his position in protest over the Anti-Spiritual Pollution campaign (q.v.). Hu was a strong supporter of the reformist political ideas of CCP General Secretary, Hu Yaobang (q.v.), whose sudden death in April 1989 set off the student demonstrations that culminated in the June 1989 Beijing massacre. In

1989, Hu Jiwei was criticized for soliciting signatures of NPC (q.v.) delegates to call for the convening of a special meeting to rescind the declaration of martial law and to dismiss Li Peng (q.v.) as state premier.

HU QIAOMU (1912–1992). From a politically prominent family of wealthy landowners, Hu Qiaomu joined the CCP (q.v.) in 1935, working with Jiang Nanxiang (q.v.) in the fields of journalism and propaganda in Shanghai (q.v.) and Shaanxi province. In 1945 Hu succeeded Chen Boda (q.v.) as personal secretary to Mao Zedong (q.v.) and also headed the New China News Agency. Hu became a member of the Central Committee in 1956 and deputy director of the Propaganda Department. Publicly criticized by Red Guards (q.v.) during the Cultural Revolution (1966–1976) (q.v.), Hu Qiaomu reappeared in 1974 as a member of the Party Secretariat and the CCP Central Committee. In 1982 he became honorary president of the Academy of Social Sciences (q.v.). He played a prominent role in the discussions of humanism and alienation in socialist society in the early 1980s. He nominally retired from his positions in November 1987 and served as honorary head of the Shakespeare Research Society until his death in 1992. Hu Qiaomu's son was arrested on corruption (q.v.) charges, but was later released after the purge of Hu Yaobang (q.v.) in 1987. *See also* CHINESE ACADEMY OF SOCIAL SCIENCES.

HU QILI (1929–). Trained as a mechanical engineer and a longtime active Communist Youth League (q.v.) member, Hu Qili was branded as a follower of Liu Shaoqi (q.v.) during the Cultural Revolution (1966–1976) (q.v.) and subsequently purged. He returned in the mid-1970s as a county Party secretary in Ningxia province and then as a vice president of Qinghua University (q.v.). In the early 1980s he became director of the General Office of the CCP (q.v.) and accompanied Hu Yaobang (q.v.) to Australia. In 1985 he became a member of the Politburo (q.v.) and was put in charge of the Propaganda and Ideological Work Leading Group under the CCP Central Committee. In June 1989 Hu was removed from the Politburo and his other posts for having allowed journalists free rein during the student demonstrations, but he reemerged in April 1990 at a meeting of the NPC (q.v.) and in 1991 became a vice minister.

HU SHI [HU SHIH] (1891–1962). One of China's most prominent liberal intellectuals (q.v.), Hu Shi was a disciple of John Dewey and a major promoter of vernacular Chinese literature in the 1920s. He attended Cornell and Columbia universities, studying at the latter under

Dewey and writing his doctoral dissertation on pragmatic tendencies in ancient Chinese thought. Hu Shi was an enthusiastic advocate of experimentalism and a sometime critic of the Nationalist government. Hu was Nationalist China's ambassador to the United States from 1938 to 1942 and later became president of the Academia Sinica in Taiwan (q.v.). He died in Taiwan in 1962.

HU YAOBANG (1915–1989). Born in Hunan province, Hu Yaobang became a Red Army soldier at the age of fifteen and in 1933 engaged in youth work for the central Party leadership in the Jiangxi Soviet. During the Civil War (1946–1949) (q.v.), he served in the Political Department of the Second Field Army and later in the Southwest China Military and Administrative Council, both of which were dominated by Deng Xiaoping (q.v.). From 1957 to 1964, he headed the then recently reorganized Communist Youth League (q.v.); he was later attacked during the Cultural Revolution (1966–1976) (q.v.). Hu Yaobang reappeared in 1972 and in 1977 became a member of the CCP Central Committee and the director of its Organization Department. In 1978 he joined the Politburo (q.v.) and headed the CCP Propaganda Department and then in 1980 became general secretary of the Secretariat. He was appointed the third and last chairman of the CCP until this position was eliminated in 1982. Hu remained general secretary until his dismissal in early 1987. Hu Yaobang's death in April 1989 sparked the student pro-democracy movement that culminated in the June 4, 1989, Beijing massacre.

HUA GUOFENG (1921–). From an extremely poor peasant family, Hua Guofeng joined the Communist Red Army at the age of fifteen and in 1949 became a county Party secretary in Hunan province. After overseeing the rapid formation of APCs (q.v.) in his county, Hua was appointed, on Mao Zedong's personal recommendation, as Hunan Party secretary and during the Cultural Revolution (1966–1976) (q.v.) headed the province's Revolutionary Committee (q.v.). After supporting construction of a mausoleum in Hunan for Mao Zedong's first wife, Yang Kaihui, Hua was transferred to Beijing and headed a special group to investigate the Lin Biao affair (q.v.). Appointed to the Politburo (q.v.) in 1973 and minister of public security in 1975, Hua became premier in 1976 and was personally designated by Mao to succeed him as Party chairman, a post Hua assumed in October 1976. Hua was replaced in September 1982 at the Twelfth Party Congress but retained his position on the CCP (q.v.) Central Committee. Hua's inscription still adorns the Mao Zedong Memorial Hall (*Mao Zedong jinian tang*) in Tiananmen Square. Two workers reportedly died from toxic fumes while affixing the inscription in gold.

HUKOU. The household registration system in China was adopted in the 1950s and provides a system of control over population movement and residence by restricting the rural population to villages and townships in the countryside where they are dependent on their own labor for their livelihood. Non-agricultural or urban registration is the most prized since it carries various amenities, such as access to education, free medical coverage, grain rations, and housing. Transfer of rural to urban registry was for most Chinese virtually impossible. Since the inauguration of the economic reforms in 1978 and the growth of the floating population (q.v.), the *hukou* system has gradually broken down as large numbers of rural migrants have settled in Chinese cities without a transfer of registry and urban residents have relied more and more on the market for grain supplies and adequate health care.

HUMAN RIGHTS. The Tiananmen crackdown in June 1989 brought human-rights issues involving the PRC (q.v.) to the forefront in its international diplomacy. Prior to 1989, the PRC was not a major focus of international human rights violations as most worldwide attention was devoted to the Soviet Union and nations such as South Africa and Iran. Since 1989, however, issues involving the applicability to the PRC of "universal" standards of human rights has been a subject of both Chinese and foreign, primarily American, commentary. PRC policies in Tibet (q.v.) are also central to the human rights issue.

As a member of the United Nations (q.v.), the PRC professes "respect" for the *Universal Declaration of Human Rights*, a document that is not legally binding on its signatories but sets out a minimum standard of human rights protection. Of the three human rights treaties that carry real teeth in their implementation—the *International Covenant on Civil and Political Rights*, the *International Covenant on Economic, Social, and Cultural Rights*, and the *Convention Against Torture and Other Cruel, Inhuman, or Degrading Treatment or Punishment*—the PRC has signed only the last, which it assisted in drafting. The other two were drafted before the PRC joined the United Nations in 1971. In 1989 the PRC was criticized for its report to the UN Committee Against Torture for failing to provide sufficient details on practical measures taken by the government to stop torture, compensate victims, and punish perpetrators.

Although the PRC has yet to sign either International Covenant, it has taken part in international meetings, like the UN World Conference on Human Rights held in Vienna in June 1993, where the PRC endorsed the UN's commitment to human rights, but also expressed opposition to those countries that "impose their values" on others. The PRC signed the final Vienna document that paid lip service to the "universality" of human rights, but left the implementation to individual countries and also reaffirmed the right to development and other collective rights. In March 1994, a draft resolution criticizing the PRC before the UN's Commission on Human Rights, consisting of fifty-three UN member states, was tabled. In this resolution that was narrowly defeated the PRC was criticized for its treatment of dissidents, reports of torture, arbitrary arrests, unfair trials, and the situation in Tibet.

In 1991, the PRC responded to its critics by publishing a "white paper" titled *The Human Rights Situation in China*. This document argued for collective rights, particularly the "right to subsistence" for the Chinese people and various cultural and labor rights. The paper also contained a riposte to critics of China's practice of prison labor and its policies toward Tibet. *See also* TIBET and UNITED NATIONS.

HUNDRED FLOWERS. The term generally used to describe the CCP's (q.v.) off-and-on policy of allowing greater intellectual freedom and expression. Hundred Flowers is taken from the ancient Zhou dynasty slogan of "let a hundred flowers bloom, let a hundred schools of thought contend" and is also referred to as "double hundred." The CCP was most emphatic in tolerating liberal opinion in 1956–1957, the period most closely associated with the term. This policy switch grew out of a concern by top leaders that the Party's policy toward intellectuals (q.v.) had been highly flawed, especially its treatment of writers and scientists.

In January 1956 Zhou Enlai (q.v.) called for "bringing the existing powers of the intelligentsia into play" and in May 1956 Mao Zedong (q.v.) joined other leaders, such as Lu Dingyi (q.v.), in endorsing "freedom of independent thinking" and "freedom to criticize." Although intellectuals were initially reluctant to voice criticisms, Mao's February 1957 call for greater openness as a tonic for strengthening the vitality of the CCP and his advocacy of pluralism as an end in itself seemed to allay the intelligentsia's fears. Thus when in April 1957 the Party called on non-Communist intellectuals to participate in another of its rectification campaigns (q.v.), a flood of criticism ensued, especially from leaders of the democratic parties (q.v.). But Mao had expected non-Communist intellectuals to shower the CCP with praise for its many accomplishments in uniting the country and developing the economy; instead, such abuses as "bureaucratism (q.v.), CCP domination of the government and of intellectual affairs, the Sino-Soviet alliance, and Party sectarianism" were singled out for criticism often through the popular medium of "big-character posters" (q.v.) (*dazibao*). Proposals were also aired for free elections to trade unions and other groups, and criticism was voiced of the CCP's elaborate structure of administrative control. Concerned with the intensity of the criticism, in early June 1957 the official organ of the CCP, the *People's Daily* (q.v.), denounced the Party's antagonists, ushering in the notorious Anti-Rightist campaign (q.v.).

Since 1957, the Hundred Flowers has been the subject of considerable debate in and outside of China. For many, the Hundred Flowers smacked of a devious trap set by Mao Zedong to ferret out the Party's critics. Others, however, suggest that Mao was genuinely committed to liberalization, but was frightened by the intensity of the intelligentsia's attacks and concerned that the CCP might go the way of Hungary and experience an anti-Communist uprising. In 1961–1962, yet another Hundred Flowers period was inaugurated in the midst of China's recovery from the devastating effects of the Great Leap Forward (q.v.). This time, however, few intellectuals dared to speak out openly as the only criticism came in the form of elliptical historical allusions, such as the play *Hai Rui Dismissed from Office* (q.v.) by Wu Han (q.v.), which purportedly targeted Mao's treatment of the peasantry.

HUNGARIAN REVOLUTION (1956). The Hungarian Uprising in October 1956 had a dramatic impact on China. Internationally, the Chinese were clearly concerned about the erosion of cohesion in the "socialist camp" and thus expressed their strong support for the "leading role" of the Soviet Union in the international Communist movement. On a visit to the USSR at the height of the crisis, Zhou Enlai (q.v.) encouraged Soviet leader Nikita Khrushchev to intervene and remove the leadership of the renegade Hungarian Communist Party.

Domestically, Hungary also influenced CCP leaders, especially Mao Zedong (q.v.). Clearly impressed and worried by this popular revolt against a sitting Communist Party, Mao Zedong implemented various policies to stifle any replication in China of the events in Hungary. Although Chinese intellectuals (q.v.) and students were aware of developments in Hungary, there appeared very little desire on their part to engage in the same kind of opposition to the newly established CCP regime as reactions to Hungary on Chinese campuses were relatively mild. Nevertheless, Mao Zedong's fear that a similar revolt could break out in China shaped his political position throughout the late 1950s. As opposed to the Leninist principles upheld by Liu Shaoqi (q.v.) and Deng Xiaoping (q.v.), Mao advocated greater "democracy" and external rectification of the CCP by intellectuals (q.v.) in the 1956–1957 Hundred Flowers (q.v.) campaign.

While Liu and Deng believed in internal Party democracy—that is, criticism and debate within the CCP—Mao believed that criticism from the outside would relieve tensions in Chinese society and prevent an outburst of opposition such as had occurred in Eastern Europe. To Mao's dismay, however, Chinese intellectuals issued forth with a torrent of criticism that led the chairman to brand his intellectual critics as members of a Chinese version of the Petöfi Club that had initiated the anti-Communist movement in Hungary. Thereafter, the 1957–1958 Anti-Rightist campaign (q.v.) cracked down on CCP critics.

I

"IMPERIALISM" (*DIGUOZHUYI*). The overthrow of "imperialism"—foreign influence and control in China—was a major goal of the Chinese Communist revolution. Influenced by Lenin's theory on the role of imperialism in the international capitalist system, Chinese Communist leaders linked their domestic enemies of rural gentry and "bureaucratic capitalists" to the presence in China of foreign powers from Europe, America, and Japan. The triumph of the CCP (q.v.) in 1949 was hailed as part of the collapse of the international imperialist order and the victory of socialism over capitalism on an international scale. Yet even as China contributed to the eventual destruction of international imperialism, socialism was still engaged in a life-and-death struggle with imperialism, which after 1949 was represented primarily by the largest and most powerful capitalist nation, the United States. Thus China considered such struggles as the Korean War (1950–1953) (q.v.) and the Vietnam War (1965–1975) as integral parts of the U.S. effort to halt the world revolution. From 1949 to the late 1970s, denunciation of "American imperialism" was a staple of Chinese polemics with songs and slogans—"down with American imperialism" (*dadao Meiguo diguozhuyi*)—memorized by Chinese schoolchildren and adults alike. Beginning with the visit to China in 1972 by U.S. President Nixon and the establishment of formal diplomatic relations between the two countries, however, such rhetoric gradually disappeared from the Chinese political scene. As the conflict with the Soviet Union heated up in the 1970s and 1980s, the USSR was condemned as "social imperialist," a suggestion by China that the once socialist country had essentially become an imperialist one. The Sino-Soviet rapprochement in the late 1980s essentially put an end to this rhetoric.

"INTELLECTUALS" (*ZHISHIFENZI*). The word "intellectual" in China refers to anyone with a high school or college education, as well as to white-collar and professional workers, a group that comprises approximately 5 percent of the entire population. Compared with the former Soviet Union, intellectuals constitute a smaller percentage of the entire population but possess a strong sense of common identity.

The history of modern China since 1949 has created a peculiar dilemma for intellectuals who have been captive to a regime that needs and demands their services but which repudiates the independent ideas they are equipped to supply. Over the years the CCP (q.v.) has built up and maintained its political power through absolute control over ideology and thought. Before and after it took power in 1949, the regime singled out Chinese intellectuals and journalists who championed independent thought and advocated freedom of speech and made them targets of persecution. The 1942–1944 Yan'an Rectification Campaign (q.v.), the mid 1950s campaign against Hu Feng (q.v), and the 1957–1958 Anti-Rightist campaign (q.v.), prosecuted by Deng Xiaoping (q.v.), were all launched to establish ideological control over intellectuals inside and outside the Party. These brutal campaigns targeted specific "example" intellectuals, but were intended to persecute hundreds of thousands of others.

In the 1940s and 1950s, the CCP needed the services of China's intellectuals—its educated elite—to achieve and consolidate its rule over China. Intellectuals were needed not only for the prosaic tasks of administration of the bureaucracies of government and business (which required literacy), but also for ideological work to buttress the legitimacy of the regime. The source of abiding tension in CCP-intellectual relations, which continues in the 1990s, is that on the one hand the CCP must rely on the social prestige and creative talents of the intellectuals to articulate its policies and motivate the public, while on the other hand, as a Leninist party the CCP inherently distrusts the intellectuals as insubordinate and divisive, and as potential rivals to political legitimacy. Thus, the CCP has gone to extraordinary lengths (even greater than its counterpart in the former Soviet Union) to win over China's intellectuals to the subordinate propaganda role desired by the leaders.

The period from the 1942–1944 Rectification Campaign to the 1957 Anti-Rightist campaign was crucial in establishing CCP hegemony over intellectuals. Drawn to the Communist redoubt in Yan'an during the late 1930s and early 1940s, many Chinese intellectuals joined the Communists out of genuine patriotic loyalty and a commitment to the New Democracy (q.v.) that CCP Chairman Mao Zedong (q.v.) had promised in January 1940. Yet, despite Mao's promise of a "new culture" and a "new-democratic republic" that so attracted the intellectuals who gravitated to Yan'an, political reality consisted of a

Party dictatorship that increasingly drew on the experiences and methods of Stalinist Russia where intellectuals were subordinated to the will of the Party leadership. During the Yan'an period this involved a variety of methods that ranged from public "education campaigns," to the establishment of direct administrative Party control of the press, to a more brutal campaign known as the "rescue movement" whereby a select number of intellectuals were persecuted and liquidated: "killing one to scare the hundred."

Several years later, after the CCP won power in 1949 and established a national regime, intellectuals were once again the target of a Communist Party that was acutely sensitive to any criticism from educated circles. This time the targets were Hu Feng (q.v.) and Liang Shuming. Hu Feng, an early critic of the CCP's Thought Reform (q.v.) efforts in the 1940s, was attacked in the mid 1950s as the reputed leader of the "Hu Feng Anti-Party Clique." Opposed to the arbitrary imposition on writers of a predetermined Communist worldview, Hu Feng appealed to the CCP Central Committee for a more flexible approach to Chinese literature, only to be attacked and subsequently arrested as a symbol of resistance to Party authority. The second target was Liang Shuming, China's "last Confucian." In 1953 Liang was publicly berated by Mao Zedong for having advocated a blueprint for China's economic development based on a model of rural reconstruction that directly challenged Mao's embrace of Soviet-style central planning with its emphasis on heavy industry and urban modernization. The attack on Hu Feng and his "clique," and Mao's chilling public vilification of Liang Shuming, led to a nationwide campaign in 1954–1955 against writers and intellectuals who still believed, despite the 1942–1944 Rectification Campaign, that some measure of autonomy and independent thought would be possible under the new regime. They were wrong.

Two years later, in 1957, following the outburst of criticism by intellectuals against the CCP that had been sanctioned by Mao Zedong's call for a Hundred Flowers (q.v.), the Anti-Rightist campaign (q.v.) was launched. Hundreds of thousands of educated people throughout the country were affected and in many cases either killed or exiled for years to remote areas. The case of Chu Anping was emblematic of the sharp conflicts that emerged between a regime intent on controlling ideology and intellectuals who considered "thought" their special preserve and independent contribution to society. Intensive criticism, public denunciations, and self-criticisms and "confessions" were the primary mechanisms for subordinating intellectuals to the will of the Communist leadership and preempting their challenge to Party ideology. During the Cultural Revolution (1966–1976) (q.v.) the persecution of intellectuals continued, this time under the frenzied attacks by Red Guards (q.v.), who condemned intellectuals as the "stinking ninth category" (*choulaojiu*). Intellectuals have been a favorite target because of the traditional role that the educated elite played throughout its more than two thousand years of dynastic history.

Since 1978, intellectuals have been treated more leniently as they are now considered part of the "working class." However, intellectual dissidents in the 1978–1979 Democracy Wall movement (q.v.) and the 1989 pro-democracy movement were singled out for harsh criticism and persecution by CCP leaders who are terribly frightened by the slightest hint of opposition from educated personages whom the average Chinese still deeply admire.

"INTERNAL MATERIALS" (*NEIBU ZILIAO*). The Chinese state and Communist Party (q.v.) bureaucracies rely heavily on printed material that is not for public consumption. The largest of the circulated "internal materials" is called *Reference News* (*cankao xiaoxi*) and contains a collection of wire-service translations from the foreign media, such as Reuters and the *New York Times*. Introduced in the late 1950s to keep the Chinese leadership informed of developments outside the country, this publication was originally limited to top-ranking cadres (q.v.), but in recent years has become widely available to state employees and university students. It reportedly has a circulation of nine million, more than the largest "public" newspaper, the *People's Daily* (q.v.). Distributed through the mail, this publication is "internal" (i.e., restricted) in name only. Less widely available is *Reference Information* (*cankao ziliao*), which also publishes translated articles from abroad, but is more comprehensive. It is controlled by Xinhua (q.v.), China's national news agency. The next most restricted material is the *Internal Reference* (*neibu cankao*), which contains sensitive reports prepared by Xinhua reporters on domestic and international events. It is limited in its distribution to state and Party ministerial (*bu*) personnel. *Internal Reports* (*neibu wengao*) and *Internal Situation* (*neibu qingyang*) are two additional sets of reports prepared for perusal by China's top leadership. The most restricted materials are so-called red-head reference (*hongtou cankao*) and hand-copied documents, which are limited in distribution to the top political leadership. Books and magazines in China also frequently carry the "internal" classification, but access is not severely restricted.

"IRON RICE BOWL" (*TIEFANWAN*). A generic term in Chinese used to refer to job security for industrial workers and Party and state cadres (q.v.) under the socialist system. From 1949 until the inauguration of the economic reforms in 1978, wages in China were low and consumer goods were few, but workers in the state-run industrial sector and the government bureaucracies had total job security. In addition, housing was provided, along with free medical care and education. Over the years, however, the number of workers and their dependents at industrial facilities, such as the Baoshan Steel Plant (q.v.) in Shanghai (q.v.), increased dramatically without commensurate increases in productivity. The "iron rice bowl" ultimately became a metaphor for inefficient and lackadaisical workers, bloated employment rolls, and inflated bureaucracies that ultimately led the CCP (q.v.) leadership in 1978 to inaugurate economic reforms. The loss of the "iron rice bowl" has been a hallmark of the reforms, although the number of workers who have lost their guaranteed jobs has been relatively small. In many large state-run industrial facilities, jobs are still guaranteed and layoffs and outright firings are few. Fear of massive layoffs and subsequent social instability that might ensue has prevented China from carrying out the privatization of industry that is required for its entry into the World Trade Organization.

"IT DOESN'T MATTER IF THE CAT IS BLACK OR WHITE AS LONG AS IT CATCHES MICE" (*BUGUAN HEIMAO BAIMAO, ZHUAZHU LAOSHU JIUSHI HAOMAO*). This phrase was used by China's paramount leader Deng Xiaoping (q.v.) to justify the package of economic reforms initiated in the late 1970s. Emblematic of Deng's pragmatic approach to policy making, the phrase was first used by Deng in the early 1960s to inaugurate moderate reforms in the agricultural sector, an initiative immediately squashed by Mao Zedong (q.v.). In its original form of an old folk saying from Deng's home province of Sichuan, the cat was "yellow," not "white," but the political meaning was obvious: leftist economic ideas did not work and thus should be replaced by more moderate policies that allowed for some role for the market and economic incentives. In the early 1960s, Deng first uttered the phrase—taken from his old military comrade, Liu Bocheng (q.v.)—in suggesting that a "household contract system" (*baochan daohu*) be adopted in the countryside to replace the ill-fated people's communes (q.v.) that were hastily set up during the 1958–1960 Great Leap Forward (q.v.). "In deciding on the best production system," Deng asserted on July 7, 1962, "we might have to embrace the attitude of adopting whichever method develops agricultural production most easily and rapidly and whichever method the masses desire most." On hearing that CCP (q.v.) Chairman Mao Zedong took the exact opposite view arguing that China's peasants opposed such a system and supported rural socialism, Deng quickly withdrew the suggestion, though he was still persecuted during the Cultural Revolution (1966–1976) (q.v.) for its utterance as evidence of his "capitalist" leanings. Not until after Mao's death in 1976, did Deng resuscitate the phrase and the pragmatic policies it encompassed.

J

JI DENGKUI (1923–1988). Ji Dengkui rose up through the ranks of the Communist Party municipal and provincial apparatus in Henan province, and during the Cultural Revolution (1966–1976) (q.v.) he played an active role in setting up the Henan Revolutionary Committee (q.v.). Also during the Cultural Revolution, Ji became a vice premier and was a supporter of Jiang Qing (q.v.), but he was purged in 1980.

JIANG NANXIANG (1910–   ). A graduate of Qinghua University (q.v.), Jiang Nanxiang joined Hu Qiaomu (q.v.) during the Yan'an period (1936–1945) in editing the journal *China Youth*. In 1952 Jiang became dean of Qinghua and in 1957 first Party secretary of the Party committee at the university. As minister of education in 1965 he was attacked for being a supporter of Beijing Party Committee head Peng Zhen (q.v.) and he disappeared until 1974. From 1979 to 1982 he was minister of education and in 1982 became first vice president of the Central Party School (q.v.) in Beijing.

JIANG QING (1913–1991). The third and last wife of CCP (q.v.) Chairman Mao Zedong (q.v.) and later the prime member of the Gang of Four (q.v.), Jiang Qing was born in Shandong province under the name of Li Yunhe. In the 1930s she was a film actress in Shanghai (q.v.) where she was also a member of the CCP underground. After divorcing her first husband (who in later years opened a Chinese restaurant in Paris), Jiang Qing traveled to Yan'an in 1938 where she met Mao. Despite the reservations of the CCP Central Committee, Jiang Qing and Mao were married after the chairman secured a divorce from his second wife (who subsequently went insane). Although Mao initially promised that Jiang Qing would stay out of politics, Jiang became active in 1965 when Yao Wenyuan (q.v.) (a later cohort in the Gang) directed his acid pen at the drama *Hai Rui Dismissed from Office* (q.v.) written by Beijing (q.v.) vice mayor Wu Han (q.v.). The play, Yao suggested, was a veiled attack on Mao. During the Cultural Revolution (1966–1976) (q.v.), Jiang Qing assumed a prominent role in the Cultural Revolution Small Group (q.v.) led by Chen Boda (q.v.) and in 1967–1968 she egged on Red Guards (q.v.) to launch vicious assaults on the Party and army. With the purge of Chen Boda and the demise of Lin Biao (q.v.) in 1970–1971, Jiang's influence waned as she focused increasingly on foreign policy. After an alleged attempt to seize power, Jiang Qing was arrested in October 1976, along with members of the Gang of Four—Zhang Chunqiao (q.v.), Yao Wenyuan, and Wang Hongwen (q.v.)—in the so-called October 1976 coup. Propaganda onslaughts on Jiang Qing throughout the 1980s were filled with enormous personal invective, with sly suggestions that she had used her well-honed sexual prowess to seduce Chairman Mao and subvert his revolutionary fervor. In November 1980–January 1981, Jiang Qing was sentenced to death (with a two-year reprieve) by a Chinese court for her role in causing the death and destruction of the Cultural Revolution. In 1991 she committed suicide while still in prison. This event was noted in the Chinese press but ignored on Central China TV.

JIANG ZEMIN (1926–   ). In 1996, concurrently general secretary of the CCP (q.v.), president of the PRC (q.v.), and chairman of the Central Military Commission, Jiang Zemin is the third successor chosen by Deng Xiaoping (q.v.), following Hu Yaobang (q.v.) and Zhao Ziyang (q.v.), both of whom were purged. Jiang Zemin is originally from Shanghai (q.v.) and has a degree in electrical engineering. Early in his career Jiang worked as a trainee in the Stalin Automobile Factory in Moscow, and in the 1950s and 1960s was director of a number of industrial plants in Shanghai. In 1971 he entered the central government in the First Ministry of Machine Building and in the early 1980s he headed the Ministry of the Electronics Industry. In 1985 he became mayor of Shanghai and in 1987 at the Thirteenth Party Congress he became a member of the CCP Politburo (q.v.). During the June 1989 student demonstrations in Shanghai he averted violence, mollifying students by reading from Lincoln's Gettysburg address. Jiang was also instrumental in purging the editors of the Shanghai-based newspaper *World Economic Herald* (q.v.) which had been a beacon of liberal thought and opinion. Following the massacre in Beijing (q.v.), he was appointed by Deng as the "core" of the third generation of CCP leaders.

K

KANG SHENG (1899–1975). Born in 1899 to a family of well-off landlords, Kang Sheng was one of the most important CCP (q.v.) leaders involved in intelligence and security and liaison with foreign Communist parties. In the 1930s he was an underground Party operative in

Shanghai (q.v.) where he established early links with Li Kenong. He then went to Moscow to study Soviet security techniques and was CCP representative to the Comintern. Returning to Yan'an in 1937 with Wang Ming, Kang Sheng was reinstated as a Politburo (q.v.) member and headed the growing security apparatus, including the Social Affairs Department or secret police, and was also a top official at the Central Party School (q.v.).

During the early 1940s, Kang promoted the notorious "rescue campaign" aimed at ferreting out alleged KMT (q.v.) spies and "Trotsky-ites" in the CCP, but which ended up purging and executing many innocent intellectuals, including Wang Shiwei (q.v.), who was killed in 1947. In the late 1950s, Kang was involved with Deng Xiaoping (q.v.) in the growing dispute with the Soviet Union over ideological and other issues and at the same time strongly defended Mao's 1958–1960 Great Leap Forward (q.v.) policies.

Kang's political star rose considerably in 1962 with the purge of Peng Dehuai (q.v.), when Kang was appointed to the Party Secretariat headed by Deng. During the Cultural Revolution (1966–1976) (q.v.) he served as a critical adviser to the radical faction of Jiang Qing (q.v.) and became a member of the Politburo Standing Committee. Kang collected art, and after his death in 1975 Kang's home in Beijing (q.v.) was converted to a hotel.

KHRUSHCHEV, NIKITA. *See* SINO-SOVIET CONFLICT.

KOREAN WAR (1950–1953). The North Korean invasion of South Korea in June 1950 resulted from a decision by North Korean leader Kim Il-sung, in consultation with Josef Stalin (q.v.) and Mao Zedong (q.v.), to invade the South. At this time, Mao was determined to promote communist revolutions in Asia and apparently was spoiling for a fight with the United States. After the collapse of North Korean forces in late 1950 following the UN counterattack at Inchon, South Korea, Mao, despite some hesitation and divisions among the top leadership, decided to send Chinese troops, dubbed "volunteers," to rescue the North Korean regime and blunt UN attacks that under U.S. General MacArthur had crossed the 38th parallel in the middle of the Korean peninsula and had approached China's border at the Yalu River.

China's involvement in the war stretched from October 1950 to the signing of an armistice in July 1953 that brought the fighting to an end. Chinese troops in Korea were commanded by General Peng De-huai (q.v.), the only top military commander in the Chinese army to serve in Korea.

Mao's decision to enter the war was made over considerable resistance from within the ruling Politburo (q.v.) and after Stalin had offered and then withdrawn promises of air support against UN forces. Chinese forces consisted of thousands of former KMT (q.v.) troops who had gone over to the CCP during the Civil War (1946–1949) (q.v.) and were now sacrificed as cannon fodder in the infamous Chinese human wave assaults against UN forces.

China's total losses in the war exceeded one million men, though the Korean conflict evidently stimulated the Chinese industrial and agricultural economy in the northeast. China agreed to the armistice after the United States, under President Dwight Eisenhower, threatened use of nuclear weapons. Thousands of Chinese prisoners were allowed to go to Taiwan (q.v.) and abroad after the signing of the armistice. Mao Zedong's eldest son, Anying, was killed in a U.S. air raid during the war. During the Korean conflict the United States also provided military protection for the Nationalist regime on Taiwan against any prospective Chinese invasion.

KUOMINTANG (CHINESE NATIONALIST PARTY) (KMT). Established in 1912, the KMT was the ruling party of the ROC on mainland China from 1928 to its defeat by the Chinese Communists in the Civil War (q.v.) in 1949. After fleeing to Taiwan (q.v.) (formerly known as Formosa), the KMT has continued to exist as the dominant party in the ROC located on the island some 100 kilometers off the southeastern coast of China where it has carried out the transition from one-party dictatorship to constitutional democracy. "Kuomintang" is the Wade-Giles romanization, which is still used on Taiwan, for the Nationalist Party. In pinyin, which is used by the PRC (q.v.), the word is spelled "Guomindang."

The KMT traces its origins to the anti-imperialist and anti-warlord struggle in early twentieth-century China. The party was established by Song Jiaoren out of a fledgling political organization known as the *T'ung Meng Hwei* and several other smaller political parties. It was quickly outlawed, however, in the context of the struggle between Sun Yat-sen (China's first president) and the warlord Yuan Shikai to control the newly created Chinese Republic set up following the collapse of the Qing dynasty (1644–1911), China's last.

In 1919 following his establishment of a rival government in the southern city of Canton, Sun Yat-sen reorganized his secretive Chinese Revolutionary Party into the KMT to challenge the warlord-run government in China's north. Organizationally weak and lacking a financial base or substantial military support, the KMT was heavily dependent on local southern warlords for its survival.

After failing to achieve Western support, Sun looked to the new leaders of Soviet Russia for aid and in 1924 announced the formation of a united front (q.v.) with the newly created CCP (q.v.), which had been formed with substantial aid from the Communist International (Comintern). At this point, the KMT was reorganized along Leninist lines and, like the CCP, adopted the principles of democratic centralism (q.v.) and began to build an army along Soviet lines. Sun Yat-sen became the supreme leader (*zongli*) and generalissimo of the KMT and introduced the Three Principles of the People—nationalism, people's rights, and people's livelihood—as the party's reigning ideology.

Following Sun's sudden death from illness in 1925, party leadership shifted to a young military leader named Chiang Kai-shek. Although trained in the Soviet Union and once referred to as the "red general," Chiang quickly imposed a more conservative ideology on the KMT and in April 1927 carried out a systematic purge of his Communist allies, bringing an end to the First United Front that had been formally established in 1924.

After successfully leading a military expedition against the warlord government in the north (known as the Northern Expedition), Chiang established a new regime in the southern city of Nanking (Nanjing) on October 10, 1928 (celebrated to this day as National Day in the ROC and referred to as "double ten"). Despite persistent factionalism in the party, Chiang consolidated his rule by basing his power squarely on the KMT's growing military forces and on the semifascist party organization known as the Blue Shirts. Although formal power in the KMT lay with the Central Executive Committee and the KMT Congress, in reality Chiang exercised absolutist rule as the party's *zongcai* or exalted leader, a post Chiang assumed in 1938. Throughout the 1930s, Chiang was obsessed with destroying his Communist rivals who were held up in Jiangxi province and then Yan'an, despite increasing incursions into China by the Japanese. But in 1936 Chiang was captured by a rival warlord and forced to join with the Communists in a Second United Front to oppose the Japanese. This fragile alliance continued with the Communists throughout the Sino-Japanese War (1937–1945) (q.v.), only to quickly collapse as the Civil War (1946–1949) (q.v.) broke out and which the KMT ultimately lost to the Communists.

Although the KMT had won the support of certain elements of the Chinese population in the 1930s and 1940s, its increasing corruption (q.v.), political repression of students and intellectuals (q.v.), and profound lack of concern for the fate of the Chinese peasantry ultimately robbed it of the necessary political support to win against the Communists. KMT policies of "one party, one leader" proved an inviting target for the Communists, who successfully mobilized student protests in the cities against the KMT, while winning over peasant support in the countryside with its promises of Land Reform (q.v.). Defeated on the Chinese mainland, the KMT under Chiang Kai-shek fled to Taiwan and established the ROC on the island while claiming overall authority for the entire Chinese mainland.

The early years of KMT rule on Taiwan were marked by political repression of the indigenous population and increased reliance on the United States. In 1947, the local KMT commander in Taiwan sanctioned a wholesale massacre of native Taiwanese that effectively deprived the local population of political leadership. Following the North Korean invasion of South Korea in 1950, the United States, which had originally not intended to defend the ROC on Taiwan from a possible invasion by the newly established Communist regime in Beijing (q.v.), came to Taiwan's defense and in effect insulated it from external threat through the signing of a mutual defense treaty in 1954.

Economically, Taiwan was severely underdeveloped despite Japanese colonization since 1895. But beginning in the mid-1950s the KMT promoted policies that dramatically transformed Taiwan into a prosperous, middle-class society. Land reform, which the KMT had abjured on the mainland, was carried out (often with considerable brutality against indigenous landlords), along with an export-oriented economic strategy that stressed foreign investment, open markets, and less state intervention in the economy. By the 1960s and 1970s, Taiwan emerged as a major exporter of both cash crops and industrial products, including textiles, electronic goods, and finally computers.

Politically, however, Taiwan remained under the iron grip of one-party rule led by the aging Chiang Kai-shek. Elections that had taken place on the Chinese mainland in 1948 remained the basis for "representation" in the ROC Legislative Yuan (the nominal parliament of the ROC), while real power lay with Chiang and his military supporters. Despite periodic student protests, the regime remained stable with a politically quiescent population. In 1975, Chiang Kai-shek died and was replaced by his son Chiang Ching-kuo. Although during his youth in the Soviet Union the young Chiang had flirted with Trotskyism, he had served his father well as head of military and internal security matters. Yet, as president, Chiang Ching-kuo emerged as a moderate reformer, allowing for a more open press and increasing democratization at the local level. Following Chiang Ching-kuo's death in 1988, the ROC was taken over by native Taiwanese President Lee Teng-hui, who went even further in allowing the emergence of opposition political parties and providing for elections to the parliament, local offices, and the prime ministership.

Throughout this process of increased democratization, the KMT has adjusted accordingly, running effective campaigns, winning the votes of mainlanders and Taiwanese alike, and maintaining control of the prime ministership. In the 1994 national elections, the KMT lost the mayoralty post in Taiwan's largest city of Taipei to the opposition Democratic Progressive Party (DPP). But in the first direct election to the office of the president held in March 1996, the KMT candidate, Lee Teng-hui, won a landslide victory with over 50 percent of the popular vote and easily defeated his DPP rival, Peng Ming-min. This occurred despite military threats posed by the PRC (q.v.) in the guise of war games held off the coast of Taiwan in the weeks and days prior to the election. *See also* CHINESE COMMUNIST PARTY.

L

"LABOR UNDER SURVEILLANCE" (*GUANZHI LAODONG*). After completing prison sentences or other forms of incarceration, individuals in China are subject to long-term "surveillance" by local public security organs (q.v.) or residence committees. This was applied to so-called landlords, rich peasants, counterrevolutionaries, and rightists who managed to survive the campaigns of terror of the early 1950s. "Labor under surveillance" often lasted for years, especially for people such as landlords and rich peasants, who experienced this local oversight throughout their lives. Manual labor was considered essential for people to "reform" themselves, that is, to develop loyalty to the CCP (q.v.). *See also* REFORM THROUGH LABOR.

LAND REFORM (1946–1953). "Land to the tiller" was a central plank in the CCP (q.v.) program formulated by Mao Zedong (q.v.) in his 1940 speech entitled "On New Democracy" (q.v.). Thus, after the CCP's seizure of national power in 1949, Land Reform was carried out over a period of three years under the guise of the 1950 Agrarian Reform Law. This redistribution of land continued the policies pursued by the CCP in the 1930s during the period of the Jiangxi Soviet, which were perhaps the most radical Land Reform policies of the CCP, and in the 1940s during the Sino-Japanese War (q.v.) when the Communists built a base of support among the peasantry by redistributing land but with moderate treatment of landlords and rich peasants. In 1949, more than 500 million peasants lived in China, with fully half of the cultivated land owned by one-tenth of the population and with two-thirds of the population owning less than one-fifth of the land. Large numbers of landless peasants populated the countryside and paid upwards of 60 percent of their production in rent to the landowning classes. Still, China lacked the large estates and latifundia prevalent in other Third World countries, particularly Latin America.

The 1950 Agrarian Reform Law was relatively moderate in that it allowed rich peasants to retain their land and even let landlords hold land for their own use. However, under political pressure from above and in the context of the Korean War (1950–1953) (q.v.), both rich peasants and landlords were subject to expropriation of their property by mobilized peasants and they were often physically abused and murdered in the "struggle meetings" and "people's tribunals" established by the CCP. By 1952, more than 110 million acres of land were redistributed to over 300 million peasants, along with farm tools and draft animals. In 1953, however, this "land to the tiller" policy was quickly reversed as peasants were pressured into "voluntarily" joining the Mutual Aid Teams (q.v.), followed by the lower and higher APCs (q.v.), and finally the people's communes (q.v.). Not until the Agricultural Responsibility System (q.v.) was introduced in the late 1970s was land in China returned to the "tiller."

LANGUAGE REFORM. Since the May Fourth Movement in 1919 language reform has been a central political and literary concern in modern China. Led by such intellectual luminaries as Hu Shi (q.v.) and Guo Moruo (q.v.), the Chinese written and spoken language was transformed from an elitist and exclusive medium into one more accessible to the common people. Of greatest importance to literary reformers determined to modernize politically and culturally was the creation of a popular literature corresponding to vernacular Chinese (*putonghua*) instead of the traditional classical language (*wenyan*). After 1949, the CCP (q.v.) introduced major language reforms that followed on those initially introduced in the 1920s. In 1951, a plan was adopted to ensure universal comprehension of a standardized common language. This plan included the simplification of written Chinese characters and introduction of romanized forms based on the Latin alphabet. At the National Conference on Reform of the Chinese Written Language in October 1955 *putonghua*, based on the Beijing dialect, was adopted as the common language for the entire country and introduced as the language of instruction in schools, and the national media. By the late 1970s, *putonghua* was used by all government, Party, and educational organs. Throughout the urban areas, *putonghua* is generally understood by most of the population, even as the local dialects continue to be used in everyday language and discourse. In theory, *putonghua* is taught in minority areas only at the request of the local population.

Simplified "shorthand" characters (*jiantizi*), with fewer strokes, have replaced many traditional "complex" characters (*fantizi*) in official publications and the schools. Since 1978, however, some *fantizi* have been revived. Other aspects of reform include the adding of new meanings to existing Chinese characters, thereby reducing to 4,000 the number of individual characters that an educated person needs to master. Pinyin romanization was created in the late 1950s to facilitate the learning of Chinese characters and in conjunction with the spread of vernacular Chinese to minority nationalities. Pinyin is the accepted form of romanization used in most Western countries.

LEI FENG (1940–1962). Perhaps the most famous political model advanced by the CCP (q.v.), Lei Feng was a PLA (q.v.) soldier whose distinguishing qualities included loyalty to the Party and Chairman Mao Zedong (q.v.). A peasant soldier from Mao's home province of Hunan, Lei Feng reportedly died in 1962 at the age of twenty-two while "serving the people" when he attempted to retrieve a telephone pole that had fallen into a river. Lei left behind a diary in which he idolized Chairman Mao, expressed his eternal love for "the motherland, the people, and the Party," and described his own many good deeds as a humble soldier to assist the common people. Politically, the purpose of the Lei Feng campaign in the mid-1960s was to bolster the image of the PLA in its growing conflict with the Party leadership of Liu Shaoqi (q.v.) and others. Lei Feng was idealized as a "rust-proof screw" in the machinery of the revolution—a model of obedience to political authority that has been a staple feature of Chinese Communist ideology since 1949. Lei Feng was also canonized for never "forgetting the class hatred of the old society where people perished and families fell apart." Lei Feng was on constant political alert and "never forgot the pain of the old society when the scars of exploitation were healed." Propaganda on Lei Feng declined from the late 1970s through the 1980s, but was revived after the June 1989 pro-democracy movement was crushed, though with little apparent effect.

LI BONING (1918–). A major figure in China's water resources bureaucracy, Li Boning is a primary supporter of the Three Gorges Dam project (q.v.), the world's largest dam slated for construction from 1995 to 2013. In the late 1950s, Li Boning was the deputy director of the Capital Construction Department of the Ministry of Water Resources and Electric Power. In 1978, he was identified as a vice minister of water resources and electric power. In 1989, he became the leading member of the Central Flood Prevention and Control Office. In 1988, he was elected vice chairman of the Economic Committee of the CPPCC (q.v.).

LI CHANG (1914–). A member of the CCP (q.v.) underground at Qinghua University (q.v.) in Beiping during the 1930s, Li Chang became a prominent figure in the scientific arena after 1949 as president of Harbin Polytechnical University and a member of the presidium of the Chinese Academy of Sciences. He was denounced during the Cultural Revolution (1966–1971) (q.v.) as a follower of Liu Shaoqi (q.v.). In the early 1980s, he was involved with the Research Society in Natural Dialectics.

LI GUIXIAN (1937–). A graduate of China's University of Science and Technology in 1959–1960, Li Guixian studied at the Mendeleyev Chemical Technological Institute in Moscow from 1960–1965. During the late 1960s and 1970s, Li Guixian worked as a researcher for the Ministry of Public Security, evidently in the field of electronics. In 1983, he was appointed to the Standing Committee of the Liaoning Province Party Committee and from 1985 to 1986 was the "leading" secretary of the Liaoning Party Committee and a member of the CCP (q.v.) Central Committee. From 1986 to 1988, Li served as secretary of the Anhui Province Party Committee and in 1988 became governor of the People's Bank of China (q.v.). In 1993, Li was forced to resign his position at the People's Bank as a result of a financial scandal that reportedly involved the loss of several billion dollars.

LI HONGLIN (1925–). A former president of the Fujian Academy of Social Sciences, Li has been a constant critic of the "personality cult" (q.v.) in China and a strong advocate of political reform since the 1970s. During the 1970s, he was a deputy head of the theoretical bureau of the CCP Propaganda Department until he was forced to step down for his liberal ideas. In March 1989 he joined forty-two intellectuals in signing an open letter to the CCP (q.v.) leadership calling for the release of political prisoners and greater freedom in Chinese society. In July 1989 he was imprisoned and released in May 1990.

LI PENG (1928–). In 1997, the premier of China, Li Peng is the "adopted" son of Zhou Enlai (q.v.). Li Peng was born in Sichuan to parents active in the CCP (q.v.), both of whom were executed by the KMT (q.v.) during the early 1930s. From 1948 to 1954, Li was trained as a power engineer in the Soviet Union and from 1955 to 1979 worked in numerous positions in the Chinese power industry. In 1982 he became vice minister of the Ministry of Water Resources and Electric Power and the same year became a member of the CCP Central Committee at the Twelfth Party Congress. In 1985 he was appointed to the Politburo (q.v.) and in 1987 to its Standing Committee. He became premier in 1988. In June 1989 he reportedly issued the order approved by Deng Xiaoping (q.v.) for troops to use force against pro-democracy demonstrators. In the early 1990s, Li Peng led China's effort to restore its reputation in the international arena after the 1989 crackdown with visits to India, Europe, Japan, Vietnam, and the United Nations where he met briefly with U.S. President George Bush. In May 1993, Li reportedly suffered a mild heart attack, but returned to work later in the year. A strong proponent of the controversial Three Gorges Dam project (q.v.), Li led the successful effort to overturn previous opposition to the dam and win NPC (q.v.) approval in April 1992 for the projected eighteen-year construction project. Li Peng's term as premier is set to expire in March 1998.

LI RUI (1917–). Li was Mao Zedong's (q.v.) secretary on industrial affairs in the 1950s. In the 1950s and 1960s, Li Rui also served as a vice minister in the Ministry of Water Resources and Electric Power. He was purged for his support of Peng Dehuai (q.v.) at the Lushan Plenum (q.v.) and was denounced as an "anti-Party element" during the Cultural Revolution (1966–1976) (q.v.), spending some twenty years in prison. Li Rui returned to prominence in 1979, was elected to the CCP Central Committee in 1982, and was vice director of the Organization Department of the Party from 1983 to 1985. He has led the effort to halt plans for construction of the massive Three Gorges Dam project (q.v.) on the Yangtze River. Since the 1989 Tiananmen crackdown, Li has continued to oppose the dam, which was approved for construction in 1992, penning letters of opposition to CCP General Secretary Jiang Zemin (q.v.). He is formally "retired" and now serves as an adviser to the Energy and Resources Research Institute in China.

LI RUIHUAN (1934–). Trained as a construction worker in the 1950s, Li Ruihuan cut his teeth during the Great Leap Forward (1958–1960) (q.v.) as a member of the young carpenters' shock brigade building the Great Hall of the People in Tiananmen Square, one of the world's largest buildings. In 1976 he was the director of the work site for the Mao Zedong Memorial Hall and in 1979 became a model worker. In 1982 he became mayor of Tianjin city and helped to clean up the city's notoriously polluted water supply. In 1987 he became head of the Tianjin Party Committee as well as a member of the Politburo (q.v.). With very little formal education, since 1989 Li has frequently weighed in on issues of ideology and culture. In the debate over the Three Gorges Dam project (q.v.), Li Ruihuan is said to have thoroughly quizzed the engineers and dam designers about the technical feasibility of the project.

LI WEIHAN (1896–1984). An early associate of Mao Zedong in Hunan, Li Weihan traveled to France in 1920 for education, though he quickly returned to China for the CCP's (q.v.) founding congress in Shanghai (q.v.) in July 1921. Also known as Luo Ming, Li became a member of the Politburo (q.v.) in 1927, but was soon thereafter denounced as a coward for attempting to terminate the ill-fated Autumn Harvest Uprising launched by the Communists against the KMT (q.v.). Li subsequently emerged in the early 1930s as a strong supporter of de facto Party leader Li Lisan and was an early opponent of the Russian Returned Student faction (also known as the Twenty-Eight Bolsheviks) who attacked the "Luo Ming line" as well as Mao Zedong (q.v.). In Yan'an, Li headed the Communist Party School and was a top official in the Shaan-Gan-Ning Border government. After 1949 Li became heavily involved in minority (q.v.) and nationality issues and also helped guide the early campaigns to seize private business and establish total state control of the economy. Director of the United Front Department from 1944 to 1965, Li in the late 1950s launched attacks on "rightists" in China's eight democratic parties (q.v.), including against his own brother. In 1964, however, Li was himself removed from his post and later attacked by Zhou Enlai (q.v.) for "capitulationism in united front work." A frequent critic of Mao Zedong, Li Weihan emerged after 1978 as a supporter of political reform and urged Deng Xiaoping (q.v.) (whom Li had once saved from political persecution) to attack "feudalism"—that is, the Party's autocratic traditions. *See also* FEUDALISM.

LI XIANNIAN (1909–1992). Born to poor peasants in Hubei, Li Xiannian was trained as a carpenter and then joined the Communists in the late 1920s. Rising to the top of the CCP (q.v.) hierarchy as a military commander, Li Xiannian became a member of the CCP Central Committee in 1945 and after 1949 became mayor of Wuhan city in Hubei province and a vice premier. He was made a member of the CCP Politburo (q.v.) in 1956 and became minister of finance in 1957. He continued to serve on the Politburo throughout the Cultural Revolution (1966–1976) (q.v.) and remained a central figure in economic and financial affairs throughout the 1980s. From 1983 to 1988, Li Xiannian served as China's president (q.v.).

LI XIMING (1926–). A graduate of Qinghua University (q.v.) in civil engineering and architecture, Li Ximing served as a vice minister in the Ministry of Power in the late 1970s. From 1982 to 1984 he was minister of urban and rural construction and environmental protection, and from 1984 to 1992 he was secretary of the Beijing Municipal Party Committee and from 1984 to 1987 first political commissar (q.v.) of the Beijing Military Garrison. In 1987, he was appointed to the Politburo (q.v.), a post that he held until 1992. Following the June 1989 military crackdown in Beijing (q.v.), which he championed, Li Ximing's political star faded somewhat. In 1994, he became titular head of the Three Gorges Dam project (q.v.).

LI XIN (1918–   ). A former secretary to Kang Sheng (q.v.), Li Xin was appointed in the late 1970s as deputy director of the Special Cases Investigation Group set up to persecute political opponents of the "Two Whatevers" faction (q.v.) in the CCP (q.v.). He was closely associated with Wang Dongxing (q.v.), Hu Sheng (q.v.), Wu Lengxi (q.v.), and Xiong Fu (q.v.). In the 1980s he was one of many "Party historians" involved in the Party History Research Center under the CCP Central Committee.

LI YINING (1930–   ). A 1955 graduate of the Economics Department at Peking University (Beida) (q.v.), Li Yining specializes in educational economics, comparative economics, and history of foreign economics. He has written a book on the economic theories of the American economist John Kenneth Galbraith. He is a member of the Standing Committee of the Seventh NPC (q.v.) and is a financial adviser to the China Investment Consulting Experts Committee.

"LIBERATION" (*JIEFANG*). The term used to refer to the seizure of political power in China by the CCP (q.v.) in October 1949, "liberation" is also used more broadly to mean the freeing of the Chinese people from the shackles of the past: landlords, capitalists, and foreign imperialism (q.v.). In Maoist theory the lifting of restraints from the past was to produce a great burst of revolutionary energy and creativity that was apparent in Mao's proposal for a Great Leap Forward (q.v.) in the late 1950s. Indeed, Chinese peasants genuinely referred to the 1949 Communist takeover and the redistribution of land as "liberation." The 1978 implementation of the Agricultural Responsibility System (q.v.) was often referred to by peasants as the "second liberation." In everyday speech, average Chinese still refer to 1949 as "liberation" or the "founding of the nation" (*jianguo*).

LIN BIAO (1907–1971). The "closest comrade in arms" of Mao Zedong (q.v.) during the Cultural Revolution (1966–1976) (q.v.) and his constitutionally designated successor, Lin Biao allegedly died in September 1971 after a purported attempt to assassinate the chairman. Lin was a major military leader during the 1946–1949 civil war (q.v.) when on one occasion his siege of the northeast city of Changchun led to the deaths of several hundred thousand people, including large numbers of noncombatants. After spending considerable time for medical treatment in the Soviet Union, Lin became a marshal of the PRC (q.v.) in 1955 and minister of national defense in 1959 following the purge of Peng Dehuai (q.v.). Lin Biao emerged as an important political figure in 1964 at a PLA (q.v.) Political Work Conference. In 1965, Lin issued his treatise "Long Live People's War" in which he proclaimed that Communist military forces from the world's rural hinterlands in Asia, Africa, and Latin America would surround and then overwhelm the world's urban populations in Europe and North America. In 1969 at the CCP's (q.v.) Ninth Party Congress Lin reached the pinnacle of his political power when he was canonized as Mao's official successor in the Ninth Party constitution. Lin and his entourage maintained an uneasy alliance with the radical faction surrounding Jiang Qing (q.v.), the wife of Mao Zedong. Following a political setback, in 1971 Lin allegedly joined with his notorious wife, Ye Qun (q.v.), and his son, Lin Liguo, in a foiled assassination plot against Mao. The official CCP line is that soon thereafter Lin Biao died in a plane crash in Mongolia after attempting to flee China. However, the rumor mill in China has it that he was actually poisoned by Mao Zedong at a banquet in Beijing (q.v.).

LIN MOHAN (1913–). A member of the Institute of Marxism-Leninism during the Yan'an period, Lin Mohan was also editor of the *Liberation Daily* (*Jiefang ribao*) and the journal *Chinese Culture* (*Zhongguo wenhua*). In the 1950s he became a vice minister of culture and in the early 1960s a deputy director of the CCP Propaganda Department. Branded as a "counterrevolutionary" in 1967, he reappeared in 1978 as a vice minister of culture and in the mid-1980s he became an adviser to the All-China Writers' Association.

LIU BINYAN (1925–). After joining the underground CCP (q.v.) in the 1940s in the city of Tianjin, Liu Binyan worked as a journalist with the *Beijing Youth Daily* in the early 1950s and later the *People's Daily* (q.v.). He was branded a "rightist" in 1957 for his scathing criticism of bureaucratism (q.v.) in China and sent to labor on a state farm. After returning to work in the early 1960s, he was denounced again during the Cultural Revolution (1966–1976) (q.v.), not to be rehabilitated until 1979. In 1985 he was elected vice chairman of the All-China Writers' Association; in 1987 he was expelled from the CCP (q.v.) for "bourgeois liberalization" (q.v.). Since 1988 he has been in exile in the West and was denounced in November 1989 in the *People's Daily* as the "scum of the Chinese nation." Liu's written works include *People or Monsters?* and *A Higher Kind of Loyalty.*

LIU BOCHENG (1892–1986). Trained as an army officer at the time of the Republican revolution in 1911, Liu was wounded several times and lost an eye. Thereafter he became known as the "one-eyed dragon." Liu began to support the Communists in the 1920s and went to the Soviet Union in the late 1920s for further military training. Liu commanded volunteer units during the epic Long March (1934–1935) (q.v.) and sided with Mao Zedong (q.v.) during his disputes with rival leaders promoted by Josef Stalin (q.v.) and the Comintern. Liu was appointed to the CCP (q.v.) Central Committee in 1945 and headed the Second Field Army in which Deng Xiaoping (q.v.) served as political commissar (q.v.). In 1955 Liu was elevated to the rank of marshal of the PRC (q.v.) and in 1956 he became a member of the Politburo (q.v.) at the Eighth Party Congress (q.v.). Liu reportedly protected Deng Xiaoping during the Cultural Revolution (1966–1976) (q.v.). He retired from public life in 1977 and at his death in 1986 Deng Xiaoping gave the eulogy.

LIU GUOGUANG (1923–). A graduate with a vice doctorate degree from the Moscow State Economics Institute, Liu Guoguang served as director of the Research Office of the Chinese Academy of Sciences from 1955 to 1980. In 1980 he became deputy director of the Institute of Economics under the Academy of Social Sciences (q.v.) and a professor at Beida (Peking University) (q.v.). In 1981, he became deputy director of the State Statistical Bureau and in 1982 became an alternate member of the CCP (q.v.) Central Committee and vice president of the Academy of Social Sciences. In 1985 he became director of its Institute of Economics.

LIU HUAQING (1917–). A military veteran with close ties to Deng Xiaoping (q.v.), Liu Huaqing attended a naval academy in the USSR in the early 1950s and from 1961 to 1965 was director of the Seventh Institute under the Ministry of National Defense. In 1965, Liu became deputy political commissar (q.v.) of the PLA (q.v.) Navy, and in 1967 during the Cultural Revolution (1966–1976) (q.v.) he was vice chairman of the Science and Technology Commission for National Defense and member of the Cultural Revolution Small Group for the PLA Navy. In 1968, he was attacked by Red Guards (q.v.), along with Nie Rongzhen (q.v.), for having purportedly established an "independent kingdom" in the Science and Technology Commission. In 1978, Liu became vice minister of the State Science and Technology Commission and in 1980 deputy chief of the PLA General Staff. In 1982, he was appointed commander of the Navy, and in the late 1980s he became vice chairman of the Central Military Commission. In 1992, he was appointed to the Standing Committee of the Politburo (q.v.) as China's top military man.

LIU HUAQIU (1939–   ). A specialist on American political affairs, Liu Huaqiu in 1994 was a vice minister of foreign affairs, a post that he held since 1989.

LIU SHAOQI (1898–1969). A native of Hunan province, Liu Shaoqi emerged in the 1950s as the first heir apparent to Mao Zedong (q.v.) whom Liu replaced as PRC (q.v.) state chairman in April 1959 after the political fallout over the disastrous 1958–1960 Great Leap Forward (q.v.). Author of the classic work on CCP (q.v.) membership entitled "How to Be a Good Communist," Liu's political star rose in the early 1960s as he supported a substantial loosening of state controls on the economy, especially agriculture, to help China recover from the Great Leap. Liu was attacked very early in the Cultural Revolution (1966–1976) (q.v.) as "China's Khrushchev" and as "the number one Party person in authority taking the capitalist road". He was replaced by Lin Biao (q.v.) as Mao's heir and was formally expelled from the CCP in October 1968. He later died ignominiously in a solitary cell in 1969.

LIU ZHONGLI (1934–   ). From 1973 to 1984, Liu Zhongli served in the planning commission of Heilongjiang province and in 1988 he became a vice minister of finance in the central government. In 1992, he replaced Wang Bingqian (q.v.) as minister of finance following Wang's apparent involvement in a financial scandal.

"LONG AND DRAGGED OUT PROJECT" (*DIAOYU GONG-CHENG*). This phrase refers to projects in basic capital construction that are unnecessary and are contrary to the interest of the ordinary people. The term first appeared in an editorial of the *People's Daily* (q.v.) on October 12, 1983, entitled "The Hefty Task of Construction Banks" and has often been used in reference to the Three Gorges Dam project (q.v.), which, although slated to take eighteen years to construct, will, like other large dam projects, such as the Gezhouba dam, probably take twice that long.

LONG MARCH (1934–1935). The seminal event in the pre-1949 history of the Chinese Communist movement that occurred between October 1934 and October 1935. Surrounded on three sides in their Jiangxi province redoubt known as the Central Soviet by KMT (q.v.) armies led by Chiang Kai-shek, the Communists decided on a bold move of strategic retreat to save the majority of their forces from

annihilation. Some one hundred thousand Red Army soldiers abandoned their base and headed west in a military maneuver that took
them over rugged terrain of mountains and rivers in China's western
provinces until they reached a small Communist base established in
Yan'an, in the northwestern province of Shaanxi (then known as
Shensi). During the march at the town of Zunyi, top CCP leaders
decided in January 1935 to appoint Mao Zedong (q.v.) military commander after Mao had challenged the military leadership and doctrine
of the dominant leadership group known as the Twenty-Eight Bolsheviks. Trained in Moscow and beholden to Josef Stalin (q.v.), the
Twenty-Eight Bolsheviks relied on the military advice of Comintern
adviser Otto Braun. Led by Mao and the military commander Zhu De
(q.v.), the CCP (q.v.) thereafter entrusted military leadership to Mao,
thereby reducing Soviet influence in the Chinese Communist movement. Splits soon developed among the CCP leadership ranks, however, as the powerful general Zhang Guotao rejected Mao's decision
to march toward Yan'an and instead fled to neighboring Sichuan province, thereby dividing the Communist forces. Zhang's armies subsequently relocated in Yan'an as well, though Zhang himself fled the
CCP's redoubt and quit the Communist movement altogether. From
the late 1930s onward, the Long March has been a central symbol of
the Chinese Communist movement that CCP leaders believed preceded the Party's ultimate success in winning control over all of
China.

LU DINGYI (1906–1996). After joining the CCP (q.v.) in 1925, Lu
Dingyi became active in the Communist Youth League (q.v.) and
served as a propaganda cadre (q.v.) in the PLA (q.v.). A Long March
(q.v.) veteran, he headed the Propaganda Department on and off
throughout the 1940s and 1950s. In May 1956, Lu delivered his famous speech "Let a Hundred Flowers Bloom" in which he favored
greater freedom of thought and expression, a proposal later embraced
by Mao (q.v.). Lu Dingyi became a member of the Central Committee
Secretariat in 1962 and in 1965 became minister of culture. Branded a
"counterrevolutionary" during the Cultural Revolution (1966–1976)
(q.v.), he was rehabilitated in 1979 and took part in revising China's
state constitution which was approved in 1982. That same year he
became a member of the Central Advisory Commission (q.v.). In
1986 he wrote a celebrated article commemorating the 1957 Hundred
Flowers (q.v.).

LU PING (1929–   ). A 1947 graduate of the Agricultural College of
St. John's University in Shanghai (q.v.), in the 1950s Lu Ping served
as editor in chief of the magazine *China Reconstructs*. He disappeared

during the Cultural Revolution (1966–1976) (q.v.). In 1978, he returned to public life and was made secretary-general of the State Hong Kong and Macao Affairs Office and in 1985 deputy secretary-general of the Basic Law Drafting Committee for Hong Kong. In 1987 he was appointed deputy director of the Hong Kong and Macao Affairs Office.

LU YOUMEI (1934–   ). Trained as a hydrologist in the 1950s, Lu Youmei served as an engineer from 1956 to 1970 at the Liujia Gorge Hydropower station on the Yellow River and from 1974 to 1984 in the Ministry of Water Resources and Electric Power. In 1988 he was appointed vice minister of energy resources. In 1992 he became the president of the Three Gorges Project Development Corporation, the quasi-private organization charged with constructing the Three Gorges Dam (q.v.) on the Yangtze River in central China.

LUO RUIQING (1906–1978). One of the earliest members of the Red Army and a senior military and political officer throughout the 1930s and 1940s, in the 1950s Luo Ruiqing became minister of public security. He helped establish the system of "reform through labor" (q.v.) and defended the execution of alleged "counterrevolutionaries" in the early 1950s as having been carried out to "appease the rightful indignation of the people." In 1959, Luo rose up the ranks after the purge of Peng Dehuai (q.v.) and became army chief of staff and was appointed to the Central Military Affairs Commission. In 1965 he was replaced and became a major target in the Cultural Revolution (1966–1976) (q.v.) during which time he sustained serious injuries at the hands of Red Guards (q.v.). Rehabilitated in the late 1970s, in 1978 he traveled to West Germany for medical treatment where he died, somewhat mysteriously, from a heart attack during an operation on his leg.

LUSHAN CONFERENCE (1959). This conference was the Eighth Plenum of the CCP's (q.v.) Eighth Central Committee that became a critical turning point in the CCP's ill-fated policies of promoting the 1958–1960 Great Leap Forward (q.v.). Held in August 1959 at the CCP's mountaintop retreat on Mt. Lu in Jiangxi province, the conference was marked by an unprecedented conflict between CCP Chairman Mao Zedong (q.v.) and his defense minister Peng Dehuai (q.v.) over the issue of continuing the radical social and economic policies of the Great Leap. After extensive visits to the countryside where he inspected the devastating impact on the rural economy of the backyard steel furnaces (q.v.) and the people's communes (q.v.), Peng had concluded that the fundamental policies of the leap and its guiding ideological line of "putting politics in command" (q.v.) were flawed and needed to be reversed as soon as possible. Peng voiced his concerns in a letter delivered to Mao Zedong—the major proponent of the leap—at the conference. Although Mao also endorsed a substantial slowdown in the Great Leap's ambitious policies of dramatically increasing steel production and relying on the people's communes for dramatic increases in grain output, Mao denounced Peng's letter as "bourgeois" and called for extensive criticism of the defense minister and his supporters in the top leadership, such as Zhang Wentian and Huang Kecheng. Peng Dehuai was forced to make a "self-criticism" (q.v.) at the meeting and even before the meeting was over a nationwide campaign against "rightism" was launched to ferret out purported supporters of Peng and other critics of the Great Leap. Although Peng lost the political battle, he won the war over policy as the Party ordered substantial reductions in the ambitious planned production targets for steel, coal, food, and cotton, thereby signaling the first significant slowdown in the frenetic effort of the Great Leap to alter radically China's economy in one fell swoop. The divisions revealed at the Lushan Conference between Mao's "leftist" policies and the "right" opposition would continue to fester throughout the 1960s and ultimately lead to Mao Zedong's dramatic attack on Party leaders and rank-and-file cadres (q.v.) during the Cultural Revolution (1966–1976) (q.v.).

LUSHAN CONFERENCE (1970). This conference marked a split between Mao Zedong (q.v.) and his personally chosen successor Lin Biao (q.v.). Mao's "closest comrade in arms" and minister of defense, Marshal Lin Biao was named at the CCP's (q.v.) 1969 Ninth Party Congress as Mao's constitutionally designated heir after the purge during the Cultural Revolution (1966–1976) (q.v.) of Liu Shaoqi (q.v.), Mao's first heir apparent. In the context of a restoration of the CCP apparatus that had largely been destroyed during the Cultural Revolution and a concomitant reduction in the influence of the PLA (q.v.), Lin Biao's cordial relationship with Mao was suddenly rent with tensions that spewed forth at this conference. Despite Mao's repeated opposition to reestablishing the largely honorific post of the presidency (q.v.), which had disappeared at the beginning of the Cultural Revolution, Lin Biao raised this issue at the conference and further irritated the chairman by promoting a theory of "genius" that Mao had also rejected. Underlying the tension between the two was Mao's growing concern with the military threat of the Soviet Union and the rise to prominence in the foreign policy arena of the more moderate Zhou Enlai (q.v.). Intensely anti-American, Lin Biao was concerned with Zhou's proposals for rapprochement with the United

States and did not believe that the Soviet Union was China's primary enemy—a position advocated by both Zhou and Mao. Following his political loss of face at the Lushan Conference and obvious vulnerability to Mao's lack of faith in his successor, Lin allegedly attempted an ill-fated coup d'état against Mao Zedong—code named Project 571 (q.v.)—that failed and ultimately led to Lin's reported death in an air crash while trying to escape to the Soviet Union.

M

MANCHURIA. This is the large swath of territory in China's northeast that currently encompasses four provinces: Heilongjiang, Jilin, Liaoning, and parts of Inner Mongolia. A quarter the size of China proper yet with only one-tenth the population, Manchuria was for centuries a frontier region of the Chinese empire. Southernmost Manchuria was known as Liaodong ("East of the River") and included the Liaodong Peninsula, which had been part of ancient China since the Han dynasty (202 B.C.–A.D 220). The northernmost parts of Manchuria were incorporated into China by the Qing dynasty (1644–1911) and included large areas that were subsequently ceded to Russia. Historically, Manchuria was the place north of the Great Wall where Chinese and "barbarians" from Siberia and nearby regions intermingled and where Chinese peasants were often subject to "barbarian" rule. The Qing dynasty, China's last, consisted of Manchu rulers from Manchuria who, like the Mongols, conquered the Chinese state and imposed a political structure that was a synthesis of Chinese and Manchu institutions and customs.

In the modern era, Manchuria has been the frequent target of foreign interests and conquests. Because it is rich in raw materials and situated strategically vis-à-vis Korea and Japan, Manchuria was a target for Russian and Japanese expansionism in the late nineteenth and early twentieth centuries. In 1858 and 1860, the Chinese and Russians signed the Treaty of Aigun and the Treaty of Peking, respectively, which ceded vast territories to the Russians and gave Russia permanent control over the maritime province in Manchuria between the Ussuri River and the Pacific. The Ussuri and Amur rivers in Manchuria were established as the formal borders between China and Russia.

Following the Sino-Japanese war in 1895, won by Japan, Russian influence in the region peaked in 1898 when Russia was granted a 25-year lease over the Liaodong peninsula and construction began on the strategic Chinese Eastern and the South Manchurian railways, linking the western and eastern and northern and southern sections, respectively, of Manchuria. The Chinese city of Lushun was renamed Port

Arthur and a large Russian presence was established in Harbin, largely at the expense of the indigenous Manchus. In return, Russia aided China in its confrontation with Japan over the issue of control of Korea.

In 1905, Russian expansion into Manchuria was halted by the Japanese defeat of Russian forces during the Russo-Japanese War and as Japanese forces entered Manchuria for the first time. The September 1905 Treaty of Portsmouth, mediated by the United States, restored Chinese sovereignty over Manchuria, but enhanced the Japanese presence in the region by giving Japan control of the South Manchurian Railway as far north as the city of Changchun. Japanese interests in Manchuria grew exponentially, especially after Korea was annexed in 1910.

Confronting an increasingly assertive and nationalistic China after the rise of the KMT (q.v.) in 1927, the Japanese military in Manchuria (known as the Kwangtung Army) engineered the "Mukden Incident" in September 1931 and launched an all-out military occupation of the region. In 1932, Japan announced the establishment of an independent nation named Manchukuo under the titular authority of the last Qing emperor, the Manchu ruler Puyi. A puppet state, Manchukuo, under the effective control of the Japanese army, stressed industrialization, railway and hydropower construction, and heavy capital investment, as well as dictatorial control over the population. It was from Manchuria that the Japanese attacked China proper in 1937.

The Cairo Declaration issued by the Allies in 1943 during World War II explicitly promised that Manchuria would be returned to China upon defeat of the Japanese Empire. However, the 1945 Yalta Agreement called for reestablishing Russian leases on the Manchurian cities of Port Arthur and Dairen and for partially restoring Russian rights over the Chinese Eastern and the South Manchurian railways, which had been forfeited after the 1905 Russo-Japanese War. Chinese "sovereignty" over the area was reaffirmed in anticipation of protests from the Chinese Nationalist government which had not been invited to the Yalta Conference. Stalin (q.v.), however, promised that Chiang Kai-shek and the Nationalists would be asked to organize the civil administration in the areas in Manchuria under Soviet occupation.

In August 1945 Soviet forces entered Manchuria in great strength and virtually retook the region. New "democratic unions" consisting of resistance fighters against the Japanese under the supervision of the Russians were formed to assume control of the local government. From late August to September 1945, Chinese Nationalist forces with American assistance attempted to enter Manchuria by sea and air, but were effectively blocked by the Soviet troops. In the interim, the Chinese Communists seeped into the region from their bases in north

China and established effective control over many strategic points, including several ports and airfields, and seized large stocks of Japanese weaponry. When the Soviet forces finally evacuated Manchuria in early 1946, the Chinese Communists controlled key communication lines and strategic positions.

During the ensuing Civil War (q.v.), Manchuria emerged as a major strategic area in the conflict between the Nationalists and the Communists. After the defeat of the Nationalists in 1949, Russia retained its interests and privileges under a treaty signed between China and the USSR in February 1950. These were subsequently ceded back to China after the death of Josef Stalin in 1953.

MAO DUN (1896–1981). A renowned novelist, and literary and art critic, after 1949 Mao Dun became China's minister of culture. Originally named Shen Yanbing, Mao Dun was born into a gentry family, and later attended the preparatory college of Peking University (q.v.). In 1916, he began working at the Commercial Press, first as a proofreader, then as a translator and editor. In 1920, as an emerging promising young writer, Shen Yanbing (as he was still known) founded the Literary Study Society, together with his writer friends Ye Shengtao, Xu Yishan, and others. The society emphasized realist literature and literature with a social purpose.

From 1921 to 1923, Shen was the editor of the *Short Story Monthly*, one of the most influential literary publications at the time. After teaching for a short period at a girls' school under the control of the Communists, he joined the left-wing KMT (q.v.) under Wang Jingwei in Chungking (Chongqing). But after the KMT purge of the Communists in 1927, he went to Shanghai (q.v.) and devoted most of his time to creative writing. It was at this time he started using the pen name "Mao Dun" in order to hide his identity.

Between September 1927 and June 1928, Mao Dun completed his famous trilogy "Eclipse" composed of "Disillusion," "Vacillation," and "Pursuit." The trilogy describes the life of revolutionary youth, decadent bourgeoisie, and intellectuals during the Northern Expedition era (1926–1927).

Although Mao Dun was a founding member of the League of Left-Wing Writers in 1930, he did not receive national recognition until the publication of his novel *Twilight* in 1933. An insightful and in-depth study of the complex life of Shanghai during the depression in the 1930s, *Twilight* portrays the ruthlessness and exploitation of capitalist society and confirms the Communist notion that capitalism was a cul-de-sac for China. In 1936, Mao Dun joined Lu Xun (q.v.), Hu Feng (q.v.), and other writers to form the Chinese Literary Workers Association that advocated a people's literature for the national revolutionary struggle. He also produced several short stories during this period, including "Spring Silkworm" and "The Lin Family Shop."

In May 1940 Mao headed for Yan'an where he lectured at the Lu Xun Institute. In 1941, he left for Hong Kong via Chungking where he published another novel, *Putrefaction*, which expresses sympathy for the Communist enterprise and opposition to the KMT. Afterward, Mao Dun moved to Chungking where he worked under Guo Moruo (q.v.) on the cultural committee of the political training board of the National Military Council. After the Sino-Japanese War (q.v.), Mao Dun and his wife toured the Soviet Union in 1947. Upon their return in 1948, Mao Dun founded the pro-Communist *Fiction Monthly* in Hong Kong.

After the Communist takeover in 1949, Mao Dun returned to Beijing (q.v.) and was subsequently elected vice chairman of the All-China Federation of Literary Workers (later the Writers Union) under Guo Moruo. In 1954, Mao Dun was appointed minister of culture, and was later elected a deputy to the First NPC (q.v.). During the Hundred Flowers campaign (q.v.) in 1957, Mao Dun attacked the conformity of the Communist literary community and as a result, he was subsequently removed from his position as minister of culture and, like other intellectuals (q.v.), suffered during the Cultural Revolution (1966–1976) (q.v.).

With the downfall of the radical Gang of Four (q.v.) in 1976, Mao Dun reemerged as a vice chairman of the CPPCC (q.v.), and in 1979, he was reelected chairman of the Writers Union. He died at the age of 85 on March 27, 1981.

MAO YUANXIN (1939–). Born in Hunan province, Mao Yuanxin was a nephew of Mao Zedong (q.v.). He first studied in the Soviet Union and in 1959 became a student at the Harbin Military Engineering Academy, joining the CCP (q.v.). In 1964, Mao Yuanxin became a lecturer at the Harbin Academy and during the Cultural Revolution (1966–1976) (q.v.) he rose to prominence as director of the Shenyang Municipal PLA (q.v.) Infantry School and political commissar (q.v.) of the Shenyang Military Region. Mao Yuanxin also served as Party secretary of Liaoning province and a special liaison to Mao Zedong. In October 1976, after the death of Mao Zedong, Mao Yuanxin was relieved of all his formal positions in the PLA and CCP.

MAO ZEDONG (1893–1976). Chairman of the CCP from 1938 until his death in September 1976, Mao Zedong was the paramount leader of the Chinese Communist revolution.

Mao Zedong was born in Shaoshan, Hunan province into a rich

peasant family, receiving a traditional primary education. Later he ran away from home to attend middle school. In 1911, he was enrolled in what was soon to become the Hunan First Normal School. With the help of a friend, he established the New People's Study Society which subsequently became the core of the CCP (q.v.) in Hunan. After graduation, Mao worked as a library assistant at Beida (Peking University) (q.v.) where he became involved with other activist students and was influenced by Beida professor and co-founder of the CCP, Li Dazhao. Following the 1919 May Fourth Movement, Mao helped organize a Hunan student organization. Two of Mao's journals—*Xiang River Review* and *New Hunan*—were shut down by the authorities. After becoming involved in a student strike targeted at the Hunan governor, Mao was compelled to flee Hunan, so he traveled to Beijing (q.v.) and Shanghai (q.v.) where he met Chen Duxiu, the leading intellectual who later became the first general secretary of the CCP. Mao was able to return to Hunan in 1920 and became head of the primary school attached to the Hunan First Normal School. Mao married Yang Kaihui and also opened a radical bookstore. Later, after the arrival of Comintern agent Gregory Voitinsky in China, Mao organized a Communist cell and a Socialist Youth League branch in Changsha, Hunan.

In July 1921 on a boat in a lake located in Shanghai, Mao participated in the First Party Congress of the CCP, which then consisted of sixty members. At the Third Party Congress, held in Canton in 1923, Mao was elected to the CCP Central Committee for the first time. During the first KMT-CCP United Front (q.v.), Mao was given several positions in the KMT (q.v.). In 1926, Mao became director of the sixth class of the Peasant Movement Training Institute in Canton. In December of that year, he promoted the importance of the peasant issue and called for intensified revolutionary action. In March 1927, Mao wrote a report that advocated harnessing peasant discontent as the great social force of the revolution. In mid-1927, the KMT-CCP First United Front fell apart following Chiang Kai-shek's coup against the CCP in Shanghai. This experience confirmed Mao's belief that "political power grows out of the barrel of a gun" (*qiangganzi limian chu zhengquan*). After the failure of the Autumn Harvest Uprising in September-October 1927, Mao led some of the survivors of the movement to the mountains between Hunan and Jiangxi provinces. In April 1928, Mao's troops were joined by reinforcements led by Zhu De (q.v.) at Jinggangshan. Following the establishment of the Chinese Soviet Republic in late 1931, although Mao held two top positions in the government and the military, he lacked influence in the Party which at that time was manipulated by the Twenty-Eight Bolsheviks who had trained in the USSR. By the time the Chinese

Soviet Republic collapsed during Chiang Kai-shek's final encirclement campaigns, Mao had lost all his authority within the CCP.

At the Zunyi Conference in 1935, Mao reassumed control over
Communist military forces. In 1938 he was made chairman of the
CCP. After the arduous Long March (q.v.) of more than six thousand
Chinese *li* (li = one half kilometer), Mao and his forces established a
base in Yan'an. During the 1942–1944 Rectification Campaign (q.v.)
in Yan'an, Mao consolidated his political authority and in 1943 he
promulgated his personality cult (q.v.). At the 1945 Seventh Party
Congress, Mao defeated the Twenty-Eight Bolshevik faction and advocated the Sinicization of Marxist-Leninist ideology to meet the cir-
cumstances and needs of the Communist revolution in China. Mao
abandoned his second wife, He Zizhen, whom he had married in 1931
after his first wife was murdered by the KMT. He married, for the
third time, an actress from Shanghai named Lan Ping whom Mao
called Jiang Qing (q.v.). By the time the Japanese were defeated in
China in 1945, the CCP had vastly expanded its power in China.
However, since Mao's troops were outnumbered by the KMT forces,
Mao initially favored cooperation with the KMT. Nonetheless, the
diametrically opposed differences between the two parties finally trig-
gered the civil war (q.v.) that lasted from 1946–1949. On October 1,
1949, Mao proclaimed the establishment of the PRC (q.v.). In February 1950, Mao signed the Sino-Soviet Treaty of Friendship in Moscow, despite ill treatment by Josef Stalin (q.v.).

The initial politics of Mao's regime followed the mild prescriptions
of the New Democracy (q.v.). Mao was instrumental, however, in
convincing Stalin to sanction the North Korean attack on South
Korea, thereby igniting the Korean War (1950–1953) (q.v.). China's
decision to enter the war was made by Mao himself, after offers of
Soviet military assistance in the form of air support were initially
made and then withdrawn by Stalin. Throughout the 1950s, Mao's
China was under the strong influence of the Soviet Union and, until
Josef Stalin's death in 1953, the policies of the Soviet leader. During
the succession crisis in the Soviet Union, Mao supported Gregori Ma-
lenkov who ultimately lost out to Nikita Khrushchev. Although
Mao's initial relations with Khrushchev were warm, the two leaders
gradually became embroiled in a mutual animosity that ultimately led
to the Sino-Soviet conflict (q.v.). Domestically, Mao resisted family
planning policies and denounced advocates of these policies, such as
Ma Yinchu.

Beginning in 1955, Mao generally supported the radical reorganization of Chinese agriculture. In 1957 he initiated the Hundred Flowers campaign (q.v.) against the advice of top Party leaders and subsequently launched the Anti-Rightist campaign (q.v.). All these

movements brought much suffering to the intellectuals (q.v.) and alienated them from the Party. In 1958, Mao switched gears and initiated the Great Leap Forward (q.v.), which ended in a human tragedy that involved upwards of 30 million deaths. Although China gradually recovered from the post-Leap depression, Mao viewed the situation with great apprehension and grew more alienated from the intellectuals, who resented and ridiculed him. In 1962, Mao insisted on the need for "class struggle" (q.v.) in the countryside, and in 1966, he initiated the Cultural Revolution (1966–1976) (q.v.), which aimed at eliminating all opposition to his policies in the CCP. The Cultural Revolution lasted for 10 years during which Mao was elevated to near "god" status in the CCP and Chinese society. In the 1970s, Mao ended the diplomatic isolation of China by sanctioning contacts with the United States that led to the establishment of diplomatic relations. Domestically, Mao engineered the return of Deng Xiaoping (q.v.) in 1973 to run the CCP, but acquiesced to Deng's purge in 1976 following the April 5th Tiananmen Incident (q.v.). Estranged for years from his wife, Jiang Qing, Mao apparently resisted any attempts by Madame Mao to gain control of the CCP and publicly criticized her factional tendencies.

Mao Zedong died in September 1976 at the age of 82. His body is encased in a crystal sarcophagus in the Mao Zedong Memorial Hall in Beijing. The "Resolution on Some Historical Questions in the History of Our Party Since the Establishment of the PRC" (q.v.) passed in June 1981 evaluated Mao's contributions to the Chinese revolution, but made note of some of his shortcomings in his later years. In the early 1990s, the Maoist revival—or Mao Craze—in China filled the ideological vacuum created by the Tiananmen massacre.

MAO ZEDONG THOUGHT STUDY CLASSES. Organized in response to Mao Zedong's May 7, 1966, letter to Lin Biao (q.v.) in which the Party chairman urged Lin to "turn the whole country into a great school of Mao Zedong Thought," Mao Zedong Thought Study Classes were an integral part of the May 7 Cadre Schools (q.v.). Set up during the Cultural Revolution (1966–1976) (q.v.), these classes became centers for cadres (q.v.) to practice criticism and self-criticism (q.v.).

MARRIAGE LAW. Since 1949 China has formally enacted two marriage laws. The first was promulgated in May 1950 by the Central People's Government and remained in force for thirty years. The second marriage law was adopted in September 1980 by the Third Session of the Fifth NPC (q.v.) and as of 1997 remains in force.

The 1950 Marriage Law attempted to deal with iniquities in relationships between men and women and husbands and wives that had been part of Chinese tradition for centuries. This was reflected in Article 1 of the law, which affirmed that "the arbitrary and compulsory feudal marriage system, which is based on the superiority of men over women and which ignores the children's interests shall be abolished." The law then went on to outlaw such traditional practices as bigamy, concubinage, child betrothal, interference with the remarriage of widows, and the exaction of money or gifts in connection with marriage. Instead, the law called for marriage to be consummated by a "contract" based upon the willingness of the two parties in which both husband and wife could retain their family name and could inherit each other's property. The right to divorce, initiated by either party, was also written into the law, though with some restrictions (discussed below).

Children were also granted certain rights, such as that of inheriting property. There were also obligations on the part of parents, regarding the rearing and educating of children. Infanticide was strictly forbidden and declared a "criminal act." Among the restrictions included were a minimum age for marriage (male 20 years, female 18 years); prohibition to marry if one party is sexually impotent; and a stipulation that "the husband shall not apply for a divorce when his wife is with child." It was also declared that divorce could only be granted upon mediation by the subdistrict of the People's Government, a process that was obligated by the law as a means of seeking reconciliation. In practice, divorces initiated by the wife resulted in the government requiring efforts at reconciliation, while divorces initiated by the husband were more often granted outright. Application of the law was allowed a certain flexibility in national minority (q.v.) areas where unconventional marriage practices were still practiced.

The 1980 Marriage Law was promulgated largely in response to changes in China's demographic situation. Unlike the 1950 law, the new legislation required couples to practice family planning. It also increased the legal age for marriage to 22 years for the male and 20 years for the woman. Both husband and wife were also given the freedom to engage in productive work. Other prohibitions and enumerated rights included in the 1950 law were repeated in the 1980 version, such as the outlawing of bigamy, "mercenary marriages," and the rights of children following a divorce. In the 1980 law the mother was given preference in custody battles when they involved a breast-fed child. Reflecting recent social changes in China, children born out of wedlock were accorded the same rights as children of married couples. The 1950 law was declared null and void as a result of the new 1980 legislation.

MARXISM-LENINISM–MAO ZEDONG THOUGHT. This constituted the major components of China's official ideology that provided the guiding principles for the CCP (q.v.) and the Chinese state. From Marxism the Chinese took "historical materialism" (the theory that the mode of production determines the social and political structure of any society), "class struggle" (q.v.) (the idea that human history is the history of violent struggles between social classes), and "dialectical materialism" (the view that fundamental contradictions between property systems and modes of production generate the dynamic for fundamental social and political change), plus a vision for a final Communist utopia. From Lenin, China borrowed his theory of imperialism (q.v.), which professed that class struggle had reached an international level of conflict between capitalist imperialist states and the proletariat in Third World nations. Lenin's theory of the Party as the "vanguard of the proletariat" is also a centerpiece of Chinese Communist ideology.

Mao Zedong Thought is laid out in the five volumes of his *Selected Works* and contains such innovative notions as the peasantry forming the basis of the socialist revolution (undoubtedly a heretical thought to Marx, who preached that the proletariat was the vanguard revolutionary class), the "mass line" (q.v.), the emphasis on the integration of theory and practice, and the concepts of "contradictions" (*maodun*) (q.v.) and "uninterrupted revolution" (q.v.). In the CCP Central Committee 1981 "Resolution on Certain Questions in the History of Our Party" (q.v.), some of Mao Zedong's policies and decisions are criticized, but Mao Zedong Thought is deemed to be "a correct theory" that had been collectively formulated by Mao and other top CCP leaders. To "negate entirely Mao Zedong Thought," it was declared in 1978, would cause China to revert to pre-1949 conditions.

"MASS LINE" (*QUNZHONG LUXIAN*). A staple feature of Mao Zedong's (q.v.) revolutionary theory was that the masses of workers and peasants in China should be relied on by the CCP (q.v.) to achieve its revolutionary goals. Theoretically, this conflicted with Lenin's more authoritarian notion that the "spontaneity" of the general population could not be trusted and would derail the ultimate goals of the revolution. In Lenin's view, workers were burdened by a "trade union mentality" that fixated concerns on bread and butter issues at the expense of the more historically significant goal of building socialism (q.v.). Russian peasants in this formulation were even more ideologically "backward," concerned solely with narrow goals of acquiring land. For Lenin, the revolutionary intelligentsia of Communist Party members alone sparked the drive toward socialism (q.v.).

Mao's "mass line" concept was fundamentally different from that of Lenin, though the Chinese leader did not reject the critical role of the Party, nor did he impart to the worker and peasant masses anything remotely comparable to political sovereignty. Instead, the "mass line" meant that "in all practical work of our Party, all correct leadership is necessarily 'from the masses, to the masses.'" The Party would be successful if it were to incorporate the views of the masses into its political formulations and policy positions, and were to test these policies out among the masses. Of course, Mao Zedong provided no institutional mechanisms either for transmitting popular views to the CCP, or for ensuring that the Party sought popular endorsement. The "mass line" consisted of moral and political guidance from the top leaders to Party cadres (q.v.) that certainly was not followed in many cases when popular dissatisfaction and real human suffering, such as that which occurred in the Great Leap Forward (1958–1960) (q.v.), apparently had no impact on CCP policies and decisions.

MAY FOURTH MOVEMENT (1919). The Chinese Communist Party (q.v.) traces its origins to this student protest movement that broke out in Beijing (q.v.) in spring 1919. Inspired by the principles of self-determination promoted at the Versailles conference by U.S. President Woodrow Wilson, the Chinese had hoped to win back the territories controlled by foreign powers. Instead, territorial concessions in China's Shandong province were taken from Germany, as a result of its defeat in World War I, and transferred to Japan, which had been an ally of the victorious Western powers. The acceptance of this decision by the Chinese government infuriated students, intellectuals (q.v.), and some workers, who organized major street protests. The movement quickly expanded into a demand for fundamental "democratic and scientific" changes in Chinese society. Exhibiting a profound cultural iconoclasm, leaders of the May Fourth Movement, such as Chen Duxiu, a Peking University (q.v.) professor, advocated totalistic changes in Chinese government, society, and culture. This included calls for transforming the country's written language from its classical origins into a more colloquial form and access to broader education for the population. University and popular journals flourished during the late 1910s and early 1920s as the general level of public opinion increased. At the end of the May Fourth Movement, the CCP was organized in 1921 by Chen Duxiu and many other veterans of the May Fourth Movement. *See* LANGUAGE REFORM.

MAY SEVENTH CADRE SCHOOLS. Established in the 1960s on the basis of a letter written by Mao Zedong (q.v.) to Lin Biao (q.v.) on May 7, 1966, these schools were assigned the task of sending cadres (q.v.) to the countryside to engage in manual labor. In reality, they were no different from the Draconian labor reform camps that the CCP (q.v.) had set up to incarcerate political criminals and other people designated by the regime as socially and politically undesirable. In the Maoist perspective, CCP cadres had spent too much time in their offices shuffling papers, where they remained aloof from the interests of the workers and peasants whose interests the CCP theoretically promoted by "building socialism." The first such "schools" were set up in the northeast, often on farms in remote areas where cadres performed menial tasks and grew their own food. These experiences were to counter the pervasive tendency among cadres toward "bureaucratism" (q.v.) that had, in the Maoist view, infected the CCP and all Chinese government organizations. Altogether, 3 million officials and cadres spent varying amounts of time at such "schools" while they retained their official positions and salaries. After a few weeks or months, they returned to their official duties. The May 7 cadre schools were abolished sometime in the 1970s.

MAY SIXTEENTH CIRCULAR. Issued on May 16, 1966, by the CCP (q.v.) Central Committee, this document revoked the "February Outline" and disbanded the first Cultural Revolution Small Group (q.v.) that had been established by Beijing mayor and veteran CCP leader Peng Zhen (q.v.) to carry out Mao's initial calls for a "cultural revolution." To Mao's consternation, Peng and his Cultural Revolution Small Group had tried to limit the issues of the "cultural revolution" (q.v.) to literary matters among a small group of Chinese intellectuals. This circular represented Mao's attempt to expand the revolution to major political issues involving the structure of the state, the course of CCP policies, and the composition of the leadership. A new Cultural Revolution Small Group was set up to report directly to the Standing Committee of the Politburo (q.v.) that was under Mao's control. Ultra-leftist (q.v.) organizations during the Cultural Revolution were called "May 16 Corps" to legitimize their radical political objectives.

MEETINGS TO RECOLLECT PAST BITTERNESS. The Chinese Communist government has constantly emphasized in its propaganda the great contrasts between the "past bitterness" of the general population prior to the Communist takeover in 1949 and the "present happiness" of the people after 1949. This message was institutionalized in mass meetings held throughout the Maoist years (1949–1976) at which older workers and peasants with vivid memories of the past would recall to younger audiences the sufferings that they had endured under the previous KMT (q.v.) regime. These descriptions were often supplemented by such activities as the preparation of meals for the young people composed of extremely scant fare such as wild fruits and plant roots, which were similar to the meals that many of the poor had depended on for sustenance before 1949. This "class education" aimed at presenting stark contrasts between the KMT past and the Communist present. Not all such meetings were successful, however, as some politically naive workers and peasants contrasted the Communist present to the KMT past in unfavorable terms. "The food was really good back then [i.e., prior to 1949]" was how some peasants described the past to the young students, to the obvious consternation of CCP (q.v.) propagandists.

MILITARY AFFAIRS COMMISSION (MAC). This body is directly under the authority of the CCP Politburo (q.v.) and its Standing Committee (q.v.) and is charged with maintaining Communist Party control over the PLA (q.v.). The primary function of the MAC is to appoint and remove military personnel, especially the commanders of the key military regions (q.v.). Through its control of the General Political Department, the MAC is also responsible for the political education of PLA troops, a tradition that dates back to the 1930s when the Revolutionary Military Committee headed by Mao Zedong (q.v.) performed this role. There are from ten to twenty top military and Party leaders on the MAC, all of whom also serve on the Politburo and the Central Committee of the CCP. The MAC chairman is China's commander in chief; historically this has been the Party chairman (and later general secretary). This was not the case, however, from 1981 to 1989 when Deng Xiaoping (q.v.) served as MAC chairman—a key strategic post—although he did not still hold the Party's top position. Deng's effort to install his first designated successor, Hu Yaobang (q.v.), as chairman of the MAC failed and helped precipitate Hu's fall from power in 1987. Since 1989, however, the MAC chairmanship has been held by Jiang Zemin, concurrently CCP general secretary, thereby reestablishing the previous tradition initially introduced by Mao Zedong. The MAC includes a standing committee composed of the vice chairmen (traditionally, the minister of defense, concurrently) and the PLA chief of staff. In 1995, China's top military officers, including Admiral Liu Huaqing, General Zhang Zhen, and General Chi Haotian, were MAC members. Approval of the MAC chairman is needed to move an entire army, as evidently occurred during the June 1989 Beijing massacre. A state MAC also exists and includes generally the same members as that of the CCP MAC, yet without apparent authority.

MILITARY REGIONS. *See* PEOPLE'S LIBERATION ARMY.

MINISTRY OF FOREIGN ECONOMIC RELATIONS AND TRADE (MOFERT). Established in 1982, MOFERT was created by merging the Ministry of Foreign Trade with the Foreign Investment Control Commission and the Import-Export Commission. It was designed to coordinate policy in both trade and foreign investment matters, including joint ventures, and to gain greater control over China's growing economic relations with the outside world. This involves the establishment of a licensing system for both imports and exports, the imposition of export duties to curb the export of goods in short supply, and the setting up of offices at China's major trading ports. MOFERT also plays a role in mapping out China's overall economic strategy in its foreign economic relations.

MINORITIES. Some 91 million people in China belong to more than 50 officially recognized minority groups, constituting about 8 percent of the country's total population. The largest of the minority groups are the Zhuang (13 million) in the Guangxi Autonomous Region in the southwest; Chinese Muslims or Hui (7 million) and Uygurs (6 million) in the Xinjiang Autonomous Region in the northwest; Mongols (3 million) in Inner Mongolia; and Tibetans (4 million) in Tibet (q.v.) or Xizang. Others include the Yi, Miao, Manchus, and Koreans, totaling approximately 16 million. Minorities constitute a majority of the population in Tibet and Inner Mongolia and they inhabit more than 90 percent of China's strategic border areas.

Immediately after 1949, central policy toward minorities in China relied heavily on coercive measures that were used to incorporate minority areas, such as Tibet and Xinjiang, under Chinese rule. Yet under the guise of constitutionally defined "autonomous regions" most minorities in China were granted limited self-governance and considerable freedom to practice their indigenous cultures, including the use of their native languages. From the Anti-Rightist campaign (1957–1958) (q.v.) and Great Leap Forward (1958–1959) (q.v.) through the Cultural Revolution (1966–1976) (q.v.), however, the Center imposed tighter controls on minority areas and extended political campaigns and persecutions into the minority areas. Local minority political leaders, such as Ulanfu (q.v.) of Inner Mongolia, were accused of "local nationalism" and purged, while minority cultural artifacts, such as temples and religious shrines, were wantonly destroyed, particularly by Red Guards (q.v.) during the Cultural Revolution. Minorities were also forced, contrary to past policies, to learn the Chinese language and to reorganize their social and economic systems along the "socialist" lines dictated by Beijing (q.v.). Central policies such as "planting grain everywhere" were imposed, for instance in Tibet, with catastrophic consequences because the area's climatic conditions were ill-suited to this policy. Since 1976, Beijing has relaxed its policies toward minorities and encouraged minority elites to join the CCP (q.v.) while promoting prominent minority leaders, such as Ulanfu, to high-level positions. Yet ethnic tensions exist in both Tibet and Xinjiang where armed conflicts have broken out, such as during the April 1990 "holy war" in the city of Kashgar. *See also* HAN.

MOVEMENT TO RESIST U.S. AGGRESSION AND AID KOREA. The Korean War (q.v.) commenced in June 1950 with the North Korean invasion of South Korea. Chinese troops, called "volunteers," intervened on the side of North Korean forces in October 1950. The "Movement to Resist U.S. Aggression and Aid Korea" aimed at mobilizing domestic support—material and psychological—for the Chinese war effort in Korea. Supplies of food and clothing were gathered for troops at the front, while an intense anti-American campaign was whipped up among the population. Americans who had stayed behind in China after the Communist takeover in 1949, and had up until the war lived in relative freedom, were then rounded up, imprisoned, and in many cases accused of spying. The movement came to an end after the Korean armistice in July 1953.

"MUTUAL AID TEAMS" (*HUZHU ZU*). The most rudimentary form of mutual cooperation in the Chinese countryside, the Mutual Aid Teams (MATs) were first experimented with by the CCP (q.v.) in the 1940s in the "liberated" areas of northwest China. After 1949, the formation of MATs throughout the Chinese countryside constituted the first stage in the reorganization of rural production. By late 1952, 40 percent of all rural households were organized into teams. In 1955 MATs were replaced by the APCs (q.v.).

Mutual Aid Teams were implemented throughout China after the promulgation of the Decision on Mutual Aid and Cooperation in Agriculture in 1951 by the Central Committee of the CCP. Theoretically, peasant participation in the MATs was voluntary, but considerable political pressure was brought to bear by rural Party cadres (q.v.) on individual peasant households. One type of temporary MATs were organized on a seasonal basis (sowing and harvest) and were generally quite small, constituting less than ten peasant households that worked on individually owned land that had been distributed during Land Reform (q.v.). Labor, tools, and draft animals were shared, but with no transfer of ownership or control. Another type of year-round fixed Mutual Aid Teams were larger-scale, generally comprising from ten to thirty peasant households. Work points (q.v.) were allocated and tools and draft animals were subject to common ownership. Agricultural production was carried out in the permanent MATs along with sideline production and a rudimentary division of labor for technical work, though land ownership was left essentially untouched for everyone except the landlords. A third type of MATs were, in effect, lower forms of APCs, involving the pooling of shares of land and labor. The move to APCs began to be implemented in 1953 with the promulgation of the Decision on the Development of APCs by the CCP as MATs were effectively abandoned for a higher form of "socialized" agriculture.

N

NATIONAL PEOPLE'S CONGRESS (NPC). The highest government organ in China, the NPC has constitutional powers similar to legislative bodies in other nations, yet without the real authority because this still lies with the CCP (q.v.). Eight NPCs have been convened, three at four-year intervals from 1954 to 1964, and five at five-year intervals from 1975 to the present. During the Cultural Revolution (1966–1976) (q.v.) and in the midst of the Lin Biao affair (q.v.), the NPC did not meet, and seven years transpired between the Fourth NPC in 1975 and the Fifth in 1982. The number of delegates to the NPC have varied from 1,200 in the 1950s to around 2,000 in the 1980s and 1990s when the Sixth through the Eighth NPCs were convened. Representation to the NPC is malapportioned, with a ratio of one delegate to every one million rural residents and one delegate to every 130,000 urban residents.

Full NPC sessions meet for a period of about two weeks usually immediately following the meeting of the CPPCC (q.v.). These sessions are devoted to reports by government officials, which are discussed, and formally approved by votes of the delegates. Four different state constitutions have been approved by the NPC since 1954. During the sessions, regional groups of delegates meet and engage oftentimes in real policy debates, though most NPC sessions are noted for their strict formality and rubber-stamping of government reports. An internal CCP document leaked by a Chinese reporter in the early 1990s indicated that all NPC decisions are cleared ahead of time by top Party leaders, all of whom sit in major government and NPC positions. Many delegates "elected" to the NPC are model workers and peasants with little legislative experience or acumen. Yet in the early 1980s intense debate among delegates was allowed— apparently at the behest of Deng Xiaoping (q.v.)—as part of the reform of the political structure. In April 1992, for example, 30 percent of the delegates refused to vote in favor of a resolution authorizing construction of the controversial Three Gorges Dam project (q.v.). And at the Eighth NPC in March 1993, 11 percent of the delegates voted "no" or abstained in the reelection of Li Peng as state premier, obviously in reaction to Li's role in the 1989 Beijing massacre. Overall, however, in spite of the enormous size of the NPC, its sessions are generally politically quiescent.

The executive arm of the NPC is its Standing Committee which meets when the full NPC is not in session. Elected theoretically by the NPC, the Standing Committee members exercise all the powers of the full body, including the enactment and amending of all laws and formal reorganization of the state structure. The Standing Committee is often used as a rostrum to question major Party initiatives. Most members of the Standing Committee hold high positions in the CCP. Throughout the 1980s, Standing Committee chairman Peng Zhen (q.v.) espoused his conservative views. Although he is said to have pushed for a more independent role for the NPC, he reportedly blocked an effort by reformers to pass a law granting full authority to factory managers, which would have undermined the authority of Party secretaries in the industrial sector. In effect, the Standing Committee of the NPC was used to block further political reforms within the CCP. Qiao Shi (q.v.), a strong advocate of greater legalization in China's political culture, was appointed chairman of the Standing Committee in 1993.

Theoretically, the NPC exercises authority over the entire state apparatus in China. This includes the courts, the State Council (q.v.), and the various state ministries, the state Central Military Commission, and the Procuracy (q.v.). Provincial, county, district, and township people's congresses are also subordinate to the NPC, to which these bodies send delegates. *See also* GOVERNMENT STRUCTURE, MILITARY AFFAIRS COMMISSION, and PROCURACY.

NATIONALIST PARTY. *See* KUOMINTANG.

NEIBU MATERIALS. See INTERNAL MATERIALS.

"NEW AUTHORITARIANISM" (*XIN QUANWEIZHUYI*). This theory propounded in the mid to late 1980s by supporters of CCP (q.v.) General Secretary Zhao Ziyang (q.v.), professes that the modernization of a backward country, such as China, inevitably must pass through a phase when the political system must be centered around a strong, authoritarian leader who serves as the motivating force for change, rather than following a democratic path. Reform and modernization in China require a politically powerful person, such as the kind who has emerged in the East Asian countries of Singapore under Lee Kuan Yew or Taiwan under Chiang Ching-kuo. The new authoritarianism did not emphasize the body politic but the strong leader, who is able to lead a country to realize its modernization smoothly by firmly establishing a free market and an institutionalized structure of legally protected property rights. Only with accumulated power and the use of autocratic authority can such changes be carried out. Similar to Western doctrines of "enlightened despotism" in the eighteenth century, this theory largely disappeared from the Chinese media after Zhao Ziyang's purge following the 1989 Tiananmen crisis.

NEW CHINA NEWS AGENCY (XINHUA). China's national news agency, Xinhua operates under the direct authority of the State Council and is responsible for releasing Party and state documents and important news. Xinhua also gathers and distributes news dispatches from around the world. The Xinhua branch in Hong Kong operated as the de facto representative of the Chinese government in the former British colony until its reversion to China on July 1, 1997.

NEW DEMOCRACY. Mao Zedong's political program for China outlined in a speech by the same name in January 1940 during the Sino-Japanese War (1937–1945) (q.v.). In it Mao declared that the ongoing Chinese revolution "was part of the world revolution" aimed at changing the colonial, semi-colonial, and feudal form of Chinese society into an independent country. Reflecting the CCP's (q.v.) alliance with the KMT (q.v.) in the Second United Front (q.v.), the speech was moderate in tone and in its political proposals, with appeals directed to China's "bourgeois-democratic" forces and promises of their "proper representation" in a system of government based on elections and universal suffrage. Capitalist property, Mao also promised, would not be confiscated, nor would capitalist production be restrained. Land would be redistributed from landlord to peasant under a program of "land to the tiller." Overall, China under the "New Democracy" would have neither a bourgeois nor proletarian dictatorship. Mao's speech "On New Democracy" is in the *Selected Works of Mao Zedong*, Volume II. It is frequently cited by dissident Chinese intellectuals to challenge the CCP dictatorship that, they claim, has violated the basic principles of the "new democracy" since 1949.

NIE RONGZHEN (1899–1992). A participant in the 1919 May Fourth Movement (q.v.) and in the 1920s a natural science student in Belgium and the Soviet Union, during the Long March (q.v.) Nie served under Lin Biao (q.v.). In 1945 he was elected to the CCP (q.v.) Central Committee and in 1949 helped "liberate" Beijing (q.v.). In the early 1950s he was acting PLA (q.v.) chief of staff and one of China's ten marshals. He was also a vice chairman of the National Defense Council. In 1958 he became chairman of the Science and Technology Commission. He was a member of the Politburo (q.v.) from 1966 to 1969 and from 1977 to 1985. During the Cultural Revolution (1966–1976) (q.v.) Nie was instrumental in developing China's nuclear weapons and in insulating the country's nuclear and missile program from interruption by Red Guards (q.v.). In 1983 Nie was elected vice chairman of the Central Military Commission (q.v.). In 1985 he resigned from all his posts. *See also* ATOMIC BOMB.

NIE YUANZI (1921–). Born in Henan province, Nie Yuanzi joined the CCP (q.v.) in 1938 and after 1949 worked for several years for the Harbin municipal government. In 1964, she was appointed secretary of the Party branch in the philosophy department at Beida (Peking University) (q.v.). In May 1966 during the Cultural Revolution (1966–1976) (q.v.), Nie won fame when her big-character poster (q.v.) denouncing the university Party committee for suppressing the student movement was singled out for praise by Mao Zedong (q.v.). This event effectively inaugurated the Cultural Revolution on Beijing's (q.v.) college campuses. During the Cultural Revolution, Nie held the following positions: director of the Leading Group of the Capital University and Middle School Red Guards (q.v.); member of the New Beida Commune; and deputy director of the Beijing Revolutionary Committee (q.v.). At the 1969 Ninth CCP Party Congress, she became an alternate member of the Central Committee, but subsequently lost this position and her Party membership after falling out of political favor. In 1983, Nie was sentenced to seventeen years in prison for "instigating counterrevolutionary crimes" and was deprived of her political rights.

NIXON VISIT (1972). *See* U.S–CHINA RELATIONS.

O

OCTOBER 6TH COUP (1976). *See* JIANG QING.

"ON CONTRADICTIONS" (*MAODUN LUN*). The concept of "contradictions" (*maodun*) is central to Mao Zedong Thought. In an August 1937 speech, Mao laid out his basic notions of contradictions in which he asserted that "internal contradiction" was present "in every single thing" and that this explained all motion and development. Conflict and change were normal aspects of any society and so perfect harmony and consensus, as in traditional Confucian society, were unattainable. In 1957, Mao elaborated on this theory in a speech titled "On the Correct Handling of Contradictions Among the People" in which he postulated that neither socialism nor even communism would end the contradictions between social classes that had produced "class struggle." Mao also referred to two kinds of contradictions: "antagonistic contradictions" between "ourselves and the enemy" and "non-antagonistic contradictions" among the people, including the workers, the peasants, and the other revolutionary classes. According to Mao, "antagonistic contradictions" should be dealt with harshly, but "non-antagonistic contradictions" could be handled with greater moderation. Mao's political purpose in espousing this theory in 1957 was to negate the efforts within the Soviet Union and also among some CCP (q.v.) leaders to terminate "class struggle" and to justify his assaults on political opponents in the CCP, ultimately leading to the Anti-Rightist campaign (q.v.) and the Cultural Revolution (1966–1976) (q.v.).

"ON TEN MAJOR RELATIONSHIPS" (*SHIDA GUANXI*). In a speech delivered in April 1956, CCP (q.v.) Chairman Mao Zedong (q.v.) espoused perhaps his most moderate views on economic and social development in China. Contrary to the one-sided approach to economic development that he would later articulate during the Great Leap Forward (1958–1960) (q.v.) with its emphasis on grandiose schemes and crash programs, "On Ten Major Relationships" outlined a model of development stressing a balance between heavy and light industry, coastal and inland industries, economic construction and national defense, and the interests of the state, the cooperatives, and the individual. Politically, the speech also called for an equalization of interests between the Center and the localities, between revolution and counterrevolution, between Party and non-Party people, and between right and wrong inside and outside the CCP. Socially, Mao stressed an equilibrium between the interests of the Han majority and the various minority nationalities and, internationally, he called for a balanced approach to China's relations with the outside world. Proponents of moderate policies in China would constantly cite this speech as justification in Maoist terms for their proposals.

ONE-CHILD POLICY. The "one child per family" program is the centerpiece of China's current population control campaign. Couples who have only one child receive benefits in the form of monthly subsidies of five yuan for the child until the age of 14, free child health care, subsidized school fees, and preferential housing allocation. Parents who have more than one child (except for those with legal exemptions) may be fined up to 15 percent of one's annual salary, and be denied promotion in one's place of employment. There are no incentives for parents to remain childless. The policy was adopted nationwide in 1980 after extensive experimentation as a response to the expected rise in China's overall birthrate due to the "baby boom" from 1962 to 1970. The policy is credited with reducing the number of expected births by about 35 to 50 million. It is estimated that one-fifth of all Chinese families have one child (approximately 35 million families), almost all of whom live in the urban areas. Difficulties in enforcing the policy stem from the fear by parents that one child, especially if it is a female, will not be sufficient to provide for them in old age. Widespread preference for male offspring is another reason for the difficulties in enforcing the policy, especially in the rural areas. In the mid-1980s, the State Family Planning Commission announced relaxations in the enforcement of the policy as farmers with "special economic difficulties" were allowed to have a second child at an appropriate interval following the birth of the first child. Ethnic minorities (q.v.) and couples in which both the husband and wife are single children can also legally have a second child. And the planned period of the one-child policy was reduced from the initial estimate of 30 to 40 years to only five years (1985–1990). However, no formal termination of the program has been announced. Charges that the policy has encouraged female infanticide and coerced abortions have led to central government efforts to crack down on such practices that are illegal under Chinese law. The imbalances in the sex ratios of female to male infants in 1982 of 100:108 have been cited as possible consequences of the one-child policy, though this figure is no different from that in South Korea where no such policy exists. By 1984, China's birthrate was down to 17.5 per thousand, with a growth rate of 1.1 percent, though in 1985 it rose to 21 per thousand and 1.5 percent, respectively. Persuasion, propaganda, social and medical monitoring, and abortion are all employed to control the population. In 1988, the UN Population Crisis Committee rated China's family planning policy as "excellent," though some critics in the West contend that the one-child policy is a violation of human rights. Indeed, some Chinese fleeing to the West have cited the one-child policy as the reason for their escape. In China, it is the social consequences of the policy that are feared, namely the spoiling of the one child, especially if it is a son, by parents, grandparents, and neighbors, producing an entire generation of children that some have characterized as "little emperors."

ONE COUNTRY, TWO SYSTEMS. This is the guiding concept promulgated by the CCP (q.v.) leadership to incorporate Hong Kong, Macao, and Taiwan into the PRC (q.v.). While mainland China will remain "socialist," these territories will be allowed to retain their "capitalist" social system as Special Administrative Regions for a considerable period of time after "reunification with the motherland." In this way, the process of incorporation will be less disruptive. The concept was introduced by Deng Xiaoping (q.v.) in the late 1970s and early 1980s in proposals made to Great Britain to reunify Hong Kong after 1997 in order that the two diametrically opposed social systems of the PRC and the British colony could coexist under one sovereign government. In the Sino-British Joint Declaration on the Question of Hong Kong initialed by the PRC and Great Britain in 1984, China declared that "the current social and economic systems in Hong Kong will remain unchanged, and so will the life-style. Rights and freedoms, including those of the person, of speech, of the press, of assembly, of association, of travel, of movement, of correspondence, of strike, of choice, of occupation, of academic research, and of religious belief will be ensured by law in the Hong Kong Special Administrative Region." Private property and ownership of enterprise were also guaranteed. But because the PRC retains the power to appoint the chief executive of the Hong Kong Special Administrative Region and given that China has disbanded the local democratically elected Legislative Council in Hong Kong, there is concern that Hong Kong's autonomy will not be respected, that an authoritarian system will be gradually imposed on the colony, and corruption (q.v.) endemic on the mainland will infect Hong Kong's administrative organs and police. The PRC has offered the same concept of "one country, two systems" as a model of reunification to Taiwan, but the KMT government asserts that mainland China must first abandon its one-party Communist dictatorship and respect the Three Principles of the People advocated by Sun Yat-sen. *See also* BASIC LAW OF HONG KONG, KUOMINTANG, and TAIWAN.

"ONE DIVIDES INTO TWO" (*YIFENWEIER*). This philosophical concept became a hot-button polemical issue during the Cultural Revolution (1966–1976) (q.v.) that gained enormous political significance. "One divides into two" was defended against the opposite philosophical concept that "two merge into one." The former was defended by the radical political forces to provide a "scientific," philosophical basis for "uninterrupted revolution" (q.v.) and for the political struggle between the bourgeoisie and proletariat. In the pseudo-scientific terminology of Marxist-Leninist philosophy, Chinese radical intellectuals proclaimed that "one divides into two" was the essence of the "law of the unity of opposites," which was a "fundamental law of the universe." Applied to the political realm, it promised unending struggle as the necessary basis for progress in human history. "Two merge into one," the radicals claimed, provided the philosophical basis for class reconciliation, class cooperation, and the elimination of class struggle—"bourgeois" and "revisionist" (q.v.) viewpoints that purportedly indicated the presence of "capitalist roaders" (q.v.) in the CCP (q.v.). This polemical and philosophical debate essentially ended with the Cultural Revolution and the death of Mao Zedong (q.v.) in 1976.

ONE-MAN MANAGEMENT. *See* ENTERPRISE REFORM.

"OPEN-DOOR POLICY" (*KAIFANG ZHENGCE*). A fundamental tenet of the economic reforms initiated by Deng Xiaoping (q.v.) in the late 1970s, this policy aims primarily at opening China's doors to foreign investment and technology. The essence of the open door (a term also used for the U.S. mid-nineteenth century policy toward China) have been the Special Economic Zones (q.v.) and joint ventures. As of 1992, a total of 40,000 foreign investment agreements had been signed with China, totaling more than $58 billion in investment pledges and $16 billion in actual investments. In 1994 alone, China approved $82 billion in foreign investments, with $34 billion in actual investments. Hong Kong and Macao rank first in actual investment, Taiwan second, the U.S. third, and Japan fourth.

The open-door policy directly contradicted Mao Zedong's autarkic policy of economic self-reliance (q.v.) that China has all but abandoned since 1978, though not without some resistance among conservative hard-line factions in the CCP (q.v.) who fear economic dependence and the erosion of socialist ideology. Indeed, foreign investment and increased interaction with the outside world, such as student exchanges, have brought an invasion of non-Communist ideological and cultural influences that the CCP has periodically condemned as "flies and germs." Periodic campaigns against foreign influences, such as the 1983 Anti-Spiritual Pollution campaign (q.v.) and the 1986–1987 Anti-Bourgeois Liberalization campaign (q.v.), have come and gone with little apparent effect, especially on China's youth. Despite such corrosive influences, however, China's top leadership shows little inclination to reverse the fundamentals of the open door.

ORGANIZATION DEPARTMENT. *See* CHINESE COMMUNIST PARTY.

P

"PAPER TIGER" (*ZHI LAOHU*). This was a term of opprobrium and contempt first used by Mao Zedong (q.v.) in 1946 to deride the power of the United States. The Chinese defined the term as "things that possess a fierce appearance but are in essence very weak and hollow." In terms of the U.S., the Chinese suggested for many years thereafter in virulent and polemical propaganda that the U.S. possession of nuclear weapons and other modern military technology gave it an appearance of being "fierce," but in reality the capitalist system made America fundamentally "weak and hollow." According to Mao Zedong: "The atom bomb is a paper tiger that the U.S. reactionaries use to scare people. It looks terrible, but in fact it is not. Of course, the atom bomb is a weapon of mass slaughter, but the outcome of a war is decided by the people, not by one or two new types of weapons." Mao went on to claim that this was true for all "reactionaries," domestic and international. The term ceased to be used after the 1972 visit to China by U.S. President Richard Nixon.

PARTY CONGRESS. *See* CHINESE COMMUNIST PARTY.

"PARTY GROUPS" (*DANGZU*). *See* CHINESE COMMUNIST PARTY.

"PEACEFUL EVOLUTION" (*HEPING YANBIAN*). This notion is disseminated by hard-line critics of "bourgeois liberalization" in the CCP (q.v.) who criticize Western countries, particularly the United States, for the alleged campaign to undermine the Communist dictatorship and to replace it with a Western-style parliamentary system. The term was originally used by U.S. Secretary of State John Foster Dulles in the 1950s to explain the American strategy of countering Communist influence in Central and Latin America. In China, the most extensive explication of the concept came in a 1991 document entitled "The Struggle Between Peaceful Evolution and Counter Peaceful Evolution is a Class Struggle in the World Arena." In it, the Chinese government singled out the administration of U.S. President George Bush for criticism because the president had in many public statements suggested that trade and cultural ties with China would gradually bring about a transition to a more liberal, democratic society. Foreign residents of China who in the early 1990s parodied the phrase by holding a "peaceful evolution barbecue" were given warnings by Chinese state authorities.

PEKING OPERA. The primary regional opera in China, the Peking Opera assumed its present form about two hundred years ago during the Qing dynasty (1644–1911). Like all traditional Chinese theater, it combines music, singing, dialogue, dancing, acrobatics, and martial arts. Acting in Peking opera is highly symbolic, with little scenery or stage props. The music of Peking opera is made up of orchestral and percussion instruments, mainly drums and gongs. The Beijing fiddle (*jinghu*) and second fiddle (*erhu*) are also used. The vocal part of the opera is both spoken and sung. Spoken dialogue consists of the recitative and Beijing colloquial speech, the former by serious characters and the latter by young females and clowns. The music is taken from folk tunes from Hubei and Anhui provinces and from older opera forms from the south. The faces of the characters are usually painted—red indicating a good character, black an evil one, and a face with a white spot is humorous. There are more than two thousand Peking operas, including such famous repertoires as "Gathering of Heroes," "At the Crossroads," and "Farewell My Concubine." During periods of political repression and turmoil in China, such as the Cultural Revolution (1966–1976) (q.v.), Peking opera was not publicly performed.

PENG DEHUAI (1898–1974). Born in 1898 in Hunan province, Peng emerged as one of the top military figures in the CCP (q.v.). It is said that at the age of eleven Peng's father fired a gun at his young son who showed his steely nerves by not flinching. Peng soon left his family and joined local military forces. In 1919 he was profoundly influenced by the writings of Sun Yat-sen and the liberal ideas of the May Fourth Movement (q.v.). Peng joined the CCP in the late 1920s and emerged as one of the foremost military figures in the Communist movement, commanding CCP forces in a major battle with the Japanese in 1940 and leading the First Field Army during the 1946–1949 civil war (q.v.). Peng then commanded Chinese forces during the 1950–1953 Korean War (q.v.) where his troops fought the American forces to a standstill, but with extremely heavy losses on the Chinese side, including Mao Zedong's (q.v.) own son. Peng Dehuai was originally reluctant to commit Chinese forces to the Korean conflict, yet ended up being the sole top Chinese military officer to serve in the field during this risky venture. A strong supporter of a professional military in China, in the mid-1950s Peng helped introduce ranks and he became one of ten marshals. Peng's letter to Mao Zedong in August 1959 raising questions about economic policy during the Great Leap Forward (q.v.) led to his purge. Efforts to rehabilitate Peng in the early 1960s provoked Mao's wrath, and during the Cultural Revolution (1966–1976) (q.v.) Peng was denounced and paraded through the streets by Red Guards (q.v.). Peng died in 1974 in obscurity.

PENG ZHEN (1902–1997). Born of destitute peasants, Peng Zhen joined the CCP (q.v.) in 1923 and served as a political commissar (q.v.) in the Eighth Route Army. In 1945 he became a member of the CCP Central Committee and the Politburo (q.v.). From 1954 to 1966 he was mayor of Beijing (q.v.). He was the first Politburo member to be purged in the Cultural Revolution (1966–1976) (q.v.). He reappeared in 1979 and was reappointed to the Central Committee and Politburo. From 1983 to 1988 he was chairman of the standing committee of the NPC (q.v.). He "resigned" from all posts in 1987 but as one of the "revolutionary elders" (q.v.) of the CCP he reportedly played a major role in 1989 in sanctioning the crackdown on pro-democracy demonstrations.

PEOPLE'S BANK OF CHINA. Under the authority of the State Council, the People's Bank of China controls the country's banking industry. Its most important function is to control the issuance and circulation of currency and exercise unified control over interest rates for deposits in *renminbi*, the national currency, and foreign exchange rates. The People's Bank also supervises the management of credit funds, manages the state treasury, and issues bonds on behalf of the government. In addition, it draws up principles and policies for financial work in China and prepares draft financial laws and regulations for government approval. In 1979, the People's Bank was separated from the Bank of China (q.v.). Throughout the 1980s and early 1990s, China's increasing problems with inflation have placed enormous responsibility on the People's Bank, particularly during periods of economic contraction. *See also* LI GUIXIAN.

"PEOPLE'S COMMUNES" (*RENMIN GONGSHE*). Promoted primarily by CCP (q.v.) Chairman Mao Zedong (q.v.), the people's communes consisted of very large-scale organization of rural production in the Chinese countryside. Officially, the formation of the people's communes was authorized by the Central Committee of the CCP in August 1958, although Mao's green light for the communes came during the Beidaihe Conference (q.v.). After some experimentation, a nationwide campaign to establish communes was begun in December 1958. Organizationally, the people's communes amalgamated the more numerous production brigades (q.v.) and became the top level of the three-tier organization (commune, brigade, team) in the countryside. In this sense, the communes represented a significant centralization of authority and organization in the countryside. However, since the communes took over much power from the central government's Ministry of Agriculture, the communes also signified a decentralization of authority from urban-based bureaucracies to the countryside.

The people's communes integrated the income and production of several villages in an unprecedented reorganization of the Chinese countryside that Mao Zedong declared to be the basis for China's route to "communism." By early 1959, over 99 percent of the rural population was organized into 26,000 communes, the largest of which numbered over 100,000 members. Unwieldy organizations, the communes took over the traditional managerial functions of the "townships"—also referred to as "administrative villages" (*xiang*)—and were generally dominated by the commune Party branch committee that quickly assumed control over production decisions and the allocation of income. The communes ran the disastrous backyard steel furnace (q.v.) campaign and implemented many of Mao Zedong's personal radical decisions to transform agricultural production, such as the close planting of paddy rice, which also proved to be disastrous. At the height of the Great Leap Forward (1958–1960) (q.v.), communes ran canteens in which peasants ate collectively and offered free supplies of food and other staples and services. The local people's militia (q.v.) were based in the communes, which also established schools and collective nurseries as a means of achieving the "liberation" of rural women. With Mao's dictum that "politics takes command" (q.v.) pervading CCP propaganda in the communes, the emphasis was on nonmaterial incentives for peasants to increase production. The sharing of labor between villages within one communal structure was also emphasized as a way to increase agricultural production.

By 1960, it was apparent to top CCP leaders, including Mao Zedong, that the communes had contributed to a growing agricultural crisis. Excessive devotion to backyard steel production and ill-advised agricultural measures led to a dramatic falloff in total grain production that necessitated a radical retrenchment by the top leadership. Without completely dismantling the communes, in 1960 the CCP ordered that decisions regarding production and income allocation be returned first to the production brigade (generally a single village) and then to the production team (a subunit of a single village). The "egalitarianism" in the communes was thereby abandoned and material incentives were reintroduced into the rural economy. The three-tier structure, with the commune at the highest level, remained, however, but authority was significantly decentralized, with only small rural factories remaining under the control of the commune administration. The 1978 agricultural reform essentially ended the role of the communes, which in 1983 were effectively replaced as administrative organs by the reestablishment of township governments.

PEOPLE'S CONGRESSES. *See* GOVERNMENT STRUCTURE and NATIONAL PEOPLE'S CONGRESS.

PEOPLE'S DAILY (RENMIN RIBAO). The mouthpiece of the Central Committee of the CCP (q.v.), *People's Daily* is controlled by the Propaganda Department of the Central Committee. Editorials and commentaries appearing in the paper represent the policy position of the central leadership and constitute the basic Party line. *People's Daily* commentaries (*pinglun*) constitute the main subject for weekly political study sessions that have been conducted in China since 1949 and that are directed by the ubiquitous "Party groups" that exist in virtually all institutions. Other media, including provincial and local newspapers, are obliged to reproduce authoritative *People's Daily* editorials and commentaries. Thus, this paper plays a major role in shaping public opinion and outlining the parameters of acceptable political discourse. The most important editorials or commentaries of *People's Daily* appear on the newspaper's front page. The circulation of the paper is approximately 7 to 9 million and is read by virtually all important Party and government personnel. An editorial board runs the newspaper, though all major editorials and commentaries are subject to censorship (q.v.) (*shencha*) by the CCP Propaganda Department and top Party leaders. Mao Zedong (q.v.) and subsequent Chinese leaders used the newspaper to make authoritative comments on political developments and trends, and to issue commands to the CCP apparatus. Leader-authored articles have also been used to circumvent opposition within the CCP and to appeal directly to public opinion, a tactic Mao Zedong employed during the Cultural Revolution (1966–1976) (q.v.). Editors of the *People's Daily* have often been placed in precarious positions as their decisions regarding the publication of certain articles and/or editorials can bring them political difficulties and lead to the loss of their jobs, as occurred with Deng Tuo (q.v.), Wang Ruoshui (q.v.), and Hu Jiwei (q.v.). The *People's Daily* has traditionally published carefully screened letters from common citizens and in the last few years has run selective advertisements from commercial firms. *See also* CENSORSHIP.

"PEOPLE'S LIBERATION ARMY" (PLA) (*RENMIN JIEFANG JUN*). The military organization of the PRC (q.v.), the PLA includes ground, air, and naval forces that in 1995 numbered about 3.5 million men and women. The PLA traces its origins to 1927 when on August 1 (now celebrated in China as Army Day) a ragtag military force of about 30,000 soldiers was organized by Zhou Enlai (q.v.), Zhu De (q.v.), and other Communist leaders who had broken off from the Nationalists (q.v.). When the CCP (q.v.) was established in 1921, the Communists abjured the formation of independent military forces in accord with the First United Front (1924–1927) (q.v.) formed with the KMT. This decision, which was imposed on the Chinese Communists by the Soviet Union via the Comintern, proved disastrous when in April 1927 the Nationalists, under the leadership of Chiang Kai-shek, turned on their erstwhile Communist "allies" and nearly wiped out the entire CCP organization in China's urban areas, especially Canton and Shanghai (q.v.). The Chinese Workers and Peasants Revolutionary Army was formed in 1927 by Zhou Enlai and Zhu De and became the Communist Red Army. It quickly expanded into a formidable military force that by the early 1930s numbered some 80,000 soldiers who were held up in the mountain redoubt of the Jiangxi Soviet. During the Long March (1934–1935) (q.v.), Mao Zedong assumed command of the Red Army at the Zunyi Conference.

During the Sino-Japanese War (1937–1945) (q.v.) a Second United Front was established with the Nationalists, formally merging Communist and Nationalist military forces. The main force of the Red Army in North China became known as the Eighth Route Army. The scattered Communist units in the South were formed into the New Fourth Army. After the war, these two military forces merged into the PLA that in less than four years was able to defeat its Nationalist rival, despite the latter's vast superiority in numbers and weaponry, supplied primarily by the United States. Theoretically one army, the PLA was organized into several field armies (*yezhan jun*) (q.v.) that operated as nearly independent units in discrete territorial regions of the country. These included the First Field Army in the northwest region under the command of Peng Dehuai (q.v.); the Second Field Army in the southwest region under Liu Bocheng (q.v.); the Third Field Army in east China under Chen Yi (q.v.); the Fourth Field Army in the central and southern regions under Lin Biao (q.v.); and the Fifth Field Army in the north and northeast under Nie Rongzhen (q.v.) that was later placed under the direct command of the General Headquarters of the PLA. The formal designation of the Communist military forces as the PLA occurred in 1948, although some military units had adopted this appellation in 1945–1946. During the Civil War (1946–1949) (q.v.) a close relationship was established between the field army commands and the civil authorities established by the Communists through the organization of military control commissions that took over the local administration from the defeated Nationalists. The commanding military officer for any particular locality headed the military control commission and concurrently held the top spot in the civil administration overseeing economic enterprises, schools, and other institutions. At the regional level, six military regions (q.v.) (later expanded to eleven and then reduced to seven) were established for the entire country to complement the six major administrative regions through which the CCP managed Chinese society in the early 1950s. Although military control of the country formally ended in 1953, the close linkage between the field armies, the military regions, and the state and Party organization has since been maintained as various political leaders have depended on support from key military leaders and field armies (q.v.) to rise to prominence.

Authority over the military is concentrated in the central government. From 1935 to his death in 1976 Mao Zedong was the unquestioned commander of the PLA. Advocating the principle that "the Party commands the gun," Mao as CCP chairman never assumed military rank, unlike his Nationalist counterpart Chiang Kai-shek, who was referred to as the generalissimo and often appeared in military garb. In a society that assigned low social status to the military profession, this abjuring of a formal military position strengthened Mao's political authority and undoubtedly provided an advantage over such political competitors as Marshal Lin Biao (q.v.). China's other two prominent political leaders since 1949, Zhou Enlai (q.v.) and Deng Xiaoping (q.v.), also disavowed military rank. Mao's personal control over the military was evident in the late 1960s, when he ordered the PLA to intervene in the internecine conflict of the Cultural Revolution (1966–1976) (q.v.) to bring an end to factional violence and Red Guard (q.v.) terror.

In the mid-1970s a more formal structure of military authority in China was established. The commander in chief of the PLA is the chairman of the Central Military Affairs Commission (MAC) (q.v.), a Party organ that is theoretically appointed by the CCP National Party Congress but which actually enjoys a great deal of autonomy from both the CCP Central Committee and Politburo (q.v.). There is also a state Central Military Commission that was established by the state constitution in 1982, but its role remains obscure. In 1995, Jiang Zemin was MAC chairman as well as general secretary of the CCP and president of the PRC. The size of the MAC ranges from ten to twenty members, and includes the defense minister, the chief of the general staff, the directors of the general political and logistic departments, the commanders of the air and naval forces, and commanders of some major military regions. Traditionally, the vice chairmen of the MAC include the minister of defense, usually a ranking military officer, and the premier. The minister of defense is the administrative head of the PLA and oversees the PLA General Headquarters in Beijing (q.v.). This body coordinates and executes combat operations of the various service arms and has a general logistics and procurement service. The General Staff Office maintains direct control over the service arms, including the air force, navy, engineering corps, armored units, and artillery. Operationally, to move an army requires the signature of the chairman of the Central Military Commission; to move a division requires the permission of the General Staff Department and the Central Military Commission; a regiment, the regional Party committee; a battalion, an army-level Party committee; and a company, the division Party committee. CCP control over the military rank and file is exercised through the General Political Department that oversees the elaborate organization of Party cells, party "core groups," and political commissars (q.v.) in all PLA units and that carries out propaganda and political education of the troops.

At the regional level, the 3.5 million military personnel are organized in seven military regions (MR), each of which encompasses several provinces. Military personnel are generally assigned on a permanent basis to a region, which in turn is divided into military districts. The seven MRs are Beijing (the capital), Shenyang (the extreme northeast), Jinan-Wuhan (central), Nanjing-Fuzhou (south), Guangzhou (southeast), Kunming-Chengdu (southwest), and Lanzhou–Inner Mongolia (northwest). Because of their geo-political and strategic importance, Beijing, Shenyang, and Lanzhou–Inner Mongolia are the most important. The Beijing Garrison Division (*weishuqu*) includes four divisions, two of which protect the capital city, and two mechanized divisions that guard the capital's suburbs. The main force units in the PLA consist of approximately 110 infantry divisions (1.5 million men), ten armored units (130,000 men), and thirty artillery units (190,000 men). These are organized into numerically designated armies (e.g., the 38th Army in Beijing) and are subordinate to regional military commanders. Approximately sixteen army corps (out of a total of thirty-eight) are under the direct control of the MAC and can be deployed anywhere in the country by direct orders from Beijing. There are also regional divisions and regiments, consisting of approximately 800,000 personnel, and a People's Militia. The Central Guard Regiment (*Zhongyang jingwei tuan*), also known as the 8341 Unit, is responsible for protecting the CCP leadership.

The history of the PLA since 1949 has been a turbulent one. Following China's participation in the Korean War (q.v.), the Minister of Defense Peng Dehuai (q.v.), who had commanded China's forces during the war, pushed for major military modernization and professionalism. Peng's demise after the Great Leap Forward (1958–1960) (q.v.), however, led to the rise of Lin Biao (q.v.), who increased the political role of the army and inaugurated a campaign for the entire nation to emulate the PLA, all at the behest of Mao Zedong. PLA heroes, such as Lei Feng (q.v.), served as national paragons of such political virtues as "self-sacrifice" and the "primacy of politics." The politicization of the army reached its zenith in 1965 with the abolition of ranks and insignia, as the army became the symbol of the masses purportedly waging "class struggle" (q.v.) under the direct command of Mao Zedong and Lin Biao. During the Cultural Revolution (1966–1976) military officers assumed key positions of authority in the Party and state bureaucracies, and they emerged as the dominant force in the revolutionary committees (q.v.). Military resources were also made available to Red Guards (q.v.) in their attacks on the Party and its leadership. By 1967, however, Mao was forced to order in the military to put down the factional violence and to establish a modicum of law and order, which the PLA did, in some cases with brutal efficiency. In effect, the PLA took control of the country as military officers assumed supervision of economic, financial, educational, media, and public security organs (q.v.). The political influence of the military peaked at the CCP's Ninth Party Congress in 1969, which designated Lin Biao as Mao's "successor" and which witnessed the appointment of military men to 43 percent of the seats on the Central Committee. In terms of military doctrine, the PLA during the Cultural Revolution adhered to Lin Biao's vision of "people's war" in which guerrilla units with mass popular support could defeat superior "imperialist" forces—a policy that the Communist forces in the early days of the Vietnam war followed.

The Lin Biao affair in 1971—also known as Project 571 (q.v.)—brought a rapid end to the army's dominant political role. The PLA central command was subject to a massive purge of Lin's supporters from his Fourth Field Army. The PLA's role came to be defined primarily as a military one as the number of military officers on the CCP Central Committee and Politburo were drastically reduced. In 1973, an unprecedented transfer of commanders of the critical military regions was effected, although 30 percent of the Eleventh Central Committee elected in 1977 were still military men. The continued political influence of the PLA reflected its critical role in carrying out the arrest of Jiang Qing (q.v.) and the radical Gang of Four (q.v.) in 1976 following Mao Zedong's death.

Throughout the 1980s and 1990s, the focus of central Party policies has been to reduce the political role of the PLA, to reestablish military professionalism, and to engage in a major modernization of the force structure. As a former PLA chief of staff, Deng Xiaoping has commanded great respect in the military. In 1980 he personally appointed ten of the then eleven military region commanders and in 1985 effected a reduction in military regions from eleven to seven. Elected chairman of the MAC in 1981, Deng became the PLA's commander in chief, even though he refused the top position in the CCP (q.v.). Deng led a major effort to modernize the military under the doctrine of the Four Modernizations (q.v.). This involved streamlining the military command structure below the MAC, improving officer training and education, and modernizing weaponry, including strategic weapons. Fragmented command structures over air, navy, armored, and other units were consolidated under the dual authority of the military regions and their service headquarters in Beijing, especially after the PLA suffered embarrassing military reverses in its 1979 war against Vietnam. A new PLA Defense University was established to recruit military personnel with college degrees and age limits were established for commanders at all levels. Deng also effected a major demobilization of PLA troop levels in 1980 and 1985 to create a leaner force. Military modernization consisted of, for example, a long-range ICBM tested in 1980, the launching in 1982 of military satellites to protect against Soviet attack, and the construction of a single missile-carrying submarine.

In the mid-1980s, China also purchased military hardware from the U.S., under a six-year agreement that involved equipment for jet fighters and modern equipment from Western European countries such as West Germany. Yet throughout the 1980s, China's military expenditures were reduced by 25 percent from a high of $14.3 billion in 1979 as the CCP (q.v.) directed critical resources to civilian economic development. Following the PLA's intervention in the 1989 Tiananmen Incident (q.v.), however, defense outlays were dramatically increased to about $17 billion per annum, with concomitant increases in spending on a "blue water" navy and strategic weapons, with major purchases from the former Soviet Union. Still, China's military forces remain significantly inferior to comparable armies of developed states, though the future of China's military prowess is uncertain. Domestically, the PLA continues to suffer from the taint of killing civilians during the 1989 pro-democracy movement. Since 1989, the trend toward professionalization was reversed as promotion through patronage rather than merit reemerged. See also ATOMIC BOMB, PEOPLE'S MILITIA, and FIELD ARMY.

PEOPLE'S MILITIA. The CCP (q.v.) has historically emphasized the creation of local armed forces to operate in coordination with the regular military units. The people's militia played a major role in supporting the CCP's military operations during the Communist struggle for power before 1949. After the CCP takeover, local armed forces were organized throughout the country to maintain social order and to assist the regular armed forces in mobilizations, for example during the Korean War (q.v.). During the Great Leap Forward (1958–

1960) (q.v.), the people's militia was expanded as part of the general militarization of society that accompanied the Great Leap. During the Cultural Revolution (1966–1976) (q.v.), local armed forces often became involved in the intense factional struggles and were intimately involved in carrying out political violence, murder, and even cannibalism. During the latter part of the Cultural Revolution, local armed forces largely disintegrated as the regular army, the PLA (q.v.), imposed its control over Chinese society. Since 1978 and the advancement of the economic reforms, the people's militia has largely disappeared, as the Chinese government has focused on more conventional military and police forces.

PEOPLE'S REPUBLIC OF CHINA (PRC). The formal name of the Chinese Communist state since its establishment in October 1949, the PRC is officially described in the 1982 state constitution as a "socialist state under the people's democratic dictatorship led by the working class and based on an alliance of workers and peasants." The PRC is headed by a president whose official powers are extremely limited and who is appointed by the highest state organ, the NPC (q.v.). The office of the president was reestablished in the 1982 state constitution—China's fourth such constitution—after it had been deleted from the 1975 and 1978 constitutions. In 1997, the president of the PRC was Jiang Zemin, concurrently general secretary of the CCP (q.v.) and chairman of the Central Military Affairs Commission (q.v.). Citizens of the PRC are said to enjoy "freedom of speech, of the press, of assembly, of association, and of demonstration," but in reality such "freedoms" are severely curtailed by the demand enumerated in the same document that all citizens abide by the Four Cardinal Principles (q.v.) of absolute loyalty to the CCP.

Internationally, the PRC is recognized by most nations in the world, though a few states still maintain formal diplomatic links with the ROC on Taiwan (q.v.). Since 1971, the PRC has held a seat on the Security Council of the United Nations (q.v.). In January 1979 formal diplomatic relations were established with the United States.

"PERSONAL DOSSIERS" (*DANG'AN*). These are files maintained on all members of "basic units" (*jiben danwei*) (q.v.), the honeycomb-like matrix of organization primarily in China's urban areas. Defined geographically and functionally (by work), these basic units rely on the personnel dossiers as part of an elaborate system to exercise comprehensive control over all members. Files include relevant facts about one's personal history, including cases of "erroneous" behavior and political dissent, and are critical in determining an individual's ability to advance in the organization and/or to receive permission to marry, to have children, or to divorce. Entries into the files are controlled by the unit head and are under the direct control of the unit personnel department. Personnel files accompany an individual when he is transferred from one unit to another. Various proposals were aired during the 1980s by Zhao Ziyang (q.v.) to reduce or even eliminate the *dang'an*, but to no avail.

PERSONALITY CULT. Theoretically, China's Communist leaders have opposed the personality cult as a "decadent heritage left over from the long period of human history." In reality, Mao Zedong (q.v.) and Deng Xiaoping (q.v.) both promoted elaborate praise and even worship of their person to serve their own political ends. In the Communist world, personality cults began with Lenin and Stalin (q.v.), who were effusively praised by the official press in the Soviet Union and China for their "genius." Stalin in particular was lavished with such praise. This model was adopted in China in the mid-1940s when the cult of Mao Zedong began. Although some CCP (q.v.) leaders, such as Zhu De (q.v.), expressed reservations about the personality cult, "Chairman Mao" became the focus of leadership idolization in China from 1943 onward. The Korean War (1950–1953) (q.v.) and the Great Leap Forward (1958–1960) (q.v.) were two tense periods of national crisis during which Mao's leadership role was heavily emphasized and his person was accorded great stature, often on a par with both Lenin and Stalin in the international Communist pantheon. The height of the Maoist personality cult came during the Cultural Revolution (1966–1976) (q.v.) when Mao was praised as "the greatest genius of the present age" and his little red book of sayings, *Quotations from Chairman Mao* (q.v.), was accorded the status of communist canon. Red Guards (q.v.) expressed fanatical admiration for Mao and different Red Guard factions fought bloody pitched battles over competing claims of loyalty to the "Chairman" and his "sayings." Although Mao personally criticized the promotion of the cult during the Cultural Revolution in a letter to his wife, Jiang Qing (q.v.), such fanatical promotion of Mao's stature as the "great helmsman" in China did not subside until his death in 1976. CCP leaders then criticized the excesses of the Mao cult, without disavowing Mao's important historical role in CCP history. Deng Xiaoping joined in this criticism, but after 1978 Deng promoted his own cult by having published his own *Selected Works*.

The personality cult in both the Soviet Union and China has been characterized by leaders claiming authority in all realms of human behavior—politics, economics, military, art, and culture. Like Stalin and Mao Zedong, Deng Xiaoping continued this tradition by issuing statements and releasing writings on virtually all of these topics, which Party members and Chinese people are urged to "study." But unlike the Maoist years in China, however, social receptivity to the personality cult in China has faded, as witnessed during the pro-democracy movement of 1989 when Deng was subjected to popular ridicule and criticism in a manner that would have never occurred during Mao's lifetime.

"PLANNED PURCHASE AND SUPPLY" (*TONGGOU TONGXIAO*). Beginning in the 1950s, important commodities in the Chinese economy were subject to unified purchasing and marketing by state-run trading companies. This was applied especially to agricultural products such as grain (rice and wheat), edible oils, cotton, and cotton cloth. The system was expanded in the mid- and late 1950s to virtually all commodities in the Chinese economy. The state was the sole purchaser and supplier of these commodities which were then rationed to the urban and rural populations. The system involved setting quotas for each farm household based upon its requirements of food, seed, and fodder, as well as based upon the demand from grain deficit areas in the country. Private trading in these products was banned. Planned purchase and supply ensured adequate stocks of essential products and maintained staple grains and oils at very low prices. Taxes in kind were also charged to peasant producers who consistently received very low prices for their products.

After the 1978 economic reform and the introduction of the Agricultural Responsibility System (q.v.), greater flexibility in production and sale of some non-essential commodities was allowed. But fear of inflation and radical shifts in production led the CCP (q.v.) leadership to maintain planned purchase and supply over essential grain and edible oil production. Private trading now occurs but rigid price and administrative controls are still in place. The prices for farm commodities paid to rural producers have increased, but the state still prevents the emergence of a true free market in farm commodities. Price increases for grains are often offset by increases in wages for the urban population, thereby contributing to some inflationary pressure in the post-1978 Chinese economy. Radical proposals for price reforms and for the dismantling of the system of planned purchase and supply, initially supported by Deng Xiaoping (q.v.), were proposed in 1988. But panic buying in China's cities led to a quick termination of this reform.

POLICE. *See* PUBLIC SECURITY.

"POLISH DISEASE" (*BOLAN BIBING*). The phrase was coined by Chinese leaders to express their fear of a repetition in China of the social and political changes in 1989 that led to the collapse of the

Polish Communist regime. Such fears that events in Poland would influence Chinese politics began in 1956 when popular demonstrations in Poznan (and in Hungary) spooked Chinese leaders and provoked major domestic policy changes, such as the 1957 Hundred Flowers (q.v.) and Anti-Rightist campaigns (q.v.). In 1980, China's domestic political situation was once again affected by developments in Poland. Initially, Chinese leaders supported the Polish resistance against Soviet domination and their demands for internal reforms. But after hard-line leaders in China warned of serious domestic consequences if political and economic reforms were enacted in China, the situation in Poland was interpreted in graver tones, provoking Deng Xiaoping (q.v.) to retreat from his proto-democratic reform program outlined in August 1980. Fears that reforms in prices and enterprise management would unleash serious inflationary pressures and lead to massive unemployment haunted China's leaders. Their greatest fear was that a Chinese version of Solidarity or a Chinese Lech Walesa would emerge. Thus CCP (q.v.) leaders during the 1989 Tiananmen crisis (q.v.) were especially harsh in crushing the embryonic workers' movement and persecuting its leader, Han Dongfang (q.v.).

"POLITBURO" (*ZHENGZHIJU*). This is a top policy-making body in the CCP (q.v.). Organizationally, it is an executive arm of the Central Committee, which meets periodically between Central Committee meetings known as plenums. The Politburo's membership varies from year to year, but generally consists of around 12 to 20 top leaders from the CCP, the government, and the PLA (q.v.). It is generally believed that the full Politburo meets approximately once a week to consider major policy issues. In theory, it is responsible to the Central Committee for its membership and policies. In reality, the Politburo controls the makeup of the Central Committee and determines its policy decisions. There are both full and alternate members of the Politburo, with the former exercising voting power, while the latter do not. The inner workings of the Politburo are generally unknown to the outside world; it is not even known for sure whether formal votes are taken or whether it operates according to consensus building.

During the Maoist period, especially from the late 1950s onward, Chairman Mao (q.v.) generally refrained from attending Politburo meetings, thus considerably reducing its authority in the CCP. Since the death of Mao Zedong, CCP leaders have attempted to increase the institutional importance of the Politburo, though at times its role has been overshadowed by the Party Secretariat, which was also revived after 1978. The critical role of Deng Xiaoping in China's politics, although from 1989 to 1997 he was nominally retired, indicated that the Politburo, like other CCP institutions, remained relatively weak in the face of Deng's enormous personal authority. The standing committee (q.v.) of the Politburo is an even smaller executive body made up of, in 1997, seven top Politburo members. It apparently meets several times a week and on some occasions takes formal votes, such as when the decision was made to crack down on the 1989 Democracy Movement. *See also* CHINESE COMMUNIST PARTY.

"POLITICAL COMMISSAR" (*ZHENGZHI WEIYUAN*). This is a system to ensure Communist Party control over the military. It was first introduced in Russia during the Civil War and was adopted in China in the 1920s. Political commissars were installed in the Chinese military down to the company level where they conducted propaganda work and ensured CCP (q.v.) control over the disparate military forces. After 1949, the political commissar system was retained and remained a central component of the CCP apparatus of control over the PLA (q.v.). The terms "political teachers" and "political instructors" are also used to refer to these positions. The political commissar must generally countersign the orders of military commanders. The system of political commissars is controlled from the top by the General Political Department of the PLA. Supporters of greater military professionalism have periodically argued for a loosening of political controls, as occurred during the 1950s and again in the 1980s. During the late 1950s and during the Cultural Revolution (1966–1976) (q.v.), Mao Zedong emphasized the army's political role in China and greatly strengthened the authority of the political commissars. Since 1978, the political commissar system has been retained but with greater authority flowing to military commanders. The Tiananmen crisis in 1989, however, reinvigorated the role of the political commissars, especially after the loyalty of the PLA to the Communist regime was questioned by the disaffection of some military commanders and by their refusal to carry out orders to fire on protestors during the Tiananmen crisis.

POLITICAL STUDY GROUPS. *See* MAO ZEDONG THOUGHT STUDY CLASSES.

"POLITICS TAKES COMMAND" (*ZHENGZHI GUASHUAI*). This is perhaps the most famous phrase spouted by Chairman of the CCP (q.v.) Mao Zedong (q.v.) indicating his central belief that politics determines everything. "Politics is the commander, the soul," Mao stated. And thus during the Great Leap Forward (1958–1960) (q.v.) and the Cultural Revolution (1966–1976) (q.v.), "politics takes command" became the watchword of the Maoist model for the transformation of Chinese society and culture. In the Maoist vision, assuming a correct political standpoint could work miracles in the economy and society. Peasants during the Great Leap Forward (q.v.) were glorified for taking the correct political standpoint of adhering to Mao Zedong Thought (q.v.) to make enormous strides in production that later proved false. Organizationally, "politics takes command" meant that the Party branch was given total authority in the people's communes (q.v.). The same was true at the provincial and central levels of government where the CCP assumed a greater and greater role in running the country.

During the Cultural Revolution, however, "politics takes command" was used to challenge the authority of Party bureaucrats. Mao mobilized Red Guards (q.v.) and other non-CCP personages to rid the Party of his ideological and political enemies. At this time, "politics takes command" entailed adhering to Mao Zedong Thought to revolutionize society through constant turmoil and political struggle, in contrast with the ideas of Mao's revisionist critics, such as Liu Shaoqi (q.v.), who purportedly advocated putting "economics in command."

The winding down of the Cultural Revolution (1966–1976) and the emergence of the economic reforms in 1978 brought an end to "politics takes command" as the centerpiece of CCP propaganda. The phrase is no longer used, essentially disappearing with the death of Mao. In its place, the post-1978 leadership has emphasized the role of economic forces and incentives mobilizing the Chinese people to increase national wealth.

"POOR AND BLANK" (*YIQIONG ERBAI*). This term was used by Mao Zedong (q.v.) to describe the general character of the Chinese people. The overwhelming poverty of the Chinese people gave rise to desire for change and for action, and that, Mao argued, was good because it produced revolutionary fervor. The Chinese people were "blank" in that they were comparable to a "blank sheet of paper, free from any mark," on which the "freshest and most beautiful characters can be written. . . ." In this sense, Mao believed that the very ignorance of the Chinese people (literacy rates in the 1940s when the Communists achieved power were very low) would allow the CCP (q.v.) to mold the population into a compliant popular support base for the Communists. The people generally had no preconceived opposition to the CCP and that made revolutionary change possible. The exception, of course, were the intellectuals (q.v.) whose admiration for the West and for political principles of liberalism and freedom of thought made them targets of CCP "thought reform" (q.v.).

"PRACTICE IS THE SOLE CRITERION OF TRUTH" (*SHIJIAN SHI JIANYAN ZHENLI DE WEIYI BIAOZHUN*). The title of an article published on May 12, 1978, in the *People's Daily*, this phrase provided the ideological basis for Deng Xiaoping's (q.v.) pragmatism in inaugurating bold reforms. The central premise of the article was that dogma could not be blindly accepted, but should be revised according to experience and practice. Truth can only be judged according to the objective yardstick of social and scientific practice, not on its own terms. Truth was no longer a matter of propping up the authority of an old or new leader. Nor must one avoid ideological "forbidden zones" and adhere to outworn dogmas. Rather, people should "seek truth from facts"—a saying once voiced by Mao Zedong (q.v.) himself that, this article argued, was in fundamental accord with the basic tenets of Marxism. In so doing one could "emancipate the mind" and adopt a more pragmatic approach to solve social and economic problems. Ideologically, "practice is the sole criterion of truth" served as a counterweight in 1978 to the "two whatevers" (q.v.) supported by the leftist faction. Politically, the "practice criterion" mobilized support among intellectuals (q.v.) for the reformist policies of Hu Yaobang (q.v.) and his patron Deng Xiaoping that ultimately triumphed at the December 1978 Third Plenum.

PRESIDENT OF THE PRC. Formal head of state in the PRC (q.v.), the president of China in 1997 was Jiang Zemin. This position (also known as state chairman) was established by the 1954 state constitution, and was initially held by Mao Zedong (q.v.). In the midst of the controversy surrounding the Great Leap Forward (1958–1960) (q.v.), Mao relinquished the position to his designated successor at that time, Liu Shaoqi (q.v.). The presidency was abolished in the 1975 state constitution in reaction to Mao Zedong's purge of Liu Shaoqi during the Cultural Revolution (1966–1976) (q.v.). Efforts by Lin Biao (q.v.) to reestablish the position in the 1970s contributed to his political downfall. It was not until 1982 that the presidency was reestablished by articles 79–81 of the new state constitution—China's fourth—which also created a position of vice president. Since then the presidency has been held by Li Xiannian (1983–1988), Yang Shangkun (1988–1993), and Jiang Zemin (1993–1997). The president is formally elected by the NPC (q.v.) for no more than two consecutive terms that coincide with the NPC sessions. As head of state, the president receives foreign diplomatic representatives on behalf of the PRC and implements decisions of the Standing Committee of the NPC in ratifying and abrogating treaties with foreign states. The president also promulgates NPC statutes, and formally appoints and/or removes the premier, vice premier, state councillors, and ministers in charge of the state ministries and commissions. Although lacking any real power, the holder of this office and the vice president are generally top-ranking members of the CCP (q.v.) leadership and sit on major decision-making organs such as the Politburo (q.v.).

"PRINCE'S FACTION" (*TAIZIDANG*). Term for politically influential offspring of senior Chinese political and military leaders, members of the "prince's faction" rely on family ties to get key policy-making positions in the Party and/or state-run economy where they can reap enormous economic rewards, often through corruption (q.v.). Examples include: Chen Yuan (q.v.), the son of the CCP's (q.v.) longtime economic czar, Chen Yun (q.v.); Wang Jun, son of the PLA (q.v.) leader and arch conservative, Wang Zhen (q.v.); Deng Zhifang, second son of Deng Xiaoping (q.v.); and He Ping, son-in-law of Deng Xiaoping. During the 1989 Tiananmen crisis, it is said that the politically conservative members of the "prince's faction" favored a military crackdown out of fear that a political victory by the democratic movement would rob them of their positions, influence, and fat contracts with foreign investors.

PROCURACY. A unique feature of China's legal system, the procuracy parallels the organization of the court system in China and serves as both prosecuting attorney and public defender. In addition, the procuracy monitors and reviews the government bureaucracy and the courts to provide, in theory, a legal restraint on the government. In reality, the procuracy is just another arm of the state bureaucracy that serves the interests of the CCP (q.v.) dictatorship. The procurator authorizes the arrest of criminals and so-called "counterrevolutionaries" (q.v.) as charged by the public security bureau (q.v.)—that is, the police. The procuracy operates under the authority of the NPC (q.v.) and is headed by the Supreme People's Procuratorate, which supervises subordinate bodies of the procuracy down to the local levels. The procuracy in China today is similar to the censorate that existed in traditional China during the Yuan dynasty (1264–1368) onward, and to the procuracy in the former Soviet Union, as well as to the system of ombudsmen in continental European legal systems. Prior to the Cultural Revolution (1966–1976) (q.v.) the functions of the procuracy were exercised by the public security bureau, which, through its extrajudicial powers of "administrative detention" can still bypass the procuracy and even the courts.

"PRODUCTION BRIGADE" (*SHENGCHAN DADUI*). Also referred to as higher APCs, the production brigades were a middle level of collective ownership within the three-tiered system of rural production organization established after 1958. Equivalent to the "natural village" (*cun*), the brigade generally consisted of from twenty to forty households and represented a higher form of collective ownership than the production team (q.v.). After the disastrous 1958–1960 Great Leap Forward (q.v.), essential decision-making authority over land and labor reverted back to the teams; thus the brigades, like the people's communes (q.v.), became something of an organizational shell. The only exceptions were "model" production brigades, such as the infamous Dazhai brigade (q.v.), which was touted in the 1960s as an advanced form of collective agricultural production that, however, never effectively replaced the teams on a widescale basis. *See also* PEOPLE'S COMMUNES and DAZHAI BRIGADE.

"PRODUCTION TEAM" (*SHENGCHAN DUI*). Also referred to as lower APCs, the production teams were the lowest level of collective ownership within the three-tiered system of rural production organization established after 1958. Production teams—also referred to as "small groups" (*xiaozu*) and small production brigades—were an intra-village work unit that generally consisted of seven to eight households to which land, labor, implements, and draft animals were allotted. Financial accounting and allocation of work points (q.v.) to determine the distribution of income were carried out at this basic level from the end of the Great Leap Forward (1958–1960) (q.v.) onward in most areas of the country. *See also* PEOPLE'S COMMUNES.

PROJECT 571. This was the purported name of the alleged plan by Lin Biao (q.v.), the commander of the PLA (q.v.) and designated successor to Mao Zedong (q.v.), to assassinate the Chairman in 1971. It has been said that "571," which in Chinese is pronounced *wuqiyi*, can also mean "armed uprising." As it turned out, the plot involved only Lin, Ye Qun (q.v.), his wife, and Lin Liguo, his son, and a few dozen supporters. After failing to assassinate Mao, Lin and his entourage tried to flee China by air. Their plane crashed in Mongolia en route to the Soviet Union where Lin had hoped to gain refuge. There is some doubt as to whether Lin Biao died in the crash, or was actually murdered earlier in Beijing (q.v.). PLA historians have called for a full reevaluation of Lin Biao based on the belief that, in fact, he never attempted to assassinate Mao.

PROVINCIALISM. This term has been used to describe the problems of China's powerful regions in their constant conflict with the central authority in Beijing (q.v.). It denotes the centrifugal forces that are constantly at play in Chinese politics. The existence of regional political, economic, and social forces that tend to pull away from the center may be explained, to a large extent, by the vast size of the country (China is slightly larger geographically than the United States), and by the many cultures represented in China's different regions among both the dominant Han (q.v.) and the minority nationalities (q.v.). The major regions include the north, south, central, east, west, and portions of Inner Mongolia, Xinjiang, and Tibet (Xizang). Each of these regions is an entity dominated by unique features of climate, soil composition, and variations in the spoken (and at times written) language.

Centrifugal tendencies have increased since the 1978 economic reforms as the central government has allowed greater flexibility over economic (but not political) issues at the regional and local levels. The 1984 decision on economic structural reform, for instance, encouraged lateral economic relations between economic regions, thereby undermining the center's control via vertically organized state ministries. The most significant aspect of provincialism has been the increasing tensions between Beijing and the various regions over the remittance of taxes to the central authorities. Increased power at the regional level has made for less centralized and taut economic structures, but has also revived fears of warlordism and national disunity reminiscent of the 1930s.

The greatest fear of both Communist Party officials and liberal political dissidents is the increasing forces of separatism among China's minority population of Uygurs and Tibetans who, in the 1980s and early 1990s, engaged in sometimes violent opposition to rule from Beijing. Tensions have also emerged between relatively backward inland regions, such as Sichuan province, and the more prosperous coastal areas that have benefited enormously under Deng Xiaoping's (q.v.) economic reforms. Some economic regions have even sought to establish their own economic autarky by economic blockades of goods to the more economically developed areas so as to protect their local industries.

"PUBLIC SECURITY" (*GONG'AN*). Public security organs constitute China's national police force to maintain domestic law and order and to protect the dictatorship of the CCP (q.v.). Every town and district in major cities in China has a public security branch (*gong'an fenju*), subordinate to a public security bureau (*gong'an ju*), which in turn is overseen by the Ministry of Public Security (*gong'an bu*). This ministry combines the tasks of domestic law and order, border police, and internal security and includes the People's Armed Police (*renmin wuzhuang jingcha*), a separate police force that was set up in 1983 and that consists of more than half a million men. There is also a Ministry of State Security (*guojia anquan bu*)—located in the same buildings in Beijing as the Ministry of Public Security—that functions like the U.S. CIA and is responsible for collecting foreign intel-

ligence and engaging in counterintelligence. The role of public security personnel is supplemented by the People's Armed Police, which
was originally controlled by the PLA (q.v.), but is now under the
direct authority of the Ministry of Public Security. Public security
organs and the People's Armed Police have, at times, operated as
arms of local Communist Party organizations of which all police personnel are members.

The role of the public security organs is to investigate crimes and
arrest suspected criminals, and to engage in the surveillance of Chinese citizens and foreigners. Since the late 1950s, public security
units in China have had the authority to issue sentences in criminal
cases, especially against political enemies of the CCP, and to incarcerate those victims in labor reform camps for interminable periods
under the procedure known as "administrative detention" (*juliu*).
Such power still rests with public security units despite efforts by
constitutional and legal reformists under the rubric of "socialist legality" to embody the authority of prosecution in courts and the procuracy (q.v.) in the 1978 state constitution and subsequent statutes. Arbitrary arrests and detentions have increased as China confronts major
crime waves. Efforts by reformist-minded leaders in China led by Hu
Yaobang (q.v.) to reduce police abuse in the mid-1980s and to create
a police force and legal system independent of the CCP have essentially been abandoned. The police, like the judges, are answerable to
various CCP-run "adjudication committees" and "political and law
committees" that effectively dictate arrests, trials, and sentencing.

Q

QIAN JIAJU (1910–   ). A graduate of the Department of Economics
of Peking University (Beida) (q.v.) in the 1930s, Qian Jiaju remained
in China after the Communist takeover in 1949 as a leading figure in
the CPPCC (q.v.) and in the China Democratic League, one of the
eight largely powerless democratic parties (q.v.) in the PRC (q.v.). In
the 1957 Hundred Flowers campaign (q.v.), Qian criticized CCP
(q.v.) policy toward science and in 1967 was branded as a follower of
Liu Shaoqi (q.v.). He reappeared in 1981 as a member of the Democratic League and the CPPCC. He became a major critic of the docile
role played by NPC (q.v.) delegates selected from the ranks of
"model" workers and peasants who lacked legislative ability or acumen. Qian was also a major critic of the proposed gigantic Three
Gorges Dam project (q.v.) that was formally approved in April 1992
by the NPC. A strong supporter of Mikhail Gorbachev's ideas, Qian

vehemently criticized the economic austerity measures of Premier Li Peng (q.v.) in 1988 and 1989.

QIAN QICHEN (1928–   ). In 1997, Qian Qichen was China's minister of foreign affairs. Previously, he spent many years in the foreign service of the PRC (q.v.) as second secretary in the embassy in the USSR and then as ambassador to Guinea (1974–1976). From 1977 to 1982, Qian was director of the Information Department of the Ministry of Foreign Affairs and from 1982 to 1988 he was vice minister of foreign affairs. He has been minister since 1988.

QIAN WEICHANG (1912–   ). A member of the commission that drafted the Basic Law of the Hong Kong Special Administrative Region, Qian Weichang earned a Ph.D. in applied mathematics in the U.S. and once worked at the Jet Propulsion Lab at Cal Tech. In the 1950s, he returned to China and became a dean and then vice president at Qinghua University (q.v.). In June 1957 during the Hundred Flowers campaign (q.v.), he joined Qian Jiaju to criticize CCP (q.v.) policy on science in an article in the *Enlightenment Daily*, which they coauthored. He was relieved of all posts in 1958 for suggesting that layperson should not be permitted to set guidelines for experts. He was rehabilitated in 1960, but purged again during the Cultural Revolution (1966–1976) (q.v.). He returned in the 1980s and developed a new coding system for computerizing Chinese-language characters.

QIAN ZHENGYING (1923–   ). Born in the United States, Qian Zhengying returned with her family to China where she studied civil engineering and in 1941 joined the CCP (q.v.). From 1958 to 1974, she served as vice minister in the Ministry of Water Resources and Electric Power and was a member of the Grand Canal Commission and the Huai River Harnessing Commission. In 1973, she was elected to the CCP Central Committee. From 1975 to 1988 she served as minister of water resources and electric power and in 1988 she became minister of water resources where she strongly supported construction of the Three Gorges Dam project (q.v.).

QIAO SHI (1924–   ). Leader of the Shanghai (q.v.) underground student movement in the 1940s, in the 1950s and early 1960s Qiao Shi worked in the Communist Youth League (q.v.) and in the steel industry. In 1982, he was appointed director of the International Liaison Department of the CCP (q.v.). In 1984 he became a director of the CCP Organization Department. In 1985 he became a member of the Politburo (q.v.) and the Party Secretariat and in 1987 a member of the Politburo Standing Committee. In 1989 he became president of the Central Party School (q.v.) and visited Romania where he praised the great socialist successes of the Ceausescu government two weeks before its collapse. Since 1993 he has been chairman of the NPC.

QIGONG. Part of China's rich tradition of non-Western medicine, *qigong* is a health regimen that involves both breathing exercises and meditation and is said to have great healing powers. Masters of *qigong* can cut gold and crack jade, defeat others in combat, leap onto roofs, and vault over walls. It is related to studies of the *Book of Changes (Ijing)*, fortune-telling, divination, psychic arts, and Chinese geomancy (*fengshui*). Practioners of *qigong* believe that there are gods and spirits in the heavens, and that all people have souls. The world is neither physical nor conceptual, but is composed of the Way (*dao*) and elements known as the "elementary breath" (*qi*). At this level, people can directly perceive the world and master it. More than 50 million people in China practice *qigong*, including many of China's elderly leaders, who look to its healing powers to keep them fit. Since the pro-democracy movement in 1989, however, the Chinese government has cracked down on local *qigong* associations and condemned the practice as "superstitious."

QIN DYNASTY (221–207 B.C.). *See* ANTI-LIN [BIAO], ANTI-CONFUCIUS CAMPAIGN.

QINGHUA UNIVERSITY. One of the best universities in China, Qinghua was established in 1908 with funds remitted back to China from the indemnity it paid to the United States after the defeat of the Boxer rebellion by foreign armies in Beijing (q.v.) in 1900. Qinghua was for many years a liberal arts school, modeled after American universities, that consistently attempted to achieve autonomy from the Nationalist (KMT) (q.v.) government. After the Communist takeover in 1949, the liberal arts were largely abolished as institutional autonomy was totally eliminated. The university became a polytechnical institution, and is now often referred to as the "MIT of China." During the Cultural Revolution (1966–1976) (q.v.), the school was the scene of pitched battles between armed Red Guard (q.v.) factions that had formed among the student body. Like many universities and high schools during this period, Qinghua periodically shut down as its students were sent down to the countryside. After 1976, the university was reestablished along its previous polytechnic lines. Regular entrance procedures were also reinstituted to replace the highly politicized criteria employed for admission during the Cultural Revolution. Many of China's top physicists and other scientists have earned degrees from Qinghua. Qinghua has also served as the training ground for nuclear physicists from allies of the PRC, such as the Democratic Republic of Korea (i.e., North Korea) and Iraq.

QUOTATIONS FROM CHAIRMAN MAO. This small book, also known as the "little red book," of Mao sayings became the "bible" of the Red Guards (q.v.) during the Cultural Revolution (1966–1976) (q.v.). It was first compiled in 1964 by the General Political Department of the PLA (q.v.), and distributed for "study" to every soldier. This reflected the political predilections of Lin Biao (q.v.), who in 1960, after replacing Peng Dehuai (q.v.) as China's minister of defense, advocated that "everyone must study Chairman Mao's writings." The book contains more than 400 quotations taken from Mao's writings in the *Selected Works.* During the Cultural Revolution, more than 1 billion copies of the *Quotations* were distributed to Red Guards, creating a virtual paper shortage in the country. In the late 1960s, the *Quotations* was required reading for nearly the entire population of the country. The subjects covered in the book included Mao's wisdom on studying, discipline, self-reliance (q.v.), "revolutionary heroism," and even how to grow tomatoes. Children reared during the Cultural Revolution were taught to wave the "little red book" in their hands as they cried out: "Chairman Mao is the reddest sun in our hearts." After the Cultural Revolution ended in 1976, the *Quotations* virtually disappeared in China and rapidly became a collector's item for visiting foreigners.

R

RAIDI (1938–   ). A member of the Tibetan minority nationality (q.v.) and a graduate of the CCP-run Central Nationalities Institute in Beijing (q.v.), Raidi has been a longtime member of the Tibet (Xizang) Autonomous Region Communist Party. In 1985, he became the deputy secretary of the Tibet Communist Party and chairman of the standing committee of the Tibet Autonomous Region People's Congress.

"REBEL FACTION" (*ZAOFANPAI*). The most radical faction of Red Guards (q.v.) during the Cultural Revolution (1966–1976) (q.v.), the rebel faction was made up of dispossessed individuals under the CCP (q.v.) regime. These included many temporary and contract workers who lacked secure employment, youths who had been rusticated to rural areas and had surreptitiously returned to the cities, students from the Five Black Categories (q.v.), various social derelicts and criminal elements, and even some CCP members and demobilized soldiers who had run afoul of their superiors. With many axes to grind and bearing harsh grudges against the CCP establishment, members of the *zaofanpai* engaged in the most severe and often violent attacks on Party cadres (q.v.) and anyone else chosen for retribution. This largely cohered with Mao Zedong's (q.v.) goal of purging the CCP of its mainstream membership and installing a new "revolutionary" generation of leaders. *Zaofanpai* and the more conservative factions of Red Guards engaged in intense internecine conflicts that severely disrupted urban life, until Mao ordered most Red Guards to the countryside, effectively ending their central role in the Cultural Revolution. Members of the *zaofanpai* were later singled out for retribution during the anti–Gang of Four (q.v.) campaign in the mid 1970s that followed the purge of Mao Zedong's widow, Jiang Qing (q.v.), and her radical followers.

"RECTIFICATION CAMPAIGN" (*ZHENGFENG YUNDONG*). These are campaigns of political "study" and "investigation" in China that the CCP (q.v.) leadership has periodically employed to achieve ideological orthodoxy, unification of the CCP, mass compliance, and the elevation of Mao Zedong (q.v.) to supreme leadership. The first such "rectification campaign" occurred in 1942–1944 when political opponents of Mao Zedong were weeded out of the CCP and freethinking intellectuals (q.v.), such as Wang Shiwei (q.v.), were vilified and ultimately executed. The major purpose of this and subsequent "rectification" campaigns, however, was to boost the authority and personality cult (q.v.) of Mao Zedong. Thus, for the first time in CCP history, Mao's writings in 1942–1944 became the major basis for cadre "study" and discussion in political study groups (q.v.). "Criticism and self-criticism" (q.v.) by errant cadres was also a central component of the "rectification," with the intention of increasing "Party unity," but producing of greater intimidation and fear among Party cadres and especially among intellectuals and artists. The same type of campaign occurred during the 1957–1958 Anti-Rightist campaign (q.v.).

"RED AND EXPERT" (*HONG YU ZHUAN*). This was a major job requirement for the millions of Party cadres (q.v.) in China during the Mao Zedong (q.v.) era (1949–1976). The idea was to ensure that Party workers were both politically pure and professionally competent. One at the expense of the other could erode the authority of the CCP (q.v.). A Party cadre who was politically suspect but professionally competent was a threat to the CCP's ideological purity, while a Party cadre who was politically loyal but professionally incompetent could alienate the population through poor leadership and decision making. Party cadres were thus chided to avoid "'becoming expert before one becomes red' and of 'becoming expert without having to become red.'"

This standard was first promulgated in 1957 after intellectuals (q.v.) criticized the CCP during the Hundred Flowers (q.v.) for promoting people into positions of authority on the basis of political loyalty rather than merit. This reflected the fact that many Party members espoused the proper political attitudes but did not have the professional skills necessary to administer the economy and manage such institutions as schools, health care facilities, and the military. During the Cultural Revolution (1966–1976) (q.v.), radical political forces associated with Mao's wife, Jiang Qing (q.v.), emphasized only the political dimension (that is, one's "redness"). Conservative groups associated with Liu Shaoqi (q.v.) and Deng Xiaoping (q.v.) tended, on the other hand, to focus on the professional competence of Party cadres. Since 1978, the "red and expert" criterion has largely been dropped from CCP propaganda, though political loyalty to the regime is still an important factor to judge one's status in the CCP.

RED FLAG (*HONGQI*). The major theoretical journal of the Central Committee of the CCP (q.v.), *Red Flag* was published monthly from 1958 to 1979, and then bimonthly from 1980 until its termination in June 1988. When inaugurated in 1958, *Red Flag* was edited by Chen Boda (q.v.), replacing the magazine *Study (Xuexi)* as the main theoretical publication of the Party. Along with the *People's Daily* (q.v.) and the *Liberation Army Daily*, it was a major publication in the PRC (q.v.) with a national circulation of about 9 million. These three publications often joined together to publish important joint editorials. During the Cultural Revolution (1966–1976) (q.v.), *Red Flag* was generally an outlet for the radical faction and published their most important political and ideological articles, often under pseudonyms. During the post-Mao era, *Red Flag* was headed, among others, by Xiong Fu, who promoted the leftist concept of the "two whatevers" (q.v.) and who generally resisted the liberal reform campaign. In 1978, Xiong refused to publish a commentary on the topic of "practice is the sole criterion of truth" that was meant to attack leftist dogma. Instead, he supported the efforts of the hard-line conservative faction led by Deng Liqun (q.v.) and Chen Yun (q.v.) to turn back the political and economic reforms. In July 1988, *Red Flag* was replaced by *Seeking Truth (Qiushi)* (q.v.).

"RED GUARDS" (*HONGWEIBING*). A major political force during the Cultural Revolution (1966–1976) (q.v.), the Red Guards were composed of university students, high-school students, and even elementary school students. Formed in mid-1966, the Red Guards had strong backing from CCP (q.v.) Chairman Mao Zedong (q.v.), who sanctioned their role of waging battle against the established Party and government apparatus. Mao first reviewed the Red Guards at a mass rally on August 18, 1966 and donned his own "red armband" that came to symbolize his support for their organization. From 1966 to 1968, Red Guard groups rampaged through China's cities attacking Party and government personnel, intellectuals (q.v.), and teachers. They also destroyed vestiges of China's traditional culture—referred to as the "four olds" (q.v.)—such as religious temples and museums. As the Red Guards became increasingly factionalized in 1967–1968, pitched battles between competing groups broke out on China's university campuses, such as Qinghua University (q.v.) where a "one hundred day" war ensued with many casualties. The increasing violence and social and economic disruption led Mao to order in the PLA (q.v.) to bring the Red Guard violence under control. By late 1968, most Red Guards had been sent to the countryside for "further revolutionary training." Their organizations were disbanded and many Red Guards were left deeply disillusioned. *See also* FOUR OLDS.

"REFORM THROUGH LABOR" (*LAODONG GAIZAO*). This is a form of punishment in China that is also known as *laogai*. It is applied to criminals who have been sentenced, including political criminals. In jails or labor reform camps, prisoners are subject to different degrees of supervision and management in an effort to make them into "new men" by virtue of enforced manual labor. This system was initiated soon after the CCP (q.v.) took power in 1949 and was justified by CCP Chairman Mao Zedong (q.v.) to ensure that prisoners did not "eat without working." The system of labor reform camps in China is very large and the number of labor reform prisoners may now number in the millions, though not all are political prisoners. These camps are economic enterprises that produce goods for both the domestic and international markets. Sale of Chinese prison-made goods in the United States has been a major source of tension in the U.S.–China relationship (q.v.). Since the inauguration of the economic reform policies in 1978, the labor reform system has remained intact with very few changes.

RELIGION. As a Communist country, free exercise of religion has been generally suppressed and/or subject to intense state control and scrutiny since the establishment of the PRC (q.v.) in 1949. From the beginning of reforms in 1978, however, religious practice has been more open with less government persecution of religious practitioners. Prior to the Communist takeover, the vast majority of Chinese practiced a combination of Buddhism, Taoism, and ancestor worship. China also had practicing Christians, and among its 90 million national minority (q.v.) population a variety of religions, such as Islam among the Moslem (or *Hui* people) and Lamaism (a branch of Buddhism) among the Tibetans. From 1949 to 1978, religious practice was severely constrained and subject to outright persecution during periods of political radicalism, such as the Cultural Revolution (1966–1976) (q.v.). Lamaist monks and monasteries in Tibet during this era were particularly hard hit by the destructive activities of the rampaging Red Guards (q.v.). Upwards of 10,000 monasteries were destroyed during this ten-year period. Christians were also subject to persecution throughout the history of the PRC, beginning with the expulsion and imprisonment of foreign missionaries and Chinese Christians in 1949. Chinese Catholics, such as Archbishop Dominic Tang Yiming, who refused to renounce their ties to the Vatican and to join the state-affiliated Patriotic Association of Catholics, were subject to years of imprisonment and persecution. They were released only in the 1980s, usually because of illness. Since 1949, the Chinese have consistently denounced ties between Chinese Catholics and the Vatican as a violation of China's state sovereignty. Although the practice of Christianity and other religions has become more tolerated since 1978, persecution of individuals who practice outside state-affiliated organizations still occurs. Christian house churches in Chinese villages, for instance, have been closed by the state, along with Buddhist and other religious activities that the CCP finds threatening. Nevertheless, religious belief and observance have increased dramatically, especially in the countryside where traditional and newfound religions are growing at a rapid pace to fill the spiritual vacuum left by the decline of ideological fervor and to confront increased government repression.

RESOLUTION ON CERTAIN QUESTIONS IN THE HISTORY OF OUR PARTY SINCE THE FOUNDING OF THE PEOPLE'S REPUBLIC OF CHINA. Issued by the Sixth Plenum of the Eleventh Party Congress in June 1981, this official CCP (q.v.) document criticizes Mao Zedong (q.v.) for his "mistakes" in extending the 1957 Anti-Rightist campaign (q.v.) to large numbers of intellectuals (q.v.), for launching the 1958–1960 Great Leap Forward (q.v.), for purging Peng Dehuai (q.v.), and for instigating the 1966–1976 Cultural Revolution (q.v.). The document also repudiates the theory of "continuing the revolution under the dictatorship of the proletariat," which had served as the ideological underpinning for the Cultural Revolution and other radical policies. The resolution claims that from the late 1950s onward Mao Zedong's leadership degenerated into an increasingly "despotic" and "patriarchal" style and that Mao's "personality cult" (q.v.) robbed the CCP of its "revolutionary tradition" of "collective leadership" (*jiti lingdao*). The document was reportedly toned down in its criticism of Mao due to the personal intervention of Deng Xiaoping (q.v.), who made sure that Mao's leadership was defined as overwhelmingly "correct." Mao Zedong Thought (q.v.) was also reinterpreted to fit the goals of modernization pursued by the post-1978 CCP leadership. Overall, this document was much less critical of Mao Zedong than was Nikita Khrushchev's "secret speech" denouncing Josef Stalin at the 1956 Twentieth Soviet Party Congress.

"RESTRICTION OF BOURGEOIS RIGHTS" (*XIANZHI ZICHAN-JIEJI FAQUAN*). In 1975, just one year before the death of Mao Zedong (q.v.), pressure was building from reformist elements who had been recently rehabilitated in the CCP (q.v.)—primarily Deng Xiaoping (q.v)—to change dramatically the course of China's development. The Cultural Revolution (1966–1976) (q.v.) had viciously attacked all vestiges of "capitalism" and had purged from the Party individuals such as Liu Shaoqi (q.v.), who had wanted to pay greater attention to economic problems. China's economy was stagnating as individuals were prohibited from owning any private property, thereby destroying any individual incentive for accumulating wealth. As the reaction against the political radicalism and anti-development thrust of the Cultural Revolution began to build in the mid-1970s, radical forces lead by the "Gang of Four" (q.v.) mobilized the propaganda machine under their control to attack all "bourgeois rights." These "rights" referred to exchanges of commodities with money, ownership of property, and determination of wages according to work performed.

Zhang Chunqiao (q.v.), a prominent radical and member of the Gang of Four, published a major article in the CCP's theoretical journal, *Red Flag* (q.v.), advocating the creation of the necessary "ideological weapons" against "bourgeois rights" and the use of the "dictatorship of the proletariat" to ensure that "bourgeois rights" not reappear. Mao Zedong also weighed in by calling for the elimination of the differences between workers and peasants, town and country, and mental and menial labor—the ultimate goals of communism. After Deng Xiaoping reappeared in late 1973, he began to promote China's turn toward economic and technological development, but he was purged in April 1976 and thereafter the campaign against "bourgeois rights" intensified. The death of Mao Zedong in September 1976 and the arrest of the Gang of Four the next month ended the criticism of "bourgeois rights" per se and led to the promotion of significant economic reforms in which money and commodities were exchanged and wage scales more generally reflected the quality of work. Criticism of "bourgeois liberalization" (q.v.)—code words in China for political reform—did, however, continue throughout the 1980s and 1990s.

"REVERSAL OF VERDICTS" (*PINGFAN*). A judicial-political term, also meaning "rehabilitation," it refers to correcting a legal case or altering a political judgment that has been decided improperly, with corresponding compensation to those individuals whose cases were handled incorrectly or who were sentenced or executed unjustly. Historically, the term traces back to the ancient Han dynasty (202 B.C.–A.D. 220). After 1949 it was used in the case of individuals whom the Communists had wrongly persecuted during the anti-counterrevolutionary campaigns (q.v.) in the early and mid-1950s. Writing in 1957, Mao Zedong (q.v.) admitted to "mistakes in the work of suppressing counterrevolutionaries" and insisted that steps be taken to correct them. Nevertheless, during the relative freedom of the Hundred Flowers (q.v.), non-CCP members called for the establishment of an independent organ of the government to investigate the wrongful persecution of innocent people, but to no avail. CCP (q.v.) members purged during the 1950s and 1960s, especially during the Cultural Revolution (1966–1976) (q.v.), were themselves "rehabilitated" after 1978. Such mass "rehabilitations" of many top leaders, including Yang Shangkun (q.v.) and Bo Yibo (q.v.), were pushed by Hu Yaobang (q.v.) against considerable political resistance from remnant leftist forces in the CCP. Many intellectuals persecuted by the CCP, such as Wang Shiwei (q.v.), were also rehabilitated. But some CCP leaders from the past (especially those purged in the power struggles of the 1930s and 1940s) and many intellectuals persecuted by the Communists during the Anti-Rightist (q.v.) and other such campaigns, have yet to be rehabilitated. *See also* ANTI-COUNTERREVOLUTIONARY CAMPAIGN.

"REVISIONISM" (*XIUZHENGZHUYI*). In Marxist-Leninist ideology, "revisionism" refers to the negation of the "basic principles of Marxism and its universal truths" by self-proclaimed Marxist-Leninists. Revisionists are heretics who have willfully distorted the meaning of Marxism-Leninism and thus undermined the pursuit of revolutionary goals. Historically, the first revisionist was Eduard Bernstein, who in the late nineteenth century suggested that socialism could be achieved through a process of evolution instead of revolution, with Marxist parties working through, rather than against, parliamentary bodies.

For this Bernstein was roundly condemned by Lenin and other defenders of the Marxist orthodoxy. After World War II, the newly established communist-controlled country of Yugoslavia was denounced by the Soviet Union as "revisionist" for its anti-Stalinist positions and for its more liberal approaches to political and economic questions. As far as China was concerned, the Soviet Union became "revisionist" under the leadership of Nikita Khrushchev and his brand of communism that stressed economic and technical achievement over ideological orthodoxy. And within China, Liu Shaoqi (q.v.) and other top CCP (q.v.) leaders were labeled "revisionist" for their purported opposition to Maoist policies.

REVOLUTIONARY COMMITTEES. Established during the Cultural Revolution (1966–1976) (q.v.) to replace the regular CCP (q.v.) organizational structure, these committees proved to be very unwieldy and were dismantled as administrative bodies in the late 1970s. The first revolutionary committee was set up in 1967 in China's northeast province of Heilongjiang by local Red Guard (q.v.) groups. It comprised a "three-in-one combination" of "mass revolutionary rebel groups" that was mostly composed of Red Guard organizations, representatives from the PLA (q.v.) and the People's Militia (q.v.), and Maoist revolutionary cadres (q.v.) from the Party and government bureaucracies. By 1968, virtually every province and autonomous region in China had established a revolutionary committee. Below the provincial level, committees were organized in schools, factories, people's communes (q.v.), and government offices, where they were to provide for mass input into the political process. In reality, it was the PLA that effectively ran most revolutionary committees and turned them into the organized arm of radical political leaders in Beijing (q.v.). Under the leadership of Lin Biao (q.v.), the PLA sided with the leftist forces. But once Lin fell from power in 1971, the PLA took a decidedly conservative direction and thus ceased supporting the radical goals of the revolutionary committees. At the same time, the regular Party committee structure of the CCP was gradually reestablished in China's political structure with Mao's blessings in the provinces and at lower levels, thereby effectively negating the revolutionary committees. After the arrest of the Gang of Four (q.v.) in October 1976, the revolutionary committees were reduced to administrative arms of local people's congresses (q.v.). The return of Deng Xiaoping (q.v.) and the beginning of economic reform in 1978 led to the formal abolition of revolutionary committees in 1979.

REVOLUTIONARY ELDER (*GEMING YUANLAO*). Reference to senior Party leaders, such as Peng Zhen (q.v.) and Deng Yingchao (q.v.), whose long service in the CCP (q.v.) and enormous personal status was transferred into considerable political influence with or without formal position. Many "elders" were nominally retired but still had substantial impact on the political and economic decisions of the CCP. Deng Xiaoping (q.v.) was perhaps the most famous (and influential) "revolutionary elder."

RIGHTISTS. *See* ANTI-RIGHTIST CAMPAIGN.

RIVER ELEGY (HESHANG). This is a six-part documentary produced in 1988 for Central China Television by a group of academics, writers, and TV directors. Written by Su Xiaokang, an ex-Red Guard (q.v.) and Wang Luxiang, a university lecturer, and directed by twenty-six year old Xia Jun, the work weaves together a number of cultural, historical, and political themes that question the country's obsession with such national icons as the Great Wall and the dragon, and urges that the Chinese people break out of the interminable cycle of disasters and cultural stagnation that the authors tie to the cult of the Yellow River. Comparing China's "old civilization" to the "silt accumulated on the bed of the Yellow River," *River Elegy* calls for the creation of an industrial society and for further opening to the "blue water" civilizations of the West so as to infuse the country with the necessary dynamism to transform its backward culture. In this sense, *River Elegy* is reminiscent of some themes espoused in the 1919 May Fourth Movement (q.v.) that led to the establishment of the CCP (q.v.) in 1921. Combining interviews with leading reform intellectuals and footage from the Great Leap Forward (1958–1960) (q.v.) and the Cultural Revolution (1966–1976) (q.v.), the film equates Maoism and the Communist state with traditional culture and the dynastic state—both of which brought huge disasters to the country. The traditional inland worldview rooted in China's peasant society and embodied in Confucian and Maoist orthodoxies needs, the film suggests, to be supplanted by an outward oriented society, linked to the rest of the world by commerce, trade, and a cosmopolitan worldview.

Popular response to the series was overwhelming. Estimates are that more than 200 million Chinese viewed it and many thousands also purchased copies of the script or wrote letters to the TV studio. But because *River Elegy* violated many cultural and political proscriptions and had vilified such historical icons as the Great Wall, the Yellow River, and the dragon (a symbol of the emperor and of fertility), it came under intense pressure from hard-line CCP leaders, such as Vice President Wang Zhen (q.v.). Supportive of the reform faction led by CCP general secretary Zhao Ziyang (q.v.) who was deposed during the 1989 Tiananmen crisis, *River Elegy* was ultimately banned. In 1990, the CCP responded to the film with its own documentary titled *On the Road: A Century of Marxism* which lauds the accomplishments of the CCP and praises Marxism-Leninism and the leadership of Deng Xiaoping (q.v.).

RONG YIREN (1916–   ). Son of a wealthy Jiangsu province capitalist family, Rong attended St. John's University in Shanghai. He is chairman of the board of directors of the China International Trust and Investment Corporation (CITIC) (q.v.) and a managing director of the Bank of China (q.v.). Rong Yiren has helped to develop China's economic ties with foreign nations ever since his reappearance in 1972 after the Cultural Revolution (1966–1976) (q.v.). In 1987 he was appointed honorary chairman of China's National Committee for Pacific Economic Cooperation. In 1993 he was named vice president of the PRC (q.v.).

RUAN CHONGWU (1933–   ). A 1957 graduate of the Moscow Motor Vehicle Machinery College, Ruan Chongwu was an official in the Shanghai (q.v.) government and Party organizations in the early 1980s. In 1985 he was appointed minister of public security and political commissar (q.v.) of the People's Armed Police. In July 1989 he became minister of labor.

S

SATELLITE PARTIES. *See* DEMOCRATIC PARTIES.

SECRETARIAT OF THE CCP. *See* CHINESE COMMUNIST PARTY.

SEEKING TRUTH (QIUSHI). Established in July 1988, *Seeking Truth* is a biweekly journal that replaced *Red Flag* (q.v.) as the CCP's (q.v.) primary theoretical mouthpiece. Although initially set up to promulgate theories and ideas related to China's political and economic reform and opening to the outside world, the magazine has served the interests of the CCP to counter excessively liberal opinion, especially since the military crackdown in 1989.

"SELF RELIANCE" *(ZILI GENGSHENG)*. This phrase was first used by Mao Zedong (q.v.) in 1946 at the beginning of the Civil War with the KMT (q.v.). Mao rejected "dependence on foreign aid" and declared that the CCP (q.v.) would rely on its own army and people to achieve its political goals. Significant military support for the Chinese

Communists was not provided by the Soviet Union, which limited its material aid to the Chinese to outmoded Japanese weaponry captured in China's northeast at the end of World War II. Thus the CCP largely won the Civil War with weapons captured from the KMT, which helped solidify the concept of "self-reliance" among top CCP military and political leaders. In the 1950s, this policy did not prevent the PRC (q.v.) from accepting substantial aid from the USSR up until the end of the Great Leap Forward (1958–1960).

In 1960 when in the midst of the Sino-Soviet conflict (q.v.) the Soviet Union withdrew its technical experts from China and terminated work on 156 industrial and related projects, Mao reiterated China's determination to be "self-reliant." In effect, this translated into considerable international isolation on China's part as it pursued an autarkic strategy of economic growth lasting until the "opening up" that began in the early 1970s with the visit to China of President Richard Nixon. Military industries were also developed in inland areas of the country (the so-called Third Front) to support a possible military confrontation with the United States or the Soviet Union. During this period from the early 1960s to the 1970s, China generally avoided formal contacts or strategic alliances with other nations. Domestically, self reliance also led Mao to encourage each region of the country to become economically independent through the development of local small-scale industries and regional self-reliance in grain production, policies that were reversed after the inauguration of the 1978 economic reforms.

"SETTLING ACCOUNTS" (*QINGSUAN*). This term has its origins in the financial transactions and obligations in Chinese society where at the end of the lunar year people with debts, etc., "settle accounts" and clear the books. Politically, the term has become a metaphor to seek revenge against one's political enemies during the various campaigns and movements, particularly the Cultural Revolution (1966–1976) (q.v.). Since revenge carried a momentum of its own, efforts were made into the 1980s to prohibit the mutual recriminations and antagonisms that "settling accounts" entailed. At one time, the term could not be used by ordinary people, for instance at restaurants where it means to "pay the check."

SHANGHAI. Located at the eastern end of the Yangtze river delta, Shanghai is China's second largest city with 13.5 million inhabitants at the end of 1994. It is more than 6,000 square kilometers in size and is a major industrial and shipping center. Site of the Baoshan Steel Plant (q.v.), the city remains the most important industrial base in China with more than 8,000 state-run enterprises involving metallurgy, shipbuilding, light industry, and petrochemicals. In 1987 its total output was more than 100 billion yuan of which industry accounted for 97 percent. Per capita income in the city is about $2,000, considerably higher than the national average. Shanghai has been a major center for foreign investment and joint ventures. The Pudong development zone is currently under construction in the northeast part of the city to increase foreign investment. Shanghai is now the location of Nextgage, the world's second-largest department store (after Macy's in New York) built by the Japanese developer Kazuo Wada. Shanghai is also poised to benefit from the Three Gorges Dam project which will supply the city with desperately needed electrical power. However, hydrologists have expressed concern that changes in the Yangtze River brought about by the dam will have irreparable effects on the city's soil and its water supply.

SHANGHAI COMMUNIQUÉ (1972). This was the first official joint document between the United States and China that began the normalization of relations. The process ended in January 1979 when the United States and China fully normalized diplomatic relations and exchanged ambassadors.

The Shanghai Communiqué was issued during President Richard Nixon's pathbreaking trip to China in February 1972. It effectively signaled U.S. recognition of China's Communist government after more than twenty years of refusal to accept the CCP (q.v.) regime as the legitimate government of China. The text of the communiqué was not agreed upon until President Nixon's historic trip had nearly ended with his visit to the city of Shanghai (q.v.), hence the name "Shanghai Communiqué." In the document, the United States accepted the principle of "one China" and recognized that the island of Taiwan (under KMT [q.v.] rule) was "part of China." Both China and the United States agreed to disagree on whether force could legitimately be used by the Communist government to incorporate Taiwan into China. In effect, the Shanghai Communiqué allowed the U.S. and China to proceed with normal relations without really solving the knotty Taiwan issue. Ultimately, after full diplomatic recognition between the United States and China, the United States abandoned its mutual defense treaty with Taiwan and ended diplomatic relations with the island. But the passage of the Taiwan Relations Act in 1979 perpetuated U.S. defense commitments in the absence of a formal treaty. U.S. and Chinese differences over how to incorporate Taiwan back into China remain today as the Chinese insist they have the right to resort to force, while the United States rejects this position. The Shanghai Communiqué also committed both countries to avoid seeking "hegemony"—that is, domination—in East Asia, though differences remained regarding how the United States and China perceived the evolving triangular relationship between China, the United States, and the Soviet Union. *See also* UNITED STATES–CHINA RELATIONS.

SHENZHEN. *See* SPECIAL ECONOMIC ZONES.

SINO-INDIAN WAR (1962). This was a short but intense conflict between Chinese and Indian troops involving disputed claims over border lands in the Himalayas in Tibet and northern India. The focus of the conflict was competing claims over the Aksai Chin (Ladakh) territories and conflicts regarding the McMahon Line that had been established by British colonial authorities in 1914 as the territorial boundary between India and China but had been rejected by the latter. After weeks of parrying and thrusts by military units on both sides, the Chinese PLA (q.v.) attacked in force in October and November 1962 and drove Indian army units south of the McMahon Line, thereby establishing undisputed Chinese control over 3,750 square miles of territory claimed by China, in the west near the Himalayan state of Bhutan and, in the east, near the border with Burma. Once the fighting ended, the Chinese unilaterally withdrew their forces (except for border police units) 20 kilometers behind the old, disputed frontier. Indian forces lost more than 3,000 men and there were indeterminate casualties on the Chinese side. The conflict came in the midst of the U.S.-Soviet confrontation over the Cuban missile crisis and after years of growing tension in Sino-Indian affairs following the Tibetan revolt in 1959, which led the Dalai Lama (q.v.) to flee Tibet for refuge in India. India's close ties with the USSR and its increasingly cordial relations with the United States beginning in the late 1950s also contributed to the outbreak of the war. A final negotiated settlement of the border issue has never been achieved.

SINO-JAPANESE WAR (1937–1945). The war between China and Japan began on July 7, 1937, and ended with the U.S. defeat of the Japanese empire in 1945. The Chinese-Japanese conflict grew out of a long period of intensifying conflict between the two nations that began with China's unification in 1928 under the Nationalist (KMT) (q.v.) government. In the 1930s, Japan expanded its control over Manchuria, which at the time was outside of Nationalist control, and established the puppet state of Manchukuo in 1932 under the titular authority of Aisin-Gioro Puyi, the last Qing emperor. Japan then proceeded to gain control over four northern provinces in China proper in 1936 through the use of puppet troops and Chinese political leaders opposed to the Nationalist regime of Chiang Kai-shek. War erupted after the infamous Marco Polo Bridge Incident, when an exchange of gunfire between Japanese and Chinese troops just outside Beiping (Beijing) served as a pretext for Japan to commence a full-scale invasion of China, though technically war was not formally declared between the two countries until December 7, 1941. Japanese forces quickly overran huge parts of China in 1937 and 1938, forcing Chiang Kai-shek's armies to retreat to the inland city of Chongqing (Chungking) in Sichuan province, trading space for time. In the interim the Japanese captured the Nationalist capital city of Nanking and carried out systematic murder of 100,000 civilians in the notorious Rape of Nanking. All major coastal cities in China came under Japanese control through a series of puppet regimes as Chinese casualties approached one-half million. In 1939, after a failed Chinese counteroffensive, the war bogged down, with the Japanese occupying huge stretches of China with more than 2 million troops. After the U.S. entry into the war, America provided crucial assistance to Nationalist forces, while contacts were made with Communist forces holed up in Yan'an where the CCP (q.v.) successfully mobilized peasant support in the vast countryside. By 1945, CCP armies numbered almost 1 million and Communist-run border governments effectively controlled 50 million people, thereby giving the Communists a distinct advantage in the post–World War II Chinese Civil War (1946–1949). In contrast, the Nationalists emerged from the war with poor morale and weakened popular support that proved fatal in the ensuing struggle with the CCP. The Sino-Japanese War, in effect, fundamentally altered the political landscape in China.

SINO-SOVIET CONFLICT. The split between the two largest Communist states broke out in the late 1950s over diametrically opposed concepts of Communist ideology and international communism, but the conflict also reflected a fundamental clash of national interests. The initial spur to Chinese-Soviet enmity was the 1956 de-Stalinization speech (also known as the Secret Speech) delivered by then Soviet leader Nikita Khrushchev to the CPSU Twentieth Party Congress. A scathing critique of Stalin and the enormous "crimes of the Stalin era," this speech rankled the Chinese Communist leadership who still held Stalin and the Stalinist system in high regard. For Mao Zedong (q.v.), the speech reeked of "revisionism" (q.v.) and suggested that the Soviet Union under Khrushchev was forsaking its leadership role in the international Communist movement, a role the Chinese were happy to fill. From 1956 to 1958 the conflict remained essentially submerged in inter-Party statements as each accused the other of perfidy and each was concerned with the other's growing independence.

In 1958 in the midst of the Taiwan Straits Crisis (q.v.), China expected full-scale Soviet support which was not forthcoming as the

USSR was undoubtedly concerned about the reckless behavior of its Chinese counterparts in provoking a military confrontation with the U.S. and the ROC—a confrontation the Chinese would ultimately lose. At this time, Soviet leader Khrushchev accused China of warmongering. Chinese concerns over Soviet assistance and support mushroomed in 1959 when the USSR apparently sided with India in its growing border conflict with China. The coup de grace came with the 1959 decision by the Soviet Union to terminate its defense accord with China, in which the Soviets had apparently offered the Chinese technical assistance to construct an atomic bomb (q.v.). Khrushchev's short visit to China in 1959 after his trip to the United States (which coincided with the tenth anniversary celebrations of the PRC [q.v.]) failed to assuage the Chinese who accused the Soviets of siding with the United States. Khrushchev also angered the Chinese by denouncing the Great Leap Forward (1958–1960) (q.v.), claiming that the transition to communism could not be achieved in such a manner, even though some Soviets evidently sympathized with this strain of Chinese idealism.

The Sino-Soviet alliance publicly ruptured in 1960 after the Chinese denounced the ideological errors of the Soviet leadership in a *Red Flag* (q.v.) article entitled "Long Live Leninism." The Soviets decided to end all economic and military support to the PRC. This involved the termination of more than 150 scientific and industrial projects and the withdrawal from China of more than 1,000 Soviet personnel who left the country with blueprints in hand. From late 1960 to 1962, the two countries engaged in a kind of proxy war, as the Soviet Union denounced Albania, China's lonely ally among the East European Communist states, while China returned the favor by condemning Yugoslavia and its leader Tito for blatant "revisionism" as a surrogate for the Soviet Union and Khrushchev. The signing of the Nuclear Test Ban Treaty between the U.S. and the USSR in 1963 convinced the Chinese that the Soviet leadership was hopelessly revisionist and that it had surrendered in its holy war against imperialism (q.v.), an accusation the Chinese would continue to make against the USSR even as the Soviets provided substantial aid to the North Vietnamese Communists in their war with the United States.

In 1969, the Sino-Soviet conflict almost led to outright war as Russian and Chinese forces engaged in a serious military exchange near the Ussuri River along the Sino-Soviet border in China's far north. By 1970 China was openly warning of nuclear war with the USSR and undertook civil defense efforts in its major cities such as Beijing (q.v.) where a vast network of underground tunnels and facilities were built to shelter the population in the event of a nuclear exchange (the so-called underground city). The Lin Biao Incident (q.v.) in 1971 further complicated Sino-Soviet relations but, fortunately, cooler heads ultimately prevailed as both sides reverted to rhetorical conflicts, though significant military forces were maintained by both countries along the border well into the 1980s.

A brief "thaw" in Sino-Soviet relations occurred in the mid-1970s as China sought out Soviet views on the border issue and in 1980 when negotiations between the two sides were carried out after China formally ended its 1950 alliance with Moscow. These talks achieved little success, however, as China demanded the Soviet Union take action to remove the "three obstacles" to normalizing their relations by pulling out of Afghanistan (q.v.), withdrawing Soviet support for the North Vietnamese occupation of Cambodia (q.v.), and reducing Soviet troops along the Sino-Soviet border. By the late 1980s these issues were generally resolved by Soviet leader Mikhail Gorbachev, who, in a May 1989 visit to Beijing, agreed to "normalization," a policy that has continued with the Russian Federation under Boris Yeltsin, who has sought increased trade ties with China's booming economy in return for Chinese purchases of Soviet military hardware.

SINO-SOVIET TREATY OF FRIENDSHIP, ALLIANCE, AND MUTUAL ASSISTANCE (1950). Signed by CCP (q.v.) Chairman Mao Zedong (q.v.) and Soviet leader Josef Stalin (q.v.), this treaty formally established an alliance between the new Communist government of China and the Soviet Union. Stalin was initially reluctant to sign the treaty with China because he suspected the new Communist government in China would be similar to the Communist regime in Yugoslavia under Tito, which had broken with Stalin in 1948. It took the outbreak of the Korean War (q.v.) in 1950 to convince the Soviet leader of China's true Communist credentials. Although the treaty was supposed to remain in force for thirty years, it was effectively dead by the early 1960s when the Sino-Soviet conflict (q.v.) arose. Formally, the treaty was not terminated until China announced in 1979 that it would not extend the treaty, which was due to expire the following year.

The goal of the treaty was purportedly to prevent a reemergence of Japanese fascism in East Asia. In addition to its military goals, the treaty also initiated economic and cultural ties between China and the Soviet Union that flourished until 1960. In 1964, China formally accused the Soviet Union of having violated the terms of the treaty for having withdrawn more than one thousand experts working in China and for canceling more than 150 incomplete industrial and scientific projects. This Sino-Soviet Treaty of Friendship, Alliance, and Mutual Assistance should be differentiated from the Sino-Soviet

Treaty of Friendship and Alliance that was signed in 1945 and that defined the Soviet position in postwar China.

"SLAUGHTERING TEN THOUSAND ERRONEOUSLY RATHER THAN LETTING ONE GUILTY ESCAPE" (*NINGKE CUOSHA YIWAN, BUKE FANGGUO YIGE*). A popular phrase during the Cultural Revolution (1966–1976) (q.v.) among Red Guards (q.v.) who were willing to murder innocent individuals to ensure that those "guilty" of political crimes would not escape. This notion has been prominent throughout the history of the CCP (q.v.) and has blocked any effort to introduce the "assumption of innocence" into the Chinese legal code. Legally, people charged with a crime in China are assumed to be guilty and the result is that without adequate due process of law many innocents have indeed been "slaughtered" to ensure that a "guilty" one does not escape. This includes people incarcerated as well as those executed, this in a country that employs the death penalty gratuitously for hundreds of crimes.

SNOW, EDGAR (1905–1972). Perhaps the most famous American journalist to visit China, Edgar Snow is most remembered for his interviews conducted in the late 1930s with CCP (q.v.) Chairman Mao Zedong (q.v.) in the Communist redoubt of Yan'an. Snow's accounts of his talks with Mao and his visit to Yan'an in the late 1930s are recounted in his most well-known work *Red Star Over China*. Snow also worked in China for the Chinese Industrial Cooperative Movement, along with Rewi Alley (q.v.), and established a magazine advocating democracy for China that was closed down by the Japanese occupation force in northern China in 1939. Snow left China in 1941, but after the war he was hounded by the McCarthy hearings in the United States. As a result, Snow and his wife moved to Switzerland. In the 1960s and again in 1970, Snow made return visits to China where he acted as a liaison between the Chinese and American governments to establish diplomatic contacts that ultimately led to the visit to China in 1972 by President Richard Nixon. Edgar Snow died of cancer the very week in February 1972 when President Nixon was visiting Beijing (q.v.).

"SOCIALISM" (*SHEHUIZHUYI*). In orthodox Marxist terms, the creation of a socialist society in which private property is abolished and the state begins to wither away presupposes certain historically necessary changes, namely capitalist formation and the full development of an industrialized society. Karl Marx defined an abundance of material goods, creation of sophisticated technology, and the emergence of a complex division of labor as the preconditions for socialism—none of which existed in China in 1949. The failure of previous regimes to overcome the country's economic backwardness and underdevelopment created the basis for the Communists' rise to power, but it also denied them the foundations upon which to begin the transition to communism. Thus the CCP (q.v.) faced a severe dilemma: forsake the socialization of the means of production and employ capitalist measures to create the necessary social base for a socialist system; or, rely on a state machine to eliminate "prematurely" private property and take over the tasks of industrialization and technological revolution to create the foundations that Marx described. During the Maoist era (1949–1976), the former strategy was chosen, as any seed of "capitalism" was crushed by the CCP and a huge state bureaucracy emerged to organize and develop the economy toward full industrialization. Since 1978, however, the regime under Deng Xiaoping (q.v.) has recognized China's backwardness. Whereas during the 1958–1960 Great Leap Forward (q.v.), Mao Zedong (q.v.) trumpeted the beginning of China's "transition to communism," Deng's regime declared that since 1956 the country has been in the "primary stage of socialism," a historical stage that makes greater reliance on capitalist forces more ideologically acceptable. The PRC (q.v.) is now said to have "socialism with Chinese characteristics," that is, a mix of market economy with state-run industries. With income disparities growing and private wealth on the rise, however, it is difficult to predict the future, if any, of "socialism" in China. *See also* SOCIALIST SPIRITUAL CIVILIZATION.

SOCIALIST EDUCATION MOVEMENT (1962–1966). Also known as the "four cleans" (*siqing*), this mass movement was designed to eliminate corruption (q.v.), primarily in rural Party and government organizations. Fraud in the handling of accounts and in the determination of work points (q.v.) for peasants, and mismanagement of state-owned warehouses and assets, were the original targets of the campaign. In 1965, the movement was expanded to "purification" of politics and economics and rectification of ideology among Party members. The fundamental contradiction in Chinese society was declared to be that between "socialism and capitalism," which eclipsed the previous emphasis on low-level corruption and venality in the rural administrative apparatus. During the Cultural Revolution (1966–1976) (q.v.), Liu Shaoqi (q.v.) was accused of limiting the target of the Socialist Education Movement to corruption and of ignoring the more fundamental conflict between "socialism and capitalism" in the Party. As the "number one capitalist roader (q.v.) in the CCP," Liu was vilified for obstructing Mao Zedong's (q.v.) goal of carrying out a broader attack on ideological deviants in the CCP. Thus the Socialist

Education Movement was expanded and directly led to the widespread purges and political struggles of the Cultural Revolution (1966–1971).

SOCIALIST SPIRITUAL CIVILIZATION. In order to counteract the threat to its legitimacy by contact with the outside world, in the early 1980s the CCP (q.v.) launched a campaign to "build socialist spiritual civilization." Communist thinking, ideals, beliefs, morality, and discipline were to be cultivated in official propaganda and educational curricula as a counterweight to the "material civilization" associated with Western society and a modern economy. Radical leftists in the CCP attempted to use this campaign to block all reform efforts and to undermine Deng Xiaoping's (q.v.) plan to depoliticize education and professional training. The building of a "socialist spiritual civilization" was also directed at combating the attraction to Western culture by the young and the general population's enchantment with making money and enjoying consumer goods. Communist ideological principles were declared to be the "core" of "socialist spiritual civilization" that distinguished China from the West. In this sense, the campaign was reminiscent of the effort in the late nineteenth century to distinguish the Chinese "essence" (*ti*) from Western "utility" (*yong*). In the summer of 1986, reformist forces led by Hu Yaobang (q.v.) severely restricted this campaign and prevented it from expanding into a general assault on the reform program.

SONG PING (1917–   ). Song Ping studied in the 1940s in Yan'an at the Central Party School (q.v.) and the Institute of Marxism-Leninism. In the late 1950s he became vice minister of the State Planning Commission and in the 1960s he was put in charge of defense construction projects in the inland areas, the so-called Third Front. He was active in the Cultural Revolution (1966–1976) (q.v.) in Gansu province where in 1976 he read Mao Zedong's eulogy. In 1983 he became a state councillor and minister of the State Planning Commission and in 1987 he assumed the directorship of the CCP Organization Department. In 1988 he opposed Zhao Ziyang's (q.v.) proposal to create a professional civil service. In June 1989 as a member of the CCP conservative faction he became a member of the Politburo (q.v.) Standing Committee.

SONG QINGLING (1893–1981). Wife of Sun Yat-sen and later a vice chairman of the PRC (q.v.), Song Qingling was born in Shanghai (q.v.) and attended school in the United States, receiving her B.A. in 1913 from Wesleyan College for Women in Georgia. Upon returning to China, she first became secretary to Dr. Sun Yat-sen, leader of the

Chinese Republican revolution. Song and Dr. Sun married in Japan in 1914 despite her father's strong opposition to the marriage. In 1917, Sun and Song moved their base to Canton in southern China to join up with Chen Qiongming, the local warlord. A conflict between Chen and Sun over expansion into the Guangdong region and over the larger issue of national unification led Chen to stage a mutiny on June 16, 1922. During an arduous escape Song suffered a miscarriage, for which she received much sympathy from the population.

During her ten-year marriage, Song remained supportive of Sun's political ideas and ideals. Sun died on March 25, 1925. The assassination of Liao Zhongkai in 1925 and the purge of Communists and other left-wing elements in the KMT (q.v.) before the Northern Expedition in 1926 convinced Song that she should carry on the banner of her late husband. At the Second National Congress of the KMT in 1926, Song was elected to the Central Executive Committee, a position to which she was reelected at every subsequent congress until 1945. In 1927, Song openly opposed her sister Song Meiling's marriage to Chiang Kai-shek, the KMT leader and heir to Sun Yat-sen's political legacy. This led Song Qingling to join Deng Yanda, a general who had turned against Chiang, to form a Third Force as an alternative to the KMT and CCP (q.v.). After the outbreak of the Sino-Japanese War (q.v.) in 1937, Song moved to Hong Kong where, in 1938, she founded the China Defense League to channel medical relief to Communist bases in the hinterland. She was considered a Communist by most westerners, though she was not a Party member. In September 1949, she was invited to Beiping (subsequently renamed Beijing [q.v.]) as a delegate to the CPPCC (q.v.). Song became one of three non-Communist vice chairmen of the new PRC government. During the years until her death in 1981, she was a vice chairman of the Standing Committee of the NPC (q.v.) (1975–1981), honorary president of the Chinese People's Association for Friendship with Foreign Countries (1980–1981), and honorary chairman of the All-China Women's Federation (q.v.) (1978–1981). She continued with welfare work and led delegations abroad. During the Cultural Revolution (1966–1976) (q.v.), Song was labeled a bourgeois liberal and her house was stormed by Red Guards (q.v.), but she was rescued due to the personal intervention of Zhou Enlai (q.v.). She developed leukemia in 1960, but despite her weakened state she lived over twenty more years. She was named honorary president of China in 1981 and was invited to join the CCP on May 29, 1981, shortly before her death. Her only surviving sister, Song Meiling (Mrs. Chiang Kai-shek), refused to attend her funeral.

SONG RENQIONG (1909–   ). A graduate of the KMT's (q.v.) Whampoa Military Academy in the 1920s, a Long March (q.v.) veteran, and an associate of Liu Bocheng (q.v.), in 1942 Song Renqiong organized the "Death Corps" in Shanxi province and in 1945 he was elected to the CCP (q.v.) Central Committee. In the early 1950s Song was first secretary of the Southwest China Bureau and in 1954 he was recalled to Beijing (q.v.) to become a member of the National Defense Council. In the early 1960s Song became minister of the Second Ministry of Machine Building. Throughout the Cultural Revolution (1966–1976) (q.v.) he was repeatedly attacked by Red Guards (q.v.), but he returned to power in 1979 as director of the CCP Organization Department. In 1982 he became a member of the Politburo (q.v.), but he resigned in 1985 to join the Central Advisory Commission (q.v.) as a vice chairman.

SPECIAL ECONOMIC ZONES (SEZS). Located in China's coastal provinces of Guangdong in the south and in Fujian opposite Taiwan (q.v.), the SEZs have been a central feature of the economic reforms introduced in China since 1978. In economic terms, the SEZs are free trade and tax-exempt areas established to lure foreign investment, technology transfer, and trade. Imports are allowed into the zones tax free. Wages in the zones are much more flexible than in China proper and labor is hired on a contractual basis fundamentally at odds with the "iron rice bowl" (q.v.) that still exists for industrial labor in other parts of the economy. Considerable development has occurred in the real estate market of the largest such zone, Shenzhen, located across the Hong Kong border. Most of the investment into the export processing industries of the zones has come from overseas Chinese, especially from Hong Kong. The zones have also helped to increase the per capita income of both Guangdong and Fujian provinces.

The 1980 decision to create the SEZs was not without controversy in the CCP (q.v.). In the early 1980s, conservative political leaders led by Chen Yun (q.v.) opposed the zones, comparing them to the foreign "concessions" that had existed in China before 1949. There were warnings that the zones would open the door to "bourgeois liberalization" and other nefarious influences that would gradually erode the Chinese socialist system. In the midst of the 1983 Anti-Spiritual Pollution campaign (q.v.), concern grew among foreign businessmen that the anti-Western, anti-capitalist thrust of the campaign would lead to policy reversals on the zones. But the intervention of Deng Xiaoping (q.v.) to oppose conservative forces ended this threat and brought a quick end to the Anti-Spiritual Pollution campaign. Some critics still argue that the rapid development of the zones has come at the expense of other regions in China, especially the interior areas, that, it is claimed, have effectively subsidized the rapid growth along the coastal regions. Concerns have also been voiced by foreign businessmen who complain about increasing costs and bureaucratic delays in negotiating contracts. But Chinese leaders have insisted that the zones will continue to exist and may even be expanded to other key areas along the coast, and in the interior, such as the area surrounding the Three Gorges Dam project (q.v.).

SPIRITUAL POLLUTION. *See* ANTI–SPIRITUAL POLLUTION CAMPAIGN.

STALIN, JOSEF (1879–1953). China's relations with and views of the great Soviet leader have been mixed. In 1935, Mao Zedong (q.v.) emerged as the top leader in the CCP (q.v.) by supplanting the Twenty-Eight Bolsheviks, a group of young Chinese Communists, led by Wang Ming, who had been trained at Moscow's Sun Yat-sen University to do Stalin's bidding in China. Mao's victory over Stalin's men in China was finalized during the 1942–1944 Rectification Campaign (q.v.) that effectively undermined the waning authority of Wang Ming. After 1949, China adopted policies on collectivization of agriculture and industrialization that also varied from boilerplate Stalinist methods.

During the 1950s, Mao intimated that Stalin had hurt the Chinese revolution, and that if the CCP had followed his orders, it would have been destroyed. Yet, officially China's leaders, led by Mao Zedong, praised Stalin both before and after his death.

In 1939, on the occasion of Stalin's sixtieth birthday, Mao hailed Stalin as "the savior of all the oppressed" and on his seventieth birthday Mao declared "Comrade Stalin" to be the "teacher and friend of mankind and of the Chinese people." At Stalin's death in 1953, Mao lamented the passing of "the greatest genius of the present age." Following Nikita Khrushchev's "secret speech" criticizing Stalin in 1956, the Chinese issued an editorial titled "On the Historical Experience of the Dictatorship of the Proletariat," which recognized Stalin's "mistakes," while confirming his enormous achievements for the international Communist movement. Privately, the Chinese were outraged that the new Soviet leader had taken it upon himself to launch criticisms against Stalin without first consulting the Chinese leadership. "Stalin did not belong to Moscow," a Chinese official is quoted as saying at the time, "Stalin belonged to all of us."

In December 1956, following the Hungarian Revolt, which broke out in reaction to Khrushchev's attack on Stalin, the Chinese issued a second editorial titled "More on the Historical Experience of the Dictatorship of the Proletariat," which evaluated Stalin in an even more favorable light. Soviet criticisms of Stalin for "placing himself above the Party" and for fostering a "personality cult" were especially sensitive in China where Mao could be accused of the same deviations from Leninist norms. Thus, from 1956 to Mao Zedong's death in 1976, Stalin was officially revered in China as a "great Marxist-Leninist revolutionary" who deserved recognition and praise, despite his unfortunate "mistakes." Since 1978, little has been said about Stalin officially (although his picture has been removed from Tiananmen Square), though no comprehensive denunciation comparable to Khrushchev's "secret speech" has been issued.

STANDING COMMITTEE. *See* POLITBURO.

STATE COUNCIL. *See* GOVERNMENT STRUCTURE.

STATE PLANNING COMMISSION. *See* GOVERNMENT STRUCTURE.

"STRUGGLE BETWEEN TWO LINES" (*LIANGTIAO LUXIAN DE DOUZHENG*). A notion propagated by Maoists in China and many outside observers that major factional divisions in China in the 1950s and 1960s were between moderate and radical elites and their respective policy lines. In this model, where policy contends between these two basic factions, Mao Zedong (q.v.) played a key role, sometimes siding with the moderate line, but more often joining the radicals to attack and purge his "moderate" opponents, especially during the Cultural Revolution (1966–1976) (q.v.). The leftist line included support for socialist agriculture and industry, ideological purity, "uninterrupted revolution" (q.v.), militant nationalism, and opposition to Soviet "revisionism" (q.v.) and American "imperialism." The moderate line involved relying on limited market mechanisms, ideological pragmatism, an end to class struggle (q.v.), and greater accommodation with domestic and international forces, including the United States.

STRUGGLE SESSIONS. Individuals and groups targeted for "thought reform" (q.v.) and/or political criticism were grilled, interrogated, and often physically abused in sessions that could last for days. The general purpose of such sessions was to extort "confessions" and wear down an individual's resistance to pressure. The struggle session became the venue for getting an individual who was accused of being a "rightist" or a "capitalist roader" (q.v.) to admit on numerous occasions his/her "crimes." During the Cultural Revolution (1966–1976) (q.v.), struggle sessions became veritable witch-hunts in which vigilante Red Guards (q.v.) acted as prosecutors and often executioners.

Since 1978, struggle sessions have essentially disappeared from the Chinese political landscape.

SU SHAOZHI (1923–   ). An economist by training, Su Shaozhi was one of China's leading Marxist theorists and proponents of reform who in the mid-1980s headed the Institute of Marxism-Leninism–Mao Zedong Thought in the Chinese Academy of Social Sciences (q.v.). In December 1988, Su attended a forum to commemorate the decade of reform where he defended liberal thinkers such as Wang Ruoshui (q.v.) and attacked conservative ideologues such as Hu Qiaomu (q.v.). In February 1989, he signed an open letter calling for the release of political prisoners in China. He fled China after the June 1989 crackdown and since has held several university posts in the U.S.

SUN CHANGJIANG. Trained as a philosopher, Sun Changjiang contributed to the article "Practice is the Sole Criterion of Truth," published in the *People's Daily* (q.v.) on May 12, 1978. When in 1982 Wang Zhen (q.v.) replaced Hu Yaobang (q.v.) as president of the Central Party School (q.v.), the Theory Research Department was dismantled and Sun, who was its deputy director at the time, was ousted, whereupon he became a faculty member at the Beijing Teacher's College. Sun subsequently became the editor in chief of the *Science and Technology Daily* (*Keji ribao*), a post that he lost after the June 4, 1989, Beijing massacre.

T

TAIWAN. The relations between the ROC on Taiwan and the PRC (q.v.) have ranged from military conflict and confrontation between the 1950s and 1970s to increasing trade relations in the 1980s and preliminary political contacts in the 1990s. After defeated Nationalist forces on the mainland fled to Taiwan (formerly known as Formosa), the Chinese Communists planned an invasion across the Taiwan Straits to finish the Civil War. Intervention by the United States following the June 1950 North Korean invasion of South Korea, however, gave Taiwan a defensive shield provided primarily by the United States Navy's Seventh Fleet. In 1955 and 1958, Communist and Nationalist forces engaged in combat largely to contest control over the offshore islands of Quemoy and Matsu, which the United States had committed itself to defend. China's refusal to renounce formally the potential use of force against Taiwan prevented the U.S. from withdrawing its military shield and effectively prevented any resolution of the Taiwan issue.

Internationally, the PRC staked its political claims to Taiwan by requiring all nations with which it established diplomatic relations to drop recognition of the ROC on Taiwan. Domestically, the PRC strengthened this claim by maintaining representation of Taiwan on the NPC (q.v.) and by staffing a Taiwan Affairs Office in the central government. Trade between Taiwan and the mainland was limited to medicinal and other minor products and channeled through Hong Kong. In the mid-1950s, periodic offers were made from Beijing (q.v.) to the ROC leader Chiang Kai-shek for a resolution of the conflict, but without success.

The establishment of contacts and then formal ties between the United States and China in the 1970s brought an end to the ROC's representation in the United Nations (q.v.) in 1971 and a break in U.S.-ROC diplomatic and formal military ties in 1979. The 1979 Taiwan Relations Act, however, maintained a U.S. military commitment to the island as the U.S. continued to press China for a "peaceful settlement" of the Taiwan-PRC conflict, even as it recognized that Taiwan was part of China. In 1981, China unveiled a more flexible policy toward Taiwan by proposing a nine-point program that included economic and cultural exchanges, official and unofficial contacts between officials on both sides of the Straits, and a general reduction in military tensions near the offshore islands. According to Beijing's plan known as "one country, two systems" (q.v.), Taiwan would ultimately become a Special Administrative Region of the PRC (similar to Hong Kong after 1997), with a distinct economic and political system and with a high degree of autonomy. Taiwan would be represented in international affairs by the central government in Beijing, though it would be allowed to retain its own military forces and a separate legal system. Negotiations on the final status of Taiwan would be carried out between the Communist and Nationalist parties on an equal basis.

After democratic changes were introduced into Taiwan's political structure in the late 1970s by Chiang Ching-kuo (son of Chiang Kai-shek) and with the emergence after Chiang Ching-kuo's 1988 death of a Taiwan-born president, Lee Teng-hui, the government of Taiwan accepted and then promoted exchanges with the mainland. This included visits by Taiwan residents to the PRC that began in 1987. Indirect trade between Taiwan and the PRC grew to more than $3 billion by 1988 as investment in the mainland economy by Taiwanese grew to over $1 billion by the end of the decade. Joint participation by Taiwanese and Chinese athletes in Olympic events was also agreed upon as both sides established organizations (on the ROC side, the

Taiwan Straits Exchange Foundation, and on the PRC side, the Association for Relations Across the Taiwan Straits) to address common problems in the waters of the Taiwan Straits, such as fishing rights. There were no formal contacts, however, as Taiwan continued to adhere to its policy enunciated in 1979 by Chiang Ching-kuo of "three no's"—no [formal] contact, no negotiation, and no compromise. Taiwan, backed by the United States, also refused to agree to direct postal and transportation links while Beijing still refused to issue a no-force pledge. China also opposed Taiwan's adoption of its "flexible diplomacy," under which Taiwan would, if possible, establish formal diplomatic relations with nations that simultaneously recognized the PRC and the ROC, or upgrade unofficial relations with nations that formally recognized the PRC but desired increased economic ties with Taiwan, now the world's largest holder of foreign exchange reserves.

The growth of an independence sentiment on Taiwan brought on by political liberalization and the emergence of the avowedly pro-independence Democratic Progressive Party (DPP) also concerned China. The 1989 Tiananmen crackdown severely undermined popular support on Taiwan for eventual reunification with China and apparently strengthened the pro-independence sentiment. The killing of Taiwanese tourists in Zhejiang province in 1994 and an attempted Chinese government cover-up also strained relations as Taiwan investors lost some of their enthusiasm for the Chinese market and cut back on mainland investments substantially. Yet, Taiwan and China remained members of the Asia Pacific Economic Cooperation and also the Asian Development Bank.

In early 1995, Taiwan called for talks between Taipei and Beijing on common problems and issues. However, increased tensions broke out between the two sides over issues involving cross-Straits negotiations, an unofficial visit by Taiwan President Lee Teng-hui to the United States, and the holding of the first direct election for president on Taiwan in March 1996. These tensions culminated in the midst of the presidential campaign when China carried out a series of war games in the Taiwan Straits that included missile firings and live-fire exercises aimed at intimidating Taiwanese voters. Despite these threats, electoral turnout exceeded 80 percent of eligible voters and Lee Teng-hui was elected with more than 50 percent of the vote. Soon after the election, President Lee offered to travel to Beijing (q.v.) to meet with CCP leaders and resolve outstanding problems between the PRC and the ROC. *See also* TAIWAN STRAITS CRISIS and UNITED STATES–CHINA RELATIONS.

TAIWAN STRAITS CRISIS (1958). After a breakdown in Sino-U.S. talks in Warsaw, a crisis in the Taiwan Straits, which separate China from the island redoubt of the Nationalist (KMT) (q.v.) regime, broke out in August 1958. The Chinese Communists launched artillery and air force attacks against the islands of Quemoy and Matsu, two small islands off China's coast that are vital to Taiwan's strategic defense, in an apparent attempt to begin a reconquest of Taiwan. In reaction, the United States deployed air force and naval units in the region and backed up these forces with strong statements of support for Taiwan by then President Eisenhower and Secretary of State John Foster Dulles. Air combat over the Straits between PLA (q.v.) planes and American-built planes of the Chinese Nationalist Air Force resulted in heavy losses for the Communist side. After the Soviet Union's apparent refusal actively to aid China in its confrontation, China's leaders beat a hasty retreat in September and promised to renew the Warsaw Talks. As a result of China's "irresponsible" behavior during this crisis, the Soviet leadership decided to renege on its promise to share nuclear secrets with the Chinese, contributing further to the emerging Sino-Soviet conflict (q.v.).

TAN ZHENLIN (1902–1983). An early follower of Mao Zedong (q.v.) in the CCP's (q.v.) 1927 Autumn Harvest uprising, Tan Zhenlin became a political commissar (q.v.) during World War II in the Communist New Fourth Army. In 1958 he was appointed to the CCP Politburo (q.v.) and he became deputy director of the Rural Work Department under the Central Committee. In 1962 he was appointed vice chairman of the State Planning Commission. In 1967, he participated in the so-called February Adverse Current (q.v.) that attempted to halt the Cultural Revolution (1966–1976) (q.v.) and to outlaw the Red Guards (q.v.). In 1967 he was purged, but reappeared in 1973 and was reappointed to the Central Committee.

TANGSHAN EARTHQUAKE. Occurring on July 28, 1976, at 3:00 a.m. and registering 7.8 on the Richter scale, the earthquake in and around the city of Tangshan in eastern China was the third most destructive in world history. Out of the city's 1 million inhabitants, it is believed that 242,000 people were killed and 160,000 injured. After the quake it took twelve hours for China's leaders in Beijing (q.v.), 100 miles to the northwest, to discover that the city had been nearly destroyed. Troops mobilized for relief operations piled the dead into mine pits outside the city as the country's leadership refused all foreign aid. It took more than a decade for the city to be rebuilt as other major urban centers took responsibility for restoring individual neighborhoods. In Chinese history it was said that natural disasters were to foretell great political changes; at this time China was embroiled in a major power struggle because of the impending death of Mao Zedong (q.v.). Mao indeed died two months later, opening the way for the major economic and political changes inaugurated by Deng Xiaoping (q.v.) in 1978. By the 1990s, Tangshan had resumed its role as a major industrial city and as a center of foreign investment.

TAO ZHU (1906–1969). A member of the CCP (q.v.) since 1930, Tao Zhu, from the southern province of Guangdong, emerged as a major regional leader in China. Associated with Li Xiannian (q.v.), Tao was appointed chairman of the Wuhan City Military Control Commission after the Chinese Communist seizure of power in 1949. In 1953, he became vice chairman of the People's Government of Guangdong province and in 1955 he was appointed the provincial governor. In 1956, he became a member of the CCP Central Committee and in 1957 he was identified as the First Party Secretary of Guangdong. In 1961, Tao was made the First Party Secretary of the Central-South Bureau of the CCP and in 1962 he became political commissar (q.v.) of the Guangzhou (Canton) Military Region. In 1965 he became a vice premier of the Chinese government, and in 1966 he headed the Propaganda Department of the CCP and was appointed to the Politburo (q.v.). During the Cultural Revolution he was branded a "counterrevolutionary revisionist" and purged. Tao Zhu died ignominiously in 1969 at the hand of Red Guards (q.v.).

"THEORY OF BEING 'DOCILE TOOLS' " (*XUNFUGONGJU LUN*). A fundamental concept of the role of the individual in the CCP (q.v.) and the Chinese Communist revolution, this theory was expostulated by Liu Shaoqi (q.v.). Essentially it instructed CCP members to rid themselves of personal interests or aspirations. A Party member, Liu Shaoqi argued, should "serve as a docile tool and a tool easy to control." During the Cultural Revolution (1966–1976) (q.v.), Liu's theory was pilloried by Party radicals for purportedly "regarding the masses as 'beasts of burden' and 'slaves.' " In addition, Liu was criticized for having "distorted the relationship between the Party leadership and rank-and-file members as one between man and tool, between slave owner and slave, a relationship of absolute obedience." The fundamental flaw in this theory was said to be that it forced Party members to obey that which was "wrong," even though the Leninist concept of democratic centralism (q.v.) was a centerpiece of CCP doctrine. Party members, it was claimed, had been turned into "mindless machines" who were forced to "forsake the principle of struggle for the sake of organization and obedience." In its place the radicals sanctioned the principle "To Rebel is Justified" (q.v.), which led to chaos and the near disintegration of the CCP, but which since 1978 has been disavowed by the CCP leadership.

THEORY OF THREE WORLDS. A theory propounded by Deng Xiaoping (q.v.) in April 1974 in his speech before the United Nations, it replaced previous Chinese pronouncements on the state of global and international relations. According to this formulation, the "socialist camp" no longer existed, since the Soviet Union, under Brezhnev, had completely degenerated into "social imperialism." The two superpowers of the United States and the Soviet Union were members of the First World, joined together in an insatiable campaign to exploit and oppress the many poor nations of the Third World. The Second World, composed of European and other equally developed nations, also joined in the exploitation of the Third World, but they themselves were exploited by the giant superpowers. In this theory, China was a member of the Third World that had assumed the role of an international proletariat, a revolutionary force opposed to colonialism, imperialism, and "social imperialism." The theory was generally dropped in the 1980s as China focused more on world peace and economic development, while it refused to join such Third World organizations as OPEC or the Group of 24, a gathering of poorer nations in the International Monetary Fund.

THIRD PLENUM OF THE CCP (1978). The watershed meeting in December 1978 that launched China on the path to economic and limited political reform. Preceded by a Central Work Conference at which major policy initiatives were announced by Deng Xiaoping (q.v.), the Third Plenum of the Eleventh Central Committee marked the return of Deng Xiaoping as China's paramount leader and the political eclipse of Hua Guofeng (q.v.), Mao Zedong's designated successor, and such Mao flunkies as Chen Yonggui (q.v.). Politically, the plenum announced plans for a full evaluation of Mao Zedong's leadership. Economically, it called for a shift in the primary work of the Communist Party to socialist modernization, but without the grandiose plans for a "Foreign Leap Forward" previously advocated by Hua Guofeng. Instead, the plenum adopted the Chen Yun approach to "balanced development" and sanctioned radical liberalization of agricultural policy, while beginning the dismantling of the people's communes (q.v.) and other Maoist innovations in the countryside. Following the plenum, major leadership changes were announced as Hu Yaobang (q.v.) was elevated to Party chairman. A formal investigation was announced of Mao's deceased police chief, Kang Sheng (q.v.).

"THOUGHT REFORM" (*SIXIANG GAIZAO*). In 1951 Mao Zedong (q.v.) referred to "thought reform" (also translated as "ideological remolding") as "one of the important prerequisites for our country to realize thoroughly democratic reform in all respects. . . ." For the victims of this intense process, primarily Chinese intellectuals (q.v.) and artists and some Americans who were imprisoned in China after 1949, the experience has been described as classic "brainwashing." The strong appeal of liberalism and intellectual and artistic freedom have made Chinese intellectuals frequent targets of "thought reform" efforts orchestrated by the CCP (q.v.). Interrogations, the writing of "confessions," incarceration and even torture were all used to remold the "thoughts" of those who did not support the CCP or did not accept the Marxist-Leninist-Maoist worldview. As a Chinese-style inquisition, "thought reform" peaked during the 1957–1958 Anti-Rightist campaign (q.v.) and during the Cultural Revolution (1966–1976) (q.v.). Yet even after the beginning of the reforms in 1978, intellectuals and writers and artists have come under periodic assault for their beliefs in liberalism and general intellectual and academic freedom. The 1983–1984 Anti-Spiritual Pollution campaign (q.v.) and the 1986–1987 Anti-Bourgeois Liberalization campaign (q.v.) involved intense criticisms of intellectuals, though psychological and physical pressure such that occurred in the 1950s and 1960s has been generally avoided.

"THREE ANTIS MOVEMENT" (*SANFAN YUNDONG*). This was one of the first mass political movements initiated by the CCP (q.v.) after the founding of the PRC (q.v.). The official purpose of this campaign was to oppose corruption (q.v.), waste, and bureaucracy (q.v.) in Party and state organs. Mao Zedong (q.v.) referred to such problems as "the poisonous residue of the old society" that needed to be "washed clean." All CCP members were forced to reregister in the Party, and those "corrupt and degenerate" elements were targeted for expulsion or even more severe punishment. Most CCP members were spared harsh treatment, especially if they "confessed" to their purported transgressions, but a small minority were viciously attacked and in some cases executed. Criticisms were launched at huge public rallies where transgressors were first "tried" and then immediately taken out and shot. These "negative examples" were used in the Three Antis and other similar movements to frighten the majority into compliance with central demands for greater discipline and obedience to central Party policies. The campaign began with the issuance of policy documents, which became the basis for "criticism and self-criticism" (q.v.) and attacks on the targeted few. It ended in late 1952.

THREE BITTER YEARS. *See* GREAT LEAP FORWARD.

"THREE CATEGORIES OF PERSONS" (*SANZHONGREN*). These were people who, during the Cultural Revolution (1966–1976) (q.v.), had headed the most violent faction of Revolutionary Rebels (*zaofan-pai*), engaged in fighting, and/or committed acts of "smashing and looting" (q.v.). They were singled out for criticism and separation from the CCP (q.v.) after the arrest of Mao Zedong's (q.v.) widow, Jiang Qing (q.v.), and the launching of the anti–Gang of Four (q.v.) campaign in the late 1970s. In effect, the label was often arbitrarily attached to almost anyone whom the regime wanted to purge. This included active political reformers who had joined in the Cultural Revolution and were singled out for attack by conservative political leaders who were intent on stalling the reform program initiated in 1978.

THREE FAMILY VILLAGE. The newspaper column "Notes From a Three Family Village" (*sanjiacun zhaji*) was published from 1961 to 1964 in the Beijing Party Committee journal, *Frontline (Qianxian)*, and authored pseudonymously by Deng Tuo (q.v.), Liao Mosha, and Wu Han (q.v.). The thrust of both columns was mild, often including indirect criticism of socialist China, its leadership (including Mao Zedong [q.v.]), and especially lower-level cadres (q.v.) in the CCP (q.v.). Published in the aftermath of the Great Leap Forward (1958–1960) and during the Three Bad Years (1960–1962), the "Notes" and "Evening Chats at Yanshan" criticized the policy failures of the Leap and lampooned arrogant and brazen leaders who had neglected the people's interests. In the tradition of classical Confucian literati, Deng Tuo reminded the Party leadership of the fine traditions in Chinese classical statecraft, especially famine relief, and called on Party leaders from top to bottom to exercise self-discipline and traditional benevolence. The importance of personal cultural pleasures and an appreciation for the past and a cosmopolitan attitude in cultivating proper behavior were also primary themes. Deng Tuo's approach was elitist and somewhat paternalistic, but it also stressed that the CCP serve the public good and not squander its hard-won legitimacy by reckless policies and arrogant leadership.

Two years after their termination, these columns (and their authors) were viciously attacked by leftist proponents of the Cultural Revolution (1966–1976) (q.v.), most notably by the left-wing polemicist Yao Wenyuan (q.v.) in his May 11, 1966 *People's Daily* diatribe entitled "Criticizing the 'Three Family Village'—The Reactionary Nature of *Evening Chats at Yanshan* and *Notes from a Three Family Village*." Deng Tuo committed suicide six days later.

After the Cultural Revolution, the columns and their authors were "rehabilitated" in such articles as the 1979 piece "It Is No Crime to Criticize Idealism, It Is Meritorious to Propagandize Materialism—Refuting Yao Wenyuan's False Charges in 'Criticizing *Evening Chats at Yanshan* and *Notes from a Three Family Village.*' " *See also* DENG TUO.

THREE GORGES DAM PROJECT (*SANXIA GONGCHENG*). Planned as the largest hydropower project in the world, the Three Gorges Dam will be 1,983 meters long, 185 meters high, and will generate, at capacity, 18,000 megawatts of electric power. Construction of the project is under way on the Yangtze River in the scenic three gorges (*sanxia*) area and will take eighteen years to complete, at a projected cost of $30 to $100 billion. It is said that when completed the dam will help prevent downstream flooding that has claimed more than 500,000 lives in the twentieth century. 632 square kilometers of land encompassing two cities, 11 counties, 140 towns, and more than 600 villages and 1.8 million people will be displaced by the huge reservoir created by the dam. Critics in China and outside the country argue that the dam will fundamentally alter the ecology of the region and, because of sedimentation and other problems, will never be able to produce the intended electrical output, nor provide adequate flood control.

The dam was first proposed in 1919 as part of Sun Yat-sen's "Plan to Develop Industry." After 1949, CCP (q.v.) leaders periodically discussed the feasibility of such a project, but consistently rejected it, citing unresolved technical problems and costs. In 1957, critics of the project, such as Mao Zedong's secretary for industrial affairs, Li Rui (q.v.), were labeled as "Rightists," but the dam was never begun because of the economic and political turmoil during the Great Leap Forward (1958–1960) and the Cultural Revolution (1966–1976) (q.v.). Recommendations to construct the dam were revived in the mid-1980s, but construction was postponed at a key NPC (q.v.) meeting in March 1989 following domestic and foreign opposition. Following the military crackdown in 1989, many dam opponents were removed from power, and dam supporters, such as state premier Li Peng (q.v.), were then in a position to push its construction. An April 1992 NPC meeting finally approved construction of the dam and preliminary work began in 1993. Foreign financing of the dam has been sparse as the World Bank and other such international lending institutions oppose its construction as do many world environmental groups, such as Probe International in Canada.

THREE RED BANNERS. This refers to the various campaigns in the late 1950s that attempted to accelerate dramatically the country's economic growth and political transformation. The first "banner" was the General Line for Socialist Construction that Mao Zedong (q.v.) had initiated in 1957. It called for "going all out, aiming high, and achieving greater, faster, better and more economical results in build-ing socialism." In practical terms, this meant China was to move as quickly as possible to construct a modern industrial and agricultural base. The second "banner" was the Great Leap Forward (q.v.) that from 1958 to 1960 involved the CCP (q.v.) in an attempt to expand agricultural and industrial production. The goal was to "overtake" Great Britain in fifteen years through the construction of backyard steel furnaces (q.v.) and massive water conservancy projects. The third "banner" was the people's commune (q.v.), the massive rural production organization that was designed to increase both agricul-tural and industrial production in the countryside. The disastrous re-sults of the Great Leap in 1960 brought an end to the Three Red Banners, though in the early 1960s Mao Zedong tried to build support for yet another leap, an effort that ultimately failed and led to his attacks on the Party leadership during the Cultural Revolution (1966–1976) (q.v.).

TIAN JIAYING (1922–1966). In 1955 Tian was appointed to the Staff Office for the Chairman of the People's Republic where he served as one of Mao Zedong's (q.v.) many secretaries. He participated in the drafting of volumes 1–4 of Mao Zedong's *Selected Works*. He com-mitted suicide early in the Cultural Revolution (1966–1976) (q.v.), reportedly because of his split with Mao Zedong on agricultural and other policy issues.

TIAN JIYUN (1929–). From Shandong province in China's east, Tian Jiyun joined the CCP (q.v.) in the early 1950s as head of a Land Reform (q.v.) team. In the 1970s he became a financial expert in Guizhou and Sichuan provinces. In 1981 he was an official in the State Council and in 1982 he was appointed to the CCP Central Com-mittee, and the following year he was made a vice premier. In 1985 he was elected to the Politburo (q.v.) and the Party Secretariat and in 1987 he became a member of the Politburo Standing Committee. In September 1989 he was put in charge of breaking up and merging companies and firms.

TIANANMEN SQUARE INCIDENT (1976). *See* APRIL 5TH MOVE-MENT.

TIBET (XIZANG). Situated in the southwest part of China, Tibet, site of the Himalayan mountain range and Mount Everest, is known as the "Roof of the World" with an average elevation more than 16,000 feet. Tibet is home to the Lamaist religion, a branch of Mahayana Buddhism, and once had over 13,000 monasteries, which were mostly destroyed by rampaging Red Guards (q.v.) during the Cultural Revolution (1966–1976) (q.v.). Tibet's major religious sites, such as the Jokhang temple in the capital city of Lhasa and the Drepung monastery (which formerly housed 10,000 monks), are periodically opened by the Chinese authorities but have often been closed for long periods of time. Continued training of Tibetan lamas (monks) has also been a constant source of tension between Tibet's religious elite and the CCP (q.v.). In 1994, the Chinese government ordered that monastery and temple construction (and reconstruction) be stopped and an absolute cap was placed on the number of monks and nuns to be trained. Foreign travel to Tibet has also been restricted in recent years during political flare-ups.

Historically, in the seventh century, Tibet was an independent kingdom encompassing an empire that stretched into significant parts of China proper, Russia, and Inner Mongolia. By the thirteenth century Tibet was incorporated into the Chinese empire, but with Chinese control limited to external affairs. Tibetans remained sovereign on domestic matters, an arrangement that lasted until the end of the Qing dynasty (1644–1911).

With the collapse of the Qing in 1911, Tibet declared its independence from the new ROC, but the territory was quickly carved up by the 1913 Simla Conference, which convened in India and included representation from China, Tibet, and Great Britain. An inner part of Tibet was made into a southwestern province of China, while an outer part was granted full autonomy. China, however, refused to ratify the treaty. In 1950, Chinese Communist forces entered Tibet to reclaim the territory and to terminate the 1911 Tibetan declaration of independence. After some resistance, the Tibetans capitulated and an agreement was signed in which China recognized Tibet's autonomy but asserted full sovereign power. A committee headed by the Dalai Lama (q.v.) was given power to govern the domestic affairs of the territory.

In 1959, conflict broke out once again as Tibetans protested the presence of Chinese military garrisons. The Dalai Lama's refusal to suppress the uprising brought an immediate Chinese military response that forced the Dalai Lama to flee the country and seek refuge in northern India where he lives to this day with approximately 10,000 Tibetans. In 1960, the United Nations (q.v.) addressed the issue of Tibet, but only in terms of the issue of human rights, not sovereignty.

During the reform era (1978–1997) in China, the issue of Tibet has influenced Chinese domestic and international politics. Throughout the 1980s, CCP leaders pushed a number of "liberalizing" policies, such as increasing the number of Tibetan natives in the government of the region and withdrawing Han (q.v.) cadres (q.v.) from Lhasa. Central government investment was increased along with tax exemptions for Tibetan farm animals and a recognition of the right of Tibetans to own private land. As an officially recognized national "minority" (q.v.) (*shaoshu minzu*) in China, Tibetans are also exempt from the one-child family policy (q.v.). Still, the Chinese have yet to appoint a Tibetan to the top Party post in the region. Riots have also periodically broken out in the area, the most serious occurring in March 1989 when thirty people were killed and China imposed martial law that lasted until May 1990. Scores of monks were arrested, while others fled to the countryside to take up arms against Chinese rule. The question of human rights in Tibet has influenced U.S.–China relations, and in 1992 the Human Rights Commission of the United Nations took up the issue, though the commission ultimately accepted a European proposal to end the debate. Negotiations between representatives of the Dalai Lama and the Chinese government have been ongoing since 1993. *See also* DALAI LAMA.

"TO REBEL IS JUSTIFIED" (*ZAOFAN YOULI*). This was the signature slogan chanted by Red Guards (q.v.) during the Cultural Revolution (1966–1976) (q.v.) to justify attacks on CCP (q.v.) members and top leaders, such as Liu Shaoqi (q.v.). It was specifically directed at invalidating all rules and regulations in schools, work units, and Party and government organizations that opposed "revolutionary" action. The slogan was given legitimacy in 1967 by the theoretical journal *Red Flag* (q.v.) that was under the control of the radical faction associated with Jiang Qing (q.v.). As restraints on the activities of Red Guards were removed, Red Guards rampaged through China's urban areas throughout 1967 and early 1968. By 1968, however, Mao Zedong (q.v.) decided to end the increasing violence, and many Red Guards were sent for long sojourns in the countryside.

TOWNSHIP VILLAGE ENTERPRISES (TVE). A product of the Agricultural Responsibility System (q.v.), which was inaugurated after 1978, township village enterprises have grown at rapid rates soaking up surplus rural labor (estimated at 200 million workers nationwide), which was freed up with the abolition of socialist agriculture. Owned by townships (*xiang*) and villages (the successors to the people's communes [q.v.] and the production brigades [q.v.]) and by individual households or groups of households, these small-scale enterprises produced a gross output value in 1984 of 170 billion yuan, employing more than 50 million workers, or about 16 percent of the total rural labor force. Approximately 70 percent of the enterprises are industrial, producing machinery, building materials, and textiles, 15 percent were in construction (particularly housing construction, which has boomed in China's rural areas since 1978), and 8 percent are in services. Most township village enterprises operate outside the state planning mechanism and rely on the market to acquire materials and sell their output through private and collective channels. Chinese government authorities have frequently charged the TVEs with tax evasion and corruption (q.v.). By the year 2000 it is expected that such rural enterprises will employ anywhere from 40 to 70 percent of the total labor force in the countryside.

TRADE UNIONS. Labor organizations in China are organized into the All-China Federation of Trade Unions, one of many "mass" organizations in the Chinese government structure (q.v.). The federation exercises leadership over trade unions throughout the country as a "transmission belt" for implementing central Party and government policy toward labor. The federation is headed by a chairman and vice chairman and is composed of the All-China Labor Congress and the Executive Committee of the All-China Federation of Trade Unions, which is appointed by this congress. Day-to-day work is handled by a secretariat. In 1983, the federation had 72 million members.

Communist interest in organizing trade unions began immediately after the establishment of the CCP (q.v.) in 1921. In 1922 the First All-China Labor Congress was convened in Guangzhou (Canton) in southern China and in 1925 the All-China Federation of Trade Unions was established as a CCP "front" organization at the time of the May 30th anti-imperialist mass movement. Membership in the federation peaked in early 1927, with two million organized workers. Following the April 1927 anti-Communist coup launched by Chiang Kai-shek, the federation was forced underground and from 1927 to 1949 it waged a struggle against the KMT (q.v.) in the urban areas. Membership in the federation dropped precipitously and did not recover until the 1940s when anti-Japanese sentiment and the CCP-KMT Second United Front (q.v.) provided a political opening for left-wing labor activity.

After the founding of the PRC (q.v.) in 1949, the federation was restored and took as its main task propaganda and political education for the Chinese working class. Membership grew from 10 million in 1953 to 16 million in 1957. The federation provided workers with propaganda about the political line and policies of the CCP. During the 1957 Hundred Flowers campaign (q.v.) strikes and other political activity by the working class broke out in Shanghai (q.v.) and other cities, indicating that CCP control of the working class was far from solid. During the Cultural Revolution (1966–1976) (q.v.) the federation was essentially gutted as workers joined various Red Guard (q.v.)

factions and the leaders of the federation were disgraced and purged. By 1978, however, the organization was revived and membership grew. During the 1989 pro-democracy movement, the then head of the federation, Zhu Houze, threatened to call a general strike to back up student demands for political reforms. A rank-and-file worker, Han Dongfang (q.v.), challenged the federation by setting up an alternative labor organization, claiming the federation was nothing but a mouthpiece for the CCP leadership. Following the 1989 Tiananmen crackdown, Zhu Houze was sacked and Han Dongfang was arrested. In 1994, major work slowdowns, strikes, and industrial violence were reported, indicating that the CCP's fear of labor unrest was indeed justified.

"TRANSFER TO LOWER LEVELS" (*XIAFANG*). Fear of "bureaucratism" (q.v.) and an insulation of government and Communist Party officials from the Chinese population led to periodic transfers of personnel to lower-level organizations and to the countryside where they engaged in manual labor. At the height of the Cultural Revolution (1966–1976) (q.v.), even top Party leaders were "sent down," some of whom did not survive the ordeal. Non-government intellectuals (q.v.) and urban youth were also periodically "sent down," especially from 1968 onward when violence among Red Guard (q.v.) factions in the cities led Mao Zedong (q.v.) to order students into the countryside. Many urban youth languished in the countryside for decades and, if they married local residents, they lost their all-important urban household registration or *hukou* (q.v.). By the mid- to late 1970s, most urban youth had returned to the cities, many reentering colleges and universities. Since 1978, the CCP (q.v.) has not used *xiafang* of government personnel as an administrative tool to fight "bureaucratism."

TUNG CHEE-HWA (1938–   ). A conservative shipping tycoon who advocates stability over expanded democracy, Tung Chee-hwa was appointed the chief executive of the Special Administrative Region of Hong Kong after the transfer of sovereignty from Britain to China on July 1, 1997. He was named to this position by China's president, Jiang Zemin, and officially nominated by a handpicked elite of pro-China businessmen and professionals from Hong Kong. Tung fled with his family from Shanghai at the age of 12 and was educated in Britain. He is fluent in English and has long work experience in the United States. His family's financially ailing company was rescued in the 1980s with a $120 million bailout loan backed by China. Up until the July 1, 1997, handover, Tung was a member of the inner circle of local advisers to the governor of Hong Kong appointed by Britain, though he also maintained close contacts with both Beijing and Taiwan.

"TWO WHATEVERS" (*LIANGGE FANSHI*). In the aftermath of the death of CCP (q.v.) Chairman Mao Zedong (q.v.), a fierce struggle broke out among contending leaders to inherit the mantle of Mao's leadership and to gain control of the Chinese Communist state and Party apparatus. Appointed by Mao as his successor, Hua Guofeng (q.v.) tried to secure his legitimacy in the CCP and to resist any backsliding from radical Maoist policies by asserting that "whatever policies Chairman Mao had decided, we shall resolutely defend; whatever instructions he issued, we shall steadfastly obey." Pegged as the "two whatevers," this slogan became the clarion call of Hua and the various leftist political leaders who tied their star to Mao and who resisted the return of more moderate CCP leaders, especially Deng Xiaoping (q.v.). As a riposte, in 1977 the ever-creative Deng suggested that the "two whatevers" had damaged Mao Zedong Thought (q.v.) and that Mao himself would never have agreed with the slogan. "The 'two whatevers' are unacceptable," Deng retorted and, in its place, he suggested that "we should use genuine Mao Zedong Thought taken as an integral whole to guide the Party," a formulation that allowed much greater flexibility in policy formation and ideological creativity by the post-Mao leadership. With Hua Guofeng's political defeat by Deng Xiaoping at the December 1978 Third Plenum of the Eleventh Central Committee of the CCP, the "two whatevers" disappeared from China's political landscape along with most of the radical leftist leaders and their polemics.

U

ULANFU (1906–1988). Born in 1906 in rural Inner Mongolia, in 1922 Ulanfu and his brother attended the Beiping Mongolian-Tibetan School. In the spring of 1924, Ulanfu became a member of the Chinese Communist Youth League (q.v.) and in the following year he joined the CCP (q.v.). Ulanfu and his brother then went to Moscow where Ulanfu entered Sun Yat-sen University where he became acquainted with a classmate, Wang Ruofei, who later became Ulanfu's superior in underground Party work. Ulanfu returned to China in 1930 and joined the underground and barely escaped arrest as Wang Ruofei was arrested and incarcerated. In 1932, when Japanese forces in China threatened the northern Chinese provinces of Jehol and Chahar, Ulanfu became involved in organizing the Mongol anti-Japanese guerrilla forces. After the Xi'an incident in 1936 and the outbreak of the war against Japan, Ulanfu served in the Pai Haifeng Suiyuan Mongolian Peace Preservation Corps as a political commissar (q.v.). In 1941, he fled to the communist redoubt in Yan'an and became head of the Nationalities' Institute of the Anti-Japanese Military and Political University under Gao Gang (q.v.). In 1944, he became the chairman of the Suiyuan Border Region government.

In September 1949, Ulanfu was appointed to the Standing Committee of the preparatory committee of the CPPCC (q.v.). In October, he became a member of the Central People's Government Council, which was the PRC's (q.v.) chief executive body until 1954. In 1952, Suiyuan was incorporated into the Suiyuan Inner Mongolia Military District. Ulanfu became chairman of the Suiyuan People's Government. In 1956, he became a top CCP leader when he was elected to full membership in the Central Committee after its Eighth National Congress (q.v.) and he became an alternate member of the Politburo (q.v.).

In 1967, during the Cultural Revolution (1966–1976) (q.v.), Ulanfu was attacked and deposed by the CCP army that had entered Inner Mongolia. Ulanfu was rehabilitated in 1973 and was elected to the CCP Tenth Central Committee in the same year. In 1977, he was appointed head of the CCP United Front Department (q.v.) and a member of the Eleventh Central Committee as well as a member of the Politburo. In 1978, Ulanfu became the vice chairman of the Standing Committee of the Fifth CPPCC, and in 1982 he was reelected to the Politburo at the Twelfth Party Congress. From 1983 to 1988, Ulanfu served as vice president of the PRC.

"ULTRALEFTISM" (*JIZUO*). This was a catchall term used first in the late 1950s after the Lushan Plenum to attack the Great Leap Forward (q.v.) and then in the late 1960s to attack radical elements in the Cultural Revolution (1966–1976) (q.v.). From 1966 to early 1967, CCP (q.v.) Chairman Mao Zedong (q.v.) seemingly threw all his support to the extreme left in its attacks on top Party leaders and the CCP apparatus. But in spring 1967 as Red Guards (q.v.) began to target military commanders and the PLA (q.v.), as well as the foreign ministry headed by Zhou Enlai (q.v.), the tide began to turn against the extreme left, as Mao gradually pulled back his support and came down on the side of order and stability as the threat from the far left was spinning out of control.

At this point Mao sanctioned criticism of "ultraleftism" as it was accused of attempting to "overthrow the proletarian headquarters of Mao Zedong" and of "seizing state power." Fiery political leaders whom Mao and his wife, Jiang Qing (q.v.), had recently embraced were now singled out for attack. This included Wang Li, Guan Feng, and Qi Benyu, leftist polemicists who had stoked the ideological fires of the Cultural Revolution. Lower level "ultraleftists" were executed. In the Orwellian language of the Cultural Revolution, "ultraleftists" were now described as "ultraleft in form, but ultraright in essence," a suggestion that all along these activists had been anti-Communist and opposed to Chairman Mao.

The attack on "ultraleftism" turned into a permanent purge of leaders responsible for the Cultural Revolution, except Mao Zedong. It even involved left-wing army leaders, such as Yang Chengwu, who was accused of plotting against Mao by promoting an extreme version of the personality cult (q.v.). The attacks against "ultraleftists" as political "swindlers" continued with the purge of Chen Boda (q.v.), the Lin Biao affair (q.v.) in 1971, the purge of Jiang Qing and the Gang of Four (q.v.) in 1976–1977, and the general reversal of the policies of the Cultural Revolution throughout the 1980s.

"UNINTERRUPTED REVOLUTION" (*BUDUAN GEMING*). This is a central concept in Chinese Communist ideology that was heavily promoted during the Mao (q.v.) years, especially during the Cultural Revolution (1966–1976) (q.v.). Also known as "continuous revolution," the term required that Chinese society remain in a constant state of turmoil and political struggle to ensure the "ultimate liberation of the working class and the people as a whole." Mao Zedong was especially fearful that China, like the Soviet Union, would gradually stabilize around a highly centralized political structure that would focus solely on economic and technical developments managed by a professional class, and with little input by the masses of workers and peasants. "Uninterrupted revolution" would inoculate China against such "revisionism" (q.v.) and prevent a subsiding of the purported revolutionary fervor of the masses. Since 1978, the Cultural Revolution has been officially condemned in China and the idea of "uninterrupted revolution" effectively dropped in both theory and practice.

UNITED FRONT. A centerpiece of CCP (q.v.) strategy inherited from the dictates of Soviet leader Lenin and the Comintern in the early 1920s, united front refers to alliances between the CCP and its natural constituency of workers and poor peasants with classes and political parties that are periodically defined as collaborators in the revolutionary struggle. During the pre-1949 period two formal united fronts were established with the KMT (q.v.) (1924–1927 and 1936–1945) to combat common enemies, in the first case the northern warlords, and in the second, the Japanese. In each case, CCP leaders developed an appropriate ideological rationale that justified such political arrangements and created a United Front Department in the CCP apparatus. After 1949, united front policies involved periodic CCP efforts to build alliances with nonproletarian social elements, particularly merchants and "bourgeois" intellectuals (q.v.). These policies were undermined and even assaulted during radical phases of CCP rule, such as during the Three Antis campaign (q.v.) in the 1950s and the Cultural Revolution (1966–1976) (q.v.) when "class struggle" (q.v.) was the dominant theme in contrast to the emphasis on "unity" in the united front strategy. The continued existence of the democratic parties (q.v.) and the CPPCC (q.v.) are both part of united front strategy. *See also* NEW DEMOCRACY and CHINESE COMMUNIST PARTY.

UNITED NATIONS. From "liberation" (q.v.) in October 1949 to its official reentry into the United Nations in 1971, China was effectively cut off from involvement in the world body as the "China seat" on the Security Council was held by the government of the ROC on Taiwan (q.v.). During this period, China was sometimes the target of United Nations action, such as the 1951 embargo on the export of strategic equipment to China that coincided with China's entry into the Korean War as an enemy of the UN-sanctioned police action. Yet China consistently insisted that it had a right to sit at the United Nations and often joined other Third World leaders, such as President Sukarno of Indonesia, in making this demand. China did not refrain, however, from criticizing ongoing UN actions, such as its 1962 condemnation of the world body's role in the Congo, where China apparently had political and economic interests at odds with those of the United States. During this period, especially during the Cultural Revolution (1966–1976) (q.v.), the United Nations was often condemned by China as an "instrument" of U.S. imperialism and a vehicle for American advancement of "neocolonialism" since it was the United States that consistently blocked China's entry. In the early 1960s, China received increased support from Asian, Latin American, and African UN members, but its hopes for entry were dealt a serious blow when the General Assembly decided that the question of China's entry was an "important question" requiring a two-thirds vote. The UN resolution on Tibet in 1960, albeit mildly worded, further antagonized China's relations with the world body. Throughout the 1960s, China insisted that its entry come at the expense of the ROC and that Taiwan not be allowed to remain in the UN under the rubric of a "two Chinas" policy.

The decision in 1970–1971 by the United States to fundamentally alter its relationship with the PRC (q.v.) led to China's seat in the UN and the ouster of the ROC from Security Council and the General Assembly. Since the twenty-sixth assembly, China has been a member of the UN and it has gradually entered all the organizations under the control of the world organization. In the 1970s, China pursued a relatively belligerent tone in the world body, condemning Russian proposals for a collective security pact in Asia and championing the political and economic interests of developing countries. On matters that the Chinese deemed to be in opposition to their interests or values, China simply abstained, such as on peacekeeping and the UN World Disarmament Conference. Yet the Chinese did not challenge the basic organizational structure of the UN and generally made their financial contributions to the world body. During the 1980s, the Chinese shifted their strategy somewhat and adopted positions on various issues, such as the Angolan Civil War, in terms of how they affected the Soviet Union, China's major nemesis in world affairs. Despite its condemnation of USSR vetoes, China also used its veto on matters before the Security Council, such as over the issue of Bangladesh's entry into the world body. After the 1989 reconciliation between the USSR and China, however, China moderated its tone and took a more active part in the consultative-consensual process of Security Council decision making, tolerating peacekeeping efforts of the UN by refusing to veto such UN-sanctioned operations as the 1990 war against Iraq.

On human rights issues, however, China has consistently opposed efforts by the United States and other nations to have China officially criticized by the UN Human Rights Commission, most recently in 1997 when China succeeded in blocking debate on a draft resolution in Geneva. As for related issues of international law, China has generally accepted the sovereignty-centered principle of the Westphalian legal order in opposing any major extension of international legal authority, though its support for many UN resolutions, such as the solution to the crisis in Cambodia (q.v.), indicates implied acceptance of a strengthened international legal regime. In the specialized agencies of the UN—FAO (Food and Agricultural Organization), WHO (World Health Organization), ICAO (International Civil Aviation Organization), etc.—China has taken a low profile, avoiding extensive involvement in the technical minutiae of decision making. China's delegates continue to infuriate and amuse other representatives. This was evident in the 1995 discussion of the UN-sponsored Climate Control Conference in Berlin where the Chinese delegate asserted that in order to avoid tough international pollution controls China "would always be a developing country," a position directly at odds with well-known official development goals of the PRC. *See also* CAMBODIA and SINO-SOVIET CONFLICT.

UNITED STATES–CHINA RELATIONS. Since 1949, relations between the United States and the PRC (q.v.) have varied from outright hostility and conflict to relatively friendly political and economic ties. During the Chinese Civil War (1946–1949), the United States, through the Marshall Mission, attempted to mediate the conflict between the KMT (q.v.) and the Communists, but ultimately failed. Although U.S. aid under the Truman administration to the KMT during the civil conflict was limited, Mao Zedong (q.v.) and the Chinese Communists identified the U.S. as a major ally of its domestic enemy.

In the aftermath of the Communist victory, Mao decided to "lean to one side" and align with the Soviet Union with which he signed a Treaty of Friendship, Alliance, and Mutual Assistance in 1950. Initially, the United States left open the possibility of immediate recognition of the PRC after its formal establishment on October 1, 1949. The American ambassador remained in Nanking (the KMT national capital) waiting for a gesture of goodwill from the new Communist leadership. (During World War II American military and State Department personnel had established informal ties with the Communist leaders in Yan'an via the Dixie Mission and, thus, some basis of mutual trust and reconciliation was thought to exist.)

But mistrust and indignation quickly surfaced as the new government in Beijing (q.v.) subjected American corporations to rough treatment, seized U.S. consular buildings, arrested U.S. consul Angus Ward on espionage charges, and persecuted Christian missionaries, while the U.S. showed continuing sympathy for Chiang Kai-shek and his plight. Unlike its European allies, such as Britain, the United States did not recognize the new regime, and maintained formal diplomatic ties with the ROC on Taiwan (q.v.). The invasion of South Korea by North Korea in June 1950 led the United States to establish a defensive perimeter in the Taiwan Straits by deploying the Seventh Fleet, while in China American students and missionaries who had remained behind after the withdrawal of the U.S. diplomatic mission were arrested and imprisoned on charges of "spying." The Chinese intervention in the Korean conflict in October 1950 brought the military forces of the PRC and the United States (operating under a UN mandate) into direct conflict until the Korean armistice was signed in 1953.

Thereafter, throughout the 1950s and 1960s, China and the United States maintained a stance of mutual hostility, though some informal contacts and efforts to alter the relationship did occur. At the 1954 Geneva Convention terminating the first Indochina War, China's Foreign Minister Zhou Enlai (q.v.) offered his hand in friendship to U.S. Secretary of State John Foster Dulles, but Dulles refused to shake his hand. At the 1955 Bandung Conference (q.v.) in Indonesia, China offered to open formal negotiations with the United States to produce a comprehensive détente in East Asia and in the Taiwan Straits. But because of irreconcilable divisions over the Taiwan question—the United States insisted that China first renounce the use of force against Taiwan, something Beijing was unwilling to do—no such meetings were ever convened.

The Formosa Resolution passed by the U.S. Congress in 1955 extended American protection to Taiwan's offshore islands of Quemoy and Matsu, while the United States government formally declared that the legal status of Taiwan remained officially unresolved. After China provoked a crisis in 1955 over Quemoy, the two countries decided to initiate contacts in Geneva and later in Warsaw. Ostensibly, these meetings, which continued to 1970, focused on outstanding issues left over from the Chinese Civil War and the Korean conflict, namely the fate of eighty Americans still held in China and 3,000 Chinese students in the United States. Although periodically suspended, the Geneva and Warsaw encounters provided the United States and China with a venue to discuss a range of political, economic, and military issues that divided the two nations. Yet with U.S. Secretary of State John Foster Dulles's commitment to an unrelenting anticommunism, full rapprochement between the two sides remained virtually impossible.

Conflicts involving the United States and China, such as the 1958 Taiwan Straits Crisis (q.v.), only exacerbated this mutual hostility. The United States built up an anti-communist alliance in East and Southeast Asia by establishing military ties with Japan and South Korea and by defensive alliances largely aimed at China, such as the Southeast Asia Treaty Organization (SEATO). In this period, China remained aligned with the Soviet Union, the main antagonist of the United States. A visit to Taiwan in 1960 by U.S. President Dwight Eisenhower was met in China with an anti-American propaganda week that spread agitation throughout China's major cities and towns. Chinese proposals for bilateral talks on Taiwan, for the establishment of a nuclear-free zone in Asia, and for the mutual exchange of journalists went nowhere as China took every opportunity to denounce the actions of the United States, going so far as to direct personal insults at both Presidents Eisenhower and Kennedy.

Hostility in U.S.–China relations continued throughout the mid- and late 1960s, inflamed by American involvement in the Vietnam War (1965–1973). While China feared the establishment of a permanent American military presence in Vietnam and Thailand, the United States considered the Vietnamese Communists an extension of Chinese military and political power. China's vitriolic denunciation of "U.S. imperialism" as a "paper tiger" (q.v.) was aimed at mobilizing support for the Chinese position in the Third World, including Latin America. China even weighed in on domestic American affairs with impassioned declarations by Mao Zedong supporting American Blacks in the civil rights struggle. America was the symbol of the much-hated capitalism and the powerful U.S. presence in East Asia thwarted the restoration of Chinese hegemony that had existed for more than two millennia. The United States also protected the KMT regime on Taiwan and blocked China's "rightful" place on the Security Council in the United Nations (q.v.). Direct confrontations between the two were avoided, however, as potentially explosive conflicts over U.S. violations of Chinese "air space" were handled with rhetorical rather than actual combat.

From 1966 to 1969 Chinese foreign policy was effectively paralyzed by the Cultural Revolution (q.v.), though China now directed its animosity at *both* the United States and the Soviet Union, which it accused of dividing up the world into bipolar spheres of influence. In 1969, however, the United States and China began to prepare for serious negotiations, but because of domestic complications in both countries and the impact of international events, especially the U.S.-led invasion of Cambodia (q.v.), efforts at reconciliation did not really begin until 1970. Despite tensions over Southeast Asia and blustery comments on "world revolution" by Mao Zedong, the United States under President Richard Nixon took the initiative by easing American economic sanctions against China and permitting American citizens to visit the PRC. As U.S. troops began their withdrawal from Vietnam, and China became more concerned with threats from the Soviet Union, the United States and China finally agreed to break the ice after two secret visits to Beijing by President Nixon's assistant for national security affairs, Henry Kissinger, produced an agreement for a formal trip to China by the president in February 1972. This relatively cordial visit by the U.S. president led to a mutual declaration by both sides in the Shanghai Communiqué (q.v.) on the central issue of Taiwan in which the United States "acknowledg[ed]" Taiwan as part of China and called for a "peaceful settlement" of the issue. Liaison offices were quickly established in both capitals and scientific and trade ties were set up.

After President Nixon's resignation, President Ford visited the PRC in 1975. The Communist takeover in Vietnam in 1975 did not produce any visible increase in U.S.–China tensions, but rather raised Chinese anxieties over growing Vietnamese "hegemony" in Southeast Asia. The United States and China agreed to coordinate their policies on Cambodia and shared concerns about Soviet expansionism, though the United States, in hopes of solidifying a Soviet-American détente, resisted Chinese efforts to enlist the United States in a broad anti-Soviet alliance. In 1979 the United States and China established formal diplomatic relations, as the United States broke diplomatic ties with Taiwan and announced its intention to terminate the mutual defense treaty within a year. Passage in 1979 of the Taiwan Relations Act, however, maintained American commitments to the island and allowed the U.S. to continue limited arms sales to the ROC. In 1979, Deng Xiaoping (q.v.), the architect of China's economic reforms, visited the U.S. and received tacit American approval for his plan to invade Vietnam. U.S. President Carter also granted China Most-Favored Nation (MFN) trade status and authorized increased military-to-military contacts, and intelligence sharing, though China requested (and did not receive) permission to purchase U.S. arms.

In the early 1980s, U.S.–China relations went through a period of tension and disillusionment. In addition to President Ronald Reagan's campaign promise to upgrade United States relations with Taiwan, this dramatic downturn in relations was caused by increased Chinese textile exports to the United States, restrictions on American technology transfer to China, potential sales of U.S. aircraft to Taiwan, and defections by Chinese citizens to the United States. As some of these issues were resolved in 1982, however, improved Sino-American ties culminated in President Reagan's trip to the PRC in 1984, an agreement on coproduction of military technology, a new textile accord, and dramatic increases in scholarly exchanges between U.S. and Chinese researchers. A visit to the United States by PRC Premier Zhao Ziyang won China's commitment to enforce nonproliferation of nuclear weapons to Third World countries, while the United States liberalized its technology export controls to China as trade between the two countries expanded rapidly in the mid-1980s. By 1987–1988, however, new tensions emerged over apparent violations by China of its pledge on nonproliferation of nuclear technology as evidence emerged of Chinese sales of such technology to Pakistan, of Silkworm (M11) missiles to Iran via North Korea, and of intermediate range ballistic missiles to Saudi Arabia that posed a direct threat to Israel.

1989 proved to be a watershed year in U.S.–China relations involving the issue of human rights (q.v.). In February 1989, during a visit to China by U.S. President George Bush, Chinese police forcibly detained the famous dissident, astrophysicist Fang Lizhi (q.v.), preventing him from attending a reception for the U.S. visitors. Then in June 1989 the military crackdown in Beijing by the PLA resulted in severe condemnation of the Chinese government by the United States and the imposition of a variety of political and economic sanctions, including termination of high-level diplomatic exchanges and an end of military relations. Yet President Bush refused to lift China's MFN status, though he allowed Chinese students to remain indefinitely in the United States out of fear of retribution if they were to return to

China. President Bush also provided safe haven in the U.S. embassy in Beijing for Fang Lizhi (who remained there for one year before being allowed to emigrate to the U.S.). Yet the Bush administration also quickly backtracked on its sanction package by authorizing secret visits to Beijing by high-level U.S. officials and allowing the sale of Boeing aircraft to China to go forward.

In 1990, the United States won China's tacit support for its tough line against Iraq in the UN, despite reports China had supplied Saddam Hussein with substantial military supplies, including nuclear technology, after the start of the Persian Gulf War. In addition to conflicts over human rights and a growing U.S. trade deficit, persistent reports of Chinese missile and nuclear technology sales to the Middle East and Pakistan inflamed the Sino-American relationship throughout the early 1990s, though President Bush denounced any move to "isolate" China through tougher actions. President Bill Clinton came to office promising a tougher stand on the human rights issue, but after one year with little response from Beijing, the Clinton administration decided to delink the MFN debate and human rights. A U.S. policy of "active engagement" was pursued, which yielded major trade agreements on protection of intellectual property rights in China, even as the United States trade deficit with China soared to nearly $40 billion a year and there was little progress on the human rights front.

In early 1995, the United States supported China's entry into the World Trade Organization—the successor to GATT—but under conditions Beijing found unacceptable. In 1996, tensions grew over a number of issues: China's threat of military force against Taiwan during the island's March presidential campaign; China's unwillingness to enforce an agreement brokered with the United States in 1995 to protect intellectual property rights covering computer software, musical recordings, and movies; Chinese sales of nuclear technology to Pakistan; involvement by Chinese state-owned companies in the illegal export of weapons, such as the AK-47, to the United States; and the absence of high-level visits between American and Chinese leaders. Despite these conflicts, however, the U.S. supported renewal of MFN for China and the two countries continued to cooperate on a range of such issues as international environmental protection and restrictions on the development of nuclear weapons by North Korea.

USSURI RIVER. *See* SINO-SOVIET CONFLICT and MANCHURIA.

UYGUR PEOPLE. *See* MINORITIES.

V

VIETNAM. Since 1949, China's relations with Vietnam have ranged from alliance to outright hostility and military conflict and finally to grudgingly tolerable bilateral relations. During the 1954 Geneva Conference that ended the First Indochina War, China pressured its Vietnamese counterparts into accepting the negotiated agreement, despite Vietnamese Communist reservations concerning the creation of a South Vietnamese regime subject to American influence. From 1954 to 1958, China in tune with the "spirit of Bandung" (q.v.), pursued this moderate line in its relations with Vietnam, but in 1958 China took a slightly more aggressive posture by supporting North Vietnamese opposition to American military aid to South Vietnam. Still, relations between China and Vietnam consisted mainly of economic and commercial ties as China granted North Vietnam substantial loans (in rubles) and technical aid for economic development projects. China was less concerned with supporting the "struggle" of the South Vietnamese Communist movement (Vietcong) than with opposing the transformation of South Vietnam into an American "colony" and a military base from which the U.S. could threaten China.

With the American bombing of North Vietnam following the Gulf of Tonkin incident, China called for a reconvocation of the Geneva Conference, just as it established a permanent delegation to the South Vietnamese Communist political arm, the National Liberation Front. As the military conflict in Vietnam in 1966 and 1967 heated up, China provided strong rhetorical support for the Vietnamese Communists, yet without committing itself to substantial military aid as both Mao Zedong (q.v.) and Lin Biao (q.v.) evidently opposed active Chinese intervention in the conflict. China officially recognized the Provisional Revolutionary Government of the Republic of South Vietnam created in June 1969 and provided Vietnam with increased economic and military aid. It also then opposed convocation of a new Geneva Conference, ignored the Paris talks between the United States and Vietnam, and denounced purported Soviet-American "collusion" in the international arena, as increasing internecine conflict of the Cultural Revolution (1966–1976) (q.v.) led to disruptions in the delivery of Soviet and Chinese military supplies to Vietnam.

Ho Chi-minh's death in 1969 brought the Chinese and Vietnamese leadership closer together, at least temporarily, but ties became strained by the sudden rapprochement between China and the United States as a result of the U.S. initiatives in 1971 and 1972 by President Richard Nixon. The 1973 Paris Accords ending U.S. involvement in Indochina were hailed by the Chinese as a continuation of the "Geneva spirit" of 1954, while the 1975 attack by North Vietnamese forces against the South evidently received no encouragement from China. From 1975 to 1979, China resisted Vietnam's growing "hegemonic" role in Southeast Asia by condemning Vietnam's 1978 assault on Cambodia (q.v.), culminating in the 1979 invasion of North

Vietnam by PLA (q.v.) units. This war to "punish" Vietnam for its Cambodian incursion ended poorly for Chinese forces, which suffered substantial casualties, sometimes self-inflicted, as a result of poor interunit coordination and communications.

Following China's withdrawal from Vietnamese territory, the two Communist countries have maintained an uneasy relationship, though in recent years mutual state visits and economic agreements have reduced tensions and created greater normalcy in their relations. Continuing disputes over the Spratley Islands in the South China Sea (to which both nations lay territorial claim) and Vietnam's adoption of an open-door economic policy toward the West, have kept Sino-Vietnamese relations on thin ice.

W

WAN LI (1916–). Wan Li fought with Communist forces throughout the 1930s and 1940s, and after 1949 he assumed various positions in Beijing (q.v.) Party and government organizations. Branded during the Cultural Revolution (1966–1976) (q.v.) as a follower of Liu Shaoqi (q.v.), Wan Li reappeared in 1971 only to be dismissed, along with Deng Xiaoping (q.v.), after the April 1976 Tiananmen Incident (q.v.). In the late 1970s, Wan Li reappeared again and assumed a position in Anhui province where, with Wan's apparent blessing, radical changes in agricultural policy took place. In 1982 Wan was appointed to the Politburo (q.v.) and assumed the role of acting premier during Zhao Ziyang's (q.v.) travels abroad. In 1988, he became the chairman of the NPC (q.v.) Standing Committee. Wan cut short his visit to the United States and Canada and returned to China during Beijing's 1989 pro-democracy demonstrations. During the 1992 NPC session that passed the resolution approving construction of the Three Gorges Dam project (q.v.), Wan, despite his credentials as a reformer, summarily cut off debate and effectively prevented dam opponents from mobilizing opposition among NPC delegates.

WAN RUNNAN (1946–). General manager of the Stone Corporation since 1984, after the June 4, 1989, crackdown, Wan was placed on a wanted list. He escaped to Paris to become secretary of the Federation for a Democratic China.

WANG BINGQIAN (1925–). A longtime specialist in finance and economics, Wang Bingqian became minister of finance in 1980. He also served as a governor of the World Bank representing the PRC (q.v.) and was China's delegate to the IMF and to meetings of the

China–U.S. Joint Economic Committee. In September 1992, he was forced to resign under pressure because of a nationwide financial scandal.

WANG DONGXING (1916–   ). A leading figure in China's security forces, since the 1930s Wang was a member of various guard units for CCP (q.v.) leaders. In 1949 Wang Dongxing became director of the Security Office of the Central CCP Secretariat. In the same year, he accompanied Mao Zedong (q.v.) to Moscow as his personal bodyguard and was also appointed deputy director of the Eighth Bureau of the Ministry of Public Security. From 1955 to 1969, Wang was vice minister of public security and leader of the 8341 Division, which protected the top leaders. During the Cultural Revolution (1966–1976) (q.v.) he was appointed director of the General Office of the CCP Central Committee and became a member of the CCP Central Committee in 1969 at the Ninth Party Congress. In 1973 he was promoted to the Politburo (q.v.) and in 1977 he became a vice chairman of the CCP and a member of the Politburo Standing Committee. As commander of the security forces in Beijing (q.v.), Wang played a key role in the arrest of the Gang of Four (q.v.). In February 1980, he was removed from all Party and state posts, but in 1982 was made an alternate member of the Central Committee. In 1985 he nominally retired, joining the Central Advisory Commission.

WANG HESHOU (1908–   ). Trained as an engineer at Tangshan University and a 1930 graduate of Sun Yat-sen University in Moscow, Wang was a Communist Party operative in the northeast during the 1940s. In the 1950s, he was minister of heavy industry, joining the CCP (q.v.) Central Committee in 1956 as an alternate member. Purged in the Cultural Revolution (1966–1976) (q.v.), Wang headed the Central Discipline Inspection Commission in 1978.

WANG HONGWEN (1932–1992). Wang rose during the Cultural Revolution (1966–1976) (q.v.) from a labor leader in Shanghai (q.v.) to the heir apparent of Mao Zedong (q.v.), before being purged in 1976 as a member of the notorious Gang of Four (q.v.). Very little is known about him before his emergence in politics during the Cultural Revolution. As a young man in his late teens or early twenties, Wang joined the Chinese People's Volunteers during the Korean War (1950–1953) (q.v.) and he reportedly became a member of the CCP (q.v.). At the end of the war, Wang was assigned as a worker to the No. 17 Cotton Mill Factory in Shanghai, a major facility under the direct control of the Ministry of Textile Industries. Very soon, Wang became a member of the personnel office in the factory and a workshop Party committee secretary.

In June 1966, Wang was a key figure in stirring up the "revolutionary" wave in the No. 17 Cotton Mill in response to Mao Zedong's May 16 Circular (q.v.) that targeted the "enemies" of the Cultural Revolution. Wang was also active in writing big-character posters (*dazibao*) (q.v.) denouncing the Party secretary at the factory. This bold action was later singled out by Mao as the first significant big-character poster of the Cultural Revolution in Shanghai. Wang expanded his attacks and targeted cadres (q.v.) holding high-level ranks: Chen Pixian, first Party secretary of Shanghai and Cao Diqiu, mayor of Shanghai. When the Maoist faction began to take control of Beijing (q.v.), Wang and others traveled to the capital and were warmly received by the Cultural Revolution Small Group (q.v.) headed by Jiang Qing (q.v.), and by Mao Zedong.

Back in Shanghai in September 1966, Wang organized the Shanghai Workers Revolutionary Rebels General Headquarters (SWRRGH) and further expanded his attacks. One incident resulted in bloodshed. Zhang Chunqiao (q.v.) was sent by the CCP Central Committee to mediate the matter and ended up giving official recognition to Wang's organization in the name of the Cultural Revolution Small Group. From that point on, the Shanghai Revolutionary Rebels became the mainstay of the Cultural Revolution in south and central-south China and Wang's political career was smooth sailing: he became the vice chairman of the Shanghai Revolutionary Committee (q.v.) and chairman of the No. 17 Cotton Mill Revolutionary Committee. In January 1971, Wang became secretary of the reconstructed Shanghai Municipal Party Secretariat whose first secretary was Zhang Chunqiao and second secretary was Yao Wenyuan (q.v.). In August 1973, Wang became vice chairman of the presidium of the CCP Tenth Party Congress. He was elected a member of the Tenth CCP Central Committee and became a member of the Politburo (q.v.). For a brief time in the mid-1970s, he reportedly controlled access to the increasingly ill Mao Zedong. But despite Wang's high positions, in October 1976, Wang, along with Jiang Qing, Zhang Chunqiao, and Yao Wenyuan, was arrested and incarcerated as the Gang of Four. They were put on public trial in 1980 and purged from the Party permanently. At the trial, Wang confessed his errors and was given a relatively light sentence. Wang died in 1992 of a liver ailment in a Beijing hospital.

WANG MENG (1934–   ). The son of a philosophy professor, Wang Meng joined the Communist Youth League (q.v.) in 1949 when he was a middle school student, and he began to study political science. In 1958, Wang Meng published his first novel, entitled *The Young*

Newcomer in the Organization Department. As a result, he was immediately attacked as a "rightist." Forced to work as a laborer, Wang remained virtually silent for twenty years, exiled in Xinjiang province in China's far northwest where he lived with Uygur peasants. In 1978, Wang was rehabilitated and returned to Beijing (q.v.) where he published his novelette *Butterfly* for which he was awarded a national prize. In 1982, Wang was identified as the vice president of the China PEN Center and was elected as an alternate member of the CCP (q.v.) Central Committee by the Twelfth Party Congress. In 1983, Wang Meng became editor in chief of *People's Literature* (*Renmin wenxue*) and a vice chairman of the All-China Writers' Association. In 1986, he was appointed minister of culture and in 1987 he became editor in chief of *Chinese Literature.* Following the Tiananmen crackdown in Beijing in June 1989, Wang "voluntarily" retired from his post as minister of culture and was subject to increasing political criticism. In 1991 he tried to sue the Chinese government for libel over criticism of his story, "Hard Porridge," which, the government claimed, was a subtle attack on Deng Xiaoping (q.v.).

WANG RENZHI (1933–). A member of the Policy Research Office under the State Council from 1978 to 1982, Wang Renzhi became editor in chief of *Red Flag* (q.v.) until it folded in 1988 and he assumed directorship of the CCP (q.v.) Propaganda Department. In 1988, he became a member of the Propaganda and Ideological Work Leading Group. Wang was one of the last Chinese leaders to visit the former USSR.

WANG RENZHONG (1917–1992). A Long March veteran, throughout the 1950s Wang Renzhong was an official in Hubei province, where he was later attacked during the Cultural Revolution (1966–1976) (q.v.). He reemerged in 1978 to become a member of the CCP (q.v.) Central Committee. He also became active in agricultural policy. In 1980 he became director of the CCP Propaganda Department (until 1982) and an active member of the NPC (q.v.) in financial and economic affairs.

WANG RUOSHUI (1926–). Trained as a Marxist philosopher and from 1980 to 1983 deputy editor of the *People's Daily* (q.v.), Wang Ruoshui studied at Beida (Peking University) (q.v.) from 1946 to 1948 and then traveled to the Communist "liberated" areas in north China. In the 1950s he worked for the Beijing Municipal Party Committee and in the theory department of *People's Daily.* He took part in the 1950s in the criticisms of Hu Shi (q.v.) and Liang Shuming and from 1960 to 1962 he was involved in the polemics regarding "the identity of thought and existence." In the late 1970s he criticized the "personality cult" (q.v.) of Mao Zedong and wrote on alienation in a socialist society. For the latter he lost his post at the *People's Daily* in 1983 and in 1987 he was expelled from the CCP during the anti-Bourgeois Liberalization campaign (q.v.). In February 1989, Wang signed a letter to CCP (q.v.) leaders calling for political liberalization. In February 1995 Wang joined eleven other intellectuals (q.v.) in petitioning the central government for a radical change in the political structure toward a constitutional democracy and an end to official corruption (q.v.).

WANG RUOWANG (1917–). After joining the CCP (q.v.) during the anti-Japanese war (q.v.), Wang traveled to Yan'an where he became involved with a wall newspaper called *Light Cavalry* (*Qingqidui*) that exposed the darker sides of the CCP. As a result he was exiled to Shandong by secret police chief Kang Sheng (q.v.). After being rehabilitated he became a journalist in post-1949 China, but was branded a "rightist" in 1957 for writing several "critical essays" (*zawen*) during the Hundred Flowers (q.v.) period. He was rehabilitated once again in 1962, whereupon he launched into criticisms of the CCP for its policies during the Great Leap Forward (1958–1960) (q.v.). He was singled out for attack by Shanghai (q.v.) Party boss Ke Qingshi, an event that evidently contributed to the death of Wang's wife. Jailed in 1966 as a "counterrevolutionary," Wang was rehabilitated for a third time in 1979. At the height of the "wounded literature" (q.v.) describing the human suffering brought on by the Cultural Revolution (q.v.), Wang wrote *Hunger Trilogy*. This largely autobiographical account portrays prison conditions during the Nationalist (KMT) (q.v.) regime as relatively less inhumane in comparison to conditions during the communist period. A Communist Party member for 50 years, Wang was expelled from the CCP in 1987. In 1989 he supported the pro-democracy demonstrations and was imprisoned for more than a year from 1989 to 1990. He now lives in exile in the United States.

WANG SHIWEI (1908–1947). The first intellectual (q.v.) to be persecuted and executed by the CCP (q.v.) during the Yan'an Rectification Movement (1942–1944) (q.v.), Wang Shiwei was born in Henan province to a scholar's family. He attended a preparatory school for study in the United States in Henan where he acquired a basic knowledge of English. Poverty stricken, Wang Shiwei found a low-level position in the KMT (q.v.) headquarters in Nanking (Nanjing). After the start of the Sino-Japanese War (q.v.) in 1937, Wang went to Yan'an and became involved in translating the works of Marx and Lenin into Chinese. During the Yan'an rectification, he published a series of critical essays titled "Wild Lilies." In 1942, Wang was wrongly accused of several crimes: "counterrevolutionary," "Trotskyite spy," "hidden KMT spy," and "member of the Five Member Anti-Party Gang" for which he was subsequently executed. In February 1982, the CCP Organization Department rendered a decision that denied the existence of the so-called Five Member Anti-Party Gang and officially rehabilitated (*pingfan*) (q.v.) Wang. Wang Shiwei is survived by Liu Ying, his widow, who is still alive and resides in Hubei province.

WANG ZHEN (1908–1993). Born to poor peasants, Wang Zhen attended only three years of elementary school and was then forced to work on the railway. Wang joined the CCP (q.v.) in 1927. Two weeks after his marriage, his wife was executed by the KMT (q.v.). After fighting under CCP General He Long, in the 1940s Wang became commander of the Yan'an garrison and was appointed by Mao Zedong (q.v.) to oversee the rectification of the intellectuals (q.v.), including Wang Shiwei (q.v.), who was executed on orders from He Long. After 1949 Wang Zhen was stationed in Xinjiang province where, with Deng Liqun (q.v.), he helped put down local Muslim resistance to Chinese Communist control. In 1956 he was appointed minister of state farms and reclamation and also became a member of the CCP Central Committee. Wang retained his posts throughout the Cultural Revolution (1966–1976) (q.v.) and in 1978 he became a member of the Politburo (q.v.) and the Central Military Commission. From 1982 to 1987 Wang headed the Central Party School (q.v.) and in 1988 became the vice president of China.

"WEAR SMALL SHOES" (*CHUAN XIAOXIE*). This phrase refers to Party cadres who suppress, take revenge on, and persecute others who adhere to political views different from their own.

WEI GUOQING (1913–1989). Wei Guoqing joined the CCP (q.v.) in 1929 and rose through the military hierarchy in the Third Field Army of Peng Dehuai (q.v.). In 1954 he contributed to the Vietnamese defeat of the French at Dien Bien Phu by directing Chinese-supplied artillery. Thereafter, he returned to his home province of Guangxi, in China's southwest, to become Party secretary. In 1966 Wei was the political commissar of the Guangzhou Military Region. He survived the Cultural Revolution (1966–1976) (q.v.), though he was occasionally criticized by the Red Guards (q.v.). In the late 1960s and early 1970s he headed the Revolutionary Committee (q.v.) in Guangxi where he tolerated massive violence committed against the Zhuang minority nationality (q.v.) that ultimately degenerated into cannibalism. Nevertheless, Wei was appointed to the Politburo (q.v.) in 1973 and from 1977 to 1982 he was director of the General Political Department of the PLA (q.v.). In 1985 he resigned his Party posts. *See also* ZHENG YI.

WEI JINGSHENG (1950–   ). China's most prominent dissident, Wei is from an Anhui province cadre (q.v.) family. He was trained as an electrician. During the Cultural Revolution (1966–1976) (q.v.) he was a Red Guard (q.v.) and also imprisoned. In 1979 at Beijing's *Xidan* Democracy Wall (q.v.), Wei called on Deng Xiaoping (q.v.) to initiate a "fifth modernization" (q.v.) of democracy and human rights, arguing that Deng's Four Modernizations (q.v.) stressing economic development and scientific and military modernization could not be achieved without democracy. Wei was arrested in March 1979 and sentenced in October 1979 for 15 years on counterrevolutionary charges and for revealing "state secrets" to a foreigner. Wei was released in 1993 in an apparent attempt to win China's bid to host the 2000 Olympics. He disappeared six months later and was sentenced in late 1995 for 14 years on charges of sedition.

"WHAT I SAY IS WHAT COUNTS" (*YIYANTANG*). This phrase, criticizing the tendency of some Party and government officials to engage in arbitrary action, has appeared in CCP (q.v.) documents and speeches by top leaders. It was held to be inconsistent with the principle of democratic centralism (q.v.) that theoretically guarantees discussion of issues within the CCP. During the Maoist era, it was also apparently used by Mao Zedong's (q.v.) detractors within the CCP and the Party's propaganda organizations as an elliptical criticism of the Chairman's frequent tendency to make arbitrary decisions on critical national issues such as agriculture and the Great Leap Forward (1958–1960) (q.v.). Rather than criticizing Mao face to face—a virtual impossibility in China that carried enormous risks—phrases such as *yiyantang* focused on Mao Zedong's arbitrary leadership that some CCP leaders believed robbed them of their legitimate role in the Party's top decision-making bodies and that often led to economic, financial, and political disasters. Since 1978, the phrase has reappeared in official and unofficial propaganda in China and perhaps is aimed at Deng Xiaoping's (q.v.) tendency also to act as the CCP patriarch.

WHATEVERIST FACTION. *See* TWO WHATEVERS.

WHITE-HAIRED GIRL (*BAIMAO NÜ*). Revolutionary ballet-opera composed by He Jingzhi (q.v.) in the 1940s, the *White-Haired Girl* was promoted by Jiang Qing (q.v.) during the Cultural Revolution (1966–1976) (q.v.). Inspired by the socialist realist traditions of Soviet art under Josef Stalin (q.v.), the ballet combines military drill, folk steps, clutched weapons, and clenched fists as major motifs. The story line focuses on a girl from a poor peasant family whose young lover goes off to join the CCP's (q.v.) Eighth Route Army. After her father commits suicide rather than submit to the oppression of the local landlord, the girl flees into the mountains where, because of lack of salt in her diet, her hair turns white. The story ends when she is reunited with her young lover who, with his contingent of Communist soldiers, discovers her mountain redoubt.

"WOMEN WITH BOUND FEET" (*XIAOJUE NÜREN*). This phrase was used by Mao Zedong (q.v.) during a critical July 31, 1955, conference of CCP (q.v.) secretaries of provincial, municipal, and autonomous region Party committees. Incensed that the pace of agricultural cooperativization was too slow and that newly formed co-ops were being dismantled in parts of the country, Mao launched an attack against what he saw as foot draggers among top leaders whom he likened to "women with bound feet." While Mao proclaimed in his report at this CPPCC (q.v.)-convened meeting that a "new upsurge in the socialist mass movement is imminent throughout the countryside," Mao vociferously claimed that "some of our comrades are tottering along like women with bound feet and constantly complaining, 'You're going too fast.'" In the Chairman's view, rural society was ready for the "socialist upsurge"; only the Party cadres (q.v.) were holding it back. In reality, many top leaders, such as Liu Shaoqi (q.v.), had genuine concerns about the impact on food production and general morale in the countryside of an excessively fast pace of cooperativization that they had dubbed a "rash advance." Famines in Zhejiang province and peasant protests against the formation of the cooperatives evidently provoked these social dislocations that some top leaders took as a warning signal to halt or at least to slow down cooperativization. In the face of Mao's severe and very politically effective condemnations, opposition to rapid cooperativization dissolved. Mao's July 1955 démarche thus had its intended effect as plans previously approved by central bodies for a slower pace were cast aside and Mao's more ambitious targets were adopted.

"WORK POINTS" (*GONGFEN*). These were the centerpiece of the system for allocating income in agricultural producers cooperatives (q.v.) prior to 1978. Peasants earned work points for certain tasks, with the harder and more physically demanding labor carrying greater value. The system generally favored men over women, who performed more menial tasks with a lower number of work points. Actual income earned by an individual was based on the total accumulated income of the cooperative (i.e., the production team [q.v.]) as the greater annual income of the co-op increased the value of the total accumulated work points for each laborer. If a cooperative member wanted a larger income he/she had to earn more points to increase the total income of the coop. Actual distributed income was determined after deducting production expenses and monies for reserve funds, welfare, and dividends on the land. Corruption (q.v.) among production team leaders and staff in the computation of points and allocation of monies led to widespread discontent with the system in the rural areas and contributed to the emergence of the Agricultural Responsibility System (q.v.) in the late 1970s. Suppression of individual and family interests to that of the collective also undermined incentives for work.

"WORK TEAMS" (*GONGZUO DUI*). These are groups of Party cadres (q.v.) organized by CCP (q.v.) authorities to carry out specific objectives or political movements. Work teams were generally sent to lower levels of the Party organization and organizations at the grassroots to expedite and lead a particular political movement, such as the 1952 Three Antis campaign (q.v.), the 1962–1966 Socialist Education movement (q.v.), and the 1966–1976 Cultural Revolution (q.v.). Under the guise of "correcting" political views, the teams in fact operated as judge and jury in dealing with ideological and political crimes. Work teams forced confessions and publicly denounced offenders, exacerbating political and ideological divisions within work units. The teams generally disbanded after the movement ended and cadres returned to their regular duties and functions. During the Socialist Education Movement, work teams were initially deployed to the lower levels by Liu Shaoqi (q.v.) to operate on a clandestine basis and to engage in confidential interviews with willing informants hostile to the local leadership. Mao's unilateral withdrawal of the teams in 1965 was a first step in the assault by the CCP chairman on top Party leaders whom he claimed were pursuing the "capitalist road" (q.v.). Work teams were also deployed following the 1989 Tiananmen crisis to stifle dissent among Party and government organs, especially in the media.

WORLD ECONOMIC HERALD (*SHIJIE JINGJI DAOBAO*). A beacon of liberal opinion in the 1980s, this newspaper was founded in 1980 by Qin Benli, a veteran journalist and high-ranking Party cadre (q.v.) who had previously edited Shanghai's (q.v.) *Wenhui Daily* and had been denounced as a "rightist" in 1957. Published jointly by the Chinese World Economists' Association and the Shanghai Academy of Social Sciences, the *World Economic Herald* was initially concerned solely with international economics, but it gradually expanded its coverage to include domestic political issues. With a circulation that ultimately reached 300,000 readers, the paper was known for its bold style of "hitting line balls"—that is, writing stories that bordered on the politically impermissible. Unlike other media in China, the *World Economic Herald* was able to avoid direct Party censorship because its sponsor was not a local Party committee. The editor in chief, Qin Benli, was also protected by his close association with CCP (q.v.) reformers, including general secretary Zhao Ziyang (q.v.). The paper was independent of government subsidies, depending on advertising and subscribers for financial support.

Throughout the 1980s the paper published articles by advocates of reform on such politically sensitive topics as the separation of the Party and government, the rule of law, and integration of China into the world economy. After publishing particularly provocative articles, the office and personnel of the *World Economic Herald* were visited by CCP (q.v.) work teams (q.v.), but the newspaper managed to survive because of its support from the Center. After the 1989 Tiananmen crisis, however, the paper was finally shut down when it published a compilation of articles by prominent reformers, such as Dai Qing (q.v.), in memory of former Party general secretary Hu Yaobang (q.v.), whose death in April 1989 had sparked the crisis. Qin Benli died two years later and many *World Economic Herald* reporters were either imprisoned or fled abroad. *See also* CENSORSHIP.

"WOUNDED LITERATURE" (*SHANGHEN WENXUE*). Named after a short story entitled "The Wounded" (*Shanghen*) written in 1978 by Lu Xinhua, this literary genre examined sympathetically the scars left by the Cultural Revolution (1966–1976) (q.v.) on an entire generation of youth. Popular in 1977 and 1978, it created an ethos of exposure and a pessimistic theme in Chinese literature that contrasted sharply with the socialist realism promoted by the CCP (q.v.) since Mao Zedong's (q.v.) authoritative statement on the political content of literature and art in 1942. The basic thematic line of the "wounded literature" was to depict the scars due to the physical and mental suffering incurred during the political movements of the CCP, especially the Cultural Revolution. Initially, "wounded literature" harmonized well with the CCP-directed campaign against the Gang of Four (q.v.). It included works such as "The Class Counselor" (*Banzhuren*) by the Sichuan writer Liu Xinwu, perhaps the very first example of "wounded literature" published in November 1977. Others included "A Youth Like This" by Zhang Jie, a work that was read over the Central People's Broadcasting Station to the entire nation. In 1978, "wounded literature" expanded its message to include issues of cadre corruption (q.v.) and privilege and the insulation of the political system from popular control. It was thus quickly replaced by a more provocative and more pointedly political "literature of protest" that included such works as *People or Monsters?* by Liu Binyan (q.v.).

WU DE (1913–1995). A labor organizer in the 1930s and 1940s, Wu De became president of Tianjin University in 1952 and the vice mayor of Tianjin city. In 1956 he was named an alternate member of the CCP (q.v.) Central Committee and from 1958 to 1966 he was a political commissar (q.v.) of the Jilin Military Region. Following the purge of the Beijing (q.v.) Party Committee at the start of the Cultural Revolution (1966–1976) (q.v.), Wu became second secretary of the Beijing Municipal Revolutionary Committee (q.v.) and political commissar of the Beijing Military Garrison. In 1971 he became secretary of the Beijing Party Committee and a member of the Cultural Revolution Small Group (q.v.). He was appointed to the Politburo (q.v.) in 1973 and in 1975 he was made a vice chairman of the NPC (q.v.). In 1980 he was removed from all Party and state posts.

WU HAN (1909–1969). Son of a poor peasant, Wu Han became a worker-student and graduated from China's prestigious Qinghua University (q.v.) in 1934. One year later he was appointed a professor of history at Qinghua. In 1948 he joined the Communist movement and in 1950 he was appointed vice mayor of Beijing (q.v.). In 1953, he was appointed chairman of the Democratic League, one of China's eight so-called democratic parties (q.v.). In 1954 he became a member of the NPC (q.v.) representing Beijing. In 1955, Wu Han became a member of the Department of Philosophy and Social Sciences of the Academy of Sciences, and in 1964 he became president of the Beijing Television University. Criticism of Wu Han's play, *Hai Rui Dismissed from Office* (q.v.) launched the beginning of the Cultural Revolution (q.v.). In 1966, Wu Han was subject to "struggle" by Red Guards (q.v.) and in 1969 he died during the frenzied attack on intellectuals (q.v.) at the height of the Cultural Revolution. Wu Han's play was rehabilitated in 1978 at a forum of writers in Beijing. Wu Han also authored many books on the history of the Ming and Yuan dynasties.

WU JIANG (1917–). Trained as a philosopher, during the early 1960s Wu Jiang was director of the Philosophy Department of the CCP's (q.v.) theoretical journal *Red Flag* (q.v.). In the late 1970s, Wu was director of the Theory Research Department of the Central Party School (q.v.) where he assisted Hu Yaobang (q.v.) in criticizing the "two whatevers" (q.v.) and also participated in the debate over the

"criterion of truth" (q.v.). In 1982, when Wang Zhen (q.v.) dismantled the Theory Research Department of the Party School, Wu was
transferred to the Chinese Academy of Socialism where he served as
honorary vice president.

WU LENGXI (1920–). From 1952 to 1965, Wu Lengxi was director
of the New China News Agency (Xinhua) (q.v.) and in 1958 he also
became chief editor of the *People's Daily* (q.v.). Like most cadres
(q.v.) in the fields of culture and propaganda, Wu was purged during
the Cultural Revolution (1966–1976) (q.v.). He was rehabilitated in
1972 and in 1982 he became minister of radio and TV, but was relieved of his posts in 1987.

WU YI (1938–). A graduate of the Beijing Petroleum Institute, Wu
Yi became a vice major of Beijing in 1988. In 1994, she became
China's minister of foreign trade and economic relations.

WU ZUGUANG (1917–). One of China's premier wartime dramatists
and author of more than forty plays and film scripts, Wu Zuguang
was labeled a "rightist" in 1957 and sent to northeast China for physical labor. He returned in 1960 only to be sent back to the countryside
in 1966 where he remained for ten years. In 1980 his play *Itinerant
Players* was performed in Tianjin, but in 1987 Wu was once again
criticized as a "bourgeois liberal" and expelled from the Party. In
spring 1989 Wu joined other intellectuals in signing a petition to the
CCP (q.v.) leadership calling for greater political freedoms in China.

WU'ER KAIXI (1968–). A former undergraduate student at Beijing
Teachers University, the charismatic Wu'er Kaixi emerged as a leader
of the 1989 Beijing Spring (q.v.) pro-democracy movement. Following the military crackdown in Beijing (q.v.), he was number two on
the list of the twenty-one student leaders slated for arrest by the Chinese government. A Uygur, Wu'er Kaixi won his fame as a member
of the student team that carried out a "dialogue" with state premier
Li Peng (q.v.) at a nationally televised meeting in May 1989. After
the crackdown on June 4, 1989, Wu'er Kaixi managed to escape
China via Hong Kong and became a founding member of the Front
for a Democratic China (q.v.). He now lives in Taiwan and the United
States.

WUHAN INCIDENT (July 20, 1967). During the peak of the Cultural
Revolution (1966–1976) (q.v.), political and military forces in the
central China city of Wuhan reached the brink of civil war. A group
in Wuhan known as the One Million Heroes defended the existing

power structure in the city and engaged in open-pitched battles with Red Guards (q.v.) and other radical organizations. Central leaders sent from Beijing (q.v.) to resolve the dispute were arrested by the city leadership upon their arrival. They were released only after the personal intervention of Zhou Enlai (q.v.) and the deployment of central military forces. Wuhan city leaders were arrested and incarcerated and the One Million Heroes was disbanded. The Wuhan Incident demonstrated to the central government that the Cultural Revolution had to be restrained, which, in fact, occurred in 1968.

X

XI ZHONGXUN (1913–   ). A political commissar (q.v.) in the First Field Army (q.v.) during the Civil War (q.v.) and a director of the CCP (q.v.) Organization Department, Xi was elected to the CCP Central Committee in 1956. In 1962 he disappeared as a result of his close association with Peng Dehuai (q.v.). In 1978 he reappeared as a Party and military official in Guangdong province and in 1981 he headed the NPC (q.v.) Legal Commission and in 1982 he became a member of the Politburo (q.v.) until 1987.

XIA FANG. See TRANSFER TO LOWER LEVELS.

"XIA HAI." Literally meaning "going to the sea," this phrase was popular in China throughout the 1980s and 1990s and was applied to young entrepreneurs who traveled to southern China, especially Guangdong, to make their fortunes in the booming economy. This group included people from all walks of life, intellectuals (q.v.), workers, professionals, and even formerly imprisoned political dissidents. The long-range effect is to perhaps create in China a stable middle class similar to that which has emerged in the newly industrialized states of East Asia such as South Korea, Singapore, and Taiwan (q.v.).

XIA YAN (1900–1995). Educated in Japan, Xia Yan joined with Lu Xun in 1930 to establish the League of Left-Wing Writers. Xia translated foreign works into Chinese, such as Maxim Gorky's *Mother*, and wrote film scripts, such as *Fascist Germs*. In 1949 he became deputy director of the Propaganda Department of the CCP (q.v.) East China Bureau and in 1954 he became a vice minister of culture. In 1965 he was labeled as "bourgeois" for his film script *Lin's Shop*, which was based on a short novel by Mao Dun (q.v.), and he was accused of serving as Liu Shaoqi's "agent" in literary and art circles. After the

Cultural Revolution (1966–1976) (q.v.), Xia reappeared in 1977 and became minister of culture until the early 1980s. In 1980 he was elected vice president of the Chinese PEN Center and in 1990 he was president of the Society for Japan Studies.

XIANG NAN (1916–   ). A longtime Communist Youth League (q.v.) member, Xiang Nan was also a specialist in agricultural machinery. He disappeared from public view from 1964 to 1977, but in 1982 he was appointed as the Party secretary in the coastal province of Fujian. In 1987 he was relieved of his posts and joined the Central Advisory Commission (q.v.). In 1990 he became president of the Foundation of Underdeveloped Regions in China.

XIE FEI (1932–   ). After joining the CCP (q.v.) in 1949, Xie Fei served in various posts in China's southern province of Guangdong. In 1983, he was appointed secretary of the Guangdong Provincial Party Committee and in 1986 he became the secretary of the Guangzhou (Canton) Municipal Party Committee. In 1987, he was appointed to the CCP Central Committee at the Thirteenth Party Congress and in 1988 became a member of the NPC (q.v.). He became a member of the Politburo (q.v.) at the Fourteenth Party Congress in 1992.

XINHUA. *See* NEW CHINA NEWS AGENCY.

XIONG FU (1916–   ). A journalist in central China in the 1950s, Xiong Fu was purged during the Cultural Revolution (1966–1976) (q.v.) and returned to become editor in chief of *Red Flag* (q.v.) from 1978 to 1987. In May 1982 he published an article in *Red Flag* entitled "On the Principle of Democracy in the Relationship Between Leaders and the Masses."

XU WEICHENG (1930–   ). A member of the Communist Youth League (q.v.), in the late 1950s and early 1960s, Xu Weicheng served as an editor of *Youth News* in Shanghai (q.v.). During the Cultural Revolution (1966–1976) (q.v.) he was reportedly a member of the radical "rebel faction" (*zaofanpai*) of Red Guards (q.v.) and a protégé of the radical Gang of Four (q.v.). In the early 1980s, he became a member of the Beijing Party organization and in 1987 launched frenzied attacks in the *Beijing Daily* on intellectuals (q.v.) as part of the overall onslaught against "bourgeois liberalization" (q.v.). Xu apparently had a hand in crafting the April 26, 1989, *People's Daily* (q.v.) editorial (based on comments by Deng Xiaoping [q.v.]) that condemned the pro-democracy movement as a "planned conspiracy and turmoil." In 1990, he was elevated to the position of deputy director of the CCP Propaganda Department.

Y

YAN JIAQI (1942–). A vice president of China's Political Science Society, Yan Jiaqi was trained in the 1950s as an applied mathematician and later studied philosophy. In the mid-1980s, Yan was director of the Political Science Institute of CASS and he served in the Office of Political Reform. He helped to shape Zhao Ziyang's (q.v.) proposals for developing a modern professional civil service and for eliminating lifelong tenure of political leaders. After giving speeches in Tiananmen Square during the 1989 pro-democracy demonstrations, Yan fled China and in Paris helped found the Front for a Democratic China (q.v.).

YAN MINGFU (1931–). A graduate of the Harbin Foreign Languages Institute, Yan Mingfu became a cadre (q.v.) in the General Office of the CCP (q.v.) in the late 1950s before disappearing during the Cultural Revolution (1966–1976) (q.v.). In 1985, he reappeared and became director of the United Front Department (q.v.) of the CCP Central Committee and a member of the Secretariat. He was purged following the June 4, 1989, Beijing massacre for trying to negotiate a peaceful end to the pro-democracy student movement, but returned to government service in 1991 as a vice minister of the Ministry of Civil Affairs.

YAN'AN WAY. This is a reference to the political and economic policies formulated by the Chinese Communists during the period from 1936 to 1945 when the central leadership was headquartered in the small provincial town of Yan'an in northwest Shaanxi (Shensi) province that also served as the capital of the CCP (q.v.) Shaan-Gan-Ning Border government. After the CCP seized power in 1949, the "Yan'an Way" gained enormous symbolic significance that was exploited by Mao Zedong (q.v.) and later Deng Xiaoping (q.v.) to impose their vision on the CCP and Chinese society in general. The heart of the "Yan'an Way" is the mass line (q.v.) propagated by Mao Zedong to foster close cooperation and a spirit of egalitarianism between CCP cadres (q.v.) and the peasantry. The "Yan'an Way" is also associated with the tradition of CCP-led Rectification campaigns (q.v.) and the advent of Mao Zedong Thought (q.v.) as the dominant ideology in the Party. Most important, Yan'an came to symbolize the selflessness and willingness on the part of CCP leaders and cadres to sacrifice for national goals, a legacy that was subsequently invoked by CCP leaders in the 1949–1997 period to combat increasing arrogance and bureaucratism (q.v.) among the leadership and rank and file of the Party. Part of the CCP's "golden age," from the 1950s to the 1970s, Yan'an was a major site for domestic and international tourists. The "myth" of the "Yan'an Way" was punctured, however, by the memory of the CCP intellectual Wang Shiwei (q.v.) who as a staff translator in Yan'an during the 1940s had criticized the perks and privileges among the CCP leaders and ultimately was purged and executed.

YANG BAIBING (1920–). A full general in the PLA (q.v.), Yang Baibing was a key figure in the late 1970s and early 1980s in the strategic Beijing Military Region where he served as political commissar (q.v.) until 1987. At the November 1987 Thirteenth Party Congress, Yang was appointed director of the PLA General Political Department, the key central organ responsible for maintaining loyalty to CCP leaders among the troops. In 1988, Yang also became a member of the Central Military Affairs Commission and in November 1989 was appointed to the Secretariat of the CCP (q.v.) Central Committee and became secretary-general of the Central Military Affairs Commission. Yang Baibing and his half brother, Yang Shangkun (q.v.), China's former president, lost their positions on the powerful Military Affairs Commission at the October 1992 Fourteenth Party Congress as Deng Xiaoping (q.v.) apparently became concerned about the rising power of the "Yang family clique." Yang Baibing, however, remained a member of the Politburo (q.v.) and the CCP Central Committee.

YANG RUDAI (1926–). A member of the CCP (q.v.) since 1952, Yang Rudai headed a county land reform team in the early 1950s in his native province of Sichuan ("four rivers") in China's southwest. From 1955 to 1970, Yang was secretary of the Renshou County Party Committee, and from 1971 to 1976 he was chairman of the county Revolutionary Committee (q.v.) and its Party secretary. In 1977, he was elected vice chairman of the Revolutionary Committee of Sichuan province and in 1979 he became a member of the Standing Committee of the Sichuan Party Committee. In 1981, he was made the secretary of the Sichuan Party Committee and in 1982 he was elected to the CCP Central Committee at the Twelfth Party Congress. In 1987 he was elected to the Politburo (q.v.) of the Thirteenth Central Committee. He resigned from his position as secretary of the Sichuan Party Committee in 1993.

YANG SHANGKUN (1907–). Yang was a member of the Twenty-Eight Bolsheviks who trained in Moscow in the late 1920s. In the

1940s he headed a drama troupe performing propaganda plays for Communist troops. In 1945 he became head of the General Office of the CCP (q.v.), a post he held until the Cultural Revolution (1966–1976) (q.v.). He became a member of the Central Committee in 1956 but fell out of favor with Mao in the early 1960s, reportedly after bugging Mao's residence (a fact apparently discovered by one of Mao's mistresses). In 1966 he was branded a counterrevolutionary and did not reappear until 1978. In 1982, he was appointed to the Politburo (q.v.) and became permanent vice chairman of the Central Military Affairs Commission. From 1988 to 1993 he served as president of the PRC. During this period, Yang and his half brother, Yang Baibing, became known as the "Yang family clique" for their influence in the military. Both lost their positions after the October 1992 Fourteenth Party Congress allegedly after Deng Xiaoping (q.v.) caught wind of their plans to place all the blame for the 1989 Tiananmen massacre on Deng following his death.

YAO WENYUAN (1931–   ). Born in Zhejiang province, Yao Wenyuan is the son of the leftist writer Yao Pengzi. As a middle school student in 1948 in Shanghai (q.v.), he joined the CCP (q.v.). After the Communist takeover of Shanghai, Yao became a resident correspondent for the *Literary Gazette*, the official publication of the All-China Writers' Union. He emerged as a young and fierce literary critic during the 1955 campaign to denounce Hu Feng (q.v.). As an arduous contributor to *Wenhui Daily* and *Liberation Army Daily*, Yao finally attracted Mao Zedong's (q.v.) attention in 1957. Around 1963, Yao, together with Zhang Chunqiao (q.v.), became close allies of Mao's wife and resident radical, Jiang Qing (q.v.). In 1965, publication of Yao's article entitled "On the New Historical Play 'Hai Rui Dismissed from Office'" eventually led to the downfall of Peng Zhen (q.v.), the then mayor of Beijing (q.v.). At the Ninth Party Congress in April 1969, Yao was elected a member of the Politburo (q.v.). In spring 1976, together with Zhang Chunqiao and Jiang Qing, he was the key figure in starting a nationwide media campaign against Deng Xiaoping (q.v.) in an effort to hold on to the policies and practices of the fading Cultural Revolution. Yao was arrested in October 1976 and together with the other three members of the Gang of Four (q.v.), he was put on public trial in 1980. Yao was sentenced to twenty years in prison and was released in Fall 1996.

YAO YILIN (1917–1994). Trained in chemistry, Yao Yilin led armed uprisings in eastern China in the 1940s. After 1949 he became vice minister of commerce and negotiated trade agreements with the Soviet Union. In 1958 he was appointed to the Bureau of Finance and

Commerce under the State Council and in 1960 he was named minister of commerce. Criticized during the Cultural Revolution (q.v.) as a "three anti-element of the Peng Zhen (q.v.) clique," he returned in 1973 and became involved in foreign trade issues. He joined the CCP (q.v.) Central Committee in 1977. In 1980 he became director of the State Planning Commission, a member of the Finance and Economics Leadership Small Group headed by Zhao Ziyang (q.v.), and in 1985 he was appointed to the Politburo (q.v.). In 1988 he was acting premier during Li Peng's absence and chairman of the State Three Gorges Project Examination Committee.

YE JIANYING (1897–1986). Born to wealthy merchants, Ye Jianying was an instructor at the KMT (q.v.) Whampoa Military Academy. He joined the CCP (q.v.) in 1927. He studied military science in Moscow and participated in the Long March (q.v.), siding with Mao Zedong's (q.v.) major nemesis, Zhang Guotao. In 1945 he became a member of the Central Committee and after 1949 he served as a vice chairman of the National Defense Council. Six years later he was promoted to the rank of marshal in the PLA (q.v.). In 1966 he was appointed to the Politburo (q.v.). In 1967 he became vice chairman of the Central Military Affairs Commission and in 1973 he was named a member of the Politburo Standing Committee. He became minister of national defense in 1975. Four years later he proposed holding the crucial Conference on Guidelines in Theory Work that promoted liberal political reforms. He resigned in 1985 from his posts and died one year later.

YE QUN (1917–1971). Born in Fujian province on China's eastern coast, Ye Qun was the wife of Lin Biao (q.v.), who, in 1969, was the officially designated successor of Mao Zedong (q.v.). Ye Qun began her political career in the 1935 December Ninth Student Movement and later traveled to the CCP (q.v.) redoubt in Yan'an. During the Cultural Revolution (1966–1976) (q.v.), Ye Qun was a member of Lin Biao's personal organization that sought to seize power from Mao Zedong. After 1967, Ye held several important positions in the Central Committee: deputy director of the All-Military Cultural Revolution Group; director of the Lin Biao Office; and member of the CCP Military Commission Work Group. After the 1969 Ninth Party Congress, Ye Qun was promoted into the CCP Central Committee and became a member of the Politburo (q.v.). After Lin Biao's effort to seize power during the 1970 Lushan (q.v.) Second Plenum of the Ninth Congress failed, Ye Qun joined her husband in organizing a coup against Mao Zedong. The purported assassination attempt against Mao failed in September 1971, and Ye, together with her husband and her son, Lin Liguo, tried to flee China by plane, but all were killed when Zhou Enlai reportedly ordered the plane to be destroyed over the skies of Mongolia. On August 20, 1973, the CCP Central tral Committee formally removed the Party membership of Ye Qun, posthumously.

YE WENFU. A poet and a member of the military, Ye became famous for his poem titled "General You Shouldn't Have Done This" in which he criticizes a PLA (q.v.) general for using his authority to displace a kindergarten in order to expand his house. Ye subsequently gave a speech at Beijing Teachers University that, while warmly welcomed by students, offended the university Party committee and the Beijing municipal government, which singled Ye out as a typical case of "bourgeois liberalization." Deng Xiaoping (q.v.) personally criticized Ye for the same "erroneous tendency" of enriching himself at public expense for which Ye had criticized the general.

YOUTH LEAGUE (CYL). The major "mass" organization for Chinese youth, the Communist Youth League is described as a "big school for organizing youth in learning the ideas of communism, an assistant to and the reserve force of the Chinese Communist Party" (q.v.). Membership in the Youth League is reserved for youth from the ages of fourteen to twenty-eight and is an absolute must for anyone aspiring to join the Communist Party (*rudang*). In 1996, CYL membership stood at 63.7 million and the first secretary was Li Keqiang.

The Communist Youth League was founded in China in 1920, before the establishment of the CCP, and was first called the Socialist Youth League of China. Its first Congress was held in 1922 in the southern city of Guangzhou (Canton), a major base of Chinese Communist support. In 1925, it took the name of the Communist Youth League of China and by 1935 the CYL was deeply involved in organizing opposition to Japanese imperialism. Throughout the war, the CYL acted as a patriotic "front" organization for mobilizing Chinese youth of all political persuasions against the Japanese occupation forces. In 1946, the organization was renamed the New Democratic Youth League in accordance with Mao Zedong's (q.v.) call for creation of a new democracy (q.v.) in the Chinese state. This organization did not change its name to the Communist Youth League until 1957, after the official completion of the "socialist transformation" of the country. The major purpose of the CYL as a "transmission belt" of the CCP is to educate Chinese youth in the "communist spirit" and "unite all youth to participate in socialist construction and create conditions for the realization of communism."

The CYL National Congress is the highest leading organ of the

CYL, with a Central Committee and Standing Committee akin to the organizational structure of the CCP. From 1957 to 1964, the CYL was chaired by Hu Yaobang (q.v.) who fostered a liberal atmosphere of democracy and openness that anticipated his plans for political reform in the late 1970s when he was elevated to the position of CCP chairman and then general secretary. During the 1989 pro-democracy movement, student activists condemned the CYL for its ideological and administrative dependence on the CCP, prompting efforts to organize alternative youth groups.

YU GUANGYUAN (1915–). A veteran of the anti-Japanese 1935 December Ninth Movement, in the 1950s Yu Guangyuan became actively involved in developing China's scientific establishment, especially in the field of physics, and the philosophy of natural science. During the 1957–1958 Anti-Rightist campaign (q.v.) he launched attacks against other philosophers. In 1962 Yu became a professor at Beida (Peking University) (q.v.). In 1967 he was branded a "counter-revolutionary" and purged, but returned in 1977 as vice minister of the State Scientific and Technical Commission. In the early 1980s Yu headed a number of societies dealing with economic development and was elected to the presidium of the Academy of Sciences. The intellectual mentor of Yan Jiaqi (q.v.), in 1988 Yu became president of the Society for the Study of Marxism-Leninism–Mao Zedong Thought. After the 1989 Beijing massacre, the *Beijing Daily* criticized Yu for "negating the people's democratic dictatorship."

YU HAOCHENG (1928–). In 1982, Yu was a vice president of the Political Science Society and a legal and constitutional expert who was also head of the *Masses* (*Qunzhong*) publishing house run by the Ministry of Public Security. In February 1989 he signed a petition by intellectuals (q.v.) calling for greater freedoms and for the release of political prisoners. After June 1989, he was placed under surveillance by the Ministry of Public Security for his role in the pro-democracy demonstrations.

Z

ZHANG CHUNQIAO (1917–). A guerrilla fighter during the 1940s, in the early 1950s Zhang Chunqiao became managing director of the PLA's (q.v.) *Liberation Army Daily* in Shanghai (q.v.). In 1959 he was appointed to the Politburo (q.v.) of the Shanghai Municipal Party Committee and director of its Propaganda Department. In 1966 he became deputy head of the Cultural Revolution Small Group (q.v.)

helping to initiate demonstrations by radical Red Guard (q.v.) Revolutionary Rebels known as *zaofanpai*. Zhang headed the "Shanghai People's Commune" that later became the Shanghai Revolutionary Committee (q.v.). In 1969 he became a member of the CCP (q.v.) Central Committee and the Politburo (q.v.). In 1975 he was appointed a vice premier and director of the PLA General Political Department. In October 1976 he was arrested as a member of the Gang of Four (q.v.). At the trial of the gang in 1980–1981, along with Jiang Qing (q.v.), he was unrepentant and was sentenced to death with a two-year reprieve. As of 1997, Zhang had not been executed, but remained incarcerated.

ZHANG PINGHUA (1906–). A Long March (q.v.) veteran and a political commissar (q.v.) in the Eighth Route Army, in the early 1950s Zhang Pinghua became a prominent member of the Wuhan Municipal Party Committee and the Hubei Provincial Party Committee. He became a member of the Central Committee in 1956 and Party secretary in Hunan until his purge in 1967 as a "counterrevolutionary double dealer of Liu Shaoqi (q.v.) and Deng Xiaoping (q.v.)." He returned in 1971 and from 1977 to 1978 headed the CCP (q.v.) Propaganda Department. In 1982 he became a member of the Central Advisory Commission (q.v.) in nominal "retirement."

ZHANG XIANYANG (1938–). Director of the Marx-Engels Research Office of the Institute of Marxism-Leninism–Mao Zedong Thought under the Chinese Academy of Social Sciences (q.v.), Zhang was involved in criticizing the theory of the "two whatevers" (q.v.) and was one of the earliest critics of Mao Zedong's (q.v.) theories of "overall dictatorship" and "the continuation of the revolution under proletarian dictatorship." In 1987, Zhang was ousted from the CCP (q.v.) in the campaign against "bourgeois liberalization."

ZHANG YIMOU (1950–). Born in Xi'an in Shaanxi province, Zhang Yimou is one of China's most renowned living movie directors. During the Cultural Revolution (1966–1976) (q.v.), Zhang worked in the countryside and in a factory. He entered the Beijing Film Art Institute in 1978. In the early 1980s, Zhang was the photographer for the film *The Yellow Earth*, the first of a number of films by China's fifth generation of film directors, and played the hero Wang Quan in the film version of *The Old Well* by the novelist Zheng Yi (q.v.). Zhang Yimou also directed *Red Sorghum*, which won the "Golden Bear" award at the 1988 Berlin Film Festival. In the early 1990s, Zhang directed *Raise the Red Lantern* and *Ju Dou*.

ZHAO ZIYANG (1919–   ). Born to a landlord family in Hua county in Henan province where large numbers of Chinese Jews reside, Zhao Ziyang attended middle school and then joined the CCP (q.v.) in 1938. During the 1940s he worked in rural areas and after 1949 worked in the CCP's Central-South China Sub-bureau of the Central Committee. In 1955 he became deputy secretary of the Guang-dong Party Committee. In the early 1960s he proposed a system of counter-vailing powers in the CCP. In 1967 he was paraded through the streets by Red Guards (q.v.). He disappeared during the Cultural Revolution, but was appointed secretary of the Inner Mongolia Party Committee in 1971 and secretary of the Guangdong Party Committee in 1973. In 1976 he headed the Sichuan Party Committee and in 1979 he was made a member of the Politburo (q.v.). In September 1980 he was appointed premier and in 1987 he became general secretary of the CCP. In June 1989 he was dismissed from all his posts in the wake of the pro-democracy movement, but retained his Party membership. Since 1989 he has been under house arrest.

ZHENG YI (1947–   ). Born in Sichuan province, Zheng Yi is one of China's greatest contemporary writers. During the Cultural Revolution (1966–1976) (q.v.), he was forced to work in the countryside in a mountainous region of Shanxi province as a carpenter and in a coal mine. After 1978, he studied in the Chinese Department of Shanxi Normal College and began to publish short stories and plays, including his most famous, *The Distant Village* (*Yuan cun*) which was later made into a movie entitled *The Old Well*. In the mid-1980s, Zheng Yi traveled to Guangxi province where he did an extensive investigation of the officially sanctioned cannibalism among the Zhuang national minority in the province's rural areas during the Cultural Revolution (1966–1976). He later published a book entitled *Scarlet Memorial* (*Hongse jinianbei*) documenting these events and revealing the role of local CCP (q.v.) officials in the killings. After the 1989 military crackdown, Zheng Yi fled to the U.S. where he now resides.

ZHOU ENLAI (1898–1976). Born in Jiangsu province, Zhou Enlai was raised by his uncle in Shanghai (q.v.) and later studied at Nankai Middle School and Waseda University in Tokyo. The May Fourth Movement (q.v.) in 1919 brought Zhou back to China where he became involved in political activities, including the establishment of the Awakening Society that formed the nucleus of the CCP (q.v.). Zhou formally became a member of the CCP in 1922 and later traveled to England, Belgium, and Germany.

In 1924, Zhou returned to China and held important political positions in Canton, including head of the political department at the

KMT's (q.v.) Whampoa Military Academy, a training facility for revolutionary soldiers. Zhou was removed from the KMT posts in 1926 after a clash occurred between the CCP and KMT. When the CCP's military arm took control of Wuhan, Hubei province, in late 1926, Zhou became head of the CCP's new military department. At the April-May 1927 CCP Fifth Congress, Zhou was elected a member of the Central Committee and its Politburo (q.v.). In mid-1928, he participated in the Sixth Party Congress in Moscow and emerged as a CCP leader, second only to Li Lisan. Zhou returned to China in late 1928 and was targeted by Li Lisan as the scapegoat for the Chinese Red Army's failure to hold the city of Changsha in Hunan province. In 1931, Zhou joined Mao Zedong (q.v.) and Zhu De (q.v.) in the Jiangxi Soviet and held important political and military positions in the Chinese Soviet Republic. Zhou gained international attention when he successfully negotiated the release of Chiang Kai-shek during the Xi'an Incident in 1936 and the agreement to form the Second United Front.

With the establishment of the PRC (q.v.) in 1949, Zhou became premier, a position he held until his death. Zhou also played an important role as a diplomat at the 1954 Geneva Conference on Indochina and at the meeting of the twenty-nine nonaligned nations in Bandung (q.v.), Indonesia, in 1955. Zhou's role in the Great Leap Forward (1958–1960) (q.v.) and the Cultural Revolution (1966–1976) (q.v.) was controversial in that he appeared to support Mao Zedong's (q.v.) radical line. At the same time, however, Zhou personally intervened to save a number of prominent CCP cadres (q.v.) and intellectuals (q.v.) and ordered the PLA (q.v.) to protect the most important historical sites from Red Guard (q.v.) violence. Zhou played a major role in the sudden demise of Lin Biao (q.v.) in 1971 by personally ordering the shooting down of Lin's plane as it flew over Mongolian airspace. Zhou was also crucial in achieving the reestablishment of Sino-U.S. relations (q.v.) in 1972. At the Tenth Party Congress in 1973, Zhou became the number two leader in China, but he was indirectly attacked by the Gang of Four (q.v.) in the 1973–1975 Anti-Lin, Anti-Confucius campaign (q.v.). Zhou died of cancer in 1976 at the age of seventy-eight after being denied medical attention. Demonstrations in Tiananmen Square on April 5, 1976, known as the first Tiananmen Incident, by mourners who were prevented from memorializing Zhou Enlai signaled a major shift in China's internal politics. *See also* April 5th Movement.

ZHOU HUI (1919–). Secretary of the Hunan Provincial Party Committee from 1957–1963, Zhou Hui disappeared during the Cultural Revolution (1966–1976) (q.v.). In 1978, he became Party secretary in Inner Mongolia and a member of the CCP (q.v.) Central Committee. In 1982 he wrote an article praising the Agricultural Responsibility System (q.v.). In 1987 he was relieved from his posts soon after the fall of Hu Yaobang (q.v.).

ZHOU JIE (1927–). A close associate of Hu Yaobang (q.v.), in the mid-1980s Zhou Jie was deputy director of the Central Committee General Office. He also served as Hu Yaobang's main speech writer, a vice minister of the Economic Reform Commission, and a member of the Political Reform Office established by Zhao Ziyang (q.v.). Zhou was a strong supporter of Zhao's plans to institute "inner Party democracy" (*dangnei minzhu*) and to reduce the role of Party committees in state-run enterprises. *See also* ENTERPRISE REFORM.

ZHOU YANG (1907–1989). In 1930 Zhou Yang was secretary of the League of Left-Wing Writers in Shanghai (q.v.). During the Sino-Japanese War (q.v.) he defended the concept of "literature of national defense" in controversies with Ba Jin (q.v.) and others. In the early 1950s Zhou joined in persecuting his old rival Hu Feng (q.v.), but during the Cultural Revolution (1966–1976) (q.v.) he was branded a "three-anti element" and publicly denounced along with the famous journalist Lu Dingyi (q.v.). Zhou Yang reappeared in 1977 as an adviser to the Chinese Academy of Social Sciences (q.v.), a vice chairman of the All-China Writers' Association, and, until 1982, a deputy director of the CCP Propaganda Department.

ZHU DE (1886–1976). One of the founders of the Red Army and the CCP's top military leader during the Civil War (1946–1949) (q.v.), Zhu De was born in Sichuan province to a family of tenant farmers. A member of Sun Yat-sen's early revolutionary organization, the *T'ung Meng Hwei* and the secret society known as the *Gelaohui*, Zhu participated in the 1911 Republican revolution and was a member of the KMT (q.v.). He also joined the CCP (q.v.) in the early 1920s during the First United Front (q.v.). In the early 1920s, Zhu De also went to Europe and attended lectures at the University of Göttingen in Germany where he became acquainted with Marxism. After returning to China, Zhu played a role in the 1927 Northern Expedition directed by Chiang Kai-shek against northern warlords and in August 1927 participated in the CCP's aborted Nanchang Uprising. In 1928, Zhu forged a cooperative relationship with Mao Zedong (q.v.) that would last throughout the period of the Chinese Soviets and the Yan'an period. In 1934, he became a member of the Politburo (q.v.) and was the commander in chief of the Long March (q.v.), the Eighth Route Army, and later the People's Liberation Army (q.v.). One of ten marshals in the PRC (q.v.), in 1954 Zhu relinquished his command of the PLA and in 1959 was appointed a member of the NPC (q.v.) Standing Committee. During the 1960s and 1970s, Zhu largely stayed clear of politics, though he was attacked during the Cultural Revolution (1966–1976) for allegedly having questioned the personality cult of Mao Zedong.

ZHU HOUZE (1931–). In the 1950s and early 1960s, Zhu Houze was involved in Communist Youth League (q.v.) work in Guiyang, Guizhou province. After being sent down to the countryside in the Cultural Revolution (1966–1976) (q.v.), he became secretary of the Guizhou Party Committee and director of the CCP (q.v.) Propaganda Department in 1985. In 1987 he was relieved of these posts and became deputy director of the Rural Development Center under the State Council. In 1988 he became secretary of the All-China Federation of Trade Unions until he was purged after the fall of Zhao Ziyang (q.v.).

ZHU MUZHI (1916–). Director of the New China News Agency (q.v.) in the 1950s, in the 1960s Zhu Muzhi became a member of the China Journalists Association. He became a member of the CCP (q.v.) Central Committee in 1973 and in 1977 he became a deputy director of the CCP Propaganda Department. In 1978 he became a member of the Central Discipline Inspection Commission (q.v.). From 1982 to 1986 he was minister of culture. In 1988 he became a member of the Propaganda and Ideological Leading Group under the Central Committee.

ZHU RONGJI (1928–). Zhu Rongji graduated from the Electric Motor Engine Department of Qinghua University (q.v.) and worked from 1951–1966 in the State Planning Commission. In the late 1970s he worked in the Ministry of Petroleum and in 1983 he was appointed vice minister of the State Economic Commission. In 1987 Zhu became a member of the CCP (q.v.) Central Committee and in 1988 he became mayor of Shanghai (q.v.). After a stint at the China International Trust and Investment Corporation (CITIC) (q.v.), in 1992 he became a vice premier and was put in charge of cooling down the Chinese economy. He became a member of the Standing Committee of the Politburo (q.v.) at the Fourteenth Party Congress.

ZHUANG PEOPLE. See MINORITIES.

ZOU JIAHUA (1926–). A graduate of the Moscow Engineering Institute, in the 1950s and 1960s Zou Jiahua served as director of a machine-tool plant in Shenyang city and then he worked in the First Ministry of Machine Building. In 1974 he was identified as a member of the PLA (q.v.) Science and Technology Commission for National Defense and in 1977 he was elected to the CCP (q.v.) Central Committee. In 1983 he became vice minister of the Commission of Science, Technology, and Industry for National Defense and in 1985 he was named minister of ordnance industry. In 1988 he became a state councillor and minister of machinery and the electronics industry, and in 1991 he was appointed head of the State Planning Commission and a vice premier. He joined the Politburo (q.v.) in 1992 at the Fourteenth Party Congress.

Selected Bibliography

A wealth of English-language materials are available on the People's Republic of China. Included in this bibliography are major books by university and commercial publishers; articles on politics, economics, and society in professional journals (primarily, *The China Quarterly*, *Asian Survey*, *The Journal of Asian Studies*, and *The Australian Journal of Chinese Affairs* renamed *The China Journal* in 1995); contemporary films on China; and databases available on the Internet. Also listed are translations of Chinese-language newspapers and radio transmissions provided by various outlets of the Foreign Broadcast Information Service (FBIS), United States Department of Commerce. Chinese-language books published in the PRC, Hong Kong, and Taiwan are increasingly available in the United States through specialized commercial outlets and research libraries at major universities, but they are not included here except for those that have been translated into English. Several commercial publishers in the United States specialize in publishing books on contemporary China and Chinese-language translations, such as M. E. Sharpe, Inc., Armonk, New York, and Westview Press, Boulder, Colorado.

The bibliography is arranged topically and begins with a comprehensive list of reference materials. Travel guides and accounts have been generally excluded, and only a few works of art, literature, and poetry are listed. This reflects, in part, the dearth of such works published in China from 1949 to 1978. Major Chinese literary works and belles lettres published since the economic and social reforms began in 1978 have been much richer and more numerous and are included below. English- and Chinese-language sources on contemporary China have also flourished since 1978 mainly because of greater openness in China and increased access to Chinese society and sources by outside researchers that were generally unavailable during the 1949 to 1972 period of China's general isolation from the outside world. Many works on China have been published in Europe, especially in France, and in Japan, but, with the exception of the English-language works published in Britain, these are generally not listed here. On-line sources on the Internet in and outside the PRC are listed in a separate section at the end of the bibliography.

251

Reference Works and Films

Bartke, Wolfgang. *Atlas of China*. 1st ed. Beijing: Foreign Languages Press, 1989. 1st edition.

———. *Who's Who in the People's Republic of China*. Armonk, N.Y.: M. E. Sharpe, Inc., 1981.

———. *Who's Who in the People's Republic of China*. 2d and 3d eds. Munich: K.G. Saur, 1987 and 1991.

Blunden, Caroline, and Mark Elvin. *Cultural Atlas of China*. New York: Facts on File, 1983.

Boorman, Howard L., ed. *Biographical Dictionary of Republican China*. New York: Columbia University Press, 1967–1979, 56 vols.

Chaffee, Frederic H., et al. *Area Handbook for Communist China*. Washington, D.C.: U.S. Government Printing Office, 1967.

Cheng, Peter. *A Chronology of the People's Republic of China From October 1, 1949*. Totowa, N.J.: Rowman and Littlefield, 1972.

———. *A Chronology of the People's Republic 1970–1979*. Metuchen, N.J.: Scarecrow Press, 1986.

The Challenge From Asia: China and the Pacific Rim. Videorecording. Princeton: Films for the Humanities, 1989.

China Briefing. 1980–1994. Boulder, Colo: Westview Press.

China Directory in Pinyin and Chinese. Tokyo: Radiopress, 1978–.

China, Facts and Figures Annual. Gulf Breeze, Fla.: Academic International Press, 1978–.

China, Financial Sector Policies and Institutional Development. Washington, D.C.: World Bank, 1990.

China Official Yearbook. Hong Kong: Dragon Pearl Publications Ltd., 1983–.

China Report: Agriculture. Arlington, Va.: Foreign Broadcast Information Service, 1979–1987.

China Report: Economic Affairs. Arlington, Va.: Foreign Broadcast Information Service, 1979–1987.

China Report: Plant and Installation Data. Arlington, Va.: Foreign Broadcast Information Serivce, 1978–1985.

China Report: Political, Sociological, and Military Affairs. Arlington, Va.: Foreign Broadcast Information Service, 1979–1994.

China Report: Science and Technology. Arlington, Va.: Foreign Broadcast Information Service, 1979–1996.

China Statistical Yearbook. State Statistical Bureau, PRC, 1981–.

China, The Mandate of Heaven. Videorecording. Ambrose Video Publishing, 1991.

Daily Report: PRC. Springfield, Va.: Foreign Broadcast Information Service, United States Department of Commerce.

Hinton, Harold C., ed. *The People's Republic of China: A Handbook*. Boulder, Colo.: Westview Press, 1979.

————, ed. *The People's Republic of China, 1949–1979: A Documentary Survey.* Wilmington, Del.: Scholarly Resources, 1980. 5 vols.

Hook, Brian, ed. *The Cambridge Encyclopedia of China.* 2d ed., Cambridge: Cambridge University Press, 1982.

Hsieh, Chiao-min. *Atlas of China.* New York: McGraw-Hill, 1973.

Johnston, Douglas, and Hungdah Chiu, eds. *Agreements of the People's Republic of China, 1949–1967.* Cambridge: Harvard University Press, 1968.

Joint Publication Research Service: China. Washington, D.C.: United States Department of Commerce.

Ju Dou. Videorecording. Miramax Films, 1990.

Klein, Donald W., and Anne B. Clark. *Biographic Dictionary of Chinese Communism, 1921–1965.* Cambridge, Mass.: Harvard University Press, 1971. 2 vols.

Leung, Edwin Pak-wah. *Historical Dictionary of Revolutionary China, 1839–1976.* Westport, Conn.: Greenwood Press, 1992.

Liu, William T., ed. *China: Social Statistics.* New York: Praeger, 1989.

Long Bow Group, Inc. *The Gate of Heavenly Peace: The Epic and Explosive Documentary on the Events Leading Up to the Tiananmen Square Uprisings.* Videorecording. Directed by Carma Hinton and Richard Gordon. Produced by Peter Kovler, USA, 1995.

Population Census Office of the State Council, ed. *The Population Atlas of China.* Oxford: Oxford University Press, 1987.

Red Sorghum. Videorecording. New York: New Yorker Films, 1991.

Sivin, Nathan, ed. *The Contemporary Atlas of China.* Boston: Houghton-Mifflin, 1988.

Sorich, Richard. *Documents on Contemporary China, 1949–1975: A Research Collection.* Greenwich, Conn.: Johnson Associates, 1976.

Tanis, Norman E., et al., comp. *China in Books: A Basic Bibliography in Western Languages.* Greenwich, Conn.: JAI Press, 1979.

Tibet Information Network, Human Rights Watch/Asia. *Cutting Off the Serpent's Head: Tightening Control in Tibet, 1994–1995.* New York: Human Rights Watch, 1996.

Tregear, Thomas R. *China, a Geographical Survey.* New York: Wiley, 1980.

Twitchett, Dennis, and John King Fairbank, gen. eds. *The Cambridge History of China.* Cambridge: Cambridge University Press, 1978–.

U.S. Government. *Directory of Chinese Government Officials.* 1963–1991.

Wang, Richard T. *Area Bibliography of China.* Lanham, Md.: Scarecrow Press, 1997.

Who's Who in Communist China. Hong Kong: Union Research Institute, 1970. 2 vols.

General Works: Books and Articles

Biography

Chi, Hsin. *Teng Hsiao-ping: A Political Biography.* Hong Kong: Cosmos Books, 1978.

Evans, Richard. *Deng Xiaoping and the Making of Modern China.* New York: Viking, 1994.

Franz, Uli. *Deng Xiaoping.* Boston: Harcourt Brace Jovanovich, 1988.

Goodman, David S. *Deng Xiaoping and the Chinese Revolution: A Political Biography.* London: Routledge, 1994.

Li, Zhisui, with Anne Thurston. *The Private Life of Chairman Mao: The Memoirs of Mao's Personal Physician.* New York: Random House, 1994.

MacFarquhar, Roderick, Timothy Cheek, and Eugene Wu, eds. *The Secret Speeches of Chairman Mao: From the Hundred Flowers to the Great Leap Forward.* Cambridge, Mass.: Council on East Asian Studies, Harvard University, 1989.

Pye, Lucian. *Mao Tse-tung: The Man in the Leader.* New York: Basic Books, 1976.

Rand, Peter. *China Hands: The Adventures and Ordeals of the American Journalists Who Joined Forces with the Great Chinese Revolution.* New York: Simon & Schuster, 1995.

Rice, Edwin. *Mao's Way.* Berkeley and Los Angeles: University of California Press, 1972.

Ruan, Ming. *Deng Xiaoping: Chronicle of an Empire.* Nancy Liu, Peter Rand, and Lawrence R. Sullivan, trans. Boulder, Colo.: Westview Press, 1994.

Schram, Stuart R. *The Political Thought of Mao Tse-tung.* New York: Praeger, 1963.

————. *The Thought of Mao Tse-tung.* Cambridge: Cambridge University Press, 1989.

————, ed. *Chairman Mao Talks to the People: Talks and Letters: 1956–1971.* New York: Pantheon Books, 1974.

————, ed. *Mao's Road to Power: Revolutionary Writings, 1912–1949.* Armonk, N.Y.: M. E. Sharpe, Inc., 1992–1995. 3 vols.

Selected Works of Deng Xiaoping. Beijing: Foreign Languages Press, 1984, 1992, 1994. 3 vols.

Selected Works of Mao Tse-tung. Beijing: Foreign Languages Press, 1965, 1977. 5 vols.

Shambaugh, David. *The Making of a Premier: Zhao Ziyang's Provincial Career.* Boulder, Colo.: Westview Press, 1984.

Terrill, Ross. *Madame Mao: The White Boned Demon, a Biography of Madame Mao Zedong.* New York: Simon & Schuster, 1992.

————. *Mao: A Biography*. New York: Harper & Row, 1980.

Wilson, Dick, ed. *Mao Tse-tung in the Scales of History*. Cambridge: Cambridge University Press, 1977.

Witke, Roxane. *Comrade Chiang Ch'ing*. Boston: Little, Brown & Co., 1977.

Yang, Zhongmei. *Hu Yaobang: A Chinese Biography*. Translated by William A. Wycoff, trans. Armonk, N.Y.: M. E. Sharpe, Inc., 1988.

Domestic and International Economics

Andors, Stephen. *China's Industrial Revolution: Politics, Planning and Management, 1949 to the Present*. New York: Pantheon Books, 1977.

Ash, Robert. "The Agricultural Sector in China: Performance and Policy Dilemmas during the 1990s." *The China Quarterly* No. 131 (September 1992): 545–76.

Barnett, A. Doak. *China's Economy in Global Perspective*. Washington, D.C.: The Brookings Institution, 1981.

Bartke, Wolfgang. *The Economic Aid of the People's Republic of China to Developing and Socialist Countries*. Munich: K. G. Saur, 1989.

Baum, Richard, ed. *China's Four Modernizations: The New Technological Revolution*. Boulder, Colo.: Westview Press, 1980.

China's Economy Looks Toward the Year 2000. Washington, D.C.: Government Printing Office, 1986. 2 vols.

De Keijzer, Arne. *China: Business Strategies for the '90s*. Berkeley: Pacific View Press, 1979.

Dirlik, Arif. *After the Revolution: Waking to Global Capitalism*. Hanover: Wesleyan University Press, 1994.

Donnithorne, Audrey. *China's Economic System*. New York: Praeger Publishers, 1967.

Eckstein, Alexander. *Communist China's Economic Growth and Foreign Trade: Implications for U.S. Policy*. New York: McGraw-Hill, 1966.

Feuerwerker, Albert. *China's Early Industrialization*. Cambridge, Mass.: Harvard University Press, 1958.

Granick, David. *Chinese State Enterprises: A Regional Property Rights Analysis*. Chicago: University of Chicago Press, 1990.

Hay, Donald, et al. *Economic Reform and State-Owned Enterprises in China, 1979–1987*. Oxford: Clarendon Press, 1994.

Howe, Christopher. *China's Economy: A Basic Guide*. New York: Basic Books, 1978.

————, ed. *Shanghai: Revolution and Development in an Asian Metropolis*. Cambridge: Cambridge University Press, 1981.

Lardy, Nicholas R. *Agriculture in China's Modern Economic Development*. Cambridge: Cambridge University Press, 1983.

————. *China in the World Economy.* Washington, D.C.: Institute for International Economics, 1994.

————. *Economic Growth and Distribution in China.* Cambridge: Cambridge University Press, 1978.

————. "Redefining U.S.–China Economic Relations." National Bureau of Asian and Soviet Research, *NBR Analysis Series Paper*, No. 5, 1991.

Lardy, Nicholas R. and Kenneth Lieberthal, eds. *Chen Yun's Strategy for China's Development.* Armonk, N.Y.: M. E. Sharpe, Inc., 1983.

Lee, Peter N. S. "Enterprise Autonomy in Post-Mao China: A Case Study of Policy-Making, 1978–83." *The China Quarterly*, No. 105 (March 1986).

————. *Industrial Management and Economic Reform in China, 1949–1984.* New York: Oxford University Press, 1987.

Lew, Alan A., and Lawrence Yu. *Tourism in China: Geographic, Political, and Economic Perspectives.* Boulder, Colo.: Westview Press, 1995.

Lim, Edwin. *China: Long-Term Development Issues and Options.* Baltimore: Johns Hopkins University Press, for the World Bank, 1985.

Lyons, Thomas P. *Economic Integration and Planning in Maoist China.* New York: Columbia University Press 1987.

Mann, Jim. *Beijing Jeep: The Short Unhappy Romance of American Business in China.* New York: Simon & Schuster, 1989.

Moser, Michael, ed. *Foreign Trade, Investment and the Law in the People's Republic of China.* Oxford: Oxford University Press, 1984.

Naughton, Barry. *Growing Out of the Plan: Chinese Economic Reform, 1978–93.* Cambridge: Cambridge University Press, 1995.

Nolan, Peter. *The Political Economy of Collective Farms: An Analysis of China's Post-Mao Rural Reforms.* Boulder, Colo.: Westview Press, 1988.

Nolan, Peter, and Dong Fureng, eds. *Market Forces in China, Competition, and Small Business: The Wenzhou Debate.* London: Zed Books, 1989.

Overholt, William H. *The Rise of China: How Economic Reform is Creating a New Superpower.* New York: W. W. Norton & Co., 1993.

Pearson, Margaret. *Joint Ventures in the People's Republic of China: The Control of Foreign Direct Investment under Socialism.* Princeton: Princeton University Press, 1991.

Perkins, Dwight. *China: Asia's Next Economic Giant?* Seattle: University of Washington Press, 1986.

————. *Market Control and Planning in Communist China.* Cambridge, Mass.: Harvard University Press, 1966.

Perry, Elizabeth, and Christine Wong, eds. *The Political Economy of*

Reform in Post-Mao China. Cambridge, Mass.: Harvard University Press, 1985.

Potter, Pitman B. *The Economic Contract Law of China: Legitimation and Contract Autonomy in the People's Republic of China*. Seattle: University of Washington Press, 1992.

Rawski, Thomas G. *Economic Growth and Employment in China*. Oxford: Oxford University Press, 1979.

Reynolds, Bruce, ed. *Reform in China, Challenges and Choices*. Armonk, N.Y.: M. E. Sharpe, Inc., 1987.

Richman, Barry M. *Industrial Society in Communist China*. New York: Random House, 1969.

Riskin, Carl. *China's Political Economy: The Quest for Development Since 1949*. Oxford: Oxford University Press, 1987.

Solinger, Dorothy J. *Chinese Business Under Socialism: The Politics of Domestic Commerce, 1949–1980*. Berkeley and Los Angeles: University of California Press, 1984.

———. *China's Transition From Socialism: Statist Legacies and Market Reforms, 1980–1990*. Armonk, N.Y.: M. E. Sharpe Inc., 1993.

Stavis, Benedict. *Making Green Revolution: The Politics of Agricultural Development in China*. Ithaca: Rural Development Monograph, No. 1, Cornell University Press, 1974.

———. *The Politics of Agricultural Mechanization in China*. Ithaca: Cornell University Press, 1978.

Tidrick, Gene, and Jiyuan Chen, eds. *China's Industrial Reform*. Oxford: Oxford University Press, 1987.

Tong, James. "Fiscal Reform, Elite Turnover, and Central-Provincial Relations in Post-Mao China." *Australian Journal of Chinese Affairs*, No. 22 (July 1989).

Walder, Andrew G. *Communist Neo-Traditionalism: Work and Authority in Chinese Industry*. Berkeley and Los Angeles: University of California Press, 1986.

———. "Wage Reform and the Web of Factory Interests." *The China Quarterly*, No. 109 (March 1987).

Wang, N.T. *China's Modernization and Transnational Corporations*. Lexington, Mass.: Lexington Books, 1984.

Wong, Christine P. W. "Between Plan and Market: The Role of the Local Sector in Post-Mao China." *Journal of Comparative Economics* 11, No. 3, 1987.

———. "The Economics of Shortage and Problems of Reform in Chinese Industry." *Journal of Comparative Economics* 10, No. 4, 1986.

Woodward, Kim. *The International Energy Relations of China*. Stanford: Stanford University Press, 1980.

World Bank. *China: Between Plan and Market*. Washington, D.C.: World Bank, 1990.

————. *China Updating Economic Memorandum: Managing Rapid Growth and Transition*. Washington, D.C.: World Bank, 1993.

Yeung, Yue-Man, and Xuwei Hu, eds. *China's Coastal Cities: Catalysts for Modernization*. Honolulu: University of Hawaii Press, 1991.

Yi, Gang. *Money, Banking, and Financial Markets in China*. Boulder, Colo.: Westview Press, 1994.

The Cultural Revolution

Ahn, Byung-joon. *Chinese Politics and the Cultural Revolution*. Seattle: University of Washington Press, 1976.

Bao, Ruo-wang (Jean Pasqualini), and Rudolph Chelminski. *Prisoner of Mao*. New York: Coward, McCann and Geoghegan, 1973.

Chen, Jo-hsi. *The Execution of Mayor Yin and Other Stories from the Great Proletarian Cultural Revolution*. Bloomington: Indiana University Press, 1978.

Chen, Xuezhao. *Surviving the Storm: A Memoir*. Ti Hua and Caroline Greene, trans. Armonk, N.Y.: M. E. Sharpe, Inc., 1990.

Cheng, Nien. *Life and Death in Shanghai*. New York: Grove Press, 1986.

Dittmer, Lowell. *Liu Shao-ch'i and the Chinese Cultural Revolution: The Politics of Mass Criticism*. Berkeley and Los Angeles: University of California Press, 1974.

Domes, Jurgen. *China After the Cultural Revolution: Politics Between Two Party Congresses*. Berkeley: University of California Press, 1977.

Gao, Yuan. *Born Red: A Chronicle of the Cultural Revolution*. Stanford: Stanford University Press, 1987.

Hinton, William. *Hundred Day War: The Cultural Revolution at Tsinghua University*. New York: Monthly Review Press, 1972.

Lee, Hong Yung. *The Politics of the Chinese Cultural Revolution: A Case Study*. Berkeley and Los Angeles: University of California Press, 1978.

Liang, Heng, and Judith Shapiro. *After the Nightmare: A Survivor of the Cultural Revolution Reports on China Today*. New York: Alfred A. Knopf, 1986.

Ma, Bo. *Blood Red Sunset: A Memoir of the Chinese Cultural Revolution*. Howard Goldblatt, trans. New York: Viking, 1995.

MacFarquhar, Roderick. *The Origins of the Cultural Revolution*, 2 vols. New York: Columbia University Press, 1974 and 1983.

Pusey, James R. *Wu Han: Attacking the Present Through the Past*. Cambridge, Mass.: East Asian Research Center, Harvard University, 1969.

Rosen, Stanley. *Red Guard Factionalism and the Cultural Revolution in Guangzhou (Canton)*. Boulder, Colo.: Westview Press, 1982.

Schram, Stuart R., ed. *Authority, Participation and Cultural Change in China.* Cambridge: Cambridge University Press, 1973.

Tsou, Tang. *The Cultural Revolution and Post-Mao Reforms: A Historical Perspective.* Chicago: University of Chicago Press, 1986.

Wen, Chihua. *The Red Mirror: Children of China's Cultural Revolution.* Boulder, Colo.: Westview Press, 1995.

White, Lynn T., III. *Policies of Chaos: The Organizational Causes of Violence in China's Cultural Revolution.* Princeton: Princeton University Press, 1989.

Democracy Movements and the Legal System

Barmé, Geremie, and John Minford, eds. *Seeds of Fire: Chinese Voices of Conscience.* Hong Kong: Far Eastern Economic Review, Ltd., 1986.

Barmé, Geremie, John Mindord, and Linda Javin, eds. *New Ghosts, Old Dreams.* New York: Times Books, 1992.

Black, George, and Robin Munro. *Black Hands of Beijing: Lives in Defense of China's Democracy.* New York: John Wiley, 1993.

Calhoun, Craig. *Neither Gods Nor Emperors: Students and the Struggle for Democracy in China.* Berkeley and Los Angeles: University of California Press, 1994.

Che, Muqi. *Beijing Turmoil: More Than Meets the Eye.* Beijing: Foreign Languages Press, 1990.

Chen, Erjin. *China: Crossroads Socialism: An Unofficial Manifesto for Proletarian Democracy.* Robin Munro, trans. London: Verso, 1984.

Cohen, Jerome Alan. *The Criminal Process in the People's Republic of China 1949–1963: An Introduction.* Cambridge, Mass.: Harvard University Press, 1968.

Cohen, Jerome Alan, R. Randle Edwards, and Fu-mei Chang Chen, eds. *Essays on China's Legal Tradition.* Princeton: Princeton University Press, 1980.Des Forges, Roger V., Ning Luo, and Yen-bo Wu, eds. *Chinese Democracy and the Crisis of 1989: Chinese and American Reflections.* Albany: State University of New York Press, 1993.

Fang, Lizhi. *Bringing Down the Great Wall: Writings on Science, Culture and Democracy in China.* James H. Williams, trans. New York: Alfred A. Knopf, 1991.

Feigon, Lee. *China Rising: The Meaning of Tiananmen.* Chicago: Ivan Dee, 1990.

Friedman, Edward. *National Identity and Democratic Prospects in Socialist China.* Armonk, N.Y.: M. E. Sharpe, Inc., 1995.

Goldman, Merle. *China's Intellectuals: Advise and Dissent.* Cambridge, Mass.: Harvard University Press, 1981.

————. *Literary Dissent in Communist China*. Cambridge, Mass.: Harvard University Press, 1967.

————. *Sowing the Seeds of Democracy in China: Political Reform in the Deng Xiaoping Era*. Cambridge, Mass.: Harvard University Press, 1994.

Han, Minzhu, ed. *Cries for Democracy: Writings and Speeches from the 1989 Chinese Democracy Movement*. Princeton: Princeton University Press, 1990.

Hicks, George, ed. *The Broken Mirror: China After Tiananmen*. Chicago: St. James Press, 1990.

McCormick, Barrett L. *Political Reform in Post-Mao China: Democracy and Bureaucracy in a Leninist State*. Berkeley and Los Angeles: University of California Press, 1990.

Nathan, Andrew J. *Chinese Democracy*. New York: Alfred A. Knopf, 1985.

————. *China's Crisis: Dilemmas of Reform and Prospects for Democracy*. New York: Columbia University Press, 1990.

Ogden, Suzanne, Kathleen Hartford, Lawrence R. Sullivan, and David Zweig, eds. *China's Search for Democracy: The Student and the Mass Movement of 1989*. Armonk, N.Y.: M. E. Sharpe, Inc., 1992.

Oksenberg, Michel, Marc Lambert, and Lawrence R. Sullivan, eds. *Beijing Spring, 1989, Confrontation and Conflict: The Basic Documents*. Armonk, N.Y.: M. E. Sharpe, Inc., 1990.

Saich, Tony, ed. *The Chinese People's Movement: Perspectives on Spring 1989*. Armonk, N.Y.: M. E. Sharpe, Inc., 1990.

Schell, Orville. *Discos and Democracy: China in the Throes of Reform*. New York: Pantheon, 1988.

————. *Mandate of Heaven: A New Generation of Entrepreneurs, Dissidents, Bohemians, and Technocrats Lays Claim to China's Future*. New York: Simon & Schuster, 1994.

Simmie, Scott, and Bob Nixon. *Tiananmen Square: An Eyewitness Account of the Chinese People's Passionate Quest for Democracy*. Toronto: Douglas and McIntyre, 1989.

Unger, Jonathan, ed. *The Pro-Democracy Protests in China: Reports from the Provinces*. Armonk, N.Y.: M. E. Sharpe, Inc., 1991.

Wasserstrom, Jeffrey N., and Elizabeth J. Perry, eds. *Popular Protest and Political Culture in Modern China*, 2d ed. Boulder, Colo.: Westview Press, 1994.

Yan, Jiaqi. *Toward a Democratic China: The Intellectual Autobiography of Yan Jiaqi*. Honolulu: University of Hawaii Press, 1992.

Yi, Mu, and Mark V. Thompson. *Crisis at Tiananmen: Reform and Reality in Modern China*. San Francisco: China Books and Periodicals, 1989.

Education and Political Socialization

Chan, Anita. *Children of Mao: Personality Development & Political Activism in the Red Guard Generation.* Seattle: University of Washington Press, 1985.

Orleans, Leo. *Chinese Students in America: Policies, Issues, and Numbers.* Washington, D.C.: National Academy Press, 1988.

Pepper, Suzanne. *China's Education Reform in the 1980s: Policies, Issues, and Historical Perspectives.* Berkeley: Institute of East Asian Studies, University of California, 1990.

Schoenhals, Martin. *The Paradox of Power in a People's Republic of China Middle School.* Armonk, N.Y.: M. E. Sharpe, Inc., 1993.

Seybolt, Peter J., comp. *Revolutionary Education in China: Documents and Commentary.* White Plains, N.Y.: International Arts & Sciences Press, 1973.

Seybolt, Peter J., and Gregory Kuei-ke Chiang, eds. *Language Reform in China: Documents and Commentary.* White Plains, N.Y.: M. E. Sharpe, Inc., 1979.

Unger, Jonathan. *Education Under Mao: Class and Competition in Canton Schools, 1960–1980.* New York: Columbia University Press, 1982.

Environment

Dai, Qing. *The River Dragon has Come: The Three Gorges Dam and the Fate of the Yangtze River.* Armonk, N.Y.: M. E. Sharpe, 1997.

———. *Yangtze! Yangtze!: Debate Over the Three Gorges Project.* Nancy Liu, et al., trans. London and Toronto: Earthscan Publications Ltd. and Probe International, 1994.

He, Bochuan. *China on the Edge: The Crisis of Ecology and Development.* San Francisco: China Books and Periodicals, Inc., 1991.

Luk, Shiu-Hung, and Joseph Whitney, eds. *Megaproject: A Case Study of China's Three Gorges Project.* Armonk, N.Y.: M. E. Sharpe, Inc., 1993.

Nickum, James E., ed. *Water Management Organization in the People's Republic of China.* Armonk, N.Y.: M. E. Sharpe, Inc., 1981.

Richardson, S. D. *Forests and Forestry in China.* Washington, D.C.: Island Press, 1990.

Ross, Lester. *Environmental Policy in China.* Bloomington: Indiana University Press, 1988.

Ryder, Gráinne. *Damming the Three Gorges: What Dam-Builders Don't Want You to Know.* Toronto: Probe International, 1990.

Smil, Vaclav. *The Bad Earth: Environmental Degradation in China.* Armonk, N.Y.: M. E. Sharpe, Inc., 1984.

————. *China's Environmental Crisis: An Inquiry into the Limits of National Development.* Armonk, N.Y.: M. E. Sharpe, Inc., 1993.

Van Slyke, Lyman P. *Yangtze: Nature, History, and the River.* Reading, Mass.: Addison-Wesley, 1988.

Foreign Relations, Military Affairs, and International Law and Organization

Atlantic Council and National Committee on U.S.–China Relations. *United States and China Relations at a Crossroads.* Washington, D.C. and New York: Atlantic Council and National Committee on U.S.–China Relations, 1993.

Barnett, A. Doak. *The Making of Foreign Policy in China: Structure and Process.* Boulder, Colo.: Westview Press, 1985.

Chang, Gordon. *Friends and Enemies: The United States, China, and the Soviet Union, 1948–1972.* Stanford: Stanford University Press, 1990.

Ching, Frank. *Hong Kong and China: For Better or For Worse.* New York: Asia Society and Foreign Policy Association, 1985.

Clubb, O. Edmund. *China and Russia: The Great Game.* New York: Columbia University Press, 1971.

Cohen, Jerome Alan, and Hungdah Chiu. *People's China and International Law.* Princeton: Princeton University Press, 1974.

Cohen, Warren I. *America's Response to China: A History of Sino-American Relations,* 3d ed. New York: Columbia University Press, 1990.

Copper, Franklin. *China's Foreign Aid: An Instrument of Peking's Foreign Policy.* Boston: D. C. Heath, 1976.

Dreyer, June Teufel, ed. *Chinese Defense and Foreign Policy.* New York: Paragon, 1989.

Ellison, Herbert J., ed. *The Sino-Soviet Conflict: A Global Perspective.* Seattle: University of Washington Press, 1982.

Fairbank, John King. *The United States and China,* 4th ed. Cambridge, Mass.: Harvard University Press, 1983.

Fingar, Thomas, and Paul Blencoe, et al., eds. *China's Quest for Independence: Policy Evolution in the 1970s.* Boulder, Colo.: Westview Press, 1980.

George, Alexander. *The Chinese Communist Army in Action: The Korean War and its Aftermath.* New York: Columbia University Press, 1967.

Gilkey, Langdon. *Shantung Compound.* San Francisco: Harper & Row, 1966.

Gittings, John. *The World and China, 1922–1972.* New York: Harper & Row, 1974.

Godwin, Paul, ed. *The Chinese Defense Establishment: Continuity and Change in the 1980s*. Boulder, Colo.: Westview Press, 1983.

Goncharov, Sergei N., et al. *Uncertain Partners: Stalin, Mao, and the Korean War*. Stanford: Stanford University Press, 1993.

Harding, Harry. *A Fragile Relationship: The United States and China Since 1972*. Washington, D.C.: The Brookings Institution, 1992.

Harrison, Selig. *China, Oil, and Asia: Conflict Ahead?* New York: Columbia University Press, 1977.

Ho, Samuel, and Ralph W. Huenemann. *China's Open Door Policy: The Quest for Foreign Technology and Capital*. Vancouver: University of British Columbia Press, 1984.

Hopkirk, Peter. *Trespassers on the Roof of the World: The Secret Exploration of Tibet*. New York: Kodansha International, 1995.

Hsiung, James C., and Samuel Kim, eds. *China in the Global Community*. New York: Praeger Publishers, 1980.

Jacobson, Harold. *China's Participation in the IMF, the World Bank, and GATT: Toward a Global Economic Order*. Ann Arbor: University of Michigan Press, 1990.

Jagchid, Sechin, and Van Jay Symons, *Peace, War, and Trade Along the Great Wall: Nomadic-Chinese Interaction Through Two Millennia*. Bloomington: Indiana University Press, 1989.

Jencks, Harlan W. *From Muskets to Missiles: Politics and Professionalism in the Chinese Army, 1945–1981*. Boulder, Colo.: Westview Press, 1982.

Joffe, Ellis. *The Chinese Army After Mao*. Cambridge, Mass.: Harvard University Press, 1987.

Kim, Samuel S. *China, the United Nations, and World Order*. Princeton: Princeton University Press, 1979.

———. *The Third World in Chinese World Policy*. Princeton: Center of International Studies, 1989.

———, ed. *China and the World: Chinese Foreign Policy in the Post-Mao Era*. Boulder, Colo.: Westview Press, 1984.

———, ed. *China and the World: Chinese Foreign Relations in the Post-Cold War Era*, 3d ed. Boulder, Colo.: Westview Press, 1994.

Kleinberg, Robert. *China's "Opening" to the Outside World: The Experiment with Foreign Capitalism*. Boulder, Colo.: Westview Press, 1990.

Lewis, John Wilson, and Litai Xue. *China Builds the Bomb*. Stanford: Stanford University Press, 1988.

———. *China's Strategic Seapower: The Politics of Force Modernization in the Nuclear Age*. Stanford: Stanford University Press, 1994.

Lilley, James R., and Wendell L. Willkie II, eds. *Beyond MFN: Trade with China and American Interests*. Washington, D.C.: American Enterprise Institute Press, 1994.

Madsen, Richard. *China and the American Dream: A Moral Inquiry.* Berkeley and Los Angeles: University of California Press, 1995.

Maxwell, Neville. *India's China War.* London: Jonathan Cape, 1970.

Nelsen, Harvey. *The Chinese Military System: An Organizational Study of the Chinese People's Liberation Army.* Boulder, Colo.: Westview Press, 1977.

Oksenberg, Michel. "A Decade of Sino-American Relations." *Foreign Affairs,* Vol. 61, No. 1 (Fall 1982).

Roberti, Mark. *The Fall of Hong Kong: China's Triumph and Britain's Betrayal.* New York: John Wiley & Sons, Inc., 1994.

Ross, Robert S. *The Indochina Tangle: China's Vietnam Policy, 1975–1979.* New York: Columbia University Press, 1988.

———. *Negotiating Cooperation: The United States and China, 1969–1989.* Stanford: Stanford University Press, 1996.

Segal, Gerald, ed. *Chinese Politics and Foreign Policy Reform.* London: Kegan Paul International, 1990.

Service, John S. *The Amerasia Papers: Some Problems in the History of US-China Relations.* Berkeley: Center for Chinese Studies, University of California, 1971.

Shambaugh, David. *Beautiful Imperialist: China Perceives America, 1972–90.* Princeton: Princeton University Press, 1991.

Sutter, Robert G. *China-Watch: Toward Sino-American Reconciliation.* Baltimore: Johns Hopkins University Press, 1978.

Swaine, Michael D. *The Military and Political Succession in China: Leadership, Institutions and Beliefs.* Santa Monica: RAND, 1992.

Van Ness, Peter. *Revolution and Chinese Foreign Policy: Peking's Support for Wars of National Liberation.* Berkeley and Los Angeles: University of California Press, 1970.

Whiting, Allen. *China Crosses the Yalu: The Decision to Enter the Korean War.* New York: Macmillan, 1960.

———. *The Chinese Calculus of Deterrence: India and Indochina.* Ann Arbor: University of Michigan Press, 1975.

Whitson, William. *The Chinese High Command: A History of Communist Military Politics, 1927–71.* New York: Praeger Publishers, 1973.

———, ed. *The Military and Political Power in China in the 1970s.* New York: Praeger Publishers, 1972.

Yabuki, Susumu. *China's New Political Economy: The Giant Awakes.* Boulder, Colo.: Westview Press, 1995.

Yahuda, Michael. *China's Foreign Policy After Mao: Towards the End of Isolationism.* New York: Macmillan, 1983.

Yang, Richard H., et al. *Chinese Regionalism: The Security Dimension.* Boulder, Colo.: Westview Press, 1994.

Zagoria, Donald S. *The Sino-Soviet Conflict, 1956–1961.* New York: Atheneum, 1964.

History

Bianco, Lucien. *Origins of the Chinese Revolution, 1915–1949*. Stanford: Stanford University Press, 1971.
Chow, Tse-Tsung. *The May 4th Movement: Intellectual Revolution in Modern China*. Cambridge, Mass.: Harvard University Press, 1960.
Fairbank, John King. *China: A New History*. Cambridge, Mass.: Harvard University Press, 1992.
———. *China Watch*. Cambridge, Mass.: Harvard University Press, 1987.
Isaacs, Harold R. *The Tragedy of the Chinese Revolution*, 2d ed., Stanford: Stanford University Press, 1961.
MacFarquhar, Roderick, and John King Fairbank, eds. *The Cambridge History of China: The People's Republic of China*. Vols. 14 and 15. Cambridge: Cambridge University Press, 1987 and 1991.
Meisner, Maurice. *Mao's China: A History of the People's Republic*. New York: Free Press, 1977.
Saich, Tony, and Hans van de Ven, eds. *New Perspectives on the Chinese Communist Revolution*. Armonk, N.Y.: M. E. Sharpe, Inc., 1995.
———, ed. *The Rise to Power of the Chinese Communist Party*. Armonk, N. Y.: M. E. Sharpe, Inc., 1996.
Salisbury, Harrison E. *The New Emperors: China in the Era of Mao and Deng*. Boston: Little, Brown & Co., 1992.
Selden, Mark. *The Yenan Way in Revolutionary China*. Cambridge, Mass.: Harvard University Press, 1971.
Sinclair, Kevin. *The Yellow River: A 5,000 Year Journey Through China*. New South Waks: Child & Associates.
Snow, Edgar. *The Long Revolution*. New York: Random House, 1972.
———. *Red Star Over China*. London: Gollancz, 1937.
Spence, Jonathan D. *The Gate of Heavenly Peace: The Chinese and Their Revolution, 1895–1980*. New York: Viking Press, 1981.

Human Rights

Amnesty International. *China: Violations of Human Rights*. London: Amnesty International, 1984.
———. *Political Imprisonment in the People's Republic of China*. London: Amnesty International, 1978.
China Rights Forum: The Journal of Human Rights in China. New York: Human Rights in China, 1989–.
Edwards, R. Randle, Louis Henkin, and Andrew J. Nathan, eds. *Human Rights in Contemporary China*. New York: Columbia University Press, 1986.
Seymour, James D., ed. *The Fifth Modernization: China's Human*

Rights Movement, 1978–1979. Stanfordville, N. Y.: Human Rights Publishing Group, 1980.

Wu, Hongda Harry. *Laogai: The Chinese Gulag.* Boulder, Colo.: Westview Press, 1992.

Literature, Culture, Philosophy, and Journalism

Berry, Chris, ed. *Perspectives on Chinese Cinema.* London: BFI Publishers, 1991.

Chang, Jung. *Wild Swans: Three Daughters of China.* New York: Simon and Schuster, 1991.

Chinese Studies in Philosophy: A Journal of Translations. Armonk, N.Y.: M. E. Sharpe, Inc., quarterly.

Clark, Paul. *Chinese Cinema: Culture and Politics Since 1949.* Cambridge: Cambridge University Press, 1987.

Dai, Qing. *Wang Shiwei and "Wild Lilies": Rectification and Purges in the Chinese Communist Party, 1942–1944.* Armonk, N.Y.: M. E. Sharpe, Inc., 1994.

Howkins, John. *Mass Communication in China.* London: Longman, 1982.

Hsu, Kai-yu, et al., ed. *Literature of the People's Republic of China.* Bloomington: Indiana University Press, 1980.

Jernow, Allison Liu. *"Don't Force Us to Lie": The Struggle of Chinese Journalists in the Reform Era.* New York: Committee to Protect Journalists, 1993.

Kinkley, Jeffrey C., ed. *After Mao: Chinese Literature and Society, 1978–1981.* Cambridge, Mass.: Council on East Asian Studies, Harvard University, 1985.

Kraus, Richard C. *Pianos and Politics in China: Middle Class Ambitions and the Struggle Over Western Music.* Oxford: Oxford University Press, 1989.

Laing, Ellen Johnston. *The Winking Owl: Art in the People's Republic of China.* Berkeley and Los Angeles: University of California Press, 1988.

Lee, Chin-chuan, ed. *China's Media, Media's China.* Boulder, Colo.: Westview Press, 1994.

Link, Perry. *Evening Chats in Beijing: Probing China's Predicament.* New York: W. W. Norton & Co., 1992.

Link, Perry, ed. *Stubborn Weeds: Popular and Controversial Chinese Literature After the Cultural Revolution.* Bloomington: Indiana University Press, 1983.

———, Richard Madsen, and Paul G. Pickowicz, eds. *Unofficial China: Popular Culture and Thought in the People's Republic.* Boulder, Colo.: Westview Press, 1989.

Liu, Binyan. *People or Monsters? And Other Stories and Reportage from China after Mao.* Perry Link, ed. Bloomington: Indiana University Press, 1983.

Liu, Haiping, and Lowell Swortzell, eds. *Eugene O'Neill in China: An International Centenary Celebration.* New York: Greenwood Press, 1992.

Mackerras, Colin. *The Performing Arts in Contemporary China.* Boston: Routledge and Kegan Paul, 1981.

Mackinnon, Stephen R., and Oris Friesen. *China Reporting: An Oral History of American Journalism in the 1930s & 1940s.* Berkeley and Los Angeles: University of California Press, 1987.

Martin, Helmut, and Jeffrey Kinkley, eds. *Modern Chinese Writers: Self-Portrayals.* Armonk, N.Y.: M. E. Sharpe, Inc., 1992.

McDougall, Bonnie S., ed. *Popular Chinese Literature and Performing Arts in the People's Republic of China, 1949–1979.* Berkeley and Los Angeles: University of California Press, 1984.

Munro, Donald J. *The Concept of Man in Contemporary China.* Ann Arbor: University of Michigan Press, 1977.

Schwarcz, Vera. *The Chinese Enlightenment: Intellectuals and the Legacy of the May Fourth Movement of 1919.* Berkeley and Los Angeles: University of California Press, 1986.

Schwartz, Benjamin. *Communism and China: Ideology in Flux.* Cambridge, Mass.: Harvard University Press, 1968.

———. *In Search of Wealth and Power: Yen Fu and the West.* Cambridge, Mass.: Harvard University Press, 1964.

Unger, Jonathan, ed. *Using the Past to Serve the Present: Historiography and Politics in Contemporary China.* Armonk, N.Y.: M. E. Sharpe, Inc., 1993.

Wagner, Rudolf G. *The Contemporary Chinese Historical Drama: Four Studies.* Berkeley and Los Angeles: University of California Press, 1990.

Wang, Ruowang. *Hunger Trilogy.* Kyna Rubin, trans. Armonk, N.Y.: M. E. Sharpe, Inc., 1991.

Political Affairs and Government Policy-Making

Bachman, David. *Bureaucracy, Economy, and Leadership in China: The Institutional Origins of the Great Leap Forward.* Cambridge: Cambridge University Press, 1991.

———. *Chen Yun and the Chinese Political System.* Berkeley: Institute of East Asian Studies, University of California, 1985.

Barmé, Geremie. *Shades of Mao: The Posthumous Cult of the Great Leader.* Armonk, N.Y.: M. E. Sharpe, Inc., 1996.

Barnett, A. Doak. *Cadres, Bureaucracy, and Political Power in Communist China*. New York: Columbia University Press, 1967.

———. *China's Far West: Four Decades of Change*. Boulder, Colo.: Westview Press, 1993.

Barnett, A. Doak and Ralph N. Clough, eds. *Modernizing China: Post-Mao Reform and Development*. Boulder, Colo.: Westview Press, 1986.

Baum, Richard. *Burying Mao: Chinese Politics in the Age of Deng Xiaoping*. Princeton: Princeton University Press, 1994.

Bennett, Gordon. *Yundong: Mass Campaigns in Chinese Communist Leadership*. Berkeley: Center for Chinese Studies, University of California, 1976.

Burns, John P. *The Chinese Communist Party Nomenklatura System: A Documentary Study of Party Control of Leadership Selection*. Armonk, N.Y.: M. E. Sharpe, Inc., 1989.

———. *Political Participation in Rural China*. Berkeley and Los Angeles: University of California Press, 1988.

Burns, John P., and Stanley Rosen, eds. *Policy Conflicts in Post-Mao China*. Armonk, N.Y.: M. E. Sharpe, Inc., 1986.

Burton, Charles. *Political and Social Change in China Since 1978*. Westport, Conn.: Greenwood Press, 1990.

Butterfield, Fox. *China: Alive in the Bitter Sea*. New York: Times Books, 1982.

Chang, Parris. *Power and Policy in China*. University Park: Pennsylvania State University Press, 1976.

———. "The Rise of Wang Tung-hsing: Head of China's Security Apparatus." *The China Quarterly*, No. 73 (March 1978).

Ch'i, Hsi-Sheng. *Politics of Disillusionment: The Chinese Communist Party Under Deng Xiaoping, 1978–1989*. Armonk, N.Y.: M. E. Sharpe, Inc., 1991.

Chinese Law and Government: A Journal of Translations. Armonk, N.Y.: M. E. Sharpe, Inc., bimonthly.

Ding, Xueliang. *The Decline of Communism in China: Legitimacy Crisis, 1977–1989*. Cambridge: Cambridge University Press, 1994.

Dittmer, Lowell. *China Under Reform*. Boulder, Colo.: Westview Press, 1994.

———. *China's Continuous Revolution: The Post-Liberation Epoch, 1949–1981*. Berkeley and Los Angeles: University of California Press, 1987.

Domenach, Jean-Luc. *The Origins of the Great Leap Forward: The Case of One Chinese Province*. A. M. Berrett, trans. Boulder, Colo.: Westview Press, 1995.

Domes, Jurgen. *The Government and Politics of the PRC: A Time of Transition*. Boulder, Colo.: Westview Press, 1985.

Fewsmith, Joseph. *Dilemmas of Reform in China: Political Conflict and Economic Debate*. Armonk, N.Y.: M. E. Sharpe, Inc., 1994.

Forster, Keith. *Rebellion and Factionalism in a Chinese Province: Zhejiang, 1966–1976*. Armonk, N.Y.: M. E. Sharpe, Inc., 1990.

Goldstein, Avery. *From Bandwagon to Balance-of-Power Politics: Structural Constraints and Politics in China, 1949–1978*. Stanford: Stanford University Press, 1991.

Goodman, David S. G. *Centre and Province in the People's Republic of China: Sichuan and Guizhou, 1955–1965*. Cambridge: Cambridge University Press, 1986.

Guillermaz, Jacques. *The Chinese Communist Party in Power, 1949–1976*. Boulder, Colo.: Westview Press, 1976.

Hamrin, Carol Lee. *China and the Challenge of the Future: Changing Political Patterns*. Boulder, Colo.: Westview Press, 1990.

Hamrin, Carol Lee, and Timothy Cheek, eds. *China's Establishment Intellectuals*. Armonk, N.Y.: M. E. Sharpe, Inc., 1986.

Hamrin, Carol Lee, and Suisheng Zhao, eds. *Decision-Making in Deng's China: Perspectives from Insiders*. Armonk, N.Y.: M. E. Sharpe, Inc., 1995.

Harding, Harry. *China's Second Revolution: Reform After Mao*. Washington, D.C.: The Brookings Institution, 1987.

———. *Organizing China: The Problem of Bureaucracy, 1949–1976*. Stanford: Stanford University Press, 1981.

Hsu, Immanuel C. Y. *China Without Mao: The Search for a New Order*. Oxford: Oxford University Press, 1982.

Joseph, William A. *The Critique of Ultra-Leftism in China, 1958–1981*. Stanford: Stanford University Press, 1984.

Kau, Michael Ying-Mao, ed. *The Lin Piao Affair: Power, Politics, and Military Coup*. White Plains, N.Y.: International Arts and Sciences Press, 1975.

Kau, Michael Ying-Mao, and Susan Marsh, eds. *China in the Era of Deng Xiaoping: A Decade of Reform*. Armonk, N.Y.: M. E. Sharpe, Inc., 1993.

Ladany, Laszlo. *The Communist Party of China and Marxism, 1921–1985: A Self-Portrait*. Stanford: Hoover Institution Press, 1988.

Lampton, David M., ed. *Policy Implementation in Post-Mao China*. Berkeley and Los Angeles: University of California Press, 1987.

Lewis, John Wilson. *Leadership in Communist China*. Ithaca: Cornell University Press, 1963.

———, ed. *Party Leadership and Revolutionary Power in China*. Cambridge: Cambridge University Press, 1970.

Leys, Simon. *Broken Images: Essays on Chinese Culture and Politics*. New York: St. Martin's Press, 1990.

———. *Chinese Shadows*. New York: Viking Press, 1977.

Lichtenstein, Peter M. *China at the Brink: The Political Economy of Reform and Retrenchment in the Post-Mao Era.* New York: Praeger Publishers, 1991.

Lieberthal, Kenneth G. *Governing China: From Revolution Through Reform.* New York: W. W. Norton & Co., 1995.

———. *Revolution and Tradition in Tientsin, 1949–52.* Stanford: Stanford University Press, 1980.

Lieberthal, Kenneth G., and Bruce J. Dickson. *A Research Guide to Central Party and Government Meetings in China, 1949–1986.* Armonk, N.Y.: M. E. Sharpe, Inc., 1989.

Lieberthal, Kenneth G., and David M. Lampton, eds. *Bureaucracy, Politics, and Decision Making in Post-Mao China.* Berkeley and Los Angeles: University of California Press, 1992.

Lieberthal, Kenneth G., and Michel Oksenberg. *Policy Making in China: Leaders, Structures, and Processes.* Princeton: Princeton University Press, 1988.

Lifton, Robert Jay. *Thought Reform and the Psychology of Totalism: A Study of "Brainwashing" in China.* New York: W. W. Norton & Co., 1961.

Liu, Allan P. I. *Mass Politics in the People's Republic: State and Society in Contemporary China.* Boulder, Colo.: Westview Press, 1996.

Liu, Binyan. *China's Crisis, China's Hope: Essays from an Intellectual in Exile.* Cambridge, Mass.: Harvard University Press, 1990.

———. *A Higher Kind of Loyalty.* Zhu Hong, trans. New York: Pantheon Books, 1990.

Manion, Melanie. *Retirement of Revolutionaries in China: Public Policies, Social Norms, Private Interests.* Princeton: Princeton University Press, 1993.

O'Brien, Kevin J. *Reform Without Liberalization: China's National People's Congress and the Politics of Institutional Change.* Cambridge: Cambridge University Press, 1990.

Ogden, Suzanne. *China's Unresolved Issues: Politics, Development, and Culture,* 3d ed. Englewood Cliffs, N.J.: Prentice Hall, 1994.

Oksenberg, Michel, and Steven Goldstein. "The Chinese Political Spectrum." *Problems of Communism* (March–April 1974).

Pye, Lucian. *The Spirit of Chinese Politics,* new ed. Cambridge, Mass.: Harvard University Press, 1992.

Schoenhals, Michael. *Doing Things With Words in Chinese Politics: Five Studies.* Berkeley: Institute of East Asian Studies, University of California, 1992.

Schurmann, Franz. *Ideology and Organization in Communist China.* Berkeley and Los Angeles: University of California Press, 1966.

Seymour, James D. *China's Satellite Parties.* Armonk, N.Y.: M. E. Sharpe, Inc., 1987.

Shirk, Susan L. *Competitive Comrades*. Berkeley and Los Angeles: University of California Press, 1982.

———. *The Political Logic of Economic Reform in China*. Berkeley and Los Angeles: University of California Press, 1993.

Shue, Vivienne. *The Reach of the State: Sketches of the Chinese Body Politic*. Stanford: Stanford University Press, 1988.

Solomon, Richard H. *Mao's Revolution and the Chinese Political Culture*. Berkeley and Los Angeles: University of California Press, 1971.

Su, Shaozhi, et al. *Marxism in China*. Nottingham: Spokesman, 1983.

Sullivan, Lawrence R., ed. *China Since Tiananmen: Political, Economic, and Social Conflicts*. Armonk, N.Y.: M. E. Sharpe, Inc., 1995.

Teiwes, Frederick C. *Politics and Purges in China: Rectification and the Decline of Party Norms 1950–1965*. Armonk, N.Y.: M. E. Sharpe, Inc., 1993.

———. *Politics at Mao's Court: Gao Gang and Party Factionalism in the early 1950s*. Armonk, N.Y.: M. E. Sharpe, Inc., 1990.

Terrill, Ross. *China in Our Time: The Epic Saga of the People's Republic from the Communist Victory to Tiananmen Square and Beyond*. New York: Simon & Schuster, 1992.

Townsend, James. *Political Participation in Communist China*. Berkeley and Los Angeles: University of California Press, 1967.

———. *Politics in China*, 3d ed. Boston: Little, Brown & Co., 1986.

Vogel, Ezra. *Canton Under Communism: Programs and Politics in a Provincial Capital, 1949–1968*. Cambridge, Mass.: Harvard University Press, 1969.

———. "From Friendship to Comradeship." *The China Quarterly*, No. 21 (January-March 1965).

———. *One Step Ahead in China: Guangdong Under Reform*. Cambridge, Mass.: Harvard University Press, 1989.

Wang, James C. F. *Contemporary Chinese Politics: An Introduction*, 5th ed. Englewood Cliffs, N.J.: Prentice Hall, 1995.

Population, Women, and Minorities

Andors, Phyllis. *The Unfinished Liberation of Chinese Women, 1949–1980*. Bloomington: Indiana University Press, 1983.

Avedon, John F. *In Exile from the Land of Snows*. New York: Alfred A. Knopf, 1984.

Banister, Judith. *China's Changing Population*. Stanford: Stanford University Press, 1987.

Barlow, Tani E., ed. *Gender Politics in Modern China: Writing and Feminism*. Durham, N.C.: Duke University Press, 1993.

Benson, Linda, and Ingvar Svanberg, eds. *The Kazakhs of China: Essays on an Ethnic Minority*. Stockholm: Almqvist & Wiksell International, 1988.

Croll, Elisabeth, ed. *The Women's Movement in China: A Selection of Readings, 1949–1973*. London: Anglo-Chinese Educational Institute, 1974.

Croll, Elisabeth, Delia Davin and Penny Kane, eds. *China's One-Child Family Policy*. New York: St. Martin's Press, 1985.

Dreyer, June Teufel. *China's Forty Millions: Minority Nationalities and National Integration in the People's Republic of China*. Cambridge, Mass.: Harvard University Press, 1976.

Gladney, Dru C. *Muslim Chinese: Ethnic Nationalism in the People's Republic*. Cambridge, Mass.: Council on East Asian Studies, Harvard University, 1991.

Heberer, Thomas. *China and Its National Minorities: Autonomy or Assimilation?* Michael Vale, trans. Armonk, N.Y.: M. E. Sharpe, Inc., 1989.

Honig, Emily, and Gail Hershatter. *Personal Voices: Chinese Women in the 1980s*. Stanford: Stanford University Press, 1988.

Jaschok, Maria, and Suzanne Miers, eds. *Women & Chinese Patriarchy: Submission, Servitude and Escape*. Atlantic Highlands, N.J.: Zed Books, 1994.

Johnson, Kay Ann. *Women, the Family, and Peasant Revolution in China*. Chicago: University of Chicago Press, 1983.

Orleans, Leo A. *Every Fifth Child: The Population of China*. Stanford: Stanford University Press, 1972.

Wolf, Arthur P. and Chieh-shang Huang. *Marriage and Adoption in China: 1845–1945*. Stanford: Stanford University Press, 1980.

Wolf, Margery. *Revolution Postponed: Women in Contemporary China*. Stanford: Stanford University Press, 1985.

Young, Marilyn B., comp. *Women in China: Studies in Social Change and Feminism*. Ann Arbor: Center for Chinese Studies, University of Michigan, 1973.

Yue, Daiyun, with Carolyn Wakeman. *To the Storm: The Odyssey of a Revolutionary Chinese Woman*. Berkeley and Los Angeles: University of California Press, 1985.

Rural Affairs

Bennett, Gordon. *Huadong: The Story of a Chinese People's Commune*. Boulder, Colo.: Westview Press, 1978.

Bernstein, Thomas. "Stalinism, Famine and Chinese Peasants—Grain Procurement during the Great Leap Forward." *Theory and Society*, 13, No. 3 (1984): 339–77.

———. *Up to the Mountains and Down to the Villages: The Transfer of Youth from Urban to Rural China.* New Haven: Yale University Press, 1977.

Byrd, William A., and Qinsong Lin, eds. *China's Rural Industry: Structure, Development, and Reform.* Oxford: Oxford University Press, 1990.

Chan, Anita, Richard Madsen and Jonathan Unger. *Chen Village: The Recent History of a Peasant Community Under Mao and Deng.* Berkeley and Los Angeles: University of California Press, 1992.

Friedman, Edward, Paul Pickowicz and Mark Selden. *Chinese Village, Socialist State.* New Haven: Yale University Press, 1991.

Friedman, Edward, Paul Pickowicz, and Mark Selden, with Kay Ann Johnson. *Chinese Village, Socialist State.* New Haven: Yale University Press, 1991.

He, Liyi, with Claire Annee Chik. *Mr. China's Son: A Villager's Life.* Boulder, Colo.: Westview Press, 1993.

Hinton, William. *Fanshen: A Documentary of Revolution in a Chinese Village.* New York: Monthly Review Press, 1966.

Huang, Shu-min. *The Spiral Road: Change in a Chinese Village Through the Eyes of a Communist Party Leader.* Boulder, Colo.: Westview Press, 1989.

Madsen, Richard. *Morality and Power in a Chinese Village.* Berkeley and Los Angeles: University of California Press, 1984.

Mosher, Steven W. *Broken Earth: The Rural Chinese.* New York: Free Press, 1983.

Oi, Jean C. *State and Peasant in Contemporary China: The Political Economy of Village Government.* Berkeley and Los Angeles: University of California Press, 1989.

Parish, William L., ed. *Chinese Rural Development: The Great Transformation.* Armonk, N.Y.: M. E. Sharpe, Inc., 1985.

Parish, William L., and Martin King Whyte. *Village and Family in Contemporary China.* Chicago: University of Chicago Press, 1978.

Perkins, Dwight. *Rural Small-Scale Industry in the People's Republic of China.* Berkeley and Los Angeles: University of California Press, 1977.

Perkins, Dwight, and Shahid Yusuf. *Rural Development in China.* Baltimore: Johns Hopkins University Press, 1984.

Potter, Sulamith Heins, and Jack M. Potter. *China's Peasants: The Anthropology of a Revolution.* Cambridge: Cambridge University Press, 1990.

Siu, Helen F. *Agents and Victims in South China: Accomplices in Rural Revolution.* New Haven: Yale University Press, 1989.

Siu, Helen F., and Zelda Stern, eds. *Mao's Harvest: Voices From China's New Generation.* Oxford: Oxford University Press, 1983.

Skinner, G. William. "Marketing and Social Structure in Rural China."

Journal of Asian Studies, 1, No. 24, (November 1964), Part I; 2, No. 24, (February 1965), Part II; 3, No. 24, (May 1965), Part III.

Walker, Kenneth R. *Food Grain Procurement and Consumption in China*. Cambridge: Cambridge University Press, 1984.

Zweig, David. *Agrarian Radicalism in China, 1968–1981*. Cambridge, Mass.: Harvard University Press, 1989.

Science, Medicine, and Technology

Bowers, John Z., J. William Hess, and Nathan Sivin, eds. *Science and Medicine in Twentieth-Century China: Research and Education*. Ann Arbor: Center for Chinese Studies, University of Michigan, 1988.

Chen, C.C. *Medicine in Rural China: A Personal Account*. Berkeley and Los Angeles: University of California Press, 1989.

Chen, Junshi, T. Colin Campbell, et al., eds. *Diet, Life Style and Mortality in China: A Study of the Characteristics of 65 Chinese Counties*. Ithaca: Cornell University Press, 1990.

Henderson, Gail, and Myron Cohen. *The Chinese Hospital: A Chinese Work Unit*. New Haven: Yale University Press, 1984.

Kleinman, Arthur. *Social Origins of Distress and Disease: Depression, Neurasthenia, and Pain in Modern China*. New Haven: Yale University Press, 1986.

Lampton, David M. *Health, Conflict, and the Chinese Political System*. Ann Arbor: Center for Chinese Studies, University of Michigan, 1974.

Rosenthal, Marilyn M. *Health Care in the People's Republic of China: Moving Towards Modernization*. Boulder, Colo.: Westview Press, 1987.

Saich, Tony. *China's Science Policy in the 80s*. Atlantic Highlands, N.J.: Humanities Press International, 1989.

Simon, Denis Fred, and Merle Goldman, eds. *Science and Technology in Post-Mao China*. Cambridge, Mass.: Council on East Asian Studies, Harvard University, 1989.

Suttmeier, Richard P. *Research and Revolution: Science Policy and Societal Change in China*. Lexington, Mass.: Lexington Books, 1974.

———. *Science, Technology and China's Drive for Modernization*. Stanford: Hoover Institution Press, 1980.

World Bank. *China: The Health Sector in China*. Washington, D.C.: World Bank, 1984.

Society, Ethnicity, and Religion

Davis, Deborah, and Ezra Vogel, eds. *Chinese Society on the Eve of Tiananmen: The Impact of Reform*. Cambridge, Mass.: Harvard University Press, 1990.

———— and Stevan Harrell, eds. *Chinese Families in the Post-Mao Era.* Berkeley and Los Angeles: University of California Press, 1993.

Dikötter Frank. *The Discourse of Race in Modern China.* Stanford: Stanford University Press, 1992.

Falkenheim, Victor, ed. *Citizens and Groups in Contemporary China.* Ann Arbor: Center for Chinese Studies, University of Michigan, 1992.

Fried, Morton. *Fabric of Chinese Society: A Study in the Social Life of a Chinese County Seat.* New York: Praeger Publishers, 1953.

Frolic, B. Michael. *Mao's People: Sixteen Portraits of Life in Revolutionary China.* Cambridge, Mass.: Harvard University Press, 1980.

Garside, Roger. *Coming Alive: China After Mao.* New York: McGraw-Hill, 1981.

Kraus, Richard C. *Class Conflict in Chinese Socialism.* New York: Columbia University Press, 1981.

Kristof, Nicholas D., and Sheryl WuDunn. *China Wakes: The Struggle for the Soul of a Rising Power.* New York: Times Books, 1994.

Levy, Marion Joseph. *The Family Revolution in Modern China.* New York: Octagon Books, 1963.

Lewis, John Wilson, ed. *The City in Communist China.* Stanford: Stanford University Press, 1971.

Liang, Heng, and Judith Shapiro. *Son of the Revolution.* New York: Alfred A. Knopf, 1983.

Lin, Zhiling, and Thomas W. Robinson, eds. *The Chinese and Their Future: Beijing, Taipei, and Hong Kong.* Washington, D.C.: American Enterprise Institute Press, 1994.

Lindbeck, John M. H., ed. *China: Management of a Revolutionary Society.* Seattle: University of Washington Press, 1971.

MacInnis, Donald E., comp. *Religious Policy and Practice in Communist China: A Documentary History.* New York: Macmillan, 1972.

Mozingo, David, and Victor Nee, eds. *State and Society in Contemporary China.* Ithaca: Cornell University Press, 1983.

Pasternak, Burton. *Marriage and Fertility in Tianjin, China: Fifty Years of Transition.* Honolulu: East West Center, University of Hawaii, 1986.

Rosenbaum, Arthur Lewis. *State and Society in China: The Consequences of Reform.* Boulder, Colo.: Westview Press, 1992.

Shanor, Donald, and Constance Shanor. *China Today.* New York: St. Martin's Press, 1995.

Smith, Christopher J. *China: People and Places in the Land of One Billion.* Boulder, Colo.: Westview Press, 1990.

Tyson, James, and Ann Tyson. *Chinese Awakenings: Life Stories from the Unofficial China.* Boulder, Colo.: Westview Press, 1995.

Watson, James L., ed. *Class and Social Stratification in Post-Revolution China*. Cambridge: Cambridge University Press, 1984.

Watson, Rubie, and Patricia Ebrey, eds. *Marriage and Inequality in Chinese Society*. Berkeley and Los Angeles: University of California Press, 1991.

Whyte, Martin King. *Small Groups and Political Rituals in China*. Berkeley and Los Angeles: University of California Press, 1974.

Whyte, Martin King, and William L. Parish. *Urban Life in Contemporary China*. Chicago: University of Chicago Press, 1984.

Zhang, Xinxin, and Sang Ye. *Chinese Lives: An Oral History of Contemporary China*. New York: Pantheon, 1987.

Zheng, Yi. *Scarlet Memorial*. T. P. Sym, trans. Boulder, Colo.: Westview Press, 1996.

Selected Internet Sites (August 1997)

China Daily, Business Weekly
www.chinadaily.net/

China infohighway communications
www.chinatoday.com/

China Journal (Canberra)
online.anu.edu.au/RSPAS/ccc/journal.html

China News Digest
www.cnd.org:8011/

Council on East Asian Libraries
www.darkwing.uoregon.edu/~felsing/cstuff/cshelf.html

Far Eastern Economic Review
www.feer.com

Finding News About China
freenet.buffalo.edu/~cb863/china.html

Hong Kong Standard
www.hkstandard.com/

Inside China Today
www.insidechina.com/china.html

International Institute for Asian Studies (Leiden)
iias.leidenuniv.nl/index.html

South China Morning Post
www.scmp.com/news/index.idc?

Tour in China
www.ihep.ac.cn/tour/china_tour.html

Voice of America
gopher://gopher.voa.gov/11/newswire

About the Authors

Lawrence R. Sullivan is an associate professor of political science, Adelphi University, Garden City, New York. He received his Ph.D. in political science from the University of Michigan in 1976. He has written many articles on contemporary Chinese politics and environmental affairs. He is coauthor of *Chinese Communist Materials at the Bureau of Investigation Archives, Taiwan* (1976); coeditor of *Beijing Spring, 1989, Confrontation and Conflict: The Basic Documents* (1990), and *China's Search for Democracy: The Student and Mass Movement of 1989* (1992); coeditor and cotranslator of Dai Qing, *Yangtze! Yangtze! Debate Over the Three Gorges Project* (1994), and editor of *China Since Tiananmen: Political, Economic, and Social Conflicts* (1995).

Nancy R. Hearst is the librarian at the John King Fairbank Center for East Asian Research, Harvard University. She is the guest editor and translator of "The Anti-Spiritual Pollution Drive—A Former *People's Daily* Editor Remembers," by Wang Ruoshui, *Chinese Studies in Philosophy* (Summer 1996); guest editor with Tony Saich, "An Internal Study of Mao Zedong's Erroneous 'Left' Thinking in his Later Years," by Li Rui, *Chinese Law and Government* (1996); with Tony Saich, "Newly Available Sources on CCP History from the PRC," in *New Perspectives on State Socialism in China*, ed. Timothy Cheek and Tony Saich (Armonk, N.Y.: M. E. Sharpe, 1997); and compiler, "China Chronology," in *China Briefing*, ed. William A. Joseph (1991, 1992, 1994, and 1996).